American Indian
Sovereignty

M000250751

ALSO BY J. MARK HAZLETT II

*The Libertarian Party and Other Minor Political Parties
in the United States* (McFarland, 1992)

American Indian Sovereignty

The Struggle for Religious, Cultural and Tribal Independence

J. MARK HAZLETT II

McFarland & Company, Inc., Publishers
Jefferson, North Carolina

LIBRARY OF CONGRESS CATALOGUING-IN-PUBLICATION DATA

Names: Hazlett, J. Mark, II, 1958– author.
Title: American Indian sovereignty : the struggle for religious, cultural,
    and tribal independence / J. Mark Hazlett   II. Description: Jefferson,
    North Carolina : McFarland & Company, Inc., Publishers, 2020 |
    Includes bibliographical references and index.
Identifiers: LCCN 2020030104 | ISBN 9781476681429 (paperback) ∞
    | ISBN 9781476640099 (ebook)
Subjects: LCSH: Indians of North America—Legal status, laws,
    etc.—History. | Indians of North America—Government
    relations—History. | Indians of North America—Ethnic identity. |
    Indians of North America—Politics and government. | Self-determination,
    National—United States. | Sovereignty.
Classification: LCC KF8390 .H39 2020 | DDC 342.7308/72—dc23
LC record available at https://lccn.loc.gov/2020030104

BRITISH LIBRARY CATALOGUING DATA ARE AVAILABLE

ISBN (print) 978-1-4766-8142-9
ISBN (ebook) 978-1-4766-4009-9

Cover Image: Drumsticks used during a Pottawatomie Pow Wow
(iStockphoto)

Printed in the United States of America

McFarland & Company, Inc., Publishers
 Box 611, Jefferson, North Carolina 28640
  www.mcfarlandpub.com

This work is the culmination of several years of work, with the countless contributions of numerous people, too many to name them all. They have granted me the honor of their friendship, teaching, advice, criticism and most of all, their patience.

To my wife Michelle. I especially want to thank you for your never-ending support, love and endless source of rationality in this crazy, illogical world we seem to live in at times. Friends will never realize how right they were when they nicknamed you Gisiss Ikwe, Sun Woman. You have been a light in my life, guiding my footsteps and keeping me from stumbling. Without you, I believe I would just wander through this world, without a clear path, purpose or direction. Thank you ever so much for agreeing to share this path of life with me and helping me over its obstacles.

To my son, Evan Mark, Song of the Hawk. You amazed me and made me open my eyes to the wonders, joys and thrills of life from the day you were born. You have given my path humor and laughter, love and yes, sometimes, worry. You have made me a very proud father, and as you serve our nation, both the United States and Native Tribe, you will make us all proud. May your life be blessed with continued light and song.

To my daughters, Sabyn Iris, Quiet Storm, and Sarah Lynne, She Claws The Sky. I have watched you blossom into beautiful and compassionate young women. You have allowed me to be a child again and have often reminded me of the joys and peace of heart of being young again. May your futures be guided by the principles of peace and happiness.

As you all grow up together, remember that you have made me want to be a better father.

Finally, to those who are struggling to find themselves, to gain recognition in the chaos of this world, to understand your place and where you fit into this great mystery we call life, whether you be Native or not, I can only offer one simple phrase of advice: *Mi taku oyasin*. We Are All Related.

Table of Contents

Acknowledgments

There are so many people who have supported and influenced me over the years and whose advice, thoughts and teachings have influenced this work, that thanking each person individually is impossible. Instead, I give each of you all a great *niawe*, or thank you. I am incredibly appreciative of you all.

There are a few select people, however, who have stood above the others and have had an even greater impact upon me both personally and professionally, and these I feel need special mention. First, my father, Joseph, needs to be thanked. Besides being a father, he was a teacher and professor for over 40 years, and a man of true spiritualism. His style, humor and professionalism helped set the stage for my career. The most memorable compliment he ever gave me is when he told me I was a scholar. He meant that I was not afraid to do research, to discover things on my own and learn new materials. He has since passed, but his presence still serves as my guide, not only in my profession, but with my family.

Others have also granted me the honor of walking with me along this path in life. Their friendship, support and assistance have been extraordinary. Glenn Longie, of the Turtle Mountain Ojibwe in North Dakota, who has always been there for both me and my wife. We met over 25 years ago, and he is responsible for guiding many of my initial footsteps on my path of self-discovery and catching me when I have stumbled. He directed me to others who would have a profound influence upon my learning. Larry and Joan Stillday would be two of these people who would guide me, celebrate with me, watch me falter and then pick me up more than a few times along the way. Randy Verdun, friend and former chief of the Biloxi Chitimacha Choctaw tribe in Louisiana, and his tribal members, welcomed me and mine into their lives without hesitation. Finally, I want to thank "Red Dawn" and the many others who have honored me with friendships over the years—sharing our complaints, issues, jokes and perspectives on life in general.

In my current phase of life, my colleagues at both the university and secondary levels have been wonderful in their support, understanding and encouragement. Among them, Vic Noto stands out as instrumental in getting me back on the path to completing this work after it went fallow. I also would like to mention an old friend, Dave Folz, for his unwavering friendship throughout the years. I would also be remiss if I did not thank Scott, Donnas, Ashley, Allison, Rebecca, Teri, Michael and many others too numerous to mention individually for their support and friendship during good and bad times.

Although our paths together have been often separated by miles and time, you all have been in my heart and prayers. Thanks to you again.

Finally, I want to acknowledge the countless students, Native and non-Native, whom I have had the honor of teaching over the last 30 odd years, from middle school to graduate school. You have all listened to me teach and discuss about my heritage, asked me questions, tried to understand, suffered my bad jokes, and you have been very respectful and interested in me, my background and ideas. You are truly the hope for a better future in this world, and I am so very proud to have been your teacher.

Megwitch.

Preface

Much has been written on the topic of tribal sovereignty in regard to landholdings; though the focus of this work is the long and continuing battle over American Indian lands, culture and religion; it also expands the idea of "sovereignty" beyond the ownership and control of traditional tribal lands or reservations. In this book, I argue that American Indian property also includes those aspects that make someone "Indian." In other words, the concept of "property" includes not only tribal lands, but also American Indian identity, religion and culture. To any American, the ability to exercise sovereignty over these parts of oneself is just as, if not more critical, than control over one's land and belongings. We, as Americans, hold these things sacrosanct, and as such they should be free from attacks and corruption by others. Most people would assume that these rights are inherent to their being, an unassailable right of self-possession, but this is not the case with American Indians, who have a long and continuing history of having their religions attacked and corrupted by outsiders, their native culture both demeaned, banned, and "borrowed," their lands stolen and environments polluted, their treaties with the U.S. government easily brushed aside and ignored, and who did not even receive U.S. citizenship until the 1920s. It seems almost unfathomable that the *original* Americans must fight for the right to control these aspects of themselves. Yet for centuries, there has been consistent and constant efforts to master American Indians and wrest their sovereignty from them.

This research examines the efforts to master Native peoples, their lands and environments, their cultures and religions. The loss of land and tribal sovereignty over it has been well documented, but less attention has been paid to the loss of cultural and religious sovereignty. Sovereignty over all of these aspects has eroded since the first contacts with non–Natives. "Cultural sovereignty" is defined as the ability of a person to be free from attacks by

1

the dominant society that trivialize and delegitimize their culture. Likewise, this has also applied to Native religions. One does not have to look very hard at all to see that the American Indian has a long way to go in this regard to regain their cultural sovereignty. Religious sovereignty is defined as Indians possessing the freedom and ability to practice their traditional beliefs without legal limits or interferences. I also include in this definition that non–Indians will not portray themselves as Natives, perverting the Indian belief system and practices for profit and other personal gain.

American Indians have been under constant attack for centuries. Whether it be by a federal or state law removing children from Native families because English is not the primary language, or whether it is something as innocuous as a Halloween costume, movie or cartoon that demeans and makes fun of their ethnicity or Native regalia, the original peoples of this country are often trivialized and forgotten in American society. This disrespect and alienation of their culture has caused many Natives to simply give up, to deny their heritage like some members of my own family have done. These individuals find it too difficult to hold onto their heritage in the face of constant mockery and derision. They succumb to being "white," because to do otherwise is to invite ridicule from society or, in some cases to actually lose their right to own real property. They have clearly lost their sovereignty.

The lack of true understanding of American Indians and their culture has always been a motivation for me. I do my best to decry and expose imposters and those who want to harm true Native culture for ego and/or profit, and have worked against the plethora of Native stereotypes. For example, when a local college allowed a non–Native to portray himself as a healer, masquerade as an Indian, and harass and embarrass true Natives, this spurred me to reveal him for what he really was—a fake. Recently, a local all-girls high school decided after many years to stop using the Sioux Indian Tribe as a class mascot. Students had made up tribal names for themselves, posed in pseudo–Indian costumes and made up other aspects of the Lakota (the true name of the Sioux) culture to fit their perceptions and needs. While many saw this practice as racist, several alumni and current students have publicly complained about the school's decision to stop this practice as being "too" politically correct. This has intensified my own efforts to educate non–Natives and show them how harmful these stereotypes really are to the Native peoples. Situations like these are often teachable moments, and the lack of understanding at times is astounding.

The fact that there are currently all sorts of self-help books being published by non–Natives claiming to have some secret tribal knowledge or calling themselves "intertribal pipe carriers," all for the purpose of making a profit off the naïve is upsetting to me. When the sweat lodge that was used by my friends and myself for spiritual rejuvenation was desecrated by a group that who used it to hang out and drink beer and have sex, the larger issue of sacred sites quickly came into the forefront of my awareness and concern. Even when I was a child, I can remember the quiet discussions and statements of dismay and disgust from my family members concerning the building of the Kinzua Dam for a recreational lake on traditional Seneca lands, flooding the Cornplanter lands and burial grounds in the process.

Some American Indian issues in this work are only discussed briefly. For example, the boarding school debacle and American Indian slavery, are extremely important but there are works that examine these topics directly and completely. For this reason, I defer to others' research expertise and knowledge in these areas. That is not the primary focus of this work, but these topics among others deserve their own vigorous investigations and conclusions.

To prepare this work, I relied not only on scholarly research, but also on personal experience and observations. I see the lack of knowledge and understanding of Native culture. Every day I see how this ignorance leads to insulting and racist behavior, intentional or not. I have personally experienced and observed discrimination toward Natives, have dealt with the "wannabes" who portray themselves as Indian for profit or ego, watched the problems of cultural sovereignty on and off the reservations, and worked with various Indian tribes on recognition issues, environmental issues, and other problems. I have danced among my brothers and sisters, sung with them, cried and prayed with them. This work is for them, for those who continue to confront these issues and attacks upon their sovereignty, and for those who wish to have a better understanding of our path.

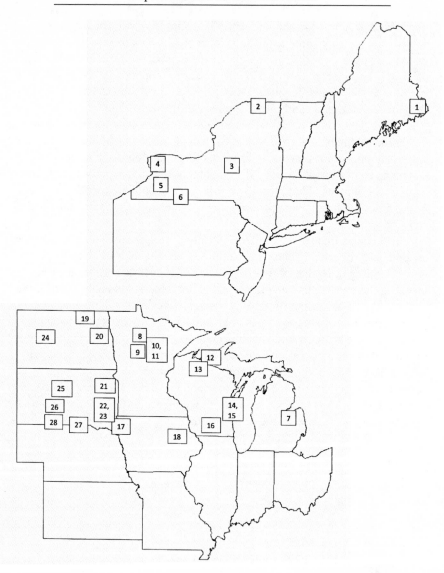

1. Passamaquody
2. Mohawk
3. Onondaga
4. Tuscarora
5. Seneca—Cattaraugus
6. Seneca—Allegany
7. Isabella Ojibwe
   (Anishinabe)
8. Red Lake Ojibwe
9. White Earth Ojibwe
10. Leech Lake Ojibwe
11. Fond du Lac Ojibwe
12. L. Anse Ojibwe
13. Bad River Ijibwe
14. Menominee
15. Oneida
16. Winnebago
17. Omaha, Winnebago
18. Sac, Fox
19. Turtle Mountain Ojibwe
20. Ft. Totten Dakota
21. Sisseton Dakota
22. Crow Creek Dakota
23. Yankton Dakota
24. Ft. Peck Dakota
25. Standing Rock Dakota
26. Cheyenne River
    Dakota
27. Rosebud Lakota
28. Pine Ridge Lakota

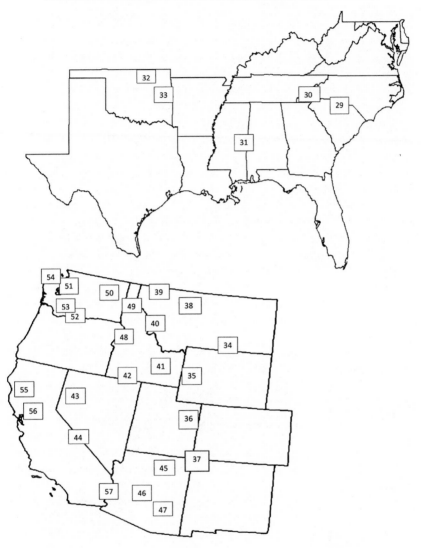

29. Catawba
30. Eastern Cherokee
31. Mississippi Choctaw
32. Osage
33. Cherokee, Choctaw,
    Creek, Chickasaw,
    Seminole, Seneca,
    Quapaw, Muscogee
34. Crow, Northern
    Cheyenne
35. Shoshone, Arapaho
36. Uintah, Duray

37. Ute, Apache, Navajo
    (Diné)
38. Cree, Ojibwe, Atsina,
    Assinboin
39. Blackfeet
40. Flathead
41. Shoshone
42. Shoshone, Paiute
43. Paiute
44. Shoshone, Paiute
45. Hopi, Navajo, Pueb-
    los

46. Pima, Yuma
47. Apache
48. Nez Perce
49. Coeur d'Arlene
50. Coluille, Spokane
51. Tulalip
52. Yakima
53. Puyallup
54. Makah
55. Hupa, Yurok
56. Varied
57. Yuma, Pima

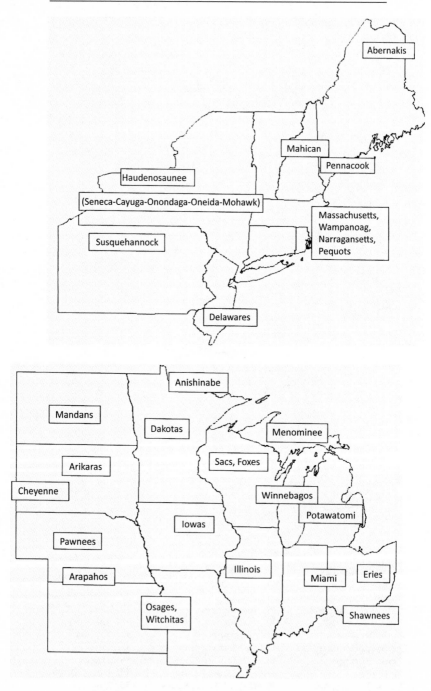

The original peoples, pre–1600 (and opposite page).

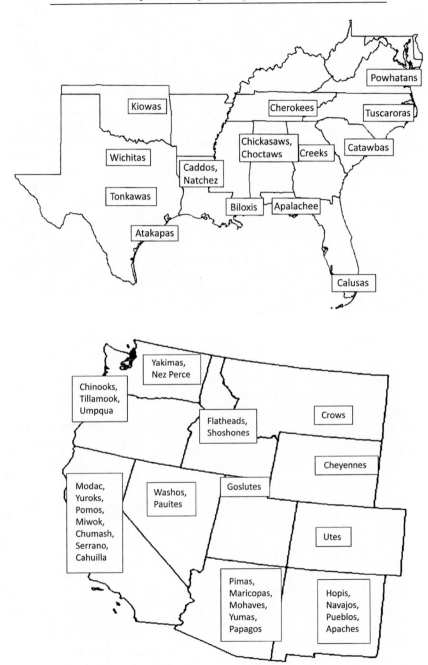

CHAPTER ONE

The Struggles Begin

> *"How smooth must be the language of the whites, when they can make right look wrong, and wrong like right."*
>
> —Black Hawk, Sauk

The Setting

As the earliest explorers landed on the Pacific and Atlantic coasts of what would be later known as North America, they did not find an uninhabited and barren land. Instead, they found a land peopled with countless numbers of tribes and cultures, full of new wonders and resources. Later, as these explorers sent settlers to establish a permanent presence in this new land, they further found that they would be dependent upon these indigenous peoples and their understanding of the land. At first, they were reluctantly grateful for the help, but as their numbers grew and the new settlers became experienced and accustomed to the new lands, they would become obstinate and decide that the land was meant to be theirs to control. The premises for this decision were varied, but the same conclusion was reached: the native peoples would not keep what they had lived with for millennia. The new settlers, mostly due to their sheer numbers, would not be denied the lands they sought. The clash of world views had begun and would continue even to this day. To fully understand this conflict, an examination of these world views needs to be undertaken.

American Indians, as the native peoples would be called,[1] held a view of the lands upon which they lived that was drastically different from the newcomers to their shores. It was, and still is, this view that would cause a great deal of pain and anger on both the newcomers' and Indian's part. It is a view that would cause military destruction of entire cultures, genocide, legal removals and terminations of tribes and groups that had existed for centuries, and a stealing of lands that would be justified *ex post facto*.

It is difficult to classify the views concerning land and property of all American Indians into one typology, but there are some dominant themes that will permit the construction of a descriptive model. It is imperative in any understanding of American Indian property rights and existing conflicts to first understand American Indian views of the land.

The American Indian View

American Indians' view of land and water reflects a cyclical and integrated world view. All things, from plants and animals to minerals and water, are animate and are a part of a greater purpose. This purpose is not meant to be fully understood, for it is part of what many tribes refer to as the Great Mystery. This Great Mystery is a plan for the natural universe that has been designed by the Great Spirit. Humans are only a small part in this overall plan, so the acceptance of the pragmatic, the *"what is,"* is integral and essential. As such, they are fully integrated and dependent upon other things in the plan, just as things in nature are integrated with humans. In other words, whenever there is an action taken by a human, there will be some reaction to it in nature, however minuscule. For example, simple motions stir the air which affect microscopic entities and this reaction continues throughout the design. Thus, greater actions such as cutting down a tree or diverting a river will have even greater effects in the natural circle of things.

Indians have conceptualized this design of nature in terms of the Sacred Circle. All things go through the circle and its parts. From creation and birth, to life, death, afterlife or spirit and rebirth. This is not the same as a belief in reincarnation. Instead, rebirth implies that one's elements will be reused by other beings. In some tribes, the person's spirit did enter a place commonly referred to as an underworld, or heaven or hell. Humans, animals, plants, soil, and water all have a path through this circle. Each item's circle is touched by others. Therefore, when one circle becomes affected, it will touch and affect the others within its sphere of influence like the ripples on a pond when a handful of pebbles are thrown into it. The seeking of balance between all things is therefore important. One cannot take from nature without offering something to restore the harmony and balance. For example, Seganagatha,[2] the Seneca prophet, taught about this need for balance throughout his life. When a plant or animal is taken from its place in nature, then to restore the balance, an offering of the sacred herb tobacco should be made to that plant's or animal's spirit thanking it for sacrificing itself.

Another tribe, the Anishinabe, have a term "mino bimaatisiiwin" which translates as the good life or continuous rebirth.[3] This concept guides all behavior and is based on the tenets that there is a reciprocity in nature and all things affect others. Actions taken today will have effects for the future, so one must be careful.

In addition to this cyclical view of life and history and the need for balance, American Indian beliefs have always professed that there is a spirituality in all things. Trees, rocks, animals and humans all share a common thread in that they all have a spirit. It is possible, some believe, to have these spirits communicate with each other or even enter each other and take one another's place. In other words, a man may become one with a tree to understand and learn from it about nature's forces. Taking from nature means the taking of spirits and thus, should not be done indiscriminately.[4] A special site or place may contain many spirits of past ancestors or deities that will share their knowledge with those who ask in the proper manner.

According to noted political historian Bernard Bailyn, the Indians had, and still have

> a sensitivity attuned to both the physical world and the ruling spiritual forces, and families with a complex array of procedures by which to adjust these external elements to serve their personal needs, the Americans [i.e., American Indians] experienced life as a delicate balance, which had to be carefully maintained. But though they were psychologically and spiritually tense and calculating, their inner lives crowded by forces and spirits of intense meaning and great power, they played out their physical lives freely and loosely in immense territories whose spaciousness was as necessary as the intricacy of their religion.[5]

Therefore, for any person to claim ownership and control over things natural, such as the land or the water, seemed somewhat pretentious by American Indian standards. How could any person claim ownership over that which only the Great Spirit controlled and what was perceived as a gift. More importantly, to claim something was owned was denying that there was a spirituality, the very essence to their belief structures. The American Indian view of the land was one of geopiety.[6] This geopietism means that land and water are held in reverence since these are part of the Great Mystery, a gift for life from the Great Spirit. Contact with these gifts is where the physical and spiritual can converge. As such, land is not perceived as a possession. Land and its use are a reciprocal relationship between an individual and the Earth Mother, where harmony and balance are treasured. It is not a commodity that was given by a deity to be exploited and consumed, but it is really an essential extension of life.[7] Land was for the most part owned by no one person, but may be lived upon by entire groups or tribes of people.[8] Territories were claimed, not necessarily out of some concept of ownership, but more out of a need for the provision of sustenance to the tribe or nation. Overall, territorial claims were part of the tribes' group identity, hence fully integrated as part of their cultural identity.

When a portion of land was finished providing its support, whether the soil being depleted or game becoming scarce, then the tribe would move to another area within their territory and allow the land to complete its cycle of death and rebirth. Seldom, if ever, was an area of land farmed until its soil became totally unproductive or an area so over-hunted that all game became extinct. These phenomena were very uncommon until the arrival of the new-comers.[9] An Indian purposely killing the land, water or animals would be committing a sin against the spirits of the area, but also against the Great Spirit.

Indian tribes, by the time that the newcomers began to arrive in numbers, had set up a loose system of territorial boundaries. It is true that these borders may have been somewhat fluid even by European standards but, nonetheless, they were respected and known by the tribes. It could be argued that tribal border wars were just as common as those occurring in Asia and Europe at this time in history.

Culture and its importance will be a central point in this work. Culture has been conceptualized in a myriad of ways. Some social scientists describe culture as a system created by people as a manner of adapting to their environment. Others describe the concept of culture as a shared system of beliefs, symbols and knowledge that tends to govern individual behavior. Yet others even go so far as to theorize that culture is some sort of manifestation of a group unconsciousness, a representation of the individual's own super-ego.[10] Culture in this work will be defined as all of these viewpoints, but even in more broad and general terms. American Indian culture will refer to the language, the dances, stories, traditions, values and beliefs, spirituality, and the tribe's history. However, whereas many writers reference American Indian culture as if it were some sort of homogeneous entity, a commonality throughout the Indian nations, this could not be further from the truth. American Indian culture is made up of hundreds, if not thousands, of smaller sub-cultures. Languages, symbols, traditions and even religion may vary even among the bands of the same Indian tribe or nation. Thus, the concept of American Indian culture must be understood to be nothing more than a convenient label for a very complex weave of traditions and histories.

The traditional values, customs and beliefs of American Indian "culture" have been maintained throughout time in the United States. This cultural identity has given the Indian peoples a source of strength to face and cope with the diverse challenges facing them.[11] There have been changes and adjustments to and within these tribal cultures the dominant Anglo society has and continues to pressure and disrupt them for whatever reasons, but the core remains and will continue to stay strong. Yet, it is this separateness, this uniqueness and set of traditions, that threatens the American Indian the most because it makes others either fear them or want to become them.

When the invaders arrived, the Indian tribes had populations with common subcultures and cultures, language, territorial claims and land base, an economic system based on hunting, trapping, and/or agriculture, and maintained a system of government which controlled what happened within their borders. Granted, some tribes were more organized in some of these criteria than others, but this does not take away from the fact that the tribes were sovereign entities before the arrival of the newcomers. Indian tribes determined their own courses of actions with respect to other Indian nations or European powers. They entered into economic, political and military alliances. From all definitions, American Indian tribes were sovereign long before the newcomers arrived to tell them otherwise.[12] Understanding this idea that American Indians were sovereign *before* the arrival of any other political power representatives will be essential.

The View of the Newcomers

The newcomers, or possibly more appropriately invaders, arrived to find what they thought to be a paradise compared to what many had left behind. It was a land rich in exploitable resources and relatively unpopulated. Most, if not all, were followers of one of the many Judeo-Christian religions which have at their base the idea that the earth is a temporary place, and to best serve God and demonstrate one's worthiness of salvation, a denial and overcoming of physical nature were needed.[13] The conquering, fixing and controlling of nature was, and to some still is, needed to show this. Hardship is a test of one's devotion.

Judaism and Christianity, in addition, normally do not include the possibility that non-human entities can have a spirit and life of their own. Plants, rocks, animals, the land and water were created for humans to utilize in their needs for life. Little or no consideration as to the effects of overuse or abuse of these entities has ever been given until more modern times. Unlike their Indian counterparts, the newcomers did not view the earth as a mother, a giver of life, and thus there was no way in which *it* could be offended.[14] The grand design established by their god was that humans were to live the best they could, and when they die, they would be rewarded in the afterlife. There was a linear ending to all life.

The newcomers had thus come with a new model of thinking, that of linear thought. Linear thinking, unlike the Indian cyclical mode of thought, sees an end to actions. Very seldom are the effects of actions considered past their immediate moment. The present is limited to the now and the future.

The past is over and has few implications for the present. Cyclical thought on the other hand, implies that the past, the present and the future are all intertwined and affect one another. Utilizing linear thinking, each action is a step leading to the next. Once the present is over, then the only concern is where to take the next step. These conceptual models led the newcomers to view the lands that the Indians controlled as under-utilized, and thus, being wasted. Others came thinking that they would save the Natives from themselves and help civilize them into salvation. The motto of the Massachusetts Bay Company depicted an Indian, standing nearly naked, spouting the phrase "please come and help us." Using biblical invocations and Lockean justifications among other legal theories, the newcomers began their assault on Indian land bases soon after settling on them.

Part of this assault was the view they held of lands in Europe. Much of the land they left was entailed and could not be sold since it was considered a life estate. This, coupled with the doctrine of *primogeniture* where all land-holdings were to go the eldest son,[15] contributed to a shortage of land for the common person. In those nations where all land was owned either by the noble class or the monarch, the possibility of the commoner owning a piece of land was almost unthinkable. Thus, when they began to land and settle on the shores of America, the opportunities that they saw were endless; this blinded them to the status of Indian tribes.

Yet, the Europeans did not settle a virgin land, rather they invaded and displaced a resident population. America was not a wide-open expanse of untouched resources, inhabited only by subhumans commonly labeled savages and described as beasts or demons. As Francis Jennings points out, the America found by these new arrivals "was more like a widow than a virgin," especially after the diseases brought over from the Old World swept through the land.[16] Hence, in reality, those coming to the shores of the new American continent only resettled the lands they found, after they had pushed its original residents off through decimation by diseases or through the destruction of their resources.

Contrasting the world views of the American Indian and the European newcomers is possible (see Table One). Whereas this description has been general, and differences do exist both in actuality and in theory, the views between the two cultures would lead to an irreparable conclusion. The Indian would have to be conquered, assimilated, or destroyed. Not only did they deserve this, but it was for their own good.

All of the notions held by the newcomers would eventually add up to a world view of the Indian peoples that would justify the dispossession of them from their lands. It would also justify their destruction as sovereign and independent nations. The Indian had to be killed, imprisoned or displaced before they would receive the noble savage or victim status. This in turn would lead

Table One. Contrasting Views of the American Indian and Newcomers[17]

American Indian	The Newcomers
Group life is primary	The individual is primary
Respects elders, experts and those with spiritual powers	Respects youth, success and high social status
Time and place viewed as being permanent, settled	Time and place always negotiable; plans for change
Introverted; avoids ridicule or criticism of others if possible	Extroverted; seeks analysis and criticism of situations
Pragmatic: accepts what is	Reformist: changes or "fixes" problems
Emphasizes responsibility for family and personal sphere	Emphasizes authority and responsibility over a wide area of social life
Observes how others behave; emphasis on how others "behave," not on what they say	Eager to relate to others, emphasize how others "feel" or "think"
Incorporates supportive non-family or other helpers, into family network	Keeps the networks of family, friends, and acquaintances separate
Seeks harmony	Seeks progress

to excessive paternalism and wardship, making an entire people into essentially cultural children. Whatever the view, their sovereignty as independent nations would be diminished. But after all, they were just Indians.

This work is concerned with rights. The concern is not necessarily with the rights that individuals hold, but with group rights, specifically those of Indian tribes. These collective rights best represent the arguments and discussions made throughout this work. Tribal members have common beliefs which makes them normatively bound to each other in a manner that each member does not act for themselves, but for the good of the tribe. Each plays a part in effectuating the shared norms and values of the tribe.[18] Tribal rights means that each member's rights are derived from the importance of protecting the group's interests as a whole.[19]

Tribal affiliation, or membership if you wish to call it that, is a collective blood right. Denial of a tribe's rights does not interfere with the aggregated individual claims, but with the very integrity of the rights of the group as a whole. However, tribal affiliation is not the same as joining a club or organization. It is one of blood and birth, even of consciousness. One must be born into the tribe, share its beliefs, norms, values, and its culture. As we will see, government officials have a difficult time visualizing and understanding this concept.

Territory, an ancestral homeland, is closely tied to both one's identity as a tribal member and to the group within the larger sphere of society. By limiting the powers and rights of a tribe over their homeland, then one limits the powers and rights of the individual members also.[20] The protection of American Indian rights means guaranteeing tribal sovereignty, and protecting this will require, as we will see, stepping outside the usual theoretical and cultural confines of thinking and understanding.[21] Courts and governments must acknowledge the territorial imperative of tribal sovereignty, and by doing so, will respect the rights of Indians as members of society.

Robert Porter, the Attorney General for the Seneca Nation of Indians, has stated the need for understanding and the influence of culture on the Indian peoples. He states:

> The communal nature of the Indian people generates a relatively cohesive family and social structure. Historically, such an existence has been critical to survival. The community orders itself ... in such a way as to impose flexible but identifiable standards on individuals that can be enforced through social pressures such as shunning, shaming, banishment and peacemaking. A [tribal] member who wishes to remain in the community must acknowledge and respect the community's norms ... [to] perpetuate harmony, strength and survival.[22]

As will be shown throughout the following chapters, the American Indian experience is primarily one of conflicts caused by the demands of group or collective rights within a society that honors and expects individualism.[23] As such, Indian policy has wavered between assimilating the Indian peoples into the newcomers' individualistic society and fostering them as a separate group with a collective identity. This is one result of a pluralistic democracy that developed in America. Promoting tribal sovereignty seems to pit a minority group against the larger polity of individuals. Hence, governments and courts just can not accept this as being even in the least bit acceptable. They fight and lobby against any efforts that Indians make to better themselves and their tribe, whether it be gaming, regulation of hunting or controlling their environment. Indian group rights are constantly being eroded and destroyed, but they still struggle against the invaders of their lands.

The Meaning of Sovereignty

Throughout much of this work, the concept of sovereignty will be bantered about and used as a foundation for numerous legal, political and social arguments. Because of this, it is necessary to try to delineate a definition of sovereignty, if this is at all possible, since social scientists and legal scholars themselves can hardly agree on a single clear and concise definition. Sovereignty can be expressed as either a right or a legal creation. The term has several connotations which involve not only the political realm, but as we will see, also the social, economic and spiritual ones as well.

Sovereignty, in its most basic form, simply refers to the right to make and enforce laws and decisions within a set and defined territory. However, this definition does not entail the idea of a divine sovereignty in the theological dimension. Therefore, in the political sense, sovereignty is a matter of authority and for some philosophers, that of supreme and unquestionable authority over the people and lands.

The philosopher Jean Bodin is usually credited with first featuring the concept of sovereignty in his writings as early as 1576.[24] His definition was developed more out of a desire to bring about order and stability to a society being torn apart by civil war than any sort of philosophical or legal evidence. To Bodin and to later writers such as Thomas Hobbes, only a supreme or absolute authority or sovereign, one that could not be challenged or even held to its own laws, could save a fractured society and territory.

In modern times, scholars do not insist that the mantle of sovereignty rests with an absolute monarch, but rather with the people of a community or nation. Territorial boundaries of nationhood have been, and probably always will be in the near future, an integral criterion for determination of a people's sovereignty. The concept now specifies to which authority a people are subject to based upon their geographical location.[25] Yet, in regard to American Indians, and elsewhere in the world where new movements of national identity and European unity are growing, this definitional criterion can be somewhat blurred, and can and has caused political and social quandaries.

It will be argued throughout this work that sovereignty can and should be equated not only with the idea of self-governance, but also with self-determination and identification in all spheres of life. This conceptualization implies that an examination of any threats to a people's sovereignty must go beyond simply examining the legal issues.

For American Indians, the debate over tribal sovereignty began when the first explorers and colonizing powers landed on American shores. Each wave of European newcomers made subsequent claims of sovereignty over the Indians based upon their own decrees, doctrines or desires. This meant that Indians lost their rights, freedoms, and independence except for those granted graciously to them by the new authority.[26] This initial stage has set Indian sovereignty on a long path of debate and controversy. Arguments erupt continually over the definition, intent and extent of both Indian tribal sovereignty and the state and/or federal government's sovereignty over the Indians.

It must be remembered that the tribal nations of both North and South

America are the indigenous peoples of the continents and all other peoples are the immigrants. As such, they have and exercise a measure of inherent sovereignty. Therefore, tribal sovereignty has a couple of major dimensions. It has the political and legal aspects meaning that the tribes can adopt their own form of government, define who is a member of the tribe, regulate relations between the tribe and other political entities, regulate domestic relations, set rules for property, settle disputes, and levy taxes, duties and fees on its members and others who are dealing with it.[27]

Sovereignty also involves a cultural and spiritual dimension, a balance and harmony between various human and non-human communities.[28] However, tribal sovereignty has not been delegated to them by any court, government, state, or nation. It is original and inherent and has only been impacted, often detrimentally, by various state and federal laws and policies.[29] Yet, even with this base, the BIA (Bureau of Indian Affairs) states that sovereignty ensures that any decision about the tribes with regard to its property or people are made with the tribes' participation and consent, implying that sovereignty is a right bestowed upon the tribes by a benevolent federal government.[30]

For the first people of this country, the "very essence of tribal sovereignty is the ability to self-govern and to protect the health, safety and welfare of [their] people within [their] territory."[31] The Indian peoples have struggled to maintain a separateness and distinctness from the rest of America in order to retain their identity as a tribe. Obviously this is a resistance to the American ideal of the cultural melting pot, but it remains a very salient point for American Indians. It is a struggle to keep an identity and culture as much as it is to keep legal and political power as a tribe, rights that they have had for millennia. And yet, it is "this desire of the tribes to remain separate which has clouded the relationship between Indians and non–Indian people,"[32] and between tribal, state and federal governments.

As Charles F. Wilkinson points out, "tribal sovereignty is the foundation that undergirds all tribal authority, whether it be taxation, environmental regulation, child welfare, tribal court jurisdiction, or a host of other specific powers."[33] He also notes that the U.S. Supreme Court in the case *Merriam v. Jicarilla Apache Tribe* ruled that his "sovereignty is not conditioned on the assent of a nonmember ... [that] sovereign power, even when unexercised, is an enduring presence that governs all contracts subject to the sovereign's jurisdiction and will remain intact unless surrendered in unmistakable terms."[34]

As will be examined, the efforts to eliminate this separateness are vast and varied and do not always come from official government policies and actions. To be sure, government acts and decisions concerning the curtailment of tribal rights, powers, or even existence have had their impacts upon the very essence of tribal sovereignty. However, other efforts abound from "non-official" avenues that are also having a similar, if not even more detrimental impact, upon the Indians and their sovereign rights and powers. Some of these attacks upon Indian culture and its many facets may be unintentional, but they are still harmful. This type of attack can be even more harmful than an official effort since it cannot be defended against using the law. These attacks are harmful to the Indian and their culture which defines them as a people, and a loss of this identity would mean a loss of self-identification.

To many Americans, this aspect of cultural sovereignty is hard to grasp. In general, American Indians see themselves as having a unique and distinct history that has shaped them and their tribe from the past to the present and far into the future. This has reinforced a desire for separateness and sovereignty, which, believe or not, has at times been accepted to some degree by governmental actions and laws. Yet, having political and legal independence is meaningless without its cultural and spiritual counterparts. It is the right to determine and protect who they are that can be just as important as having the right to govern your own people within some bordered territory. Therefore, as will be seen, the struggle for sovereignty to the Indian peoples is no different than the myriad of empowerment movements and revolutions that have characterized both the history of the Americas and the world.

In conclusion, this section, the issue of sovereignty for the Indian peoples is more than legal and political independence and relationships. It is also an issue of cultural determination and identification. This is a right that pre-existed the colonization of the Americas by non–Indians. For the Indians, the loss of culture and identity would be much more harmful than the continued loss of political and legal rights to make and enforce decisions within their own territory (which is now, of course, limited to reservations). As Peter d'Errico has stated, "ultimately, it is land and a people's relationship to land that is at issue in [Indian] sovereignty struggles. To know that sovereignty is a legal-theological concept allows an understanding of these struggles as spiritual projects,"[35] involving debates about who the Indian peoples are among other Americans.

"Sovereignty arises from within a people as their unique expression of themselves as a people."[36] It is not produced or granted by decrees or doctrines, but by the actual ability of the people to sustain themselves in a place. This is, in fact, self-determination. It is this battle that the American Indians have fought for over five hundred years which this book will address.

Structure of the Book

The purpose of this book is to explore this clash of world views and the implications that it has had on the American Indians. In particular, the examination of the conflict's effects upon property and landholdings will be undertaken. The property rights debate began well before the establishment of the present government of the United States. Therefore, the earliest doctrines that justified the genocide and dispossession of Indians from their lands are discussed in the next section. These include the discovery, conquest and other doctrines.

The focus is on real property, meaning land and its resources, and the right to control it. Having a territorial land base is needed for any nation to be considered independent and sovereign. It is from this base that other rights and powers stem. There are numerous court cases and volumes written describing and evaluating the arguments concerning the right to regulate hunting, fishing and gathering on Indian lands. Furthermore, the literature concerning the right to tax and regulate commerce in Indian Country is both complex and expansive. Yet, these areas of concern stem from having a land base, a territory to which a people can claim to be a nation. As such, although some of these cases will be examined as they pertain to land sovereignty issues, they are not be the primary discussion in this work. Instead, the work deals with the doctrines used to take Indian lands, to dispossess the Indian peoples of their sacred sites, and the ability to stop and regulate the pollution which affects the land and resources upon which the Indian peoples must live and survive.

Once a foundation of Anglo and Indian world views is established, the book focuses on how the United States government has continued to pursue the removal and dispossession of the American Indian peoples and the destruction of their culture. The most common method utilized has been through the court system, therefore the relevant court cases are discussed as they pertain to the issues of property and sovereignty. Although the time frame is somewhat limited to pre–1887, the year of the Dawes Allotment Act, references to more recent cases and decisions are made where appropriate.

Chapter Three is dedicated to a discussion of sacred site protection, access and denials. The importance of a physical setting to American Indian religious and spiritual beliefs cannot be overstated. Sacred sites as property relates not only to the Indian peoples' territorial claims, but is an important aspect of their cultural and intellectual property as well. Recent court decisions that have placed entire tribal cultures and religions in jeopardy due to the denial of access to the sites, actual site destruction, and dispossession are examined.

Environmental issues, particularly the tribal sovereignty issue of dealing with solid and hazardous wastes on reservations, are covered in Chapter Four. If Indian nations are to be considered sovereign, then this means they have the right, power and responsibility to regulate and keep their environment uncontaminated. However, the federal and state governments and private groups have not always agreed that tribes should have this right and have challenged them in judicial and legislative settings. American Indian environmentalism, both in truth and myth, are discussed, and then the focus shifts to the various areas of protection, regulation and pollution control.

The book continues with a more complete discussion of recent court decisions concerning tribal sovereignty and general land issues. Reflections and criticisms are raised due to many of the courts' opinions and their fallacies and shortfalls of logic. The secondary effects that these decisions will have for the future of the American Indian peoples are examined, for the past, the present and the future are all intertwined.

The conclusion expresses thoughts for the future of American Indian sovereignty, culture and survival, including a discussion of current issues facing American Indians and their property rights. The overall effects upon the Indian culture are examined. These concluding remarks address the issues of Indian mascots, sacred sites and hopefully, bring attention to the ongoing struggle America's First Peoples still face today.

At times, the reader may become conflicted with the facts and viewpoints presented here, yet it is this very same inner debate that has confronted indigenous peoples throughout the world whenever they have been subjected to the powers of colonization and assimilation. The purpose of this work is not to produce guilt in the non–Indian reader, but to bring to light the struggles that have faced the very first peoples of this land called America. No apology whatsoever is made for defending the rights of the Indian peoples throughout this work.

CHAPTER TWO

The Challenges Ahead

"Some of our chiefs make the claim that the land belongs to us. It is not what the Great Spirit told me. He told me that the lands belong to Him, that no people own the land; that I was not to forget to tell this to the white people when I met them in council."[1]

—KANEKUK, KICKAPOO PROPHET

Introduction

The Indian and newcomer views of the land and its resources have already been addressed a little in the previous chapter. However, the views that the invaders held of the Indians themselves for the most part, have not. These views are an integral part of the doctrines that have justified the taking and dispossessing the Indians from their lands for nearly five centuries.

The exact number of original Americans in North America when the first wave of immigrants arrived is debated and relatively unknown. Estimates range from a million to over ten million.[2] An examination of the northeastern woodlands places that number at around 300,000, but it was unevenly distributed.[3] This meant that the land was very open except for areas where villages would have existed. This openness was vital to the Indians' existence which was primarily one of hunting and gathering with a small part of their lives dedicated to agriculture. Lands tended to be owned communally and groups moved about their territory on a seasonal or needs basis.

Of course, this meant that there were no personally owned lands, and this idea would have been absurd to an individual member of a tribe. There was no personal wealth attributable to land ownership or control. Instead, the land was shared by the entire tribe on a communal basis. Tribes obviously did not always respect each other's territorial borders, especially during hard times, and there were conflicts but they were not genocidal.

Therefore, America before the invasion was:

> a diverse world—polylingual, polyethnic, regionally disparate in political and social structures, and economically multiform. Yet below these manifest differences lay the common civilization of people who lived at a distinctive level of culture. North and South, East and West, they were all villagers, most of them horticulturists, who lived in similar multifamily dwellings, acquired and prepared food in similar ways, dressed similarly in clothes of similar material, recognized similar signs of status, practiced the same division of labor, and fought wars in similar ways. Above all, they coped with their environment with similar skill. Every measure that historians have been able to devise indicates successful adaptation to the environment.[4]

When the Europeans first arrived, many were unprepared and unaccustomed to this new and strange environment and they lacked the necessary skills and knowledge to survive in the wilderness. They were in need of assistance. Every American has learned the romanticized version of how the Indians helped the first arrivals survive their first winter in this new land. Although history may point out that this happened due to the natural graces of the Indian heart, in reality it probably had a lot to do with the winning over of potential trading partners. The newcomers arrived with steel tools, muskets, fabrics and other items that were unavailable to most tribes. Therefore, when assistance was rendered, many tribes were simply establishing a trade agreement for future goods.

Francis Jennings best described this exchange of goods as a reciprocal discovery between the two cultures.[5] The Indians' cultures would be changed forever by the materials traded to them. Competition within and between the tribes for exclusive trading rights with the newcomers would help contribute to the end of traditional and time-honored ways; there would be demoralization through the introduction of alcohol; missionaries would cause schisms within and between tribes; and the dispossession from their territories due to the occupier's expansion would never be overcome.[6] However, more importantly, the Indians would become more dependent upon the new settlers, all the while the settlers were becoming less dependent upon them. Therefore, Squanto sowed the seeds of the Indians' destruction at what would become known as Thanksgiving by first showing the settlers how to survive in the New World. Soon, the Indian would become less of an asset to the settler, and more of a liability as their lands and other resources were desired.

Whatever the motivations for coming to the Americas and trading goods, no one has argued that there were not Indian peoples present when the first settlers arrived.[7] This presence of the American Indian prior to the newcomer's' arrival is foundational to their claims of sovereignty. Therefore, the newly arriving representatives of European governments needed to justify a means of dealing with these original residents.

Spain was foremost in developing a policy of dealing with the aboriginal peoples of the Americas. Theologians had argued that conquest of another people's lands could only be legitimate if the war was just. However, the problem was arranging events and circumstances to make the war just at the most opportune times (meaning having a larger army), especially since national defense was difficult to argue when the offenders lived halfway around the world.[8] Searching for a legal, religious and philosophical justification to take lands they encountered, Spanish explorers only had to turn to the history of the Crusades for a model. Pope Innocent IV (1243–1254) was one of the first to theorize about contacts with non–Christian infidel peoples. He justified Christian warfare against infidel nations as being just, and that the infidels, by virtue of their nonbelief, possessed no rights to property and they could be forcefully dispossessed by the Christian Crusaders.[9] Pope Innocent extended this theory into one that included the position that the non–Christians (infidels) belonged to the Christian faith by virtue of their creation, but did not belong to the Church. As such, the "Pope had jurisdiction and power over all men in law if not in fact."[10] Papal intervention to save the souls of the nonbelievers was essential and justified by divine law. It was the Papal duty to enlighten all non–Christians, thus authorizing conquest and conversion to both Christian and Eurocentric views and ideals. Thus, the Crusades had established the principle that war and/or conquest in the name of the church, was inherently just.

Spain and Portugal, being devoutly Catholic countries, quickly adapted Pope Innocent's decree into their mandate for exploring and claiming lands in the New World. As Williams states, this meant that the "conquest of infidel peoples and their lands could proceed according to a rule of law that recognized the right of non–Christian people either to act according to the European's totalizing normative vision of the world or to risk conquest and subjugation for violations of this Eurocentrically understood natural law."[11] This is the attitude that Columbus and his followers had when they first landed in the New World, being rescued by Chief Guacangeri of the Arawak people. They arrived with their own self-proclaimed political and religious right to conquer due to the native Arawak's divergence from the European/Christian norms of civilization.[12] More importantly, they believed the Arawak Indians to be inferior and subhuman, thus marked from birth for subjugation.[13]

Of course, Columbus' contract which granted him 10 percent of all the wealth he discovered in the New World, was a great impetus to take more land. Thus, began the history of Indian enslavement and death as well as the need for new theological and legal justifications. The Indians of the West Indies islands were enslaved to mine the gold which had been discovered there. The native revolts of 1495 were put down with such ruthless efficiency that some of the Arawak people committed suicide rather than face slavery.

By the early 1500s, Indian enslavement was justified by Papal decree stating that slavery was a way of civilizing and Christianizing the Indians. European powers had decided that "only by denying their freedom and appropriating their labor could the civilizing task of assimilation be carried out."[14] Furthermore, King Ferdinand's royal order stated that due to their excessive liberty, the Indians tended to run from their European invaders and thus, "must be compelled to work so that kingdom can be enriched, and the Indians Christianized."[15]

Land was taken from its Indian inhabitants and awarded to those who would support the church and crown through the encomienda system. The holy alliance of church and crown had taken firm hold in the New World by the early 1500s.[16] Therefore, the crusading mentality of the invaders' innate superiority over all other humans due to divine endowment continued, with nothing immoral if it benefited the conqueror's god or goals.[17]

Since the Indian had no scripture or linear theology, their beliefs and practices were seen as paganist or heathenistic, and they were infidels at best and demons at worse. The invaders operated under the belief that Christianity was founded in natural law. The Indian violated even natural law with their nakedness, their acceptance of homosexuality, their granting a woman right and control over her own body, their simple marriage and divorce proceedings, their dances and ceremonies, their reliance on dreams and magic, and their numerous other customs and traditions that the settlers encountered and could not comprehend.[18] All this added up to the justification of the Indian's inferiority and savagery. Therefore, having the Natives reduced to the status of a subhuman beasts only gave the newcomers more of an impetus for conquest. Of course, the Indians were especially savage when they attempted to defend themselves and fought against the incessant encroachment on their territory.[19] By 1503, England had also begun to dabble in trade with the various tribes, with a sideline business of kidnapping and selling of captives into slavery.[20]

In 1513, King Ferdinand had the Requerimiento drafted, which was a charter of conquest, that informed the Indians that they could either accept Christian missionaries and Spanish rule or be annihilated.[21] The charter informed the Indians of their obligation to hear and follow the Christian world view, and more importantly, that their lands had been donated by the Pope to Spain. If the Indians refused to obey, their deaths became their fault. There was no right of self-rule or autonomy within this system, nor obviously of appeal.

A new path was chosen in dealing with Indian rights and property when Francisco de Vitoria's (1480–1546) work entitled "On the Indians Lately Discovered" was published posthumously in 1557, and his conclusions were not liked by the government. Using international law as a foundation, Vitoria's conclusions can be summarized as: (1) Indians possessed natural legal rights as a free and rational people; (2) the Pope's grant of America to Spain was baseless and had no effect on the Indians' inherent rights; and (3) it is true that transgressions of the norms of the law of nations by the Indians may serve to justify their conquest.[22] In more detail, Vitoria dismissed the papal decrees giving control over all Indian lands to either the government, or to the church itself.

The Indians were not "precluded by the sin of unbelief or by any other mortal sins from being true owners [of their land] alike in public and in private law."[23] The Indians were the true owners before the arrival of the Spaniards. He went further and dismissed those who used the philosophy of Aristotle to claim the Indians were natural slaves. Instead, Vitoria pointed out that Aristotle only meant that those who were deficient by nature were to be ruled. There was no evidence that the Indians met this standard.[24]

His dismissal of world rule by the emperor or the Pope was daring for the day. Vitoria stated that the emperor was not the lord of the whole world, and even if he was, this would not give him the power or right to seize Indian lands and erect new lords and taxes over them. Furthermore, the Pope was not the civil or temporal lord of the world, and could not transfer secular power to lords and princes.[25] Therefore, the Pope had no secular power over the Indians. To wage a war against the Indians and seize their goods and land for simply refusing to recognize the Pope's dominion over them was unjustified. In other words, announcing Christianity to the Indians and then having them not accepting it immediately was not a justification for making war upon them.[26]

Vitoria's efforts placed the process of the Indian's' conquest into a legalized and rational structure, especially in regard to their land. Vitoria dismissed the idea that mere discovery overrode the Indian's title to their land, for they were the true owners of the territory.[27] Yet, the law of nations was to constrain the Indians and the discoverers. The Spaniards retained the rights of travel, residence and commerce on Indian lands as long as they caused no harm.[28] Moreover, if the Indians did not obey this set of laws, only then would a war waged against them be justified, reducing them to captivity.[29]

Vitoria denied that the doctrine of mere discovery had given Spain clear title to Indian lands. The Indians retained the title of ownership. Furthermore, unless a war waged against the Indians was legally justified, then the conquest theory could not be used as justification.[30]

The religious grounds for conquest became coupled with one of paternalism and guardianship over the Indians. It was a Christian duty and right to help a backward people, a duty mandated under the law of nations. Vitoria stated that the Indians should give unhindered freedom to the Spaniards to preach among them, and if they did so, then they could not be warred into subjugation or have their lands despoiled.[31] It was the Indians' duty under these same laws to entertain the attempts at their conversion. For refusal to hear the "truth," Spain and the other European powers could conquer and colonize Indian lands.[32] Of course, Vitoria recognized the fact that the Indians could always willingly give up the title to their land to Spain. Unfortunately, all works written before Columbus, especially those describing the harsh treatment and atrocities committed by Spain toward the Indians, were declared illegal by the Spanish Inquisition in 1577, and nearly lost forever.[33]

France, possibly more due to the location of their first settlements than anything else, embarked upon a slightly different approach in dealing with the Indians. Since many of their settlements were in areas unsuitable for farming, they turned to the trading in furs and other resources for their wealth. Trade required a reciprocal relationship, and it would obviously not work if the other partner was disliked or mistrusted. As such, France's policy was beneficial to all parties. Their limited settlements seemed compatible with Indian occupancy of the lands. Their attempts at "francization" of the Indians, converting them to French civilization, culture and religion, had little effect and thus, caused little disruption.[34]

Christianity as a justification of conquest soon became displaced by racism as the dominant conquest theme.[35] The European conquerors were "civilized," and thus superior in all ways to the "savages" found in the Americas. As Jennings states, "civilization had created a savage, [all] to kill him. Idea had begotten image, [all] to kill it."[36] The Indian was demonized, described as monsters and animals incapable of acting, or ever becoming civilized. Even Captain John Smith of Pocahontas fame described the Indians as devil worshipers.[37]

The Dutch West India Company had set up a trading post and colony at New Amsterdam (Manhattan, New York). In 1640, they tried to tax the local Indians to help pay for the fort and troops; this only resulted in the tax collector being attacked.[38] The Company responded by attacking the local Raritan Tribe which would lead to an escalation of massacres and countermassacres by both the Indians and whites which would continue well into the 1650s. The Company's policy of extermination would really be a failure in that it caused ruin to both the settlers and the Indians.[39]

As England entered into the competition for the New World, the theories and justifications for taking Indian holdings also increased and diversified. England was pressured to extend both Christianity, (albeit not Catholicism), and its sphere of military-economic influence in the Americas to rival its enemy, Spain. By the mid–1500s, efforts were well under way to break the Spanish monopoly in America. The Papal decrees giving Spain title to Indian lands were rejected by England. England's belief that there was a Christian duty to expand its control in America existed but was not a driving force as it had been for Spain and Portugal.[40] The economic justification of controlling the Indians and their lands shifted to the forefront of royal orders. "In the transformed legal discursive formation of England's seventeenth century, the Indians came to be viewed as the dehumanized entry barrier to the lawfully mandated sovereignty of the English over the underutilized, savage lands of the New World."[41]

The English settlers attempted to establish agricultural centers rather than trade centers like the French and Dutch. Overall, they had more settlers than France and Spain combined. The attitude was that the only proper usage for the land was farming. This policy was destructive of American Indian hunting practices, of native plants, and it forced the Indian to: (1) contest the English destruction of their economy; (2) convert to the white man's ways and methods; or (3) remove themselves further into the frontier where they would encroach upon other tribes and their lands.[42]

The English gained Indian land titles by: (1) claiming all of the land for the King and then, receiving a parcel from the King; and (2) companies that were empowered to settle the New World got the title via Indian permission, or simply seized it outright.[43] The Pilgrims and Puritans claimed their titles to Indian lands because the land was temporarily vacant, having been depopulated by plagues brought over by earlier explorers. According to their logic, the land was vacant by divine providence, making it theirs to possess and control.

Even though conquest became justified legally, it was limited since the Indians were usually militarily stronger than the new arrivals.[44] As economic ventures such as the Virginia Company were granted monopoly rights to settle in America, this legality took on a new meaning. The settlers of Jamestown had to accept the surrounding Powhatan Confederacy as a sovereign nation, even if just due to its size.[45] Yet, acceptance of Indian sovereignty was due to more than just size; it was due to the needs for food and other resources which the Indians were willing to trade. The purchase of lands from Chief Powhatan and this economic dependence disturbed the owners of the Virginia Company. This meant that the settlers would be less dependent upon the Company and more independent in their dealings with the Indians. England and the Company made several attempts to make Chief Powhatan a vassal, but he refused to be subjugated to English rule. Instead, Parliament and the Company's directors began to restrict trade with the Indians through a licensing system.

Both England and the Virginia Company disliked having to accept Powhatan's control over the settlement's surrounding territory. When Jamestown's Governor Yeardley agreed to getting the consent of the Indian rulers[46] before expanding the colony, both the Crown and Company reacted negatively.

If Indian title were recognized as legal, then the cost to the Crown and private ventures such as the Virginia Company would greatly increase. A new track in thinking about Indian rights and title had to be undertaken.

The answer was in an adjustment to the right of conquest. Since the Virginia Company had failed to conquer the Powhatan Confederacy, it had to be given special authority to extend English sovereignty over America. The local "infidels'" laws were obviously contrary to the laws of nature and God. Therefore, in this new twist of logic, England decided that getting any Indian ruler's consent for land meant that England would be placed under the authority of a heathen savage whose laws were in direct conflict with those of the civilized world.[47] John Smith and Samuel Purchas of the Virginia Company depicted the local Indians as savages and beasts in order to dehumanize them. This permitted them to pass along the blame for the settlement's failures and the deaths of its settlers onto the "savages."[48] The sovereignty of the "savages" was illegitimate under natural law. "A savage could never validly exercise sovereignty over land, for sovereignty, by its very definition, was a power recognized to exist in civilized peoples whose laws conformed with the laws of God and nature."[49] Hence, sovereignty, the ability to control one's own territory, became tied to the European standards of civilization and all that this entailed.

As such, no English citizen could enter into an agreement for title of land with the Indians since it was impossible for them to have title in the first place. More so, if the Indians resisted any encroachment, they could be dispossessed as violators of the laws of nature, God, and international law.[50]

Soon, European powers would battle for the right to dispossess Indians from their lands. France and England waged a war that split tribes and nations. In 1763, when the Treaty of Paris officially ended the hostilities between the two European powers, England gained control over colonization and commerce in areas formally controlled by France. England's goal was to facilitate trade with the Indians, yet limit expansion into Indian lands especially into the Haudenosaunee lands who had allied themselves with the British, all to prevent future costly hostilities. In addition, inland expansion would raise the transportation costs of manufactured goods from England, thus increasing reliance on American-made goods. Thus, a containment policy was instituted by England.

In 1764, a Board of Trade was established by Parliament to manage all political and economic relations with the Indians. Two districts were created, north and south, and the superintendents of these were to license traders, set treaties and regulate trade.[51] In the northern district, Sir William Johnson became superintendent. In defense of Haudenosaunee claims to western New York and Pennsylvania, Sir Johnson explained to the Board that the *Indian* "right of conquest" had given them these lands and the smaller resident tribes accepted the Haudenosaunee as their sovereign.[52] Therefore, all encroachments upon their lands needed to be stopped and they should be reimbursed for lands already taken. The Board failed to act on these recommendations. Meanwhile, Americans were not content to be limited in their right to expand westward. Colonial radicals turned to English libertarian philosophy to justify their right to expand into Indian lands. John Locke's work became the basic premise for taking over Indian wastelands. The Americans saw the opportunity for creating a society based on property, one that England was denying them by preventing them the right of expansion. Using Locke, the radicals' argued that since "God and His reason commanded [man] to subdue the earth, i.e., improve it for the benefit of life, and therein lay out something upon it that was his own, his labor,"[53] England and their protection of Indian lands were preventing them from fulfilling this goal. The earth and everything in it was given to humans for their support and comfort of being, according to Locke.[54] And even though the world was given in common to everyone, both God and reason did not intend for it to remain this way. As such, the Indians' failure to apply labor to their lands in the form of agriculture and having tribal ownership rather than individual title was in violation of the very basis of reason.[55] Land was for those who were industrious and rational.[56] England's containment policy was denying the Americans their right to property and was a clear violation of natural law.

There was another reason that the containment policy was disliked by the Americans. Several of the colonial governments and the upper class were getting wealthy by selling Indian lands to settlers and speculators. The granting of land patents and the selling of land sale approvals was big business. Containment meant a loss of revenue for those involved in this business. This was especially true for Virginia, whose land claims covered an extensive area. In fact, the governors of Virginia and Pennsylvania were warned several times that land speculators like George Washington were violating British law and needed to cease their activities.[57] Despite these warnings and Parliamentary Proclamations forbidding expansion westward, the colonists continued to move onto Indian lands. They were under the impression that any lands reserved for the Indians by the King really belonged to the Americans in the first place, and land syndicates rapidly bought, swindled and took every acre they could get.[58]

Some settlers had purchased their land directly from the various Indian tribes. This action was justified in that free men were simply exercising their natural law rights to purchase and acquire land, as were the unconquered Indians by freely alienating their lands to the buyers.[59] The Indians' willingness to enter the land market demonstrated their rationality. This self-serving inclusion of Indians within the natural law discourse was a blatant attempt to justify what England was denying the land speculators. "Land market capitalists assumed a mantle of zealous advocate of Indian's natural law rights in order to engage in unregulated real estate transactions."[60] In other words, the Indians were sovereign, rational, trustworthy and held land title whenever and as long as there was a purpose and they cooperated. "The speculators in Indian land grants never regarded themselves primarily as crusaders for a racially neutral form of American egalitarianism that demanded recognition of the Indian's title to their lands."[61] Instead, title was only recognized by those in the colonies who had the most to gain from doing so. Therefore, American racism and economic interests became linked in the process.[62]

As the colonies and Britain erupted in warfare, the Continental Congress was filled with representatives inundated with self-interest.[63] Competition between the landless states, as measured by the amount of Indian land titles gathered, and states such as Virginia delayed the signing of the Articles of Confederation. This led some members to propose that Congress be given sole authority to purchase Indian lands so that all states could benefit to some extent. In the 1777 session, Congress gave itself the authority to regulate all trade and affairs with the Indians as long as this power did not infringe upon any state.[64] This did not stop the competition and squabbles over who could claim Indian lands to the west. Congress eventually agreed not to void any previous Indian land grants of title, and at the same time, recognizing Virginia's claims to lands of the west.

In 1781, two pamphlets were published that stirred up public opinion concerning the Indian lands to the west. Thomas Paine's work, "Public Good," argued that these "vacant" lands should be regarded as the people's common right. He dismissed both Virginia's and Britain's claims to the area as being unreasonable. Besides, Paine believed that these lands could be utilized to settle the national debt.[65]

The second work by Samuel Wharton focused on Indian natural rights.[66] Wharton extended natural rights theory to include the Indians. Utilizing Lockean logic, he argued that the Indians had exercised their first natural right, that of self-preservation, through the acquisition and holding of property. He ridiculed Christian dictates that stated they had unilateral rights to the lands since the Indians were heathens. The Indians of the west had not been conquered, nor had their laws been altered. Therefore, they could enter into land contracts and these had to be valid. Since the Indians held title to the land as its first occupants, no one else could derive a title to it based on the doctrine of discovery since under both the laws of nature and nations, Indian title was valid.[67] Of course, Wharton was merely justifying years of land purchases from the Indians. Yet, his arguments allowed a new direction in Indian-American relations.

With the new constitution of 1787,[68] the implication seemed to be that Congress would have the ultimate authority over Indian tribes and their lands.

However, the individual states did not see it this way. Massachusetts and New York continued to purchase Indian lands directly from those tribes within their borders, and North Carolina and Georgia did not cede their western land claims until 1792 and 1801.[69] The new argument was that the Indians did not have the natural right to sell their lands to anyone they wanted, but had the right to sell only to the federal government. The natural right theory now excluded the Indian.

Both the Continental Congress under the Articles of Confederation and the new United States Congress treated the surrounding Indian tribes, mostly the Haudenosaunee, as equal and sovereign nations. Military and trade alliances were sought and peace treaties entered into freely by both sides. The 1787 Northwest Ordinance was therefore a mixed blessing to the Indians. It established a system of peaceful relations with the Indians and created a principled bill of rights for them.[70] More importantly, it declared that Indian property, rights and liberty were inviolate to unconsented invasions or disturbances. In addition, it set up the national government as the key to Indian relations rather than the individual states.[71] This was affirmed by the 1790 Trade and Intercourse Act which prohibited individuals and states from acquiring Indian lands without federal approval.[72] This was to allow an orderly acquisition of Indian lands and a controlled expansion for the new nation.

As long as the infant United States remained militarily unorganized and weak, and the population relatively small, then this period of convenient political equality with its respect for Indian sovereignty would continue. However, this would not last long and the challenges to both the ideals of American Indian equality and sovereignty soon began. The Indian became more of a hindrance and a block to expansion than a people whose rights and cultures should be respected. As stated earlier, the American Indian was no longer an asset to the Europeans, but had become a serious liability. The doctrine of Manifest Destiny was not to include the American Indian.

Challenges from the New Nation

The period of respect and equality was not to last very long after the American Revolution. As mentioned, in the years immediately following the Revolution, the United States (both its national and state governments) considered the Indians as sovereign entities in order to get much land as possible without resorting to military force. Yet, as the government's wealth, power and populations increased, the need to respect Indian rights and sovereignty began to diminish.

The statement of the Shawnee leader, Tecumseh, to Governor Harrison in 1810 lays the foundation for the upcoming disputes. Tecumseh stated:

"Sir, [Governor Harrison], you have the liberty to return to your own country. This land was given by the Great Spirit for the Red man, to keep it, traverse it, enjoy its productivity. Until lately, there was no white man on this continent. We were once happy, but have been made miserable by the whites who are never contented, but always encroaching. The way, and the only way to check and stop this evil, is, for all the Red men to unite in claiming a common and equal right in the land, as it was at first, and should be yet; for it was never divided, but belongs to all, for the use of each. That no part has a right to sell, even to each other, much less to strangers; those who want all, and will not do with less. The white people have no right to take the land from the Indians, because they had it first; it is theirs. They may sell, but all must join. Any sale not made by all is not valid.... Part do not know how to sell. It requires all to make a bargain for all. All Red men have equal rights to the unoccupied land. The right of occupancy is as good in one place as in another. There cannot be two occupations in the same place. The first excludes the others. It is not so in hunting ... but the camp is stationary, and that is occupancy. It belongs to the first who sits down on his blanket or skins, which he has thrown upon the ground, and till he leaves it no other has right."[73]

Tecumseh had foreseen the grounds and issues in the upcoming legal battles for Indian lands. The right of occupancy would be granted, then stripped away; and treaties would be signed with minor chieftains behind the backs of entire Indian nations and held to be legal in the courts. If his advice had been heeded, the legal history dealing with Indian lands would be drastically different. The first legal challenge to Indian rights, like many to follow, would not even have the Indians as a party to the case. It was primarily a result of a state government, in this instance Georgia, having financed its Revolutionary War efforts through the sale of Indian lands. Georgia rushed to accept a bid for land made by some speculators, the New England Mississippi Land Company, in order to pay off its militia in 1795. The entire legislature had been bribed to pass the act patenting the state's unceded western territory for a nominal fee.[74]

In 1796, the legislature repealed by statute the sale to the company and its director, John Peck. However, during the year, Peck had sold the land to Robert Fletcher. The legislative repeal brought into question the legitimacy of all land titles in the area. This was particularly true since the state of Georgia had failed to get a transfer of the lands from the Indians via treaty in the first place.[75] Fletcher proceeded to sue Peck to recover his money.

Hence, *Fletcher v. Peck* (1810)[76] was to be the first case used by the Supreme Court to extol the sanctity of vested rights in property and a secure meaning to the contract clause, thereby establishing a legal status for American Indian lands within the United States.[77] The justices, upon hearing the case "affirmed the prerequisite of tribal consent to the extinguishment of Indian title."[78] However, this title was only one of occupancy.[79]

The right of occupancy and not one of fee simple title was justified by Justice Marshall by the doctrine of discovery. Thus, in *Fletcher v. Peck*, the

Court stated that discovery of the lands reduced Indian title from fee simple to one of mere occupancy with no rights to own or transfer title to their ancestral lands. Georgia had acquired fee simple title and could grant land patents, yet the state was denied the right to evict its Indian tenants.[80] The right of occupancy was firmly established without the right of alienation, and occupancy could only be terminated on a consensual basis.

The Court found for Peck because Georgia's first contract was legal and its repeal was a violation of the contract clause. According to Marshall, the land grant, even if achieved by bribes, could not be annulled since it would be a violation of the Constitution. Besides, any rights the Indians held to the lands were not in contradiction to the state's claims. The lands were within Georgia and the state had the power to grant title to them, a sovereign authority to patent "vacant" Indian lands to non–Indian purchasers.[81]

Justice Johnson did dissent to this decision and argued that the Indians had absolute proprietorship of their lands.[82] He pointed out that past political practices of treaty making and land purchases by settlers and governments alike affirmed this right. The Indians' rights and title could only be ceded by agreement, and not simply because a white person had glanced upon the lands. Johnson simply expressed a line of thought that was foremost until the colonies were independent.

Yet, this "squabble among thieves"[83] set the stage for a new wave of Indian land takings, most of which were decided without the Indians' knowledge or participation. What used to be bought or taken by treaty, would now be forfeited in the courts. The Indians were no longer equal sovereign nations, but a wandering inferior people who were wasting the lands, leaving them vacant.

In *New Jersey v. Wilson* (1812)[84] the issue involved ceded lands. In 1758, the Lenape Indians (Delawares) ceded land to New Jersey in exchange for tax exempt reserved lands. In 1798, they sold these lands with legislative approval, and since the purchaser was non–Indian, the tax status was revoked.[85] The change in tax status was challenged and the Supreme Court ruled that the rights of the new landowners were the same as those granted the original Indian owners. This was not an issue of political sovereignty, but one of title transfer.[86]

The Marshall Court seriously defined Indian property and sovereignty rights in a series of cases beginning in the 1820s. The first of these was *Johnson v. M'Intosh* (1823).[87] Once again, the Indians (in this case the Illinois and Piankeshaw) were not a direct party to the case and the issues relating to them were being argued and resolved without their involvement.

The plaintiff, the Illinois Wabash Land Company, claimed lands via Indian grants of title in 1773 and 1775 and argued that the Indians had the right to grant these titles and sell the land fee simple.[88] The defendant, M'Intosh, claimed the same lands from a grant given to him in 1795 by the national government. He argued that the Indians had no right to sell to private individuals because the "civilized powers of Europe have uniformly disregarded the Indians supposed right to the territory."[89] Furthermore, the Indians were considered to be still in the state of nature and as such, had not been admitted into the general society of nations.[90] This implied that they had no political sovereignty, nor the property rights usually assumed of sovereign peoples.

Justice Marshall used this opportunity to further develop an American system of real property law, at the expense of the American Indians. He and the Court were faced with the issue of whether a land grant obtained without federal government approval conveyed title that had to be respected by the American courts.[91] Marshall, using the discovery doctrine laid out in *Fletcher*, expounded on Indian property rights and tribal sovereignty. He now used this doctrine to justify exclusive right to appropriate Indian lands and to create impairments of Indian rights.[92]

As mentioned, the doctrine of discovery was developed by the invading Europeans to systematically expand their spheres of influence. In order to ensure that the land would be open to settlement, this required the mischaracterization of the native peoples as uncivilized savages, nomads, and heathens. This doctrine of discovery, although rooted in racism, did not affect American Indian sovereignty in any form, for it was a self-imposed limitation by European powers which affected only their interests and relations in that it organized their respective spheres of influence.[93] Marshall chose to answer a deeper question than the one that the facts brought forth. The real question was whether or not private individuals or the government had the authority to purchase Indian lands. Instead, Marshall went further and negatively answered the question as to whether or not the Indians had the right to sell their lands to anyone they chose.[94]

According to Marshall, the Indians were the rightful occupants of the land, with a legal and just claim of possession and use, but their rights to sovereignty and power to dispose of their lands at will is denied by the fundamental principle that discovery gave exclusive title to those who made it.[95] In other words, the newcomer's' arrival simply reduced Indian land ownership to occupancy due to their mere appearance of Europeans on the shores of North America. The Indians therefore, had no right to alienate the title to their own land since they no longer held fee simple title to it. Only a discoverer can alienate land title.[96] Thus, the invasion of America conveyed (or reduced) the rights of the Indians to mere occupancy, but at the same time gave the new occupants fee simple title to the same lands. The doctrine of discovery justified taking the land from its occupants "who are heathens" and could not own land.[97] The Europeans had made ample compensation by bestowing upon the Indians Christianity and civilization.[98]

While Marshall pointed out that under international law, all white land titles were questionable, he inverted these same laws and replaced them with the doctrines of discovery and conquest.[99] Marshall was running contrary to nearly two centuries of legal evolution in the opposite direction in which Indian sovereignty and land rights were to be respected. He reduced the Indian to a mere nuisance on their own lands, a view that the American public would soon adopt as it sought to take more and more Indian lands.[100] The federal–Indian relationship was now to be one of landlord-tenant with the rights of the landlord being absolute.

The *Johnson* case involved two white litigants, and "effectively denied American Indian tribes recognizable full legal title to their ancestral home-lands under the doctrine of discovery, which had been adopted by Marshall and the Court as the domestic law of the United States."[101] The new rule was to be that the Indian had no theoretical, independent natural law-based right to full sovereignty over their land that any European discoverer might be required to recognize under the Law of Nations.[102]

In *Johnson*, Indian property rights were divided between the ultimate title of the colonizing sovereign and the title of occupancy reserved for the original inhabitants.[103] Yet, this compromise did not completely define Indian title, even if one of limited occupancy by permission. If it had, then there would have been no further need of legal conceptual models to delineate Indian land rights and political sovereignty. The ultimate results of this case included the creation of inferior status for Indian property rights; an established notion of conquest in American property law; a placing of Indians in an inferior cultural standing; an impairment of the Indians' ability to sell their lands; and, an overall diminished political status for all Indian tribes.[104] Once again, the law and legal philosophy had been readjusted to justify what those displacing the Indian wanted: land.

However, the reworking of the discovery doctrine is what would haunt Indian rights well into the next century. Justice Marshall stated that all of America had been claimed and granted, at some time, by the various European powers. The discovery of the land was conditioned by it being settled. This right was respected by each European competitor. Since the United States had acceded to this system, they were now the rightful discoverer. As such, the United States had the exclusive right to extinguish Indian land titles, now reduced to that of mere occupancy, through either purchase or conquest.[105] Furthermore, since the discovery principle was asserted from the beginning, and then was sustained, Marshall concluded that it had become the law of the land and was not to be questioned.[106] Indian rights of title conveyance to whomever they wished was denied by this logic, this unquestionable law of the land. Only the discoverer can have the right of purchase and thus, exclusive title. Since all past institutions recognized this fact, it should continue.

The linearity of the Europeans' logic was now set and would continue to confound Indian rights and sovereignty.

Of course, this principle of discovery utilized Christianity as its bulwark. In fact, the Christian subjugation of a non–Christian people was the underlying premise of the *Johnson* case.[107] "Accurately stated, the centuries-old right of discovery was the right of any Christian nation to locate and take possession of non–Christian lands."[108] Marshall's logic converted the discovering Christian sovereign's right of possession into a right of ultimate dominion, which included both absolute authority over and absolute authority ownership of these discovered lands.[109]

In the *Johnson* case, Justice Marshall ensured that Indian rights of ownership and sovereignty did not have to be recognized because of their uncivilized status. Hence, the discovery doctrine simply stated that the Christian trespassers had control over the lands of the infidels. To prove this point, Marshall relied on historical precedent in that "as the successor nation to Great Britain's right of dominion, the government of the United States possessed the absolute right of soil. This was all that was needed for it to have plenary power, or absolute governmental authority, over all the lands and inhabitants within the geographical limits claimed by the United States."[110] In essence, Marshall was stating that the Indians did not have the right to dispose of their land as they wished due to the discovery doctrine and, in fact, they could only dispose of any land to their discoverers.[111]

Therefore, "once the principles of Christian discovery and dominion become United States law as a result of the *Johnson* decision, the religious aspect of the original discovery doctrine was no longer needed."[112] In what would become known as the Cherokee Cases, the Supreme Court demonstrated just how far it would go to destroy Indian property rights and political sovereignty. Once again, the state of Georgia would be the venue for the debate.

The fledgling United States government had secured the Cherokee Nation's lands and their right to legal and political jurisdiction within these lands with the 1791 Treaty of Holston. The United States received other lands in return. However, by 1802, the federal government had agreed with the state of Georgia that it would at its own expense extinguish American Indian land titles within the state as soon as it reasonably could.[113] For the next twenty years, the federal government failed to act on its promise while the Georgia legislature constantly pressed for action. With the election of Andrew Jackson to the presidency, a new hope was revived in the state.

In 1825, the fraudulent Treaty of Indian Springs had been negotiated between the state of Georgia and the federal Indian commissioner and the Creek nation. It swindled the Creek out of 4.7 million acres of land.[114] Although President John Quincy Adams had initially signed the treaty, he reneged on this when he discovered the trickery involved in getting it. Incensed, the state of Georgia declared that this revocation was invalid and was a violation of state rights since the land had already been promised. Governor George M. Traup even threatened to call out the state militia if the federal government did anything to hinder the treaty's enforcement.[115] Adams caved in to Georgia's threats, and the stage was set for Georgia to expand its efforts at stealing Indian lands, especially after gold was discovered on Cherokee lands in 1828.[116]

Georgia quickly annexed Cherokee lands in 1829, annulled the Cherokee Constitution and assumed jurisdiction over all Indians residing on Cherokee lands.[117] Andrew Jackson, for his part, withheld federal monies owed to the Cherokee and pressed Congress to ratify a removal act which Congress had promised since 1802, as part of the deal to get Georgia to give up land claims in neighboring states. The removal act eventually was passed over any opposition in 1830.[118] The opportunity to test these actions came when the state arrested a Cherokee, Corn Tassel, for murder. Corn Tassel was arrested, convicted and executed before the issue of state-federal-tribal jurisdiction could be settled. The Supreme Court had issued a writ of error but Georgia ignored it, refused to appear in the Court, and carried out the execution.

The Cherokee Nation brought suit under the Article III of the Constitution giving the Supreme Court original jurisdiction in disputes between the United States, its states and foreign nations. The Cherokee sought relief from any further actions by Georgia that were in violation of the Cherokee property rights, treaties and laws. Thus, *Cherokee Nation v. Georgia* (1831)[119] did give Marshall and the Supreme Court another opportunity to either reestablish Indian property rights, or further erode and erase them altogether. The Court chose the latter.

Marshall did hold that under international law, the Cherokee were a foreign nation, but this did not apply under the U.S. Constitution. Instead, they were "domestic dependent nations" and did not have standing to invoke the original jurisdiction doctrine granted under Article III.[120] In a strange twist of logic, Marshall placed the new U.S. Constitution as being dominant to the Law of Nations. Utilizing the Commerce Clause, he stated that the Constitution had given Congress the delegated authority to regulate commerce with foreign nations, among the states and with Indian tribes. In a leap of faith, he explained how this meant that the Indians were not foreign nations under this wording. Instead, he created a new classification for the many Indian nations, declaring them to be domestic dependent nations.

This domestic dependent nation status reduced the Indian nations to that of a ward with the United States government as the guardian.[121] He placed the Indian nations in a sort of legal limbo, making them neither states nor foreign nations. However, as wards, he established a trust relationship and responsibility firmly with the federal government. Marshall did conclude that the Cherokee were capable of managing their own affairs and governing themselves. Hence, they retained sovereignty within their own borders.

Justices Thompson and Story dissented in this case. They argued that the Cherokee were in fact a foreign nation. They had never lost their independent status through conquest, and as such, could bring suit to the Supreme Court.[122] They stated that the Cherokee properly claimed protection from Georgia's laws and actions due to previously signed treaties. In addition, if the state's actions were left unstopped, then they would ruin all Cherokee laws, government and national character.[123] In fact, Thompson and Story concluded their dissent by stating that the Georgia laws were repugnant to, not protected by, the U.S. Constitution.

However, this did not stop the state of Georgia from proceeding to harass and destroy the Cherokee. The discovery of small amounts of gold on Cherokee lands in 1829 only exacerbated the urgency to remove the Cherokee from the state. A new law was passed forbidding the passage of any non–Indian into Cherokee territory without state permission.[124] Samuel Worcester, a missionary, defied this new law, entered Cherokee territory with the tribe's permission, was arrested, tried, convicted and sentenced. A second chance to define Indian rights and sovereignty was now before the Court.

Worcester v. Georgia (1832)[125] gave Marshall and the Court a chance to test the constitutionality of Georgia's laws and modify the track that was being followed concerning Indian rights. The Court did find that Worcester had standing and was a victim of laws that were repugnant to the U.S. Constitution and treaties.[126] Georgia's laws dealing with the Indians were void since all relations with the Indians were to be carried out by the federal government.

Justice Marshall veered away from utilizing the conquest doctrine to justify Georgia's actions. He did admit that it is difficult to comprehend that discovery should give rights to the discoverer that annulled pre-existing rights of ancient possessions.[127] He separated discovery from conquest by rationalizing that discovery and settlement did not constitute conquest which yields title to the conquered's property. Instead, this process granted only the right to purchase land should the Indians wish and consent to sell. Using military force to take the lands from the Indians is conquest and this act of aggression could not be recognized as legitimate in the courts.[128] The Indian nations have always been considered as distinct independent political communities that retained their original rights as the undisputed possessors of their soil.[129]

Marshall went a step further and reiterated that relevant treaties have recognized the national character of the Cherokee and their rights to self-government, lands and for the federal government to protect these rights.[130] Therefore, the ward-guardian relationship set up in the previous case was now combined to obligate the rights of the Indians with the duties of the discoverer.

The federal government had the sole responsibility to take care of the Indians, not the states. This was an echo of the English government's decision in dealing with the earlier settlers and American colonists. Specifically, Congress was charged with regulating Indian trade and commerce, as well as transfers of property and its interests outweighed those of the states. Therefore, Marshall delineated the trust responsibility that the U.S. government had to the Indians.

This decision angered both the Georgia legislature and many members of Congress. President Jackson responded by uttering his infamous statement: "Marshall made his decision, now let him enforce it."[131] A renewed effort for the complete removal of the Indian west of the Mississippi began. The Cherokee, as well as the Choctaw and other tribes throughout the United States, were asked to voluntarily leave their lands at bayonet point.[132] The end results of these two cases were: "(1) That the Indian Nations and tribes were now under the protection of the federal government and in this condition lack sufficient sovereignty to claim political independence; and (2) Do possess sufficient power and sovereignty to shield themselves from the intrusions of the states, and the federal government has the responsibility to guarantee this."[133] Justice Marshall made sure to subjugate the powers and rights of the Indians, but also those of the states, to the powers and duties of the federal government.

Mitchell v. United States (1835)[134] sanctified the Indian right of occupancy, yet this case has been largely ignored by both legal scholars and policy makers. The case has to do with Spanish sovereignty in the Florida territory. The 1763 Treaty of Paris had ceded east and west Florida from Spain to Great Britain. However, after the American Revolution, where Spain had sided with England against the colonies, Spain was able to regain control of Florida and much of the Gulf Coast. In 1795, the United States negotiated the Pinckney Treaty with Spain in which Spain allowed the new nation free navigation along the Mississippi and accepted the American version of the Floridian border. Of course, relations did not remain stable and with the War of 1812, the question of Florida's ownership was brought up again. President Monroe ordered General Jackson to invade Florida and punish the resident Indians, Seminoles and Creeks, for their raids and for harboring run-away slaves. Finally, in 1819, the Adams-Onis Treaty ceded Florida to the United States.

Panton, Leslie and Company had been operating in east Florida prior to 1783. Spain had authorized their being there. When the Company lost property due to Seminole raids (1780–1792), the company petitioned the Spanish Crown for compensation. This was given in the form of various land grants west of the Mississippi River, and the company received permission to purchase Seminole and Creek Indian lands within Florida. Over the next seven years, they purchased nearly 1.25 million acres. Colin Mitchel eventually bought these lands from the company, and purchased other deeds from the resident Indians. However, the United States claimed the same lands under the 1819 treaty.

The question of the case was whether by the time the cession by treaty took effect, did Mitchel have a right to the lands included in his grants, or had they been previously granted by the lawful authority of the King of Spain.[135] Mitchel had filed suit in 1828 under a federal law allowing the settling of Florida land claims. The Superior Court dismissed his original claim, yet he appealed to the Supreme Court in 1830. The Court gave the government five years to gather the needed evidence to refute Mitchel's claims.

Mitchel's argument was that the Indian conveyance to Spain gave the King complete title. This in turn was given to the company, and eventually to Mitchel. The U.S. argued that unless Mitchel received the lands before the 1819 treaty, he held no title to them. The government's argument stated that the Indians had no right to cede the lands to the company in the first place; and secondly, since the absolute title rested with Spain, the company could not even buy Indian lands.[136] Furthermore, the Indians' right of occupancy had been extinguished by the 1765 and 1783 treaties.

Justice Baldwin stated that the Indian occupancy title was as sacred as the fee simple title by non–Natives.[137] The Indian title did imply the power to transfer it to others; however it could proceed only with their consent. Baldwin went against the grain by stating that the cultural differences between the Indians and others was not a bar to their possessing these titles.[138] The Indians' and the company's sale of the land to Mitchel had been made with the consent of the Spanish sovereign; therefore he gained superior title over any that the United States could assert.[139]

Most importantly, Justice Baldwin recognized the fact that the Seminole Indians had transferable title rights. Their right to the land was not merely possession or occupancy, but also included that of alienation. Baldwin's statements repudiate the doctrine of discovery as explained in earlier Marshall cases. Discovery in no way diminished the political status or the property rights of the Indians.[140] Overall, Justice Baldwin's conclusions about Indian title can be summarized as: (1) That the Indian's were in possession of the lands they occupied and were to be considered the owners by their perpetual right of possession; (2) Possession could not be taken without consent; (3) Indian possession was to be considered equal to that of white possession, regardless of whether the land was hunted or cleared; (4) The Indians possessed the land until they abandoned it, sold it, or ceded it; (5) Spain had recognized this fact; (6) Spain, by entering into treaties with the Indians had accepted the Indians as equals, and accepted the land cessions and established boundaries to their lands, and thus, gave up the right of conquest; and (7) The United States had to follow this plan since no treaty had annulled earlier agreements.[141] The United States was simply assuming Spain's role and duties toward the Indians. Baldwin saw the court in this instance as acting as a court of equity.

As David E. Wilkins states, upon a more critical review of the *Mitchel* case, the conclusions one has to make are that

> (1) the doctrine of discovery elaborated by Marshall in M'Intosh and used to diminish tribal sovereignty is without credibility as a legal principle; (2) tribes are the possessors of a sacrosanct title that is as sacared as the fee-simple [title of whites]; (3) tribes may alienate their aboriginal territory to whomever they wish, and the question of whether the non-aboriginal purchaser has the authorization of a sovereign is a matter that cannot be used to reduce indigenous rights; (4) an argument based on alleged inferior tribal cultural status, regardless of its differences with Western culture, will not inhibit aboriginal sovereignty; and finally (5) tribes as collective entities and the individual members thereof are entitled to international protections of their recognized treaty rights which survived the federal government's assumption of jurisdiction upon Spanish cession of Florida.[142]

History seems to have also been forgotten in the *United States v. Rogers* (1846) case.[143] Although this was a criminal rights case involving a non–Native person within the tribe, its implications for property rights and sovereignty were numerous. The Court described the American Indian as an unfortunate race who have never been treated as independent nations by European governments, nor regarded as the owners of the territories they occupied.[144] Obviously, the history of treaty making between the various Indian nations and the European and American governments was being brushed aside as inconsequential, and it was simply being ignored. The court seriously impeded the rights of sovereignty by limiting who the tribes could claim jurisdiction over. A white person could marry into a tribe, become a member of it, but tribal jurisdiction does not extend to those not born as American Indian nor can the white person shrug off their obligations to U.S. laws.[145] The doctrine of discovery was now extended to allow interference in internal tribal issues and affairs. Federal power over a tribe need not be tied anymore to a treaty standard or commerce regulation.[146]

These cases helped bring about a new call for removal of the Indian from their traditional lands to allow expansion by any means. The new wave in removal advocates were best typified by the abolitionist Horace Greeley, who stated that, "these people [Indians] must die out, there is no help for them. God has given this earth to those who will subdue and cultivate it, and it is vain to struggle against His righteous decree."[147] A renewed Lockean rationalization was being developed for taking Indian property. There was too much land for the Indians to use. The land was simply laying idle and being wasted, thus their ownership and control was stopping those who would best use the land for profit.[148] Of course, even if the Indians were using the land, they were not using it as a more civilized people would and it still should be taken away. Therefore, undeveloped Indian land was seen as an impediment to the progress of the newcomers and something had to be done. Removing the Indians from their land was only one option. Acculturation and destruction were others. Regardless of the option selected by policy makers, the courts seemed more than willing to aid in the process.

Whereas Andrew Jackson gets, and deserves, the dishonor of forcing through Congress and enforcing the Indian Removal Act, the actual idea and goal of getting the Indians off their lands started decades earlier. As if he was predicting the future, in 1796, George Washington urged the Cherokees to become farmers and warned them that if they did not become "civilized," they would be overrun by the white settlers.[149] He was prophetic in that he believed that the treatment of the Indian would be a stain on the new nation's character and could even hinder its growth.[150]

Thomas Jefferson envisioned removing the Indian tribes from the Louisiana Purchase lands well beyond the Mississippi River, especially those tribes that were having conflicts with the American settlers. He even went so far as to propose a Constitutional amendment calling for the removal of these tribes.[151] However, it would be Andrew Jackson who would turn these wishes into a horrible and long-lasting reality.

The Indian Removal Act of 1830 "denied the American Indian the right to claim lands as their own and removed military protection, treaty rights and protection from execution by fiat that had been in place since Washington."[152] It denied the tribes the right to negotiate with the federal government, even as "domestic dependent nations" as the Court had decided.[153] The act essentially focused on the Chickasaw, Choctaw, Creek, Cherokee and Seminole Indians, but other tribes would soon be included (the Potawatomi, Sauk, Fox, Iowa, Illinois, Shawnee, Seneca, Miami, and Delaware to name just a few). The southern tribes would soon face the infamous Trail of Tears, the forced march to Indian Territory, present-day Oklahoma, in 1838–1839. It is estimated that approximately 100,000 American Indians would be removed, and over 15,000 would die en route.[154]

Jackson, in 1833, would address Congress and state that the Indian does not have the intelligence, industry, morality nor desire for any favorable change in their condition.[155] This racist attitude would set the stage for James K. Polk and the policy of Manifest Destiny that he set in motion when he took office in 1845.

Polk would use this policy as an excuse to take even more lands from the American Indians. He claimed it was the "holy duty of godly men to subjugate the heathen races."[156] He moved responsibility for dealing with the Indians from the War Department to the Department of the Interior, where by the time of the U.S. Civil War, the Office of Indian Affairs (now the Bureau of Indian Affairs) had become known as the most corrupt, patronage-ridden, wrought-with-fraud, inefficient and racist part of the federal government.[157]

The Indian system destroyed tribes so they could become pliant tools of dishonest traders, agents and missionaries.[158] Unscrupulous people flocked to join the system so as to tap into the flow of federal monies to feed their greed, with very few concerned or focused on the actual welfare of the Indian peoples.[159] Since the tribes that had been removed to new lands became even more dependent upon the federal government for their very survival, they were more often than not at the mercy of the appointed Indian agent, who controlled the contracts for goods and services on the reservations.[160] In fact, being an Indian agent was very often the path to wealth and power, all at the expense of the very people he was supposed to be concerned about.[161]

While removal was occurring in the South and East, Indian tribes in the Southwest and California were also suffering from the influx of non–Indians and their quest to remove the tribes from lands that they wanted. The tribes of California would especially suffer due to the discovery of gold on their lands. Many tribes would outright disappear due to disease, displacement or outright extermination by white militias formed for this very purpose.[162] California's tribes were so decimated, that reformers sought to separate them from white society as an alternative to their very extinction. They were to be relocated, taught to farm and guarded from wandering into white communities and to keep whites from venturing into their lands.[163] In essence, this was a form of apartheid predicated on the racism of the times, and a paternalistic humanitarian concern for the tribes.

In New Mexico, the Navajo would also undergo their own conquest and removal at the hands of the invaders. General James Carleton in the early 1860s worked to remove the Navajo over 400 miles from their homeland to an area along the Pecos River. The river was alkaline, it flooded, and it offered no forage, yet Carleton dismissed these concerns since "subjugation or destruction were the only alternatives" the Navajo faced.[164] The Navajo were to learn to read and write, and ironically, the truths of the Christian religion. As the older generations died off, Carleton assumed that they would take the old harmful habits with them and over time, the Navajo people would be civilized and contented. Of course, the idea that the Navajo's land might contain gold would also propel these policies into high gear. Fortunately, the plans failed and the Navajo would be able to eventually return to their homelands.

Later, the Court demonstrated their willingness to limit tribal sovereignty in land matters in *United States v. Cook* (1873)[165] where it decided that although the right of occupancy was unlimited, the occupied land and its resources cannot be severed or sold until occupancy is alienated. In this instance, the Indians wanted to cut and sell the timber off of the lands they occupied. The Court argued that the cutting of the timber must be for the improvement of the land, not just for profits.[166] Therefore, a strict interpretation of occupancy would be enforced to limit any chances that the Indians may enter the marketplace using resources on their own lands.

From 1778 until 1871, the United States government entered into 371 treaties with the Indian nations and tribes. These treaties obviously presumed some level of political sovereignty on the part of the Indians. It was true that treaties were a far less expensive endeavor to gain land as opposed to using the army.[167] However, before the treaty could be ratified by the Senate, modifications would be made to the initial draft developed by the Indian representatives and government negotiators and usually, the original negotiated treaty did not resemble the final draft. The changes were almost always in favor of the government and its interests. To complicate the process more, government officials were seldom worried as to who would represent the Indian tribe and sign the final draft of the treaty. A lot of times it would not be the same representatives who negotiated the original treaty tenets. Minor chieftains or religious leaders would be bribed and misled to sign the final treaty. This would lead to numerous internal conflicts and political struggles within the tribes, some of which still plague them. More importantly, this pattern would lead to the end of treaty making with the tribes and thus, give the federal government new legal and political tools to take Indian lands.

During the 1860s, there were 11 treaties signed with the Lakota, Dakota and Nakota tribes[168] of which the 1868 Treaty of Fort Laramie was the most significant. The Great Sioux Reservation was created out of this treaty. It stipulated that all military forts and outposts were to be removed from the territory, white transgressions against the Indians were to be punished, and no one was allowed to settle in the area north of the North Platte River without tribal permission.[169] However, Chief Red Cloud believed he had been deceived in the negotiations and refused to sign the final treaty.

The U.S. Congress, especially the House of Representatives which was somewhat jealous that all treaties were ratified in the Senate without their input, reacted very quickly.[170] The Resolution of 1871 was passed which effectively ended all treaty making between the United States and all Indian tribes or nations. It was attached as a rider by the House to the Indian Appropriation Act. The resolution stated:

> No Indian nation or tribe within the territory of the United States shall be acknowledged or recognized as an independent nation, tribe or power with whom the United States may contract by treaty: Provided further, that nothing herein contained shall be construed to invalidate or impair the obligation of any treaty heretofore lawfully made and ratified with any such Indian nation or tribe.[171]

The treaty system was deemed to be no longer viable by members of Congress. The courts, saw this act as Congress' intention to domesticate American Indians and as an action irrevocable under the plenary powers of

Congress.[172] The statutory taking of Indian lands soon commenced.[173] The decision in *United States v. Kagima* (1876)[174] further eroded treaties that had been made with the American Indians. The decision made in this case extended Marshall's claim that the plenary power of Congress allowed it to exercise authority over the Indians as it saw fit.[175] The federal government was to assume the role of protector over the Indians for their own good, and the treaties of the past were no more than licenses for federal intervention.

However, Congress proceeded to pass an act in 1887 that would do more damage to Indian land claims and tribal political sovereignty than any past or future court decisions could. In a further effort at assimilation, Congress passed the General Allotment Act (also known as the Dawes Act or Dawes Severalty Act) in 1887. When the treaty-making power ended in 1871, the era of new colonialism began and this act is a prime example of how the United States intended to separate the Indians from their land and destroy their cultural heritage utilizing any mechanism, whether it be economic, legal, military or social.[176]

In essence, the Dawes Act took all of the Indian land still in their possession and divided it up among the people. Any residual acreage was sold off to non–Indians. Married Indian males received 160 acres, while unmarried adult males received 80 acres. Full-blooded Indians were issued trust patents with no control over the land for a period of 25 years, after which it turned to a fee simple patent and could be sold to anyone. It was during this time that they would be expected to learn business methods; then the land would be theirs free and clear. Mixed-blood Indians received land title by fee simple patent.[177] Those who accepted their allotments could then become citizens of the state they resided in if they agreed to give up their tribal affiliations and ties.[178] The landholdings of the American Indian went from 138 to 156 million acres in 1887 to 78 million in 1900, and to just 48 million acres by the Act's end in 1934. Of this remaining land, roughly 20 million acres is desolate or arid.

Overall, the philosophy behind the act held that somehow, "private property had mystical magical qualities about it that led people directly to a 'civilized' state."[179] Congress assumed that communal ownership of the land only furthered the Indians uncivilized lifestyles and thus, prevented the land from being properly utilized and exploited.[180] Private ownership was the solution for the Indian problem, that being a failure to assimilate properly into white culture. The government must "kill the Indian but save the man."[181] However, the greed for land and the presumed cultural superiority of the whites had created a popular will to take Indian lands at any cost.[182]

Congress and the Supreme Court provided both the impetus and then the tacit consent for these actions. As has been seen, "the words that have been the most effective in 'conquering' the Indians are the words of the great legal decisions setting the premises of American Indian law as it relates to land rights."[183] The Dawes Act would just be another challenge faced by the American Indian for their very survival.

The era of assimilation quickly became replaced by policies of termination. There were numerous legislative efforts to end the Indian culture, most met with judicial ambivalence when and if challenged in the courts. These Indian policies have always reflected the white definition of what they perceive as the "Indian" problem. These policies included military subjugation and attempts to "civilize" or "save" the Indians, all in hopes of making them "another lost race in the American melting pot."[184] "To assume that white values lived and Indian civilization died, the federal government used the full power of the law."[185] This meant that laws were passed banning and criminalizing traditional Indian culture, values and norms.

Dances, feasts, medicine men and healing practices, religions and spiritual systems, languages and dress all became codified as illegal as demonstrated in the 1883 Rules of Courts of Indian Offenses.[186] Education, in the form of boarding schools where Indian children were forcibly taken from their parents and homes and shipped hundreds of miles away, was the primary method of sanctioned destruction for a millennium-old culture and way of life. In fact, it was the founder of the Carlisle Indian School, Richard Pratt, whose statement succinctly summed up this movement: "Kill the Indian and save the man."[187] Native language, the cornerstone of any culture, was formally forbidden in 1887. The attitude was simply that "a language that is good enough for a white or a black man ought to be good enough for the red man. It [was] also believed that teaching an Indian youth in his own barbarous dialect [was] a positive detriment to him."[188] Despite these efforts at genocide, most tribes and their cultures survived, even if on an underground basis.

It would not be until 1934, that the allotment process would be ended with the Indian Reorganization Act (IRA), also known as the Wheeler-Howard Act.[189] However, the IRA would pose a new set of problems for the American Indians in that it would force them further into internal conflict and subjugation to the federal government and its policies.

The Dawes Act created a mosaic of land ownership. Those lands not allotted by the passage of the IRA were to be held in trust by the federal government with the Secretary of the Interior maintaining regulatory control over the land. The foundation for the IRA began in 1933 when John Collier, the new Commissioner of Indian Affairs conducted a study of the conditions in which Indians lived, and found them to be deplorable. Disease, poverty, homelessness and death were prevalent on and off the reservations. In addition, government waste was evident where the appropriations for the Indians amounted to roughly $135.00 per Indian, yet the Bureau of Indian Affairs had one bureaucrat for every forty-three Indians.[190] As such, Collier saw the IRA

as not only restoring the Indian land base, but also restoring cultural determination and sovereignty.

Collier attempted to get Indian input into the formation of the IRA as
much as possible, although the support was not always forthcoming. Many
tribes opposed the Act for various reasons. Since many Indians had become
Christianized, there was a fear that the old religions and traditions may return
and renew problems all over again. Others saw the Act as a threat to their
own political power within the tribe. Finally, the Act set forth a one-quarter
blood quantum for tribal membership which was opposed on the grounds
that the tribes should set these themselves.[191] Non-Indians complained also
about the loss of tax revenues, the loss of Christianity's influence among the
Indians, and some even saw this act as being communist in that the American
Indian should end its soviet-style society, and being supportive of paganism
for allowing Indian culture to be renewed.[192]

Regardless of the internal and external opposition, the Indian Reorganization Act did pass for better or worse. It ended the allotment process and
gave all surplus lands back to the respective Indian nation or tribe. The further sale of Indian lands was forbidden except to members of the tribe. Furthermore, it established BIA-approved tribal constitutions and governments
if the tribe accepted the terms of the IRA. Again, this would be a double-
edged sword: Acceptance could mean more self-determination socially, culturally, and economically; yet it would mean that political sovereignty would
be given to the BIA which had to approve all tribal governments and constitutions.[193]

The tribal elections to approve the IRA were held in June 1935. Two hundred and fifty-two tribes held acceptance elections. The tally ran 174 tribes
in favor, 78 against acceptance. Of the 97,000 eligible voters, only 39,000 (39%)
voted to accept and 24,000 (25%) voted to reject the IRA.[194] Of the 174 tribes
accepting the IRA, 92 went on to write BIA-approved constitutions and of
these, 71 wrote articles of incorporation.

The Department of Interior did embark to make discriminatory regulations to punish those tribes and nations that had rejected the IRA, calling
them the "unorganized tribal governments."[195] Many tribes simply wanted to
keep their traditional forms of governance. Yet the BIA withheld federal support and condemned the traditional governments that were in place. A prime
example were the Navajos.[196] In 1923, the Department of Interior ended the
traditional government and established a new council to make it easier for
the Standard Oil Company to get oil leases on the tribal lands. Standard had
asked that the BIA convene a council meeting where the elders soundly refused
to grant any leases. The BIA proceeded to establish a new government, the
Navajo Grand Council, without tribal approval. The first act of the new council was to approve the oil leases that Standard was seeking.[197] When the IRA

came up for a vote, of the 43,135 members, only 15,900 were eligible to vote and they split: 7,608 to accept, but 7,992 to reject. Collier was incensed and held up grazing rights and federal dollars dedicated to the Diné (Navajo). This retaliatory action would finally end in 1950 with the Navajo-Hopi Rehabilitation Act that restored economic development packages to the nations.[198]

Therefore, the IRA hoped to create board-like governments for the Indian tribes and nations. It was designed to undercut and end any traditional forms of government. The traditional consensual style of decision making was transformed into the democratic majority rule which only caused divisions and rivalries within the tribes. Private property and for-profit industries replaced communal ownership and sharing. Overall, the IRA transformed the Indians by bringing to the reservations all the social, economic and political problems that non–Indians had off the reservations. These actions would culminate in the 1953 House Concurrent Resolution 108, also known as the Termination Act, which gave Congress the right to unilaterally end the trust responsibility of the federal government with selected Indian tribes and end their status as distinct tribal entities. The BIA determined that there were 78 tribes ready for immediate termination, 20 would be ready within 20 years and another 78 within 50 years. The percentage of white–Indian blood, the literacy level, the level of acceptance of the Indians by the surrounding non–Indian communities, the Indian's ability to earn a living, the business acumen of the tribe, and the level of agreement to accept the transfer of control were the criteria that the BIA utilized to place the tribes into the aforementioned three categories.[199] In order to get Congress to move forward with the plan, the new commissioner of Indian Affairs, Dillon S. Myer (who had previously been in charge of the Japanese-American internment camps) submitted a budget to Congress inflated by 70 percent.[200] Congress responded with the Concurrent Resolution 108.

From 1953 to 1959, 109 tribes with over 11,500 members and over 1.3 million acres, lost their status as tribes or nations. All the tribes in California, Florida, New York and Texas were to have their status terminated, as were selected tribes such as the Klamaths (Oregon), Menominees (Wisconsin), Anishinabé (Turtle Mountain, North Dakota) and the Kansas-Nebraska Potawatomies. The Paiutes of Utah opposed their termination, but uranium and oil interests were able to persuade Congress to go ahead with the decision.[201] The lost lands reverted to the federal government which promptly sold them to other private and corporate interests.[202]

What has been demonstrated throughout this section is that the United States government has purposely worked to deprive the original inhabitants of this land of their rights to control, enjoy and use their lands freely. From the period of the earliest treaties, until recent years, these efforts have flagrantly ignored or twisted history and legal philosophy. The policies and judicial decisions that have affirmed them are tainted with the racism of cultural genocide.

In the next section, the focus will turn to more recent efforts of the Indians to seek redress for their grievances or at least, compensation for the illegal takings of their lands. At the same time, it will be shown how the courts have been at times supportive, but for the most part, asinine in their determination of American Indian property rights. The paper will end with a discussion of some solutions to the "Indian problem."

The Continuing Conflict

In 1876, the Supreme Court ruled that the 1834 Trade and Intercourse Act did not apply to the Pueblo Indians of New Mexico.[203] The Pueblo Indians were under direct federal jurisdiction due to the Mexican-American War, and since no treaty had ever been entered with them, they were exempt from the Act's stipulations. In addition, the Court found the Pueblo Indians to be "peaceable, industrious, intelligent, honest.... Indians only in feature, complexion and a few of their habits."[204] Hence, since they were not like other Indians, they were not subject to the same restrictive laws.

However, by 1913, the Court's attitude toward the same Indians had changed. In *United States v. Sandoval* (1913),[205] the Court noted that the Pueblo's character had changed and they were, in fact, Indians. Justice Van Devanter stated: "The people of the Pueblos ... are Indians in race, customs and domestic government. Always living in separate and isolated communities, adhering to primitive modes of life, largely influenced by superstition, and chiefly governed according to the crude customs inherited from their ancestors, they are essentially a simple, uninformed and inferior people."[206] By 1922, Senator Holm O. Bursum of New Mexico would introduce legislation to end all Pueblo water and land rights. He found support in many other members of Congress and in the BIA. The action was never completed, but the damages had been done.[207]

This drastic reevaluation of the American Indian typifies the change in governmental policy and judicial attitudes to conflicts that made it to court. Now, the conflict expanded to include the states who rejected the idea that the federal government and the Indian tribes could determine what went on within the borders of Indian land. For example, in *United States v. Winans* (1905),[208] the Supreme Court rejected the state of Washington's argument that the Yakima Indians had given up the title to their lands and were not entitled to place fishing traps in the Columbia River. The state claimed that the Yakima, in giving up this title, deserved no special treatment under signed treaties. The Court disagreed and stated that treaties are not grants *to* the Indians, but *from* the Indians of certain rights.[209] The Fort Belknap Reservation in Montana relied upon this decision when they argued that they had not given up their riparian rights (water rights) just because adjoining lands were owned by non–Indians.[210] Therefore, the diversion of the Milk River would be depriving them of their rights to use the water for beneficial uses. The Court agreed. However, the state of Utah refused to obey the ruling on the grounds that the federal government has no control over state waters.[211]

The issue of occupancy appeared again in the Court in 1923. In *Cramer v. United States*,[212] the land claim made by the Hualapai Indians of Arizona was based on the right of occupancy which dated back before the 1850s. The Court ruled that the right of occupancy, even though unrecognized by treaty or an act of Congress, did establish property rights against non–Indian granters such as Cramer the railroad company he represented.[213]

Yet, in the era of termination, the old theories of conquest and discovery would grant the court the foundational basis for depriving Indians not only of their lands and resources, but even their right to occupancy without the need for compensation. The case in point is *Tee-Hit-Ton Indians v. United States* (1955).[214]

The Tee-Hit-Ton belonged to the Tlingit Tribe of Alaskan Indians. Their land, roughly 350,000 acres and 150 square miles of water in total, contained vast timber and other resources. The Department of Agriculture had sold the land's timber without compensating the Tee-Hit-Ton. The Court of Claims initially gave the group standing to sue, but did not award any damages which brought the case on appeal to the U.S. Supreme Court.

The Tee-Hit-Ton claimed full proprietary ownership of the land, or at least a recognized right to unrestricted possession, occupation and use of the land. In other words, they claimed a fee simple title in the land. It was an area owned and occupied by their tribe from time immemorial. Justice Reed writing for the Court stated that the Tee-Hit-Ton's property interest is only one of a right to use at the government's will. Congress has never recognized the claim of the Tee-Hit-Ton to the land in question; therefore, no compensation for taking the timber is due the tribe.[215] In fact, Reed went on to write that Congress never gave its recognition to any land claims of the plaintiffs. Their title was one of mere permission by the whites to occupy the area, not ownership.[216]

He justified this reasoning with the idea that "after conquest they were permitted to occupy portions of territory over which they had previously exercised sovereignty."[217] This is not a property right but merely a right to occupy which may be ended and the lands fully disposed of without any legal obligations to compensate the Indian inhabitants. In other words, the American government had conquered the Alaskan Indians when it purchased the lands from Russia. Reed's logic reflected that of John Marshall's in that "the practice of two hundred years of American history, that discovery gave an exclusive right to extinguishing the Indian title of occupancy, either by purchase or by conquest."[218] However, the Tee-Hit-Ton had neither sold their lands nor been conquered in any form whatsoever. Reed continued to invert reason by stating:

> No case in this Court has ever held that taking of Indian title or use by Congress required compensation. The American people have compassion for the descendants of those Indians who were deprived of their homes and hunting grounds by the drive of civilization. They seek to have the Indians share the benefits of our society as citizens of this Nation. Generous provision has been willingly made to allow tribes to recover for wrongs, as a matter of grace, not because of legal liability.[219]

Therefore, Indian title of occupancy can be extinguished without compensation. This was especially true since the Court likened the Tee-Hit-Ton's existence to that of nomadic tribes.[220] To put the final nail in the coffin, Reed once again pointed out that this was the right of the victor, of the conqueror to end this title. "Every American schoolboy knows that the savage tribes of this continent were deprived of their ancestral ranges by force and that, even when the Indians ceded millions of acres by treaty in return for blankets, food, and trinkets, it was not a sale but the conquerors' will that deprived them of their land."[221] In other words, every Indian tribe, band or nation has been conquered at some point in the history of the United States.[222] The Tee-Hit-Ton claim was one of sovereignty, not property. Sovereignty could be ended at the government's will. But even this argument did not preclude a payment of compensation.

Earlier, the conquest theory had left the American Indians with only the title of occupancy. Now, Reed had removed even this right by extending the conquest doctrine to allow even the right of occupancy to be ended by the economic whims of private industry or government. This decision did reverse earlier ones that did agree that compensation was due those tribes whose lands were taken, even if it was unrecognized title to those lands.[223] Now, a tribe had no legal interest in the land unless recognized by Congress as such, primarily by explicit treaty. If that land were taken by the government, no compensation was due, whereas any other taking by eminent domain would be required under the Constitution's Fifth Amendment.[224] Yet, the treaty process had ended nearly 80 years earlier. Indian tribes were now in the proverbial Catch-22.

The *Williams v. Lee* case of 1959 went even further than *Tee-Hit-Ton* in that the Supreme Court allowed the states to step in and regulate the Indian tribes when there was an absence of federal rules and regulations.[225] The Court permitted a violation of the federal trust responsibility by allowing states to do this. They did reaffirm that tribes were sovereign, distinct communities occupying their own territory, and were under federal rather than state jurisdiction. However, if the federal government failed to regulate an area, then the state pre-empted this action.[226]

The assault on Indian lands extended to the four directions. Throughout the 1950s and 1960s, the Haudenosaunee (Iroquois) saw their lands they had owned and occupied since the 1300s taken away for various hydroelectric or flood control projects. In 1957, the Tuscarora,[227] learned that they were to lose almost 1400 acres for a hydroelectric dam to be built by the New York Power Authority (NYPA) with the permission of the Federal Power Commission (FPC).

The Tuscarora fought the decision all the way to the Supreme Court. In 1960, the court ruled against the tribe, effectively opening the dam and allowing for more land takings.[228]

This all stemmed from a rockslide that had destroyed the old electric plant used by the NYPA in 1956. This created an electric shortage according to them, and an opportunity to build a new dam. In addition, a treaty between the U.S. and Canada in 1950, allowed for the development of the Niagara River for power purposes.[229] Since Congress had granted the power of eminent domain to the FPC, the time was right to assert these rights of development, which just so happened to be on tribal lands.

The Tuscarora opposed the NYPA's authority to take their lands, which was purchased as part of a 4329-acre tract in 1804. Although the FPC listened to the Tuscarora protests, it ruled in 1959 that using any other lands for the dam and reservoir would result in "delays, severe community disruption and unreasonable expense" while at the same time agreeing that the taking of the Tuscarora lands would interfere with and be inconsistent with the purposes for which the reservation was created.[230]

The Tuscarora argued on the other hand that the land in question was in fact part of the reservation via the 1784 Treaty of Fort Stanwix and the unratified 1789 Treaty of Fort Harmar. This meant that it was excluded from any such takings. The Court ruled that national interest and paternal relationship toward the Indians is not expressed in terms of property, and the Federal Power Act has deemed the acreage in question to be outside the reservation.[231] In other words, legislation overrides any treaty, Indian purchase, or ancestral ownership.

The majority concluded that the power of eminent domain could be exercised in the same manner in territory occupied by an Indian nation as it could be in any other location.[232] However, there was a strong dissenting opinion.

Justices Black, Douglas and Chief Justice Warren all agreed that this land was in fact reservation land and was entitled to protection since the act in question specifically stated "tribal lands embraced within Indian reservations" were excluded.[233] The land owned by the Tuscarora has been called and considered a reservation for 150 years, even being referred to as a reservation by the FPC itself. The land has been clearly owned by the Tuscarora tribe since 1838. In sum, the dissent argued that "despite all this and the government's continuing guardianship over the Indians and their lands throughout the years, the Court attempts to justify this taking on the single ground that the Indians, not the United States government, now own the fee simple title to this property."[234]

While the FPC and NYPA were attacking the Tuscarora, the Army Corps of Engineers was going after the Seneca in Pennsylvania. The Cornplanter Band of Seneca learned that the Corps intended to flood over 10,000 acres of their reservation land in Warren County. The Corps wanted to dam the Kinzua River for a flood control project. The land included the Cold Springs Longhouse where Handsome Lake, the Seneca prophet and founder of the traditional Gaiiwio religion preached. It was an extremely sacred place. Even though engineers hired by the tribe demonstrated that a more effective site was thirty miles downstream, the Corps refused to consider any alternative sites.[235]

The Cornplanter Reservation *was* about 12.5 miles south of the New York border. It was granted to the Seneca by the 1794 Pickering Treaty signed by George Washington, which explicitly stated that the "United States will never claim the same, nor disturb the Seneca nation in the free use of" these lands.[236]

The Seneca sought an injunction preventing the construction of the dam. In 1958, they lost this battle. The District Court dismissed the petition by stating that the power of eminent domain can be exercised over tribal lands regardless of treaty provisions.[237] Even though general acts of Congress may not apply to the Indians unless clearly stated otherwise, the Court argued, general legislation is sufficient to override treaty provisions where the intent of Congress is clearly to do so.[238] Meaning, that mere mention of doing something in any piece of legislation that may nullify a treaty is all that is needed. In this case, the treaty was nullified and the dam authorized by an appropriations bill passed by the Congress.

On appeal to the Supreme Court, the Seneca lost again.[239] The question was not whether or not the flooding was authorized by the powers of eminent domain, or even whether or not the flooding would infringe upon the rights acquired by the Seneca in the 1794 treaty. The Court agreed to both of these issues. Instead, the question was whether or not Congress had made it sufficiently clear and specific what its intentions were by legislation. Here the Court referred specifically to the Kinzua Dam Appropriations Bill which meant, in its mind, that Congress knew it would flood Seneca lands and that these lands could, and would, be taken by eminent domain.[240]

Hence, the result was that the Cornplanter Seneca were removed from their lands, lands promised to them forever by George Washington. The best lands on the other Seneca reservations were given to the Christianized Seneca, while the poorer choices were offered to the followers of the traditional religion, the Code of Handsome Lake.[241] Furthermore, this effectively destroyed the Cornplanter Seneca Tribe. The dam was completed in 1961. The battle for just compensation, however, would continue for another five years.

If there was no formal treaty or agreement between the Indian group and the government, then the Court became quick to find a new solution to the dispute, mainly passing the issue back into the political process where the odds were well stacked against the Indians. Take the *Gila River Pima-Maricopa Indian Community v. United States*[242] as an example. The Pima-Maricopa Indians had sought compensation for governmental actions that had deprived them of both land and water rights. Furthermore, they argued that the government's guardianship had reduced them to the status of wardship with no concomitant beliefs. The government at best was providing only inadequate services. Most seriously, the reduction to wardship, according to the tribe, resulted in a "stagnation of self-expression ... [and] bridled the petitioner into cultural impotency."[243] The mismanagement of their property by the federal government had to cease and they wanted compensation.

The Court of Claims upheld summary judgment and reasoned that the moral claims made must be balanced against any claims of sovereign immunity. However, it also held that any tribe seeking compensation based on actions undertaken by the government had to rely on treaties, agreements, orders or statutes that expressly obligated the government to perform specified services. The tribe, in this instance, had such documentation.[244] Therefore, the case was relegated to the political process for solution. Judge Davis did note that given the United States' historic policy of semi-apartheid, permitting the Pima–Maricopa Tribe to recover damages would only open the door wide for every other Indian group to bring forth disputes.[245]

Regardless of Davis' wishes, the door did open and more and more claims were filed not only for monetary compensation for illegal takings and failure of trust, but also for a return of lands. In 1972, the Passamaquoddy and Penobscot Indians of Maine claimed 12 million acres under a treaty signed by George Washington. The federal courts agreed that there was no ceding of lands and awarded the tribes 300,000 acres and $27 million in 1980.[246] Likewise, the Narragansett Indians of Rhode Island won recognition and received 1,800 acres that had been illegally taken by the state in 1880.

The Mandan, Hidasta and Arikara tribes lost their lands in North Dakota to the Garrison Dam project in 1944. The dam was part of an overall project consisting of 90 dams to control the Missouri River. The Garrison Dam drowned over 155,000 acres of tribal lands, every productive parcel on the Fort Berthold Reservation, and displaced 349 families without the tribes' permission or compensation.[247] It would not be until 1984 that the tribe would have the opportunity to seek redress for this illegal taking. Eventually, in 1990, after years of haggling and jurisdictional bickering over responsibility, the decision was reached that the dam had constituted an unlawful and unconstitutional taking of tribal lands.[248] The result was a settlement of $149.5 million in 1991. Still, the question remains as to whether money can erase a crime and make the guilty innocent. The tribal homelands have been lost forever, and no amount of money can bring back history.

Probably one of the most celebrated cases, and as of now still unsettled, deals with the Lakota/Dakota/Nakota Nation and the seizing of the Black Hills in South Dakota.[249] Much has been written about this case and its full meaning, both for the American Indian and for the United States, so just a summary of those points relevant to this work's purpose will be examined here.

In 1868, the Fort Laramie Treaty established the Great Sioux Reservation which included the Black Hills.[250] The Black Hills have been considered as sacred for generations by the Lakota/Dakota/Nakota peoples. It is an area of creation, as well as sustenance for them to this day. However, in 1874, an expedition of 1,000 soldiers and civilians led by George Custer found gold in the hills. Soon, miners and settlers were flowing into the area with the military's tacit consent and in clear violation of the treaty.[251]

In the winter of 1876-1877, the local bands proceeded with their winter hunt as they had for generations. The Commissioner of Indian Affairs, fearing the Indians may be planning something else, ordered their return to the reservation. Weather prevented this by the specified deadline and the military was called out to attack them. Meanwhile, in 1876 Congress passed an agreement that would cede the Black Hills to the United States. The agreement was signed by only 10 percent of the adult males, in clear violation of the treaty that required three-fourths consent before any changes would be made.[252] In 1877, the agreement was passed into an Act and the Black Hills were taken from the Indian peoples.[253]

It was not until 1922–1923 that there was any mechanism in which any Indian tribe could litigate a claim against the United States. It was at this time that the Sioux first filed for a return of the Black Hills as stipulated under the 1868 treaty, or just compensation as stated in the Fifth Amendment to the U.S. Constitution where the land was taken for public use.[254] The Court of Claims, stating that a fair and honorable deal was evidenced by the government, held that the tribes were entitled to $17.5 million (with no interest) in damages for lands taken by trespassing miners prior to 1877.[255]

The tribes sued to get their payment, but with interest from the first taking. They did not challenge the constitutionality of the unilateral abrogation of the Fort Laramie Treaty or the taking of their ancestral lands. The Court in turn, affirmed that the taking was justified, and compensation was due, but with interest attached.[256]

The Supreme Court attempted to harmonize the plenary power of Congress, its trust relationship with the Indians, and the Fifth Amendment stipulation that compensation should be given for taking one's property for public use.[257] The Sioux Nation test meant that a tribe whose recognized title to the land was, or is, taken by Congress without Indian consent must overcome the good faith effort test to recover for its lost land if it received any consideration for the land at all.[258] By good faith effort, the Court was considering whether Congress attempted to compensate the party or at least, treat it fairly. Yet, good faith is not evidence that Congress acted as a trustee rather than a conqueror or sovereign. As the ruling implies, some Indian property is not property and some takings are outside the scope of the Fifth Amendment.[259] Hence, there is an exception to the Fifth Amendment that seems to only apply to the taking of Indian lands. This ruling relegates American Indian property as "not property" and government confiscation of this un-property as "not taking," where any other group in America would be protesting such treatment.[260]

The government had acted out of eminent domain, not as a trustee to its ward. Compensation was ordered for the land at its value in 1877. The Court upheld an award of $100 million to compensate the tribes for the loss of the Black Hills. However, traditionalists in the tribes want the land not the money, and have refused to accept a penny of the award.

Justice Rhenquist dissented and argued that further awards of compensation were in conflict with decisions made in 1943 by the Court of Claims. To have Congress review and then set aside court determinations is a violation of the separation of powers, and thus, the Sioux should not have been given the opportunity to pursue their claims past the initial rulings.[261] Rhenquist continued to state that the facts of the case have not changed.[262] Therefore, Congress' granting of a second chance to litigate this claim is a step into the judicial branch.

Justice Rhenquist disagreed with the historical interpretations given in the majority opinion and claimed they were biased. He stated that they gave a one-sided view of the expansion westward.[263] He cited sources that stated that the Indian-white conflict was inevitable, one due more to cultural differences than to conspiracies or planned deceptions. In fact, Rhenquist pointed out that the Plains Indians had no conception of property, were nomadic and basically, barbaric.[264] He did admit that there was deception and tragedy as the nation (United States) expanded, but forewarned that both Indian and whites had better be careful in their interpretations of history, quoting the Bible's rule, "judge not, lest ye be judged."[265] Therefore, other than the possible argument that Congress had overstepped its authority by allowing the

Lakota/Dakota/Nakota to refile their claims, Rhenquist apparently fell into his own trap by allowing a one-sided biased interpretation of history to cloud what really may have happened. The use of history, and its interpretation thereof, leads into the final case to be reviewed.

In 1987, 36 members of the Abenaki Tribe were arrested for fishing without a license on what they claimed were their tribal lands in the state of Vermont.[266] The trial court agreed with the Abenaki defendants and in a lengthy and well-documented decision ruled that only the federal government could extinguish Indian land titles, and the Abenaki title had not been extinguished. The state appealed this decision claiming that the Abenaki were no longer a tribe, and even if they were, their title had long ago been extinguished. Therefore, in *State of Vermont v. Elliot* (1992),[267] the Vermont Supreme Court would fail to give the state's Indian citizens the same property protections that its non–Indian citizens enjoyed.[268] The U.S. Supreme Court let stand its ruling by denying certiorari in 1993.

The State Supreme Court did agree that Indian title did convey a right of occupancy, unless the tribe either abandons the land or the sovereign extinguishes this right. Therefore, the Abenaki had to provide evidence that throughout history they had not abandoned the lands, their status, or that the government had not ended their title.[269]

The Court explained that this property concept flowed from the doctrine of discovery which in turn stems from natural law. The Court agreed with earlier rulings that the discoverer had a split title to the land with the Indians retaining occupancy as their right, and absolute ownership to the land cannot be vested until this is ended. To end this title, an act or the consent of the sovereign is needed.[270] More importantly, this sovereignty, or power to end the Indians' title to the land is transferable from one succeeding sovereign to the next. In this case, from Great Britain to the Republic of Vermont, and then to the federal government upon admission into the union.

Therefore, the court argued that a cumulation of historical events can be sufficient in showing that there was an intent to extinguish Indian title, even though there may not be one specific event or act, and that the exact date of this may be indeterminable.

The Vermont Supreme Court used two basic assumptions in reaching this conclusion. The first was that Indian title can be extinguished through the increasing weight of history. In other words, the longer the period that Indian rights are ignored, the greater the reason for construing that the federal government's failure to protect Indian interests was an affirmative intent to end their title.[271] However, federal law requires clear evidence that Congress intended to end Indian title not just ignore it, or failing to take action on it for some nondescript period of time. As such, this view permits the ending of Indian title in the most casual of manners. It also denies Indians the equality under the law that non–Indians enjoy since non–Indian property will be held more sacred and inviolable than tribal rights and property.[272] Is non–Indian property title ruled extinguished simply because Congress has ignored it for some time? If so, then no title in the country is safe from being extinguished at any time.

The second assumption is that Indian lands may be taken without compensation guaranteed under the U.S. Constitution's Fifth Amendment.[273] As discussed in the *Tee-Hit-Ton* and *Sioux Nation* cases, among others, this view is based on the idea that Indian property is somehow, non-property. Indian property must be recognized as such by Congress for it to be protected. Yet, once again, this places Indian property in a lower status than non–Indian property. Therefore, courts, including the Vermont Supreme Court, have adopted an approach to Indian property rights that have had the consequence of treating the Indian as a second-class citizen with limited rights. The courts have treated the lands as unpossessed due to the Indian lifestyle, thus reducing the Indian occupants to mere animals wandering on the land.[274] Overall, these views and efforts were elaborated in order to protect non–Indian property rights and interests.

The key question in *Elliot* was whether the original Abenaki title was ever extinguished. The Court assumed Congress had no limit on its power to end Indian titles, and besides, these are unreviewable political questions.[275]

The State Court decided that the federal government had an absolute, unreviewable power to continue the conquest of the American Indian that have yet to be forced to sign a treaty with the U.S. This statement sounds ridiculous if one considers that the Indians are in fact, citizens of the U.S. They also stated that they could not determine any constitutional limits on these actions.[276] Yet, the extinguishment of Indian title was not something to be done lightly. It cannot be implied and must be a plain, unambiguous action to deprive the Indian of the benefits of society.

The Vermont Supreme Court used a series of historical events to show that the Abenaki title had been extinguished. The first was simply that the Crown of Great Britain had given the land to the settlers in the first place. This was a sovereign ending Indian title.

After the French and Indian War of the 1760s, England issued several proclamations ordering non–Indians off of Indian lands for the primary purpose of preventing future Indian wars. The first of these royal decrees was in 1761, where the Crown, concerned that white encroachment could cause a new Indian war for which it was ill-prepared, ordered all royal governors to stop granting title to Indian lands and prevent further settling of these areas.

Vermont, at this time, was a part of New Hampshire and New York. New Hampshire Governor Benning Wentworth, in violation of the British orders, made land grants to Abenaki lands with the condition that they be settled in

1763. This was, the Court argued, the second event ending Abenaki title.[277] However, even this in and of itself amounts to an illegal taking of Indian lands!

Yet, the New York governor granted the same lands. The Court determined that the royal proclamations banning the settling of Indian lands was really designed to pacify the two colonies rather than protect Indian rights.[278] England had settled the dispute between the two colonies by 1769, and the grants fell into New York territory which promptly went about trying to evict the settlers. A small revolt took place, and in 1777 the Wentworth land grant area, calling itself Vermont, declared itself a republic and to be independent from any other sovereign. This was the next event in the historical progression of Indian title extinguishment.

Finally, the last event in the historical series was the admission of Vermont into the United States in 1791. As part of the admission negotiations, Congress agreed to the land borders for the state. The Court saw this as obviously meaning that it meant to cede all Indian lands within the state. This is the final event in the Abenaki's title being extinguished.[279] "These events remove any doubt that extinguishment of Abenaki aboriginal title was complete by 1791."[280]

The Court argued that since the land was granted to non–Indians, this ended Indian title. The obvious gap in the logic is how the establishment of the state ended Indian title. In fact, the original grants were in violation of British laws.[281] The Court turned this around and stated that the British laws were only meant to pacify New York and New Hampshire, not protect the Indians from further white encroachment upon their lands. Despite all this, the fact that the proclamations were ignored does not make the original grants of land illegal and invalid.[282]

The Court continued its defense of extinguishment by choosing to ignore the 1790 Trade and Intercourse Act that also attempted to prevent non–Indian squatters from Indian lands. The state of Vermont was covered by this law when it entered the union in 1791. Yet, if the Court's assertion is that the Republic of Vermont was created in 1777 to protect its non–Indian claimants over the Indians, then the state is indeed unique. Just because Congress may have been aware of the original land grants when the state was admitted into the union does not mean that it condoned the extinguishment of Indian title like the court implied.[283]

Finally, the Court claimed that the increasing weight of history extinguished title to the land by the Abenaki. Somehow, Vermont's admission into the union as a state transferred sovereignty over the Indians to the federal government and that statehood was a clear demonstration of intent fails to answer a lot of issues. It ignores whether the state had the right to extinguish title before admission; and it fails to address whether compensation may be deserved. The Abenaki were never removed to a reservation that would indicate a giving up of certain lands in exchange for others. In fact, the court did admit that there was no legislation ever introduced that even mentioned the Abenaki.[284]

Whatever their reasons, the Vermont Supreme Court hoped that by arguing that the Abenaki land title ended sometime in the indeterminate past, the state would be excluded from state and federal liability for the unlawful taking of the lands. The Court substituted implied consent of the sovereign for a plain and unambiguous act. They totally rejected and ignored the pre-established requirement of aboriginal consent for title extinguishment, and made their ruling based simply on the ultimate fact of white settlement.[285] Essentially, the Court embraced the idea that the original sin of how the United States has dealt with the Indians is deplorable, but relegated it to some distant past and wished it to be forgotten.[286] When coupled with erroneous citation, the taking ideas and quotes out of context, and forgetting the history surrounding a preceding case, a decision can be made for anything. As Singer states, the courts have failed to realize that acknowledging Indian land claims will not necessarily displace the non–Indians on the land, but it will set up a system of compensation for past wrongs.[287] By denying the American Indian claims for compensation, the courts "will have to bear the weight of the increasing judgment of history that they have participated in the continuing conquest of American Indian nations."[288]

Summary and Concluding Remarks

Land is an important resource to the American Indians. It serves as an economic asset, as a key to their political sovereignty, and as an integral part to their culture and religion.[289] Yet, "with few exceptions, federal Indian policy has permitted the continual acquisition of large portions of Indian land often justified as necessary for the Indian's survival."[290]

Even with the efforts of Congress, state governments and the various courts, the "Indian tribes have refused to disappear despite the genocide of the eighteenth and nineteenth centuries, the neglect of the first half of the twentieth century, and the genocide-at-large that [has] continued well into this century."[291] Indian claims for compensation and restitution will continue well into the next century. These claims will continue to be "initiated and litigated in spite of the creation of elaborate judicial devices to settle these claims for all time."[292] For example, the 1946 Indian Claims Commission Act granted tribes access to the Court of Claims, but was only given the power to award monetary compensations, not the ability to return lands wrongly confiscated.

In essence, the federal government cannot seem to decide whether its relationship with the Indians is one of guardian and ward, one of trustee and beneficiary or of conqueror and conquered.

From its very beginning, the United States has been seen as a stable country, dedicated to the sanctity of private property and set on its reinforcement through the legal structure. The security of property has extended to all landholders, regardless of the amount, size or location of land owned and regardless of whether or not they intended to or have used it productively.[293] However, as has been demonstrated, this view does not seem to apply to American Indians and their land. Laws have developed that have justified the taking of Indian land as "perfectly legal and presumptively moral" in their application.[294]

As Nell Jessup Newton has succinctly stated:

> The federal courts have spun a web of rules to enforce treaties of cession whether coerced or consensual, to declare aboriginal Indian property as not property within the meaning of the Fifth Amendment to the United States Constitution, and to declare physical invasions of Indian land that result in the transfer of land from the tribe to the United States are not necessarily "takings." Outrageous self-serving justifications for seizing Indian land and destroying tribalism have alternated with frank acknowledgment of the wrongs done to native Americans and the moral duty to make amends.[295]

The U.S. government, the same government built on the foundation of private property is the "very government that confiscated the land from the Indian tribes by methods both naked and subtle despite the high sounding words of the Fifth Amendment takings clause."[296]

It is a "historic fact that practically all of the real estate acquired by the United States since 1776 was purchased not from Napoleon or any other emperor or czar but from its original owners," the Indians.[297] However, according to Cohen, the U.S. has merely purchased the powers to govern and tax these lands. He even stresses that the Indians received fair value for all of these lands, a point that many Indians and non–Indians are in disagreement about.

Cohen has suggested that the Indians were satisfied with the price paid for their lands, except of course in those cases dealing with military duress.[298] In fact, Cohen uses the fact that several of the early settlements and colonies had passed laws requiring that they receive the consent of the Indians before acquiring their land as evidence of a fair transaction.[299] He obviously and conveniently forgets that many of these sales were under the threat of military force, were signed or modified under false pretenses, were not translated properly whether by accident or purpose, or were not negotiated with the proper tribal representatives.

This view of fair transactions does not take into account the basics of contract law where all parties are to be fully aware and understand the terms of the sale, in other words, have an equal playing field. This was seldom possible with Indian land sales. As mentioned, there are numerous examples of a treaty being signed, then changed when it arrived in the Congress; or of government officials not negotiating with the proper tribal leaders; or of the use of bribes and alcohol to guarantee a treaty signature. Thus, to claim that Indian land transfers to the trespassers were legal and proper cannot be an accurate statement, unless one chooses to be naïve to history.

Should there be a concern for Indian land at all? Obviously, the Indians have struggled against the threat of cultural extinction for centuries. Should scholars, politicians and citizens be concerned for their property?

Land is an important asset for any person or community. Its acquisition is "absolutely essential to increase the tribes' material wealth and the tribes' ability to exercise its sovereign powers."[300] In an era of decreasing support for the Indians and amid cries calling for more Indian economic and social self-sufficiency, land is the solution to these problems. In other words, an era of decolonialization must be started. This will be difficult since America has been constructed on the colonialist paradigm, and most American citizens are uncomfortable with admitting the history of deals with the Indians.[301] To even suggest giving the land back to the Indians brings to mind horrible mass evictions and dispossessions.

However, this view is biased and slanted within the aforementioned paradigm. If a land return policy were instituted, there would not be the wailing and gnashing of teeth that most opponents predict. The reality of a land return policy can be constructed on the following facts: (1) Most of the land taken from the Indians is stilled owned by the national or state governments, or by corporations; therefore there would be few evictions; (2) Roughly two-thirds of all land titles are non–Indian and are legitimate; (3) The U.S. government owns an estimated 770 million acres, the states own an estimated 78 million and corporations own another 250 million acres. Therefore, there is plenty of land to return without affecting mass numbers of non–Indian landowners; (4) Even though public lands do not match the Indians' original landholdings, these can be negotiated and changed accordingly; (5) The loss of these lands would be a loss of resources for the said governments, but instead of allocating funds to support the Indians, they could purchase these resources instead.[302] Since the 1980s, many policy makers have proposed selling national lands to private interests, or at least allowing private interests to operate these lands. Why not permit the original owners to operate them, collect any fees, and maintain them as they see fit? Other than the argument that the Indians should not have more than the non–Indians, there does not seem to be a good argument against this idea.

The courts need to readjust their thinking toward Indian rights and titles. The use of history has been so convoluted, that all the inherent biases and prejudices of the dominant culture are being expressed in their opinions. "Incorrect history and inadequate memory are in and of themselves devastatingly destructive for those who have endured the gravest wrongs in the past."[303] From the Marshall era to the present, American Indian tribal sovereignty and rights have been inconsistent and malleable. The primary reason for this is to better reflect the wishes of the dominant, majority culture.[304] The Supreme Court has reversed itself, has hidden behind archaic doctrines, and has simply ignored the context and meaning of treaties, all to protect the national interest in getting and maintaining ownership of Indian lands. Those courts created to handle the claims made by Indians have not been much better.

"In adjudicating the just claims of Indian nations and peoples, however, the Federal Circuit and Court of Federal Claims have not given force to the spirit of moral restitution implicit in Congress' waivers of sovereign immunity, but instead have given succor to the sovereignty of the United States, appointing themselves not so much a court of claims but rather guardians of the public fisc."[305] The court system has acted as the trustee of the public wealth, rather than a forum of justice. They have "jealously guarded the government against attacks by the country's original owners."[306] They have done this by narrow reading of the statute of limitations, strictly construing waivers of sovereign immunity, parsimoniously interpreting the duties of the trustee, placing evidentiary burdens on the beneficiaries (Indians), and disallowing good-faith reliance on government officials' words.[307] The courts have chosen to ignore history as they proceed on the continuing conquest of the American Indian and the subduing of their culture. As such, whether the court has chosen to ignore or misinterpret the history surrounding a case, the result has been the same, the Indian loses.

In concluding this chapter, Justice Black of the U.S. Supreme Court, ironically, has best described the solemn fate of the American Indian and their lands at the hands of the government. In his dissenting opinion, he stated:

> These Indians have a way of life which this government has seen fit to protect, if not actually to encourage. Cogent arguments can be made that it would be better for all concerned if Indians were to abandon their old customs and habits, and become incorporated in the communities where they reside. The fact remains, however, that they have not done this and that they have continued their tribal life with trust in a promise of security from this government.
>
> It may be hard for us to understand why these Indians cling so tenaciously to their lands and traditional tribal way of life. The record does not leave the impression that the lands of their reservations are the most fertile, the landscape the most beautiful or their homes the most splendid specimens of architecture. But this is their home—their ancestral home. There, they, their children, and their forebearers were born. They, too,

have their memories and their loves. Some things are worth more than money and the costs of a new enterprise.

There may be instances in which Congress has broken faith with the Indians, although examples of such action have not been pointed out to us. Whether it has been done so before now or not, however, I am not convinced that it has been done here. I regret that this Court is to be the governmental agency that breaks faith with this dependent people.

Great nations, like great men, should keep their word.[308]

The American Indian people will continue their struggle to have those lands which were taken returned. What was stolen, polluted and depleted, will someday return to its original owners. The circle will be made whole once again.

CHAPTER THREE

Sacred Sites and Culture: The Spiritual Assault

"We have men among us, like the whites, who pretend to know the right path; but will not consent to show it without pay! I have no faith in their paths, but believe that every man must make his own path"[1]
—BLACK HAWK, SAUK

Introduction

There is no doubt that people around the world would be outraged if tomorrow's headlines declared that the Vatican was to be demolished by the Italian government to make way for a theme park, or if Jerusalem's Wailing Wall (or any of its other 400 sacred sites) were to be flooded for a recreational lake so local residents and tourists could go fishing and water skiing. One could only imagine the outrage if the followers of Islam were prevented from making their trek to Mecca in Saudi Arabia, or if Catholics were told that the Pope was being evicted. In fact, the world watched in horror as the Notre Dame Cathedral burned, threatening not only its architecture but the priceless stained-glass windows and holy relics held within. Within days, millions of dollars were pledged to help in the rebuilding efforts.

Moreover, if hordes of tourists began attending various church services while munching hot dogs and popcorn and guzzling beer, religious leaders would protest and demand governmental action and protection from such outrageous behavior. These sites and churches are sacred, important not only to the followers of these religions, but to the world as a whole. Indeed, history shows numerous religious conflicts erupting over both real and imagined infringements upon lands and objects that the major religions deemed sacred. Conversely, Native American sites have been consistently violated and treated

66

with none of the same respect and reverence accorded Judeo-Christian and Muslim sites.

In July 1861, General Irvin McDowell had amassed over 30,000 federal troops to prevent the Confederate army from crossing the Potomac River and marching into Washington, D.C. In order to accomplish this mission, McDowell ordered his five divisions to meet Beauregard and his army at Manassas, Virginia. Beauregard, outnumbered nearly two to one, withdrew to Bull Run to wait. On July 21, the Battle of Bull Run erupted and ended with the Union army being routed and retreating back to the capital. The federals suffered 460 dead, 1124 wounded and another 1312 missing in action out of the 20,000 who saw action. Of the 17,000 Confederate troops in combat, 387 were killed and 1582 were wounded.

The effect of the battle was more important than just the military results. Southern morale was boosted by the defeat of the Union forces so near their own capitol. Bull Run was not only the place where Jackson became a "Stonewall," but also the place for the birth of the now infamous Confederate battle flag. It would also see a second defeat of the Union forces by Robert E. Lee in August of 1862. Later, the battlefield would be where one of the first monuments to the war's fallen would be built and dedicated.

There is no doubt that the Manassas–Bull Run Battlefield is of great historical importance, basically sacred and hallowed ground. So, in 1993, when the forces of the Disney Company marched into Manassas, a new battle quickly erupted.

Disney proposed to build a $650 million theme park on 3,000 acres of land only four miles from the battlefield.[2] Their army of lobbyists, public relations specialists and lawyers was able to convince the Virginia legislature to approve a $163 million package of incentives for roads, worker training and tourism promotion.[3] Essentially, Disney got everything it asked for from the state government. The state governor was a quick ally, and succumbed to the promises of the creation of 19,000 jobs and $1.5 billion in state and county tax revenues over the next thirty years.[4]

An opposing army was quickly raised, and consisted of historians, wealthy landowners and environmentalists. They testified in Congress, protested on the steps of the state capitol and launched a letter and lobbying campaign of their own. They wanted to protect this natural area of woods, creeks and rolling hills. Their fear of unchecked development surrounding the proposed park, the possibility of debt to the local taxpayers, the destruction of their country lifestyle and the possible distortion of history by Mickey and friends all became battle cries. As author and producer Ken Burns stated, his opposition was less about the theme park than the location. He said it would have distracted visitors from the real places of history, and it would "sanitize and make enjoyable a hugely tragic moment" in the history of the country.[5]

C. Vann Woodward in a 1994 article in the *New Republic* stated:

Here is precisely the problem with Disney's America. Wedged between the Potomac and the Blue Ridge Mountains and running up to Harper's Ferry, this part of northern Virginia has soaked up more of the blood, sweat and tears of American history than any other area of the country. It has bred more founding fathers, inspired more soaring hopes and ideals and witnessed more triumphs and failures, victories and lost causes than any other places in the country. If such a past can render a soil "sacred," this sliver is the perfect venue. And it is precisely upon this sliver that Disney and its Hollywood investors propose to release their hordes of commercial developers.[6]

Disney's troops unexpectedly surrendered in October 1994, and while retreating, it shouted at its enemies about building its theme park elsewhere in the state. The anti-development groups, environmentalists, historians, and landed gentry were victorious. The battle of "authentic and inauthentic America"[7] was won by those seeking to keep the battlefield a pure, solemn and sacred site to visit, reflect and learn from the lives lost there. When the sacredness of a site is threatened, society should raise its voice in opposition as it did in this case.

However, public outcry over the desecration of sacred sites has continued, even when the area is not being directly threatened. In Missouri, at the site of the Battle of Wilson's Creek where over 535 men died during the Civil War, the park superintendent led "the fight to protect this sacred ground from encroachment."[8] The superintendent argued, "it's a crime that we don't preserve these areas for the soldiers."[9] The site was being "threatened" by home developers and the construction of a public school.

The effort at Wilson's Creek is being supported by the Civil War Preservation Trust, an organization that attempts to save battlefield sites from urban sprawl. The group works to save battle sites from developers and other commercial interests because "battlefields are nonrenewable resources."[10]

The battlefield desecration debate has also erupted in Maryland *near* the site of one of the Civil War's bloodiest battles, Antietam. Here, the fight is over billboards being erected along the routes leading to the site. The debate is over signs that are not even visible from the actual battlefield, but miles away on the roads that lead into the area.[11] The billboard that has spurred on this debate is located across the road from a new 773 home subdivision. Opponents of the sign argue that it "destroys the rural and scenic entrance to the battlefield."[12] The concern is that Antietam will become trashed like the Gettysburg area has been.

In response to the controversy, the county has passed a compromise ordinance banning new signs along the scenic routes, but this has angered both the sign companies and the critics hoping to protect the site's sacredness. The opponents' goal is to protect "the viewshed,"[13] yet the infringement upon commercial interests is sure to keep stirring the proverbial pot of contention.

Just how far can or should a group, government or people go to spare what they consider to be sacred from outside infringement, and just how far can this sphere of sacredness expand, is a question that needs to be answered.

The fight over sacred sites, both religious and secular, continue constantly. More recently, in order to celebrate entering the year of 2000, officials decided to turn the Washington Monument into a gigantic sparkler in front of a huge crowd and numerous celebrities, including the President. Whereas the thought of setting off fireworks on the monument seems innocuous enough, some called this action a desecration of a sacred place! The National Park Service (NPS), obligated to protect numerous American Indian sacred sites, albeit somewhat dubiously, even initially protested the idea. A spokesperson for the NPS was quoted as expressing concern "about whether that's the appropriate use for this monument. It's a sacred building."[14] Congressman Ralph Regula (R–Ohio) wrote a letter to the President claiming the fireworks display on the monument is "a desecration of the values inherent in our designation of such monuments."[15] Regardless of the concerns for the sacredness of the man-made obelisk of stone, concrete and mortar, the White House pressured the NPS into permitting the display.

Of course, these reactions are understandable for this and other situations that are very distasteful and disrespectful endeavors in the eyes of most people. In fact, calls will probably be made for government intervention to protect and guarantee that these areas remain safe, secure, and sacred for future generations. The difference between these reactions and others that will be examined in this chapter is that these sites involved non–Indian battles and anguish, or they were erected and constructed by non–Indians to honor one of their own, but they are not natural like a spring, mountain or tree. How could anything that was created by a higher spiritual power be sacred? It has been put there to be controlled or changed according to the European settlers and their descendants.

However, the times when the voices are silent always seem to be connected to natural sacredness. When a tract of land which was held and worked by the same group of people since pre–Columbus days was flooded for a recreational dam, no outsider cared or spoke out in opposition, not even when an ancient burial ground was dug up and analyzed, desecrating the graves. Instead, the owners were only compensated years later, the graveyard combed by archeologists for the purpose of journal publications, some of the remains shipped off to a national museum for study and storage, and the problem forgotten by the start of the next fishing season.

When the courts decided that selling snacks and beer near a sacred "church" of a local group of people was permissible, no one cared, except of course the customers of the refreshment stand and the "church" goers. When another group's lands were stolen and a gigantic carved monument placed there, not so much as a whisper of concern arose around the world. This monument was man-made, showing that man-made sacredness wins out over the natural. When grandstands were constructed so that tourists could gawk at this very same group's worship services, the only question raised was if concessions were to be sold or not.[16] When the site of a massacre becomes a misrepresented monument to the killers, the world should be outraged. Furthermore, when money is offered to buy off the silence and forgiveness of a people, does this automatically make the original crime justified? Voices should be raised to remind the world of these crimes.

The reason for the lack of concern expressed for these situations may be varied. However, one variable is common in each case: the affected groups were and are American Indian tribes. Whether the group was Seneca, Navajo, Lakota, Cherokee or some other tribe, the details may have differed slightly, but the response was almost always the same. There is little concern or protection for American Indian sacred sites. This seems to be true whether the site is religious, historical or cultural in its importance. It could be as simple as a dichotomy between the natural monument to the greatness of a higher spirituality versus the constructed monument to man's own self-worth. Whether the Indian sites are taken and developed outright, or are lost through deception or theft, tribal access is denied and the result is the same: European Americans have and will offer little or no protection for American Indian beliefs and culture. The assault has come from and occurred in the four directions.

This chapter will examine the checkered history of sacred sites and their protection from government and other intrusions via the U.S. Constitution's First Amendment.[17] It will begin with a brief general description of American Indian religion and its site specificity. From this foundation, the conflict between the non–Native's belief structures and those of the Native American will be reviewed. The varied attack strategies used on the tribes will be discussed. Finally, the chapter will conclude by looking at the court cases involving sacred sites and some of the future implications for the protection of these sites caused by these rulings.

American Indian Religions

It would be erroneous and stereotypical to treat all American Indians as a single monolithic group with the same beliefs, religions or spiritual systems. Although to the casual observer all Indians may be alike, nothing could be further from the truth. Each Indian nation and tribe has its own belief system, ceremonies, and reinforcement mechanisms. These beliefs and ceremonies may vary from band to band or tribe to tribe within a single Indian nation. Therefore, the following discussion of American Indian religious beliefs is done in a very general manner with the knowledge and respect that individual tribal traditions and nuances do exist.

In most traditional American Indian languages, there is no single word to indicate or describe their religion. In addition, the religion's teachings are not usually written or collected into a single guidebook or volume. Most tribes lacked a written language and relied mainly on orally transmitting stories, beliefs and ceremonies. Unlike western thought which isolates religion as a discrete aspect of one's social and individual life, American Indian religion permeates almost every aspect of life.[18] "Religion" enters into the social, political, economic and cultural spheres of traditional American Indian life.[19] This simply means that religion is something, an overriding guide, that cannot really be separated from the whole, demonstrating an interdependency between all life on Mother Earth.[20]

One can summarize American Indian spirituality as it pertains to the individual in several ways, but the following points describe succinctly most tribal belief systems as it pertains to the "self":

1. American Indians have a belief in a supreme creator. In this belief system, there are lesser beings as well. Many American Indian tribes identify a supreme creator, and this supreme creator is generally perceived as omnipotent. The name of the supreme creator is very seldom spoken because it is sacred.

2. Humans are threefold beings made up of body, mind, and spirit. Of the three elements, body, mind, and spirit, the spirit is the most important because in the American Indian world, spirit is the essence of being. The instrument by which the spirit expresses itself is the body. The mind is the link between spirit and body and is viewed as being the interpreter between the two.

3. American Indian tribes believe that all creation has a spiritual component. In the native world, the earth is the mother, the sky is the father, and animals are the brothers and sisters.

4. The spirit world existed before it came into a physical body, and will exist after the body dies. American Indian people conceive of immortality as circular in nature. In the American Indian belief system, once the physical body dies the spirit is free to inhabit another body. This cycle is repeated until the spirit reaches perfection and returns to the supreme creator.

5. Illness affects the mind and spirit, as well as the body. The interaction between body, mind, and spirit is common to American Indian people. In attempting to heal one or the other, all three of these entities must be dealt with simultaneously.

6. Unwellness is disharmony in body, mind, or spirit. Many American Indian people experience unwellness. Unwellness in one of the three areas will affect the other areas.

7. Natural unwellness is caused by the violation of a sacred or tribal taboo. Many American Indian tribal belief systems include a distinction between illnesses that are a result of natural causes and those that are a result of unnatural causes. Natural unwellness may be a consequence of violating a taboo. Each native tribe has its own set of taboos that may be moral, religious, or cultural in nature.

8. Unnatural unwellness is caused by witchcraft. In most American Indian tribes, an evil power is perceived to exist, and individuals must be aware of that power.

9. Each individual is viewed as responsible for his or her own well-being. Many American Indians believe that they are responsible for their own wellness. Individuals can make themselves well, and they can make themselves unwell. When individuals allow themselves to be upset, they allow themselves to experience disharmony in their lives.[21]

Each tribe, and as mentioned, sometimes even subgroups within a tribe, will vary somewhat in cultural nuances and spiritual beliefs. Thus, to make a sweeping generalization that Indian religion is this or that can be very misleading and overly simplistic. Yet, a general model can be created to explain North American Indian traditional religions. This description contains the following features:

1. A body of mythic accounts explaining cultural origins and cultural development as distinctive peoples.

2. A special sense of the sacred that is centered in natural time and natural geography.

3. A set of critical and calendrical rituals that give social form and expression to religious beliefs and permit the groups and their members to experience their mythology.

4. A group of individuals normally described as shamans (medicine men and medicine women) who teach and lead group(s) in the conduct of their ritual life.

5. A set of prescriptive and proscriptive (ethical) guidelines establishing appropriate behavior associated with the sacred.

6. A means of communicating (dreams and visions) with sacred spirits and forces.

7. A belief in dreams and visions as the principal sources of religious knowledge.

8. A belief that harmony must be maintained with the sacred through the satisfactory conduct of rituals and adherence to sacred prescriptions and proscriptions.

9. A belief that while all aspects of nature and culture are potentially sacred, there are certain times and geographical locations that together possess great sacredness.

10. The major goal of religious life is gaining the spiritual power and understanding necessary for a successful life, by entering into the sacred at certain sacred times/places.[22]

From these frameworks, some Indian nations have also willingly assumed the role as the Earth's caretakers, not its controllers or developers.[23] For example, the Hopi fall into this stewardship role. Their beliefs include the need and duty to keep the world in balance by carrying on the traditions and caring for the lands.[24] They are only one of several tribes that believe that if an area is destroyed, marred or polluted, the guardian spirits will leave the area and a connection with the Earth and its life is lost.[25] This places the entire world in jeopardy.

In addition to caring for the Earth, American Indian religions include the belief that all life is animated and humans can learn from these other forms if they know how to listen and observe.[26] Indians are engaged in special relationships of mutual respect, reciprocity and caring with the Earth and its creatures, and as a part of this, everything is as alive and as self-conscious as are humans.[27] This awareness and interrelationship is reflected in the stories, myths and teachings that are interconnected to particular lands held sacred by the tribe.[28]

Their beliefs are continued through the tribal songs, ceremonies and cultural traditions. These tend to be life affirming, showing respect for life with all of its diversity, inconveniences and inconsistencies.[29] In other words, this is all a demonstration of the Great Spirit and Great Mystery. As such, tribes have a spatial reference, a physical place to express this relationship with the natural world.[30] Various rituals and locales are needed to maintain the spiritual and earthly harmony of nature, community, and individuals.[31] This requires a physical "entering" of the sacred rather than simply praying to it. This is especially salient since nature is a reality rather than some abstract concept.

So, whereas non–Natives believe that humans can or should interfere with the universe in order to control it, Natives are more accepting of the universe as it is. There are simply things beyond human control and this is due to the spirits. In the traditional view, the spiritual plane is not simply a sphere of belief or activity separated from everyday life, it is a context within which most aspects of life are defined and given significance.[32] Life revolves around the spirits; they are real and powerful and thus require constant attention through ceremony and offerings.[33]

This traditional belief that the universe is in a spiritual balance leads many non–Natives to see Indians as passive or even fatalistic. Instead, many Indian beliefs are passive because they believe there are powers beyond human understanding and control. Therefore, one must seek a balance and harmony with this spiritual plane and hope to be whole in mind, body, emotions and spirit. Whereas non–Natives prize aggressiveness against all odds and mastering creation, Indians see themselves as dependent upon and a component of all creation, celebrating its gifts and being thankful for them.[34]

"Residents and landforms are experienced as loci of spirit beings whose collective and individual presences give meaning and sacredness to a person's perceptions of land."[35] These places are pathways to the great mysteries of life, in both the above and underworld. This means that the land is more than simply soil, minerals or other resources. It actually defines the person and their spirit. More importantly, the Great Spirit is a creative spirit that is still actively participating in this ongoing process. Hence, places are needed to receive guidance as to His intentions, actions and needs. Disturbing these sites, even slightly, will disturb the Great Spirit and limit the contact with Him.

As mentioned, American Indian religion teaches of a kinship between other beings in nature and humans, for they are the link and guides in the Great Mystery. To realize oneself, this kinship must be understood and to gain introspection, one must be humble and learn from nature and its beings. The key is one of balance and sacredness, and a place to renew this relationship. To American Indians, the sacred is more founded on idea in that it is an embedded attribute of all phenomena.[36] The assessment of this sacred attribute is a major ritual goal in traditional Indian religions. There are attempts to find access points to the spiritual world, which in turn become sacred. Each holy site contains its own spiritual power, revelations, history and purposes.

These points of entry are used for vision quests, purification ceremonies, group ceremonies and/or medicine plant gathering.[37] Therefore, "points of geographical and other natural traditions become access portals to the sacred; dreams and visions are access techniques used to enter the sacred through these portals."[38] Usually, "points of geographical transitance are joined with the sacredness of the seasons, the sun, the moon, the life cycle of the individual, and the rhythm of community life to form a complex set of sacred transitions customarily celebrated in rituals."[39] Traditional American Indian religions "view gods, people and nature as an integral whole … [and their] worship focuses not so much on revelatory events, but on spiritual renewal through ceremonies and individual relationships with holy places."[40] More importantly, "the traditional religious practices are inseparably bound to natural formations."[41]

These holy places are an integral part of traditional American Indian culture and life. These sites have a sacred value, a value which resides there for eternity, transcending human history.[42] Rarely, if ever, are these sites chosen out of mere convenience. More importantly, these sites must remain untouched and undisturbed in order to keep them pure and sacred.

In sum, native religious beliefs include the tenet that

> specific geographic areas may be understood to be places in which the people originated as well as the loci of other significant events in tribal life. They may also be believed to be the point of origin of the world and life in general and axes upon which the world turns. In these places people[s] relate ... to ancestors and relatives, including, perhaps, animals and plants as well as human relatives. Here one relates to all of the most significant powers. In some cases, interrelationships with a particular area may be understood to be crucial not only to tribal welfare and existence but to the continuing vitality of the area itself and even ... to the well-being of the whole world.[43]

Hence, the destruction and loss of a sacred site can mean the destruction of an entire religion, the entire culture, and even the people themselves.

Therefore, one aspect of traditional native religion which has proven difficult for non–Indians to grasp is this connection between worship and specific places and that the beliefs of Indians cannot easily be divorced from these lands.[44] This problem is further compounded by American Indians not having a single body of sacred literature such as the Koran, Bible or Torah.[45] Furthermore, unlike the religions of the Europeans, traditional American Indian religions are almost devoid of charismatic founders; are sometimes non-commemorative of dates or events; lack a chronology of a single deity; and probably the most dumbfounding to the non–Indian observer is that the American Indians have little or no desire to convert others to their tribal beliefs, instead respecting the various paths one takes in life. These traditional religions are active and classless in that the community is involved in the practices and are an integral part of the whole.

Western religions tend to be linear, rather than cyclical, in their celebration of specific events, prophets and messiahs.[46] Followers of these religions in America are generally used to worshiping on a single day at any number of different places (churches). American religions are portable in that they are not site dedicated. If a church becomes too small, the congregation simply purchases land elsewhere and builds a new structure. If a church loses its congregation, the site is sold and redeveloped. People can attend any number of churches, selecting one for convenience to home, because they like the minister, or for some other reason. At the same time, non–Indian religions do not require the same level of participation as do Indian religions. A final difference can be found in the very premise that Christianity requires the belief in the redemption and proselytizing to non–Christians in an attempt to convert them.[47]

The Judeo-Christian concept of a supreme and immortal deity who can be separated from any site is not really applicable to many Indian religions.[48] This means that a particular spirit or deity may be very vulnerable to changes in the physical habitat to which it is intimately and inseparably connected.[49] In other words, whereas the average citizen may have numerous choices as to where to attend worship services, traditional American Indians have only a few select areas such as a mountain, a forest, a cave, a spring or some other natural site.

In the United States, churches usually are not seen as religiously significant since the spiritual is considered separate and distinct from the location and actual structure.[50] In fact, it is not uncommon for churches to gain historical significance due to their age or architecture rather than due to some spiritual event.[51] Therefore, it is difficult for non–Indians to understand or accept the mysticism and connection given to a mountain, river, cave or other such natural site and consider it the equivalent to a church. To them, it is just nature and one mountain or spring is as good as another.

"Although [the United States] professes to cherish its First Amendment–enshrined religious liberty, our society persistently denies this right to America's original inhabitants."[52] Federal policy has a very long history of attempting to forcibly Christianize the American Indians. For example, the Bureau of Indian Affairs (BIA) outlawed native practices and rites as well as enlisted the services of various churches to help administer the reservations and run its schools.[53] The attempts to Christianize the Indians have lasted centuries and have had disastrous effects on the traditional religions, stealing its followers and denigrating its teachers, essentially destroying cultures and identities. In other words, this boils down to a debate between maintaining the traditional belief structures versus the assimilated views instilled in the minds of the younger generations. Often, this debate occurs within the tribe itself as the traditional members must fight with those who have been assimilated and seek profits over sacredness. With the differences between Indian religions and others, and the understanding that native religions have traditional sacred sites that need protected, it is now necessary to turn toward an understanding of the implications of Supreme Court rulings on American Indian religions and their practices. It will be necessary to review the doctrines used by the Court to determine if the issue is a constitutional matter deserving of their attention.

Supreme Court Doctrines and Tests

One of the first occasions where the Supreme Court applied the First Amendment to a religious belief was in *Reynolds v. United States* (1878).[54] In its decision as to whether polygamy was a protected part of a religion, the Supreme Court pointed out that the First Amendment only applied to beliefs, not to conduct.[55] If a religious practice violated the law and/or community values, then it may be regulated by the government. Hence, religious beliefs are protected, but their worship practices may be regulated.[56] Society should be protected from undue religious influences while protecting the beliefs of the religion.[57] The obvious result of this decision is that the majority of the community, which sets the laws and values of the community, may regulate those practices which it deems contrary to their own. Therefore, freedom of religion is not really freedom for the minority.

In *West Virginia Board of Education v. Barnette* (1943)[58] the Court ruled that the government could not interfere with religious rights without a compelling interest. In this case, the state of West Virginia followed the example of Pennsylvania[59] and passed a law making a salute and pledge of allegiance to the flag[60] mandatory. Failure to do so would result in expulsion from school and/or fines for the parents.

The Barnette children were Jehovah's Witnesses whose religious beliefs would not permit them to follow this law. The Court's opinion, penned by Justice Jackson, stated that the children's refusal did not interfere with anyone's rights, nor was their behavior disorderly or disturbing to the peace. Their passivity during the pledge did not create a clear and present danger. Furthermore, Jackson argued that the state's action was coercive and "transcendeds constitutional limitations on their power and invades the sphere of intellect and spirit which it is the purpose of the First Amendment to our Constitution to reserve from all official control."[61]

In essence, there is no state compelling interest to have a group of children violate their religious beliefs and conscience just to salute a symbol. The entire pledge requires an affirmation of a belief and attitude, and in doing so required any personal convictions to the contrary be foregone.

The Court narrowed the test of "compelling interest" to mean a limit on only those actions that posed a threat to public safety, peace or order in the *Sherbert v. Verner* (1963) case.[62] Therein, the Court utilized a two-step test for analyzing free exercise of religion claims. Step One, the claimant had to demonstrate that the state regulations or practices imposed a substantial burden on the exercise of the religion; and Step Two, the burden is only justified if it is advancing a "compelling state interest" that outweighs the impairment on the free exercise rights.[63] More importantly, the claimants had the initial obligation to establish that the governmental action interfaced or burdened a "sincerely" held belief.[64] This narrow construction of compelling state interest was used again in *Wisconsin v. Yoder* (1972).[65] In this instance, the Amish and their basic beliefs were the focus of government interference.

In the *Yoder* case, the Amish were resisting compulsory education requirements imposed by the state on the grounds that it interfered with their rights to free exercise of their religion. Like American Indians, the Amish religion and their everyday life are closely interrelated, and their daily life has a distinct role in the survival of their religion.[66] There were threshold criteria established to determine if the claimants met the criteria for a free access claim. First, they were required to demonstrate that they followed a recognizable religion.[67] Second, the actions for which they sought protection had to be rooted in the religion's beliefs.[68] Finally, the actions and beliefs had to be connected.[69]

Therefore, in cases brought before the Court, claimants have had to prove the sincerity of their religious beliefs, a tough test at times for anyone to meet. Some argue that this may serve to weed out those trying to use religion to hide illegal or immoral activities.[70] The Court has narrowed the scope so that it makes a factual examination of the belief without intruding into the issues of the religion.[71] In other words, the Court does not determine the nature of the belief, but how central the belief is to the claimants and how strongly they adhere to it. The Court has also applied the centrality issue as a gauge to measure the degree of connection between the practice and beliefs of the religion and as such, those practices found to be connected to the beliefs of the religion have been and are afforded protection.[72]

The balancing of interests test has been applied in religion cases. In both *Sherbert* and *Yoder*, it was determined that *only* a compelling state interest that *could not* be achieved in a less intrusive manner could override individual free exercise rights. This is especially important if there is a less restrictive alternative in existence. For if there is one, then the state must choose this route.[73] However, as will be discussed, in cases dealing with American Indian religious issues, if this means the Indian claim could override the state, then a better solution had better be found. Therefore, the Court has reversed its argument to whether the state interest, or any other, would suffer if an exemption is granted to accommodate the practice at issue.

The Supreme Court has attempted to develop an analytical framework capable of protecting the government's ability to independently and efficiently conduct its affairs, while at the same time ensuring each person's right of free expression of religious beliefs.[74] It has stated, in more recent cases, that the religious belief need not be mainstream in order to be afforded protection under the First Amendment.[75] Looking at this another way, any government action that coerces or penalizes, or for that matter, helps a religion, whether directly or indirectly, will not be permitted under the United States Constitution. Thus, the compelling interest and least restrictive means test stem from the *Sherbert* and *Yoder* rulings.[76] The problem, as will be seen, is whether protecting a sacred site from destruction is an unconstitutional help for a traditional religion. When it is, then cultural genocide has been legalized in many instances, or post hoc justified.

Coercion occurs when the government compels behavior repugnant to the religion or outlaws it outright.[77] Penalties occur when a benefit is withheld because of the religious beliefs and/or practices.[78] Courts have struggled to discern and apply in a consistent manner the appropriate test to cases involving Indian religions. In other words, since religion permeates Indian life, to the very culture and identity of the tribe itself, what constitutes coercion or a penalty in these situations is a difficult decision to make and tends to only muddy the legal waters even more. This legal confusion stems in part due to the judiciary's inability to relate to an unfamiliar cultural and religious framework.[79] It also is caused by a cultural myopia which has the courts characterizing legitimate Indian claims as non-religious in nature or non-central infringements on their practices.[80]

The Sacred Site Cases

In order to set the stage, one should remember that "although most of the Indian peoples in this country no longer own their sacred ground, what is now the U.S. was once the domain of the Indian peoples. The indigenous peoples of this continent were divested of their land through duress and treachery."[81] Notwithstanding the loss of these sites, tribes have struggled to keep those sites that remain, or at least have continued and open access to those sites that are on federal and/or state-owned lands.

The American legal system has failed to recognize that these sites may be of vital significance to Indian religions and may be the place that has witnessed momentous spiritual events.[82] Governmental agencies and courts have refused to "accord credibility to the testimony of [Indian] religious leaders. They demand evidence that a ceremony or location has always been central to the beliefs and practices of an Indian tribe and [have] imposed exceedingly rigorous standards of proof on Indians who appear before them."[83] The "trusteeship theory," first advanced by de Vitoria, which states that the government will be the guardian to their Indian wards, does not work well in these disputes. The theory is flawed in that the government may unilaterally end this relationship and may, as the sovereign power, simply refuse to be held accountable for any violations.[84]

In essence, property interests tend to outweigh American Indian free exercise of religion claims regarding sites and practices. Some courts have dismissed these free exercise claims due to the emphasis that Indians have no property interest at stake.[85] Of course, the issue of where and how the land became owned by the government in the first place comes to the forefront. For, "if the taking was unjust to begin with it seems especially egregious to use the lack of a legal interest in land to deny a free exercise claim for protection

of preexisting sacred sites."[86] The challenges faced by American Indians protecting their sacred sites have come from the four directions, thus showing
that no tribe or group has or will be left unscathed.

Therefore, many "sacred sites claims arise when the spiritual and inter-
dependent relationship of Native Americans with all living things, including
land, is threatened by development."[87] In fact, the "continuing inability of our
society to comprehend and appreciate the religions of Native Americans is
reflected in the First Amendment case law, both in the results of cases, which
frequently deny Indian religious rights, and in the flavor of the opinions, which
rarely transcend Judeo-Christian notions of religion to grasp the spirituality
of American Indian religions."[88] More importantly, of all the courts in this
nation, "the Supreme Court is unsurpassed in manifesting this disability"[89]
in accepting and understanding native religions. The courts seem to utilize
an unbalanced cost-benefit analysis in determining American Indian religious
freedom. This implies that the costs of government acceptance and recognition of the tribe's religious freedom are weighed, while the benefits of doing
this are usually ignored. Land values can be quantified, but a belief structure
has no direct economic benefit and can thus be easily dismissed as invalid.
It seems as if acceptance were given, the entire foundation from which the
newcomers have justified their conquest of the land and cultures of the Indian
would rot, as if it has not started already. Some scholars have pointed to ethnocentrism as an explanation for judicial failure to appreciate and protect
Indian religions.[90] However, whereas ethnocentrism may be the explanation,
it is really a combination of this ignorance and the unwillingness to accept
true diversity in belief and culture in the American melting pot. Of course,
this is just another stage in the ethnic cleansing which has threatened the
Indian peoples for well over five hundred years.

As the cases will reveal, the main cause of American Indian religious
discrimination may really be as simple as pure economics and land-use politics. The failure of the American Indians to utilize the Lockean theory of
land development and exploitation is a disquieting concept to much of America and especially to the courts, which represent the legality of this concept.
As will be shown in the following cases, the courts have consistently failed
to address the real issue of religious freedom while hiding behind numerous
facades of property and government interests and using a variety of tests and
doctrines to aid in these efforts at obscuring the real truth and motives.

Sequoyah v. Tennessee Valley Authority (1980)[91] was an assault from the
south and showed how the Court established tests that seemed designed to
prevent Indian religious rights and freedoms. As has been pointed out, the
courts have subjected native claims to religious freedom to much higher standards than in the *Yoder* or *Sherbert* cases. This standard is nearly impossible
to meet in that it requires an Indian plaintiff to prove that their religious

practices and exercises at specific sites are central *and* indispensable, or absolutely required by their religion.[92] When native religions rely on oral traditions and teachings rather than the written word, it becomes all the more difficult to prove these points.

In *Sequoyah*, the centrality issue was taken to a new level by the Court, focusing on the relationship between the religious practices and the site in question. In this case, the TVA wanted to construct the Tellico Dam and Reservoir which would flood the Cherokee birthplace, capital and sanctuary of Chota.[93] This area contained not only medicinal plants and ancient burial grounds, but also sacred sites for prayer, legends and cultural history. The plaintiff, Ammoneta Sequoyah, represented several individuals and bands in a class action suit to halt the dam.

The Cherokee argued that the land possessed sacred qualities, not the least of which was a place where a connection to the spirits of the buried and to the Great Spirit was maintained.[94] The plaintiffs used the Free Exercise clause of the First Amendment to pursue protection of the land's sacredness and importance to their religious beliefs.

The Sixth Circuit Court used centrality as the only measure in this dispute and ruled that the Cherokee fell short of proving that the land was indispensable to their way of life, religious ceremonies or practices.[95] Instead, the Court reasoned that the Cherokee were protecting the land for historical and cultural reasons only; therefore it did not fall within the protections offered by the First Amendment.[96] In dismissing the centrality of the Cherokee beliefs, the Court ruled that the plaintiffs were merely expressing a personal preference, not religious beliefs, with their focus and concerns over the beginnings of the Cherokee culture.[97] The dam would damage the Cherokee's family and cultural folklore and traditions more than their religion, the Court reasoned, so the claim was dismissed.[98]

Obviously, one could argue that the very use of the centrality doctrine is ethnically biased from the start. Traditional Indian religions are not separated from culture and legends. In fact, they complement each other. Thus, the very use of this doctrine precludes a true understanding of native religions.[99] Religious values and traditions are passed down from generation to generation through stories and legends. These have hidden meanings and purposes that may only be understood in a particular time frame. In other words, Indian legends are at times very similar to the stories and fables found in the Bible.

The Court, in *Sequoyah*, managed to distance the Cherokee's identity from the land in question, and by determining that the plaintiffs were expressing personal rather than group preferences. They ignored the very idea that a religion can be shared by a group while being individualized in experience.[100] Simply put, the government's property interests outweighed those of the Cherokee's religious claims.[101] Thus, the Court twisted its opinion and logic to benefit the government and its interests, not the original inhabitants of the land.

In this instance, the Court's application of the *Yoder* analysis to the context of native religion was inappropriate. It overstated the central inquiry threshold, making it impossible to be met, and failed to apply the balancing portion of the analysis.[102] Even though the plaintiffs in this case, as in others, had been able to demonstrate that the sites in question were used for religious, as well as cultural purposes (which may be one and the same), the Court simply ignored this fact, picking and choosing the elements of the case to manage the outcome. Instead, it transformed the plaintiff's case into one of showing an undue burden, rather than showing why their First Amendment rights were infringed. It also furthered the stereotype that Indian religions were not organized or structured, and thus, less worthy of recognition and protection.

The courts continued to cloud American Indian religious freedom claims in *Badoni v. Higginson* (1980).[103] This case dealt with the western door and the Diné (Navajo) Nation. The Diné claimed in their suit that the government's impounding of water to form Lake Powell, the second largest reservoir in the country, in Utah with the Glen Canyon Dam, and the use of the lake to ferry tourists to the Rainbow Bridge National Monument violated their religious free exercise since these actions interfered with and desecrated the ceremonies performed at the site.[104] According to the Diné, the bridge is the incarnation of a deity which helps to maintain the world in balance. It represents the site where the gods Monster Slayer and Born for Water returned to Earth after their journey to Father Sun. The Diné healers' ultimate goal would be for the rivers to return to their natural courses so as to return the tribes and people to harmony.[105] Lacking this option, the plaintiffs asked that the monument be closed periodically for their ceremonies, and that no alcohol be sold there since this is a desecration of the sacredness of the land and an insult to their religious and cultural beliefs.

Now, in a twist of logic that adds to the legal confusion regarding sacred sites, both the District and Circuit Courts accepted the centrality of the Diné beliefs with the site.[106] However, the government's interests of water storage, hydro-electric power and the promotion of tourism outweighed these beliefs and their freedom of expression.[107] Even though the courts agreed that the Park Service hindered the Diné right of religious exercise, it decided that its regulations did not compel them to violate the tenets of their religion.[108] The courts agreed that the site was religiously significant, but this did not matter because the government had other plans for the area, for the Diné had no property interests in the area.

Furthermore, the Court argued that closing or limiting the monument to tourism to ensure privacy during Diné religious ceremonies would constitute an impermissible support of a religion in violation of the First Amendment's establishment clause.[109] In other words, the Court believed that granting the Diné request would be supporting and facilitating a religion in violation of the Constitution. The underlying belief was that the sacred site in dispute was on public, i.e., government, land and this alone justified the intrusion and infringement upon Diné religious freedom.[110]

The Court clarified the two-step process for analyzing free exercise claims via this case. First, to determine whether the government's action created an undue burden, the nature of the burden had to have a coercive effect as it works against the practice of the religion.[111] Additionally, the plaintiff would have to prove that the belief is truly religious in origin and is held sincerely. This the Diné did do. Second, the process requires a compelling state interest with no other alternatives.[112] It was this part upon which the *Badoni* case focused, and the Court saw no other alternatives that would not cause further constitutional violations. As usual and expected, the tribe lost.

The relentless attack on sacred sites continued in *Fools Crow v. Gullet* (1983).[113] This case involved the Lakota (Sioux) and Tsistsistas (Cheyenne) peoples and the sacred Bear Butte in South Dakota. To the Cheyenne, Bear Butte is the holiest place in the world for it is where the Creator gave the sacred arrows to the prophet Sweet Medicine.[114] Since this time, the Cheyenne have been the Creator's (Ma'heo'o) own chosen people.[115] Sacred power flows from the lodge of Ma'heo'o that rests within the Butte and this, in turn, gives the People the power for new life.[116] It is obvious then, that this site is highly religious, and used for both tribal and individual ceremonies.

The state of South Dakota decided to construct roads, parking lots and grandstands to increase tourism in the area. Viewing stands were built to allow tourists to watch tribal ceremonies, ceremonies for which the tribes had to acquire a permit before they could be conducted.[117] Obviously, such actions were quite unacceptable to the Cheyenne and Lakota. While the Court did recognize the Butte as one of the most sacred sites in the Black Hills, it ruled that halting the state's plans would violate the establishment clause.

The main reason for this view is that the Court reasoned if it allowed the exclusion of tourists, it would be tantamount to establishing a government-managed religious shrine.[118] Thus, by siding with the tribes, the Court would be supporting a religion, placing the Indians in a lose if you win, lose if you lose situation. Tribes cannot win protection even if the site is held sacred by Indians and non–Indians alike.

The Court furthered demonstrated its ignorance and prejudice by stating that the state's interference with the Indians' ability to practice their religion did not force them to relinquish their beliefs or abandon their practices.[119] The religious ceremonies could, after all, argued the Court, be done elsewhere or in front of the tourists![120] The state had no constitutional duty to provide an environment where ceremonies could be carried out, for if it did it risked becoming entangled with religion.[121] The state's interest in preserving and promoting a historical landmark outweighed the religious concerns of the two nations. Of course, nowhere did anyone consider simply returning the site to the tribe.

Furthermore, not only had the Lakota and Cheyenne not shown any protected First Amendment right infringements, they had not shown the government's plans to be coercive. In this case, the "claimants had to demonstrate the coercive effects of the restrictions as it operated against their religious practices."[122] The Court simply could not see that the proposed construction had any coercive effects!

In *Fools Crow*, the Court failed the Indian people once again. The government does manage churches, albeit as historical landmarks. Furthermore, the attitude that if a religion can be protected anywhere else, no burden exists showing a clear prejudice and ignorance of America's first people. The Court twisted itself into a pretzel to reach a decision, but once again, the Indian lost as the Court again changed its test.

The Diné, along with the Hopi Nation, found their beliefs under attack once again in *Wilson v. Block* (1983).[123] The U.S. Forestry Service sought to allow private interests to expand and develop the government-owned Snow Bowl ski area located in the San Francisco Peaks in the Coconimo National Forest in Arizona. As revealed in the case, the peaks

> have for centuries played a central role in the religions of two tribes. The Navajos believe that the Peaks are one of the four sacred mountains which mark the boundaries of their homeland. They believe the Peaks to be the home of specific deities and consider the Peaks to be the body of a spiritual being or god, with various peaks forming the head, shoulders and knees of a body reclining and facing to the east, while the trees, plants, rocks and earth form the skin. The Navajos pray directly to the Peaks and regard them as a living deity. The Peaks are invoked in religious ceremonies to heal the Navajo people. The Navajos collect herbs from the Peaks for use in religious ceremonies, and perform ceremonies upon the Peaks. They believe that artificial development of the Peaks would impair the Peaks' healing power.
>
> The Hopis believe that the Creator uses emissaries to assist in communicating with mankind. The emissaries are spiritual beings and are generally referred to by the Hopis as "Kachinas." The Hopis believe that for about six months each year, commencing in late July or early August and extending through mid-winter, the Kachinas reside at the Peaks. During the remaining six months of the year the Kachinas travel to the Hopi villages and participate in various religious ceremonies and practices. The Hopis believe that the Kachinas' activities on the Peaks create the rain and snow storms that sustain the villages. The Hopis have many shrines on the Peaks and collect herbs, plants and animals from the Peaks for use in religious ceremonies. The Hopis believe that use of the Peaks for commercial purposes would constitute a direct affront to the Kachinas and to the Creator.[124]

The Peaks were managed by the Forest Service until they transferred the operation to a private company in 1977. The company submitted plans to the Forest Service and requested a permit to expand the ski area, clearing about fifty acres and constructing a new lodge. At first, this was denied by the regional forester, but the chief forester overruled this and allowed the expansion.[125]

The plaintiffs argued that the expansion would violate their First Amendment right to free exercise, the American Indian Religious Freedom Act, the fiduciary duties owed to the tribes by the government and various environmental acts. The Diné (Navajo) and Hopi argued that the Peaks are sacred to their tribes and development would be a profane act, an affront to the deities residing there causing the Peaks to lose their healing powers and benefits.[126] The proposed development would impair their prayers and ceremonies and prevent the gathering of sacred objects and plants or destroy them.[127] Their claim stipulated that these practices *could not* be performed elsewhere; thus the area was central to their beliefs.[128]

Even with these arguments, the Court determined that there was no violation of the tribe's religious rights and denied their request for an injunction stopping the development of the area. The Forest Service had presented two so-called experts on Diné and Hopi religions who were *not* from the tribes, who stated that the expansion would have little or no direct impact.[129] It is amazing that the Court would rather listen and believe non–Indian experts on Indian religion than to members of the tribes that practice that religion every day. The Court decided that the area was not central based upon the information gathered from the non–Indian experts, nor was the area indispensable, and as such, no burden was presented to the tribe's free exercise rights. In the Court's blunt words, the "plaintiffs have not shown an impermissible burden on religion."[130]

In order to be protected by the free exercise clause, "a belief or practice must be rooted in religion," stated the Court.[131] Furthermore, the Court opined that the "free exercise clause proscribes government action that burdens religious beliefs or practices, unless the challenged action serves a compelling governmental interest that cannot be achieved in a less restrictive manner."[132] In this case, by permitting the ski area expansion, the government has not regulated, prohibited, or rewarded a religious belief nor has it burdened them in any manner.[133]

The Court continued splitting legal hairs and stated, "many governmental actions may offend religious believers, and may cast doubt upon the veracity of religious beliefs, but unless such actions penalize faith, they do not burden religion."[134] The Forest Service had determined that the public interest would be best served by expanding the ski area, and this did not, whether indirectly or directly, penalize tribal beliefs. Even though these actions were inconsistent with tribal beliefs and would cause them spiritual disquiet, these were not consequences that constituted a free exercise claim.[135]

Being able to separate faith from religion was an astounding feat, one that is incomprehensible to many observers. Even more so, it shows an absolute ignorance of the site specificity of traditional American Indian religions. The decision of the Court in this case went even further by holding that the plaintiffs seeking to restrict the government's land use in the name of religious freedom must, at a minimum, demonstrate that the government's proposed land use would impair a religious practice that could not be performed at some other site.[136] In other words, the very destruction of a tribal belief structure does not violate the free exercise clause unless a government benefit is denied or conditioned in a manner that discriminates against the religion.

The Diné and Hopi plaintiffs utilized the 1978 American Indian Religious Freedom Act (AIRFA)[137] as part of their claim. The Act specifically states, "it shall be the policy of the United States to protect and preserve for American Indians their inherent right of freedom to believe, express, and exercise [their] traditional religions … including but not limited to access to sites…."[138] The components of AIRFA recognize that traditional religions are an integral, indispensable and irreplaceable part of Indian life. It also recognizes and states that federal actions in the past have prohibited the access and use of sacred sites as required in Indian ceremonies and religions, and purports that this Act will change and correct this mistake. However, the *Wilson* case and others show otherwise.

The critics of AIRFA argue that it is an act without teeth, in that it did not create a cause of action for violations of American Indian religious freedom.[139] In support of this position, it seems that courts have construed the AIRFA as a mere articulation of existing constitutional rights afforded to Indian religions, not as a direction to give deference (or understanding) to them.[140] So, even when the U.S. Congress enacts specific legislation to protect Indians, the courts are not willing to follow federal laws if it interferes with the wants and desires of non–Indian entities.

Unfortunately, as the *Wilson* case demonstrated, the only manner in which the AIRFA can be enforced properly is if the judiciary realizes, understands and appreciates the differences between traditional Indian religions and those of the Judeo-Christian heritage.[141] This means understanding the impact of natural sites upon these religions. The plaintiffs contended that the AIRFA prevented any conflict or interference with traditional religions unless it was justified by a compelling government interest.[142] However, the District Court refused such a broad reading of the AIRFA and sided with the Forest Service. The AIRFA does not declare Indian religions to be an overriding factor of federal policy. According to the Court, the only purpose of the AIRFA is to have the government treat American Indian religions as equal as others, that it is nothing more than a policy statement dictating that the federal government review its procedures and regulations, and this is the view that the courts have seemingly taken throughout the cases. The AIRFA simply requires federal agencies to consider, not defer to, Indian religious values. The government is in compliance if it solicits Indian views and implements those programs that have the least interference.[143]

To summarize, the cases have left sacred sites in the following position:

In the Indian sacred land cases, the federal courts effectively precluded attempts by Native Americans to preserve their sacred lands from destruction or alteration via government action. A compilation of all the components of the free exercise tests employed in sacred land cases, as propounded by the courts reads as follows:

1. Plaintiffs must establish that their beliefs are sincere.

2. Plaintiffs must show that the beliefs are religiously based.

3. Plaintiffs must show that the land in question is central and indispensable to the practice of their religion to the extent that the practice is incapable of being conducted elsewhere.

4. Plaintiffs must show that the government action significantly burdens their ability to practice their religion.

Once plaintiffs construct this prima facie case, the government is required to either:

a. Come forward with a compelling state interest that may not be protected in any less restrictive manner, or

b. Weigh the relative strengths of the interests asserted.[144]

This was the status of judicial reasoning when the *Lyng* case came before the court.

Lyng v. Northwest Indian Cemetery Protective Association (1988)[145] involved the peoples of the northern door. The United States Forest Service wanted to construct a road to connect two small towns in the Chimney Rock area of the Six Rivers National Forest in California so as to permit logging in an area held sacred by the local Indian tribes.[146] In 1977, the U.S. Forest Service (USFS) issued an environmental impact statement (EIS) for the area of the road.

In 1979, the EIS determined that the area was significant for the religions and ceremonies of the Yurok, Karok and Tolowa Indian tribes in the area. It concluded that the construction of the road would cause serious and irreparable damage to the sacred areas which were an integral and necessary part of the belief systems and lifeways of the Indian peoples in Northwest California.[147] The EIS recommended that the road *not* be completed and of course, the Forest Service chose to ignore this recommendation in 1982 and proceeded with its original plans.[148] Thereafter. Suit was filed by the Indians and the state of California, as well as various environmental groups.[149]

The Ninth District Court did agree to halt the road's construction since the USFS had failed to demonstrate any compelling reason for the completion of the road.[150] It decided that stopping the road *was not* a violation of the establishment clause by creating a religious preserve for a single group of believers. Since the area in dispute had been historically used by the local tribes for religious ceremonies, it was a burden on their free exercise rights to have the road built there. The District Court found that the USFS not only violated the Indians' First Amendment rights, but also the National Environmental Protection Act (NEPA), the Wilderness Act, the Water Pollution Act, the Administrative Procedures Act, and the fiduciary role that the federal government has for the Indian peoples.[151]

The Court agreed that the necessity of performing their ceremonies in isolation and without outside interference was vital to the tribes' exercise of religion rights and that the government's interest in revenue and recreation did not outweigh these concerns.[152] The court stated that the "Constitution encourages accommodation, not merely tolerance, of all religions and forbids hostility towards any."[153]

It was a short-lived victory, as the tribes had to continue their fight against the Forest Service. It was determined to build its road and appealed the 9th Circuit Court ruling to the U.S. Supreme Court which reversed the appellate court decision. Economics and property interests were once again pitted against Indian religions and their sacred places of ceremony and worship.

The Indian respondents contended that the burden on their religion was dire enough to violate their First Amendment freedom of religious exercise rights, especially since there was no demonstratable government compelling interest to complete the road and harvest the timber on both sides of it.[154] They also argued that the subsequent description and destruction of the environment would diminish the sacredness of the area, create distractions, and interfere with their religion and training.[155]

The Supreme Court brushed aside these arguments. Free exercise claims cannot be used to force or require the government to readjust its own internal affairs or policies. This was the same line of argument used in *Bowen v. Roy* (1986)[156] where the Indian plaintiffs refused to get their daughter a social security number based on religious grounds. The Court dismissed this claim by pointing out that this was an internal policy of government and it did not harm the religion or its practices. In *Lyng*, the Court stated that building the road was the same thing, and it "cannot be meaningfully distinguished from the use of a social security number…" since in neither case would the affected individuals be coerced by the government into an action, into violating their religious beliefs; nor would the government action penalize them by denying them an equal share of rights, benefits, or privileges enjoyed by other citizens.[157] It concluded that the First Amendment does not require the government to conduct its internal affairs in accordance with individual religious beliefs; nor does it allow a single person to dictate governmental internal policy or act in a manner to promote personal spiritual growth.[158]

Justice O'Connor, writing for the majority, further delineated the Court's logic (or lack thereof) by stating that it could not "determine the truth of the underlying beliefs that led to the religious objections here or in *Roy*, and accordingly cannot weigh the adverse effects on the appellees in *Roy* and compare them with the adverse effects on the Indian respondents."[159] Despite this, however, O'Connor continued, amazingly admitting that "the government does not dispute, and we have no reason to doubt, that the logging and road building projects at issue in this case could have devastating effects on traditional religious practices."[160]

Yet, the Court got itself out of this jam of acknowledging that the road would destroy the religion of the natives by pointing out that the Constitution does not allow, nor can the courts offer to reconcile various competing demands on government in such a diverse society.[161] Then, as if to demonstrate a total disregard for American Indian culture and history, O'Connor pointed out that "whatever rights the Indians may have to the use of the area, however, those rights do not divest the government of its right to use what is, after all, *its land.*"[162]

Therefore, the Court had three main issues in this case. First, O'Connor worried that the Court would become entangled in determining the legitimacy of each religion if free exercise claims to national areas were made by "non-traditional" groups. This obviously categorizes American Indians as outside the religious mainstream. Second, the Court may overstep the establishment clause by accepting some claims but not others. Finally, third, the Court may interfere with Congress' ability to manage federal lands by having a group place them into "religious servitude" if the land in dispute is settled for the plaintiffs.[163]

Justices Brennan, Marshall and Blackmun dissented in this case and recognized, in a judicially uncharacteristic manner, the importance and processes of American Indian religions. Furthermore, they recognized the differences between Western and Native religions in that American Indians regard creation as an ongoing process in which they are morally and religiously obligated to participate via rituals and ceremonies.[164] They also recognized that Indian religions have no reliance on dogmas or creeds which are at the very heart of Western religions.

The Indian respondents believe that the area in dispute is where the prehuman spirits moved to with the coming of humans to the Earth, and since these spirits are the source of religious power, the area is where great medicine is found and made.[165] The timber road is not, according to the dissenters, a compelling interest that outweighs the effect on their religion.[166] In fact, Justice

Brennan, writing for the dissent, stated that the proposed government activity would have restrained religious practice to a far greater degree than any case cited by the majority. Brennan continued and pointed out that in his view, "while Native Americans need not demonstrate, *as respondents did here*, that the government's land-use decision will assuredly eradicate their faith, I do not think it is enough to allege simply that the land in question is held sacred."[167] The plaintiffs must show a substantial threat to their religion, and once this is done the burden shifts to the government. In Justice Brennan's opinion, the plaintiffs did meet this criterion, proving the site had significant importance using both historical and contemporary evidence,[168] and it became the government's burden to prove why the project should be undertaken. Simply put, it did not do this.

If the Court had really taken the time to consider the evidence, stopping the road would not have been a violation of the establishment clause since it would have been an exception or exemption like several other religions already enjoyed.[169] However, Brennan concluded his opinion by stating:

> Similarly, the Court's concern that the claims of Native Americans will place "religious servitude" upon vast tracts of federal property cannot justify its refusal to recognize the constitutional injury respondents will suffer here. It is true, as the Court notes, that respondents' religious use of the high country requires privacy and solitude. The fact remains, however, that respondents have never asked the Forest Service to exclude others from the area. Should respondents or any other group seek to force the Government to protect their religious practices from the interference of private parties, such a demand would implicate not only the concerns of the Free Exercise Clause, but also those of the Establishment Clause as well. That case, however, is most assuredly not before us today, and in any event cannot justify the Court's refusal to acknowledge that the injuries respondents will suffer as a result of the Government's proposed activities are sufficient to state a constitutional cause of action.
>
> Today, the Court holds that a federal land-use decision that promises to destroy an entire religion does not burden the practice of that faith in a manner recognized by the Free Exercise Clause. Having thus stripped respondents and all other Native Americans of any constitutional protection against perhaps the most serious threat to their age-old religious practices, and indeed to their entire way of life, the Court assures us that nothing in its decision "should be read to encourage governmental insensitivity to the religious needs of any citizen." I find it difficult, however, to imagine conduct more insensitive to religious needs than the Government's determination to build a marginally useful road in the face of uncontradicted evidence that the road will render the practice of respondents' religion impossible. Nor do I believe that respondents will derive any solace from the knowledge that although the practice of their religion will become "more difficult" as a result of the Government's actions, they remain free to maintain their religious beliefs. Given today's ruling, that freedom amounts to nothing more than the right to believe that their religion will be destroyed. The safeguarding of such a hollow freedom not only makes a mockery of the "policy of the United States to protect and preserve for American Indians their inherent right of freedom to believe, express and exercise their 'traditional religions,'" (quoting AIRFA), it fails utterly to accord with the dictates of the First Amendment.[170]

In evaluating the *Lyng* decision, it could be said that this was merely a culmination of the failure of the judiciary to understand American Indian religions and to protect their rights under the First Amendment.[171] The majority left no room for any Indian to bring forth a First Amendment claim, while at the same time refused to protect their religious practices.[172] By separating the protection of practice from a religious belief, the Court has shown its disdain and ignorance of the fact that to traditional American Indian religions, some practices are so vital that to prevent them will ultimately destroy the religion, and maybe even the very culture of the people.[173] As a result of *Lyng*, "ceremonies and rituals that had been performed for thousands of years were [now] treated as if they were popular fads or simply matters of preference based upon the erroneous assumption that religion was only a matter of individual aesthetic choice."[174]

This distinction reflects the judiciary's bias in favor of those religions that are well-established, are portable and are not site specific.[175] The Court's actions in *Lyng* indicating that the Constitution's clauses do not provide protection for sacred sites against development also point out that the Constitution will not protect site-specific religions.

In conclusion:

> The *Lyng* court confronted and rejected traditional methods of free exercise analysis and distorted principles advanced in prior religious freedom decisions involving more conventional religious interests. To reach its conclusion that the Native American's religion was not unconstitutionally burdened, the Court essentially ignored the cautious construction and careful development of free exercise jurisprudence which had evolved since the drafting of the Constitution.[176]

The Supreme Court, thanks to this decision, had "resurrected an outmoded and embarrassing judicial attitude toward the Constitutional status of American Indians."[177] In other words, the Supreme Court placed property interests over that of the free exercise of religion rights of the American Indian.

The final case to be reviewed is that of *Pueblo of Sandia et al. v. U.S.* (1995).[178] Once again, the peoples of the southern door were under attack. The Pueblo and various environmental groups filed suit for injunctive relief against the U.S. Forest Service citing a violation of the National Historic Preservation Act (NHPA).[179]

The Forest Service wanted to expand a road, add more picnic sites and other tourist attractions in the Las Huertas Canyon in the Cibola National Forest in New Mexico. This would infringe upon the Pueblo's land which was asserted to contain numerous significant religious and cultural sites, enough to qualify the Canyon as a "traditional cultural property."[180] Of course, as before, the U.S. Forest Service had its own plans and would deem otherwise.

What is unique about this case are not the arguments, for they have been expressed countless times before, but the extent to which the USFS would go to get what it wanted. The USFS requested information about the area from local tribal leaders. However, the information requested via official letters were drawn-to-scale maps, official documents and other items of such detail that it would be nearly impossible for anyone to produce them. Furthermore, the USFS, as the Court determined, should have known that local tribal customs would restrict the divulgence of such sacred sites to any outsider, no matter what the purpose.[181]

To add insult to injury, the USFS withheld all information it did receive about the sacred sites in the Canyon from the State Historic Preservation Officer (SHPO) until the officer had concurred with the USFS decision at the initial hearing and the process had closed![182] The USFS had received affidavits and oral testimony from various tribal leaders, but simply ignored it and hid it from review by the SHPO.[183]

In the appeal, members of the Pueblo once again expressed that the Canyon contained sacred medicinal plants, religious shrines and ceremonial paths. More importantly, after the SHPO discovered that the USFS had withheld vital information about the significance of the Canyon to the Indians there, the officer now sided with the members of the Sandia Pueblo.[184]

The Court ruled that the Forest Service's request for information was not reasonable and did not qualify as a good faith effort under the NHPA.[185] The testimony and affidavits it did receive were sufficient to halt the construction.

The outright deviousness of the Forest Service came to the surface in the case. The USFS was well aware of the claims prior to its final hearing and decision in April of 1993. In fact, it had taken testimony and affidavits from Pueblo elders and religious leaders as far back as August 1989. The USFS's own anthropologist and archeologist explained in their 1992 report that the area was sacred and showed why its religious and cultural functions would be destroyed by the proposed development.[186] The sites were critical to the religious practice, cultural identity and overall well-being of the Pueblo. They also explained why communications and information from the tribe were not forthcoming and why the tribal members were reluctant to speak about these sites.[187] The report was withheld from the SHPO until concurrence was acquired in May of 1993. Yet, when the SHPO did finally get the information in January 1994, this concurrence was immediately withdrawn.[188] Hence, the Court ruled against the Forest Service, not for infringing upon the sacred sites of the Pueblo, but for failing to follow the proper administrative procedures as detailed in the law. Although the outcome was favorable to the Pueblo, no sanctions were issued against the USFS for their behavior.

However, President Clinton, in one of his final acts before leaving office, granted protection to at least part of the Pueblo's land by declaring it sacred. The declaration endorsed the Department of Interior's stance and stated that the eastern border of the Pueblo was the crest of the Sandia Mountain.[189] This disputed an 1859 Department of Interior survey. Furthermore, the Pueblo won support of the New Mexico Conference of Churches who have since urged New Mexico's Congressional delegation to support the decision. Private property on the western side of the mountain would remain untouched, and the public would still have full access to both sides, appeasing the coalition of property owners and sportsmen that wanted the eastern side to remain national forest.[190] However, the eastern side of the mountain is now given to the Pueblo for free and unrestricted religious use. At last, and at least, a partial victory.

What this review of cases has shown is that the American court system does not, or chooses to not, understand that religious freedom to the American Indian is a matter of cultural survival.[191] Instead, the government has continually suppressed and assaulted Indian religions—both in belief, faith and practice. "By denying sacred site claims, courts are ignoring, or at best marginalizing, the destructive aspect of the development of public land."[192]

However, as has been explained already, these "sacred land cases are of paramount importance to American Indian religious practices as the sites in question are not merely traditional gathering points; the land represents a physical embodiment of the Indian religion."[193] "[As] sacred sites are restricted or destroyed, so too are the religious rituals connected to those places, and without this connection of culture, the very essence of American Indian identity is threatened with destruction."[194]

The *Lyng* decision overruled the precedent holding that a governmental action which created an incidental burden on free exercise of religion need not be justified by a compelling state interest which cannot be served by a less restrictive means.[195] Now, plaintiffs must prove that the government is punishing its religion—a task nearly impossible to complete considering the ethnic bias reflected in the courts, and the inadequacy of legislation (AIRFA, RFRA, etc.) designed to protect and accommodate American Indian religions. It seems that the court moved from the balancing test to a coercion test to *determine if the tribal religion burdened the government or private commercial interests and their actions or desires.*

However, these decisions by the court can be viewed as nothing more than the culmination of a long history of governmental attempts to Christianize, and thus, assimilate the Indian into white society. From the start, Christianity was equated with civilization, and the courts seem to be continuing this effort by helping the government to suppress ceremonies, rituals and beliefs, and even entire cultures.[196] It would appear that this is nothing more than a subtle form of ethnic cleansing.

"Despite the pressures from the federal government to abandon their traditional religions, Native Americans have continued to worship at their often remote and isolated sacred sites. However, developments interfering with Native American sacred sites located on public lands have made it difficult for many traditionally religious Indians to conduct ceremonies and rituals."[197] Now a new threat has joined the government and has attacked traditional Indian religions and their sacred sites of worship and ceremony. This threat is not organized, and seems to stem more from a haughty ignorance than from anything else. It is the New Age movement and its adherents.

The New Age Threat

Whether they are called Wannabe, Waciku or as Vine DeLoria has labeled them, "New Age circuit Indians claiming to be intertribal pipe carriers,"[198] these people are now the newest and maybe the most dangerous threat ever to traditional Indian religions, their practices, ceremonies and sacred sites. "The spiritual practices of New Age movements often draw upon Native American rituals. Some Native Americans are happy to export elements of their religion to outsiders ... others resent it as insensitive to their own traditions."[199]

This fascination with American Indian culture, lifestyle and religion began a long time ago. It is "by an ironic semantic twist, [that] by the end of the nineteenth century the same Euro-Americans who had once viewed American Indians as alien savages came to embrace them as the true, the natural, the first Americans, icons of the nation and territory."[200] Of course, this has led to a lot of non–Indians playing Indians in Hollywood and in various advertisements. Regardless of the purpose, it was, and is, easier to do this for a few reasons.

First, and maybe the most obvious, is skin color. Indians vary in their skin color and tone regardless of the Hollywood and history book stereotypes. Someone with a European heritage that had darker skin could easily pass themselves off as Indian.[201] Second, since most tribes do not have written records of families and members, at least not before the mid– to late–1800s, it is easier to claim some Indian heritage and it is very difficult to have this verified or disproved.

Third, unlike other minorities, contact with American Indians is probably less common for non–Natives so there is, and was, less chance of actually divulging the truth about the person's background. Furthermore, due to the lack of contact, there has been less knowledge about the real discrimination and issues that American Indians have suffered. If the pseudo–Indian did start to suffer like the real Indians, they could and have conveniently and easily reverted to their former status to avoid further harm. Of course, if the person had claimed African American or Asian American heritage, it would have been easily identifiable through physical characteristics and the impact would have been immediate and harsh, from both the majority and minority communities. Many of these pseudo–Indians want the notoriety and attention of being Indian, but without the burden, responsibilities and problems that accompany this minority status.

Finally, "among such counter-longings, the wish to 'go native,' to find freedom and fulfillment by adopting certain versions of indigenous styles and practice, to 'Indianize' oneself, has a long and still active history."[202] Non–Indians have often created a functional Indian and it upsets them if reality fails to satisfy their stereotypes. "Inventing symbolic Indians, playing Indians, dreaming Indian—all of these phases describe the way white Americans [have] put themselves in relationship to the aboriginal population."[203] Many of these non–Indians were and are rebelling against mainstream society and they have sought an identity in what they see as a new age, not as themselves, but as pseudo–Indians, as if being Indian is a costume that can be removed when it becomes uncomfortable or dangerous. It is identification without responsibility and is a form of cultural theft, a threat to the sacred sovereignty of the Indian people.

Nowhere is this desire to be Indian more prevalent and obvious than in Germany. Germany's Hobbyism or Indianism, as it is called, is the desire to copy Native Americans from yesteryear and many modern-day Indians find this puzzling, and some find it as a threat to their history and culture. There are literally tens of thousands of Germans who don wigs, dress up as American Indians, dance in powwows, sell and buy German-fashioned Indian goods, reenact imaginary tribal battles, choose pseudo–Indian names for themselves, and at times, even make up imaginary tribes. They buy and wear sacred Eagle feathers, which are earned and to receive one is a rare and true honor to a Native American, and violate other cultural norms of many tribes.

Many trace this cult-like fascination with American Indian culture the author, Karl May, who wrote a series of fictional books about a German explorer, Old Shatterhand, and his faithful Apache companion, Winnitou, in the late 1800s.[204] Even though he claimed the books were based on actual experiences, they were all pure fiction and figments of his imagination.[205] The appeal of his novels may just be the fact that they had so little factual basis.

This behavior by the Germans enthusiasts has had detrimental effects. Many Hobbyists:

> have romanticized long-gone Native Americans to a degree that they think "latter-day" Indians are poor examples of their ancestors—whom they revere as noble savages. (German Hobbyist) Old Bull's followers believe Natives today are being perverted by modern culture and that they are not native Americans preserving native culture. Instead of empathizing with the very real struggles of natives now living in North

America, these "new Indians" of Europe see the societal problems, substance and alcohol abuse, poverty and internal difficulties within some indigenous communities as evidence supporting their conclusions. They believe their activities are keeping Native American traditions alive, because—they believe—most natives neglect or do not appreciate their own heritage.[206]

Whereas some true American Indians see these Hobbyists as an opportunity to promote and educate about their tribe and culture, others are not so sure. There is the opinion that these people are claiming the right to improvise sacred rituals and are beginning to develop a serious sense of ownership over Indian cultures.[207] Many German Hobbyists are of the opinion that "no people should be allowed to keep their culture just for themselves."[208] This can pervert history and true respect and understanding of American Indian culture, and may damage it for future generations, both Indian and non–Indian alike.

New Agers are those people who take bits and pieces of established religions and spiritual paths for their own benefit, without a full understanding and respect for the struggles, teachings and history that these religions include. They mold these selected pieces into an easy-to-follow pseudo-religion, sometimes complete with manual, into which they can fit any type of behavior or actions. They draw from paganism, witchcraft, wicca, and the ancient druids as well as Buddhism, Hinduism and American Indian religions. It is an individualistic approach to spirituality rather than a group one, where whatever makes you feel good must be right. New Agers have grasped onto palm reading, tarot cards, auras, chakras, channeling and crystal gazing in order to revamp things into an individual spiritual system. They are obviously seeking paths outside the older established religions, either because these churches have failed to adapt to this new individualism, or because today's society stresses the importance of the self and its immediate satisfaction.

Unfortunately, many of these New Agers have turned these spiritual practices and ancient teachings into near-cult-like gatherings, and have hatched schemes to deceive the lost and wandering into paying for ceremonies, crystals, and self-help books. Without fully understanding the ceremonies that they perform, they open many people to possible emotional, mental, spiritual and even physical harm.[209] Some of this group claim to have discovered social, sexual and spiritual forms and even dialects unknown to the Indian peoples themselves.[210] Usually, this knowledge is claimed to have been learned from some unknown elder or shaman that they met and studied with, a person that apparently did not want to instill this knowledge in one of his or her own people.

One could look at the New Agers with pity. However, it is their willingness to steal and destroy American Indian religious practices and sacred sites in particular that makes them a force to be feared for the damage they can do to the Indian peoples and their cultures. This is cultural theft or worse. For they are taking for their own power and egos, disregarding the effects of those they steal from.

The effort to find something that is missing from their own lives and culture has led to a vast multitude of people seeking out Indian religious leaders, whether they are real or not, in hopes of emulating their ceremonies and rituals. Yet, "as interested as whites are in Indian culture and religion, they prefer to learn from non–Indians who pose as experts in this field."[211] Whites are portraying themselves as Indians, renaming themselves using animal motifs, acting as channelers for some sacredness that true Indians have never fathomed, and are now setting themselves up as the true native spiritualists.

These actions supplant the real Indian in the areas of customs and spirituality. In other words, this gives the non–Indian the power to define who and what makes up the American Indian and their spirituality.[212] The practitioners of "white shamanism" defend their actions as being totally apolitical, or that they were trained by some mysterious elder or medicine man somewhere and they are being sent as spiritual messengers. They are aspiring to be what they believe to be a "real Indian." However, when asked to define exactly the source of their "training," they cannot or will not identify the source of their knowledge or relate any real connection to a true Indian tribe. These self-proclaimed gurus dispense healings, medicines and blessings at bogus medicine wheel gatherings, ersatz sweat-lodge ceremonies and other fad events.[213] Unfortunately, they get fanatical followers who will believe almost anything they are told, as long as it has a tinge of "Indianness" to it.

As a prime example, Patton Boyle is an Episcopal priest who has written two books supposedly depicting his studies with an American Indian shaman, while at the same time he unabashedly admits that he did not know much about American Indians or their spirituality when he wrote the books. Furthermore, he readily admits that he did not know any medicine men and did not fully understand Indian spirituality when he wrote the books.[214] In essence, he wrote the books about Indian spirituality without the knowledge, the beliefs or the cultural inheritance that a true Indian or even a valid researcher may have. He lied to the readers of his books. If an Indian author had written about Christianity without so much as meeting and talking to a Christian leader, his opinion and conclusions would surely be questioned. Instead, when a Christian priest writes a myth about Indian spirituality, he is embraced by followers as an expert. These people are seeking a true Indian spiritual leader for whatever reason, but only end up with someone who is ready to steal their ceremonies and beliefs for their own use and profit.

It is unfortunate that "some whites feel alienated by their own religious traditions and they are trying to fill a spiritual void ... trying to be something they are not."[215] These people pick and choose which aspects of Indian religion and customs they wish to follow and put them on like some costume, removing it when it becomes too difficult to wear. Fake Indian shamans abound, some claiming that they have been ordered by their tribal elders to spread the word, revealing religious secrets to the non–Indian. When they go off and try to imitate an Indian ceremony in an offensive manner, they are not filling a void but simply practicing escapism.[216] Some would argue that this is not theft. The ideas, beliefs and practices are out there to be shared by anyone for their own worship practices. It may be true that no one "owns" a ceremony, but running around "playing" Indian is racist and a form of cultural rape in that it diminishes and trivializes the culture and traditions of the true Indian. In addition, it is interesting that many African religions have similar belief structures, but no New Ager seems to be emulating them and claiming to be African.

These New Agers who use Indian ceremonies for their own gain, whether it be for money,[217] or power or ego, are attacking and essentially raping the Indian culture. Without getting into a debate over a proper definition of rape, the term as it is used here refers to an act of violence for power, not gratification. These New Agers are assimilating and Anglicizing Indian traditions and sacred ceremonies for the power it gives them over themselves and others.[218] Hence, they are more accurately known as cultural rapists. As Vine DeLoria stated:

> Today an alleged shaman can explain his or her absence from the reservation or absence of Indian blood with the excuse that after being trained by elders, the individual has then been authorized and commanded to go among all peoples and preach the Indian gospel. It seems that this surplus of shamans could severely tax the credibility of these practitioners. How can there be so many medicine people who have been commissioned to hold ceremonies for non–Indians while their own people suffer without religious ministrations?[219]

These non–Indian religious leaders simply claim to be a mystical pipe carrier in order to perform ceremonies without having to understand them, or to be held accountable if something goes wrong or if nothing happens as promised. The followers of these "spirit trained" pipe carriers or self-proclaimed ceremonial leaders and healers see the romantic side of traditional American Indian religions without having to endure the history of struggle and oppression to keep them alive.[220] In fact, it has become such a problem that at times the non–Indian experts are relied upon more for information and teachings than the real Indian religious leaders. It has gotten to the point that "non–Indians are claiming the authority to teach Native American spirituality; mixing Native and new age beliefs; and charging money for sacred ceremonies."[221] At gatherings such as powwows, these same non–Indians even look down upon the real Indians as if they are an intrusion upon their new-found way of life. In reality, they are disgusted because the real Indians are simply reminding them who they are and what they cannot become.

Native "ceremonies and ritual knowledge is possessed by everyone in the Indian community, although only a few people may actually be chosen to perform these acts."[222] Furthermore, authorization to perform these acts comes from certain medicine societies, tribal leaders, or from affirmed and accepted spiritual callings. This is something that the New Age adherents fail to grasp as they rush out on their own after seeing a movie or reading a book, and attempt to perform their own version of tribal religious ceremonies. "Some people want traditional healers to share their religious beliefs in the same manner that priests, rabbis, and ministers expound publicly the tenets of their denominations."[223] Unfortunately, these people do not share the same sense of belonging and community that the Indian culture does, and will never be able to assimilate into it. They cannot seem to shed their Judeo-Christian religious beliefs, which at their core are about converting people to their beliefs. Indian religions do not have this core tenet.

"The New Age movement has helped spark an interest in the nature-based spirituality of Native Americans among non–Indians."[224] As such, "in the 1990s, Indian religions are a hot item. It is the outward symbolic form that is most popular. Many people ... have taken a few principles to heart, mostly those beliefs that require little in the way of changing one's lifestyle. Tribal religions have been trivialized beyond redemption by people sincerely wishing to learn about them."[225] This trivialization has not only affected ceremonies and rituals, but also objects utilized in traditional Indian religions such as prayer pipes, drums and herbs. This behavior has now spread to threaten the very sites where these emulated religions are practiced.

The invasion of usurpers, now in New Age guises, have even desecrated sacred sites. "The New Age's harmonic convergence in 1987 brought thousands to ancient Indian sites ... and the unwelcome leftovers from New Age rituals have remained steady."[226] These people take rocks, stones and plants, build fires and leave behind objects such as crystals, feathers and cremated human remains that not only disrupts the archeology of the site, but defiles its sacredness.[227] As an example, the Spirit Little Cedar, known to the local Anishinabé Indians as Manidoo-giizhikens, is an ancient cedar on the shore of Lake Superior, Minnesota that has become the focus of tourists, and by those who practice witchcraft and black magic (condemned and feared by many traditional Indian religions). It has gotten to the point that access to the tree has had to be restricted by the tribal council.[228] The Cedar's well-being is being threatened by people taking pieces of it or hanging objects such as witch's amulets, upon its branches. This is desecrating its spirit. The Anishinabé have instituted what they term a cultural repossession process to stop this instance of cultural rape.

In 1993, a coalition of religious, political and environmental leaders launched an effort to protect Indian religions and their sites. One of their concerns was the "incursion[s] into sacred sites by non–Indians who destroy or damage sacred Indian lands in at least forty sites."[229] American Indian practices are being imitated and objects are being left at, or the actual sites are being disturbed in a manner in which no other religion would permit. Surely, no Judeo-Christian sect in the United States would allow anyone simply claiming to believe in some of their religious tenets to perform sacred rituals or ceremonies in their church, or to take a piece of a cathedral or holy relic home as a souvenir. If souvenir hunters rushed to Notre Dame to grab a piece of it or a holy relic, there would be an uproar and a demand for protections. Yet, exploiters and cultural rapists are permitted to continue to steal and hoard Indian relics and history while the "real" Indian fights to save their culture in the courts and legislatures. The reason for this may be as simple as the commercialization of Indian religions.[230]

The New Age cultural followers have even committed crimes in the guise of conducting ceremonies. These have ranged from simple fraud and theft, to rape and even manslaughter. During the summer of 2002, a group known as the Kokopelli Ranch led a group of people off into the woods in northern California for a vision quest and sweat-lodge ceremony. Instead of finding their inner selves or peace, two participants died in the sweat lodge from unknown causes.[231] The coroner believed it could have been cardiac problems, asphyxiation and/or toxic fumes from the herbs and materials burned in the lodge. Two others barely survived their ordeal. None of the leaders or participants claimed to be American Indian. Once again, the non-native experts on Indian spirituality have not only endangered others, but this time they succeeded in killing two people.

While the courts strip away the free exercise rights of true American Indian religions, and the culture-perverting Wannabes corrupt their ceremonies and beliefs, tourists and recreationists continue their totally selfish and self-centered acts on sacred lands. One of the best examples is that of Devils Tower in Wyoming. The 860-foot Tower has been the focus of American Indian pilgrimages, vision quests and ceremonies for centuries. This is where the Lakota people were created. However, it is also the focus for thousands of rock climbers who rivet the face of the Tower with climbing bolts, disturb ceremonies held there, and even urinate on its walls.[232] The Indians would like all climbing halted, but this is being resisted by recreational climbing companies in the area. As the owner of one of these rock-climbing companies stated:

> As far as I'm concerned, prayer bundles are a bunch of trash, and I'm very offended to have them hanging around the monument. They [monument officials] should be managing climbing based on quantifiable, scientific research on its impact on the tower,

not on one group's religious beliefs ... the Indians get to build fires in the most beautiful meadow in the park for their sweat lodge and Sun Dance ceremonies, but they don't climb that rock, which I own as an American citizen.[233]

The statement demonstrates a profound ignorance of the First Amendment and that the American Indian was here long before this person's ancestors found their way to America's shores. The Indian is America's first citizen, though obviously not in respect or in rights. If American Indians were to attempt to climb monuments in Washington, D.C., arrests would be made. More likely, the citizenry would demand retaliation. Furthermore, if a group climbed Mount Rushmore (built in the sacred Black Hills) and urinated on its faces, would American citizens merely stand by and shrug it off? Skeptical non–Indians have always sought to discredit tribal religions and sometimes have deliberately violated holy places with no apparent ill effects, thus hoping to demonstrate the false nature of Indian beliefs.[234]

Despite such statements of opposition, the National Park Service issued a climbing plan in March 1995. The plan *requested* that climbers refrain from climbing the Tower during the culturally significant month of June.[235] Furthermore, it stated that federal agencies "are to accommodate access to and ceremonial use of Indian sacred sites and to avoid adversely affecting the physical integrity of sacred sites" as per Executive Order.[236] In March 2000, the U.S. Supreme Court allowed the voluntary closure to stand and the result has been amazing. The number of climbers has dropped an average of 85 percent as of June 2000.[237]

On May 24, 1996, President Clinton issued Executive Order 13007 dealing with Indian Sacred Sites. The stated purpose was to protect and preserve Indian religious practices. Federal agencies with federal land management duties were ordered to accommodate access to and ceremonial use of sacred sites by Indian religious practitioners to the extent practicable and permitted by law.[238] Whereas the wording sounds promising, final sections of the Executive Order state that the Order is intended to "only improve the internal management of the executive branch, and is not intended to, nor does it, create any right, benefit or trust responsibility...."[239] In other words, the federal government has to show concern; but in politics, a show is all that is needed. In reality, and as the courts have amply demonstrated, the government can do nearly anything under the auspices of a "compelling interest." While the rhetoric continues, sacred sites are desecrated or destroyed.

Other sites are under attack as a result of this order. Medicine Wheel, Wyoming, is under assault from local sawmills who want the area timbered and developed. The medicine wheel is an 80-foot-diameter circle with a cross in the middle. Each direction of the wheel represents a certain aspect of human existence and spirit.[240] Tribes from around the nation have come to the site to leave prayer bundles and offerings, and to sing and pray for personal or tribal reasons. In accordance with the 1996 order, the Forest Service placed a limit on logging on 18,000 acres around the site, which rests on 264,000 acres already open to the lumber industry. These acres were declared an "area of consultation."[241] This area set aside requires that the local Indian tribes be consulted before any activity takes place there. The sawmills have opposed this ruling, claiming the Indians would have veto power over their commercial industry. A lawsuit has been filed to deny the natives the right to protect their religion and tradition, and to protect commercial interests on native sacred lands.

In a final evaluation of the Court's decisions, in several cases involving non–Indian religious rights, the courts have stated that they were not competent to evaluate, nor would they judge, the accuracy of the religion's belief.[242] Yet, in many of these cases, the Court did just that. Therefore, it has developed the position that as long as the government is not telling the Indian *what* to believe, it may go ahead and restrict, even destroy, the ability of the American Indian to practice the religions they have practiced from time immemorial.

The Legislative Remedies?

There have been numerous pieces of federal legislation that, although not specifically designed to protect sacred sites, could be used as a starting point in this process. In 1906, the Antiquities Act gave the President, via executive order, the ability to protect landmarks and structures on federal lands.[243] This could be used to protect sacred sites, but this has not been attempted.

The 1966 National Historic Preservation Act, the 1979 Archaeological Resources Protection Act and other acts established the criteria of informing and soliciting Indian input on plans that may encroach upon Indian lands or sites.[244] However, as mentioned earlier, the problem exists because many of these sites are secret, or even if the input is received this will not always guarantee that the final decision will be altered to protect the area, especially if the federal agency has made up its mind otherwise.

The 1978 American Indian Religious Freedom Act (AIRFA) has been reviewed, as has a history of losses in recent sacred site lawsuits involving claims of site protection under its auspices. The AIRFA recognized American Indian religions and required federal agencies to become aware of these and avoid unnecessary interference with these practices. But as has been pointed out, the AIRFA has no enforcement procedures. In sum, the act "declared that it was the policy of Congress to protect and preserve the inherent right of American Indians to believe, express and practice their traditional religions."[245] Thus, it is easy to simultaneously follow and ignore this as nothing more than another bureaucratic hurdle.

In 1993, Congress enacted the Religious Freedom Restoration Act (RFRA)[246] in order to restore judicial use of traditional strict scrutiny in those cases where a religion is burdened by a supposedly neutral government action.[247] Of course, in the opinion of the courts, if a traditional Indian religion's worship can be performed elsewhere, then there is no burden on their free exercise rights.[248] Worshiping at a specific site has not been seen as central and/or indispensable to traditional Indian religions. Unfortunately, American Indian religions are not as portable as Judeo-Christian ones which often only require moving the church or congregation to a new location.

The RFRA redirected the courts to employ the compelling state interest test before allowing a religion to be burdened.[249] In other words, "the law allowed government agencies to impinge on religious faith only if they had a 'compelling interest' to do so and used the 'least restrictive means.'"[250] Only then, can an individual's free exercise of religion be burdened. Of course, the RFRA was not broad enough to address all American Indian religious practices, nor did it cover sacred sites according to the U.S. government.

However, the Supreme Court has allowed the RFRA to protect some religious practices from ordinances that unfairly burdened them. In Hialeah, Florida, followers of the Santeria religion fought against local laws banning animal sacrifices as cruel to the animals and a danger to public health. The Court declared that the laws were not neutral in that they were focused directly on the Santeria Church and its worship practices.[251]

The Court explained further that the free exercise clause of the First Amendment is a guarantee of individual religious liberty. Hence, "a religious minority can be a minority of one"[252] and deserves protection! The Court continued by stating, "our national liberty is replete with instances of deliberate offered suppression of religious outsiders, by explicit targeting or by 'religious gerrymandering'; either of which is directed at a group."[253]

In the second example of where the RFRA became the focal point of defense, a dispute between the Catholic Church and the Boerne City, Texas, government provided the grounds. The church wished to rebuild to accommodate its growing congregation. The city wanted to protect the architecture and church as a historical site. The Church sued under the RFRA.

The Fifth Circuit Court agreed with the Church in that the RFRA gives special consideration to religious practices when they collide with neutral government laws.[254] The city zoning and preservation laws placed an undue burden on the religion, or in other words, the Church. When a burden takes place, the government must show a compelling interest and in this instance, the historical preservation of the church was not strong enough.[255]

When this case arrived at the Supreme Court in 1997, not only did the Court overrule the lower court, it struck down the entire RFRA as unconstitutional. Justice Kennedy, writing for the 6–3 majority, stated that the law was too broad, it was not based on evidence of widespread discrimination, and it placed too heavy a burden on the state while altering the meaning of religious freedom.[256] According to the Court:

> RFRA is not a proper exercise of Congress's enforcement power because it contradicts vital principles necessary to maintain separation of powers and the federal-state balance…. RFRA's legislative record lacks examples of any instances of generally applicable laws passed because of religious bigotry in the past 40 years. Rather, the emphasis of the RFRA hearings was on laws like the one at issue that place incidental burdens on religion. It is difficult to maintain that such laws are based on animus or hostility to the burdened religious practices or that they indicate some widespread pattern of religious discrimination in this country. RFRA's most serious shortcoming, however, lies in the fact that it is so out of proportion to a supposed remedial or preventative object that it cannot be understood as responsive to, or designed to prevent, unconstitutional behavior. It appears, instead, to attempt a substantive change in constitutional protections, proscribing state conduct that the Fourteenth Amendment itself does not prohibit. Its sweeping coverage ensures its intrusion at every level of government, displacing laws and prohibiting official actions of almost every description and regardless of subject matter. Its restrictions apply to every government agency and official, and to all statutory or other law, whether adopted before or after its enactment…. It has no termination date or termination mechanism. Any law is subject to challenge at any time by any individual who claims a substantial burden on his or her free exercise of religion.
>
> Such a claim will often be difficult to contest. Requiring a State to demonstrate a compelling interest and show that it has adopted the least restrictive means of achieving that interest is the most demanding test known to constitutional law.
>
> Furthermore, the least restrictive means requirement was not used in the pre–Smith jurisprudence RFRA purported to codify. All told, RFRA is a considerable congressional intrusion into the States' traditional prerogatives and general authority to regulate for the health and welfare of their citizens, and is not designed to identify and counteract state laws likely to be unconstitutional because of their treatment of religion.[257]

Justice Kennedy, writing for the majority, stated that the RFRA was an overextension of Congressional authority. It is outside the scope of Congress to legislatively change the interpretation of the free exercise clause of the First Amendment. This is a judicial, not legislative duty.[258] The RFRA has imposed the most demanding test known to constitutional law and applies to every level of government according to the Court. In addition, the laws being challenged under the RFRA were not motivated by religious bigotry.[259]

Therefore, Justice Kennedy and the Court concluded that the act was out of proportion to any supposed remedy or preventive measure and was meant instead, to change constitutional protections.[260] It was incongruent in its means and ends focus.

It is obvious that the majority was considering laws and actions that have affected or burdened mainstream religions, for American Indian beliefs, among others, have been under a strenuously bigoted system of attack for centuries. It is amazing that the *Lyng* decision and its effects were overlooked, and that any religion may have to demonstrate a serious history of bigotry in order to be afforded protection. What can be more narrow-minded than declaring a culture unworthy of protection, or more serious than its ultimate destruction?

Surprisingly, Justice O'Connor dissented, stating her "study of American constitutional history showed that the First Amendment guarantee of religious liberty is a right to practice religion 'even when such conduct conflicts with a neutral, generally applicable law.'"[261] O'Connor's dissent reviews the numerous colonial charters and early state constitutions to demonstrate that *individual* religious liberty was, and still is, an essential liberty. If there was a conflict between religious beliefs and civil law, "religion prevailed unless important state interests militated otherwise."[262] This is the same ideal utilized in the present day, according to O'Connor.

Justice O'Connor further expanded upon the individual religious liberty to mean "the accommodation of religious practice."[263] The accepted concept was that government should, when possible, accommodate religious practice. She explained that without this accommodation principle, several religions and sects would have faced a severe problem in the early United States. Even George Washington believed in religious accommodation. Furthermore, accommodations were granted by legislatures, not courts.[264]

Therefore, O'Connor stated, "given the centrality of freedom of speech and religion to the American concept of personal liberty, it is altogether reasonable to conclude that both should be treated with the highest degree of respect."[265] This point shows a marked difference from O'Connor's view in the 1995 *Lyng* case.

Consequently, with AIRFA considered worthless and RFRA ruled unconstitutional, there are not many options left to protect American Indian sacred sites.[266] The RFRA was obviously not meant to be capable of addressing the ingrained judicial misconceptions of Indian religions. Reliance on treaty rights or on international principles of human rights have been ambiguous in that few treaties specify worship rights on ceded lands and international claims seem to be conveniently ignored when applied to the United States. Yet, one proposal has been to switch from the past use of the ineffective free exercise claims to a use of the trust doctrine in making sacred site claims.

The Trust Doctrine

The trust doctrine imposes a fiduciary duty on the federal government that allows American Indians to challenge any government action that violates this trust.[267] The trust doctrine has already been discussed, but to briefly review, it developed from the *Cherokee* cases where the Court described the Indian Nation-United States relationship as one of a ward to its guardian. This has developed into the trust doctrine. Justice Marshall in the *Worcester v. Georgia* case elaborated on the scope and nature of this trust relationship.

Marshall stated that the Cherokee were under the protection of the U.S. via treaty, but not as a conquered nation. Instead, the Cherokee maintained their distinct community occupying its own territory outside of the state of Georgia's jurisdiction.[268] Therefore, the federal government's role as trustee included the obligation to ensure the Cherokee their lands and sovereignty.

Of course, in the years following these decisions, the trust doctrine went from a doctrine protecting a sovereign people to one used for total control and removal of these same people. By the late 1800s, Congress utilized various maneuvers and the courts assisted in a series of decisions to eliminate Indian landholding, to confine the Indian and to assimilate them. The trust doctrine's focus and purpose had indeed shifted.

Still, certain cases reaffirmed that this trust relationship and U.S. fiduciary duty to the tribes still existed, regardless of equity.[269] The courts have reaffirmed that the fiduciary duty remains and that American Indians have a guaranteed input into the determination of governmental interests involving them.[270] Hence, the importance of a sacred site to an Indian tribe constitutes the only relevant consideration as to whether it should be protected as part of the trust. These sites are as essential as the material goods or land resources argued about in the courts. If tribes would utilize this tactic when seeking sacred site protection, they would be able to avoid the First Amendment issues of religion altogether. Indian tribes, as inherent sovereigns, may lie outside the constitutional standards imposed by the Bill of Rights,[271] and tribes should use and extend the trust doctrine to include sacred sites, since this seems to be consistent with the values deemed important by the Supreme Court.[272] Since it is part of the fiduciary duty of the U.S. government to protect American Indian interests—material, cultural, and spiritual—then certainly sacred sites (both on and off the reservation) fall within this sphere of interests.

American Indian tribes must push for the expanded recognition and broader interpretation of their status as inherent sovereigns with a unique trust relationship with the federal government.[273] Therefore, Indian religious rights ought to be judged under the trust doctrine. This would obligate the government to protect the tribe's existence.[274] Hence, to do so, it must protect its traditional religion which is infused into almost every aspect of the Indian culture and life. By failing to protect their religion, the government is failing to protect the tribe, and thus, violating the trust doctrine. First Amendment rights should therefore be interpreted in terms of the trust doctrine to protect and preserve the American Indian culture and life.[275]

Trust doctrine claims were not a part of the *Lyng* or the other sacred site cases in recent years. However, if the government does have a fiduciary responsibility to protect the lives and welfare of the Indian peoples, then an avenue to protect sacred sites is opened. A trust claim would not be limited to a purely "religious" question as is the point with a First Amendment claim.[276] Instead, a trust doctrine claim could include a full array of cultural and lifestyle issues. This is important for as has been explained, traditional religion cannot be unwrapped from its influences upon tribal culture, life, economy and other areas.

Since traditional religions and cultures are so intertwined, it will be more difficult for courts to separate them using the trust doctrine and federal fiduciary responsibility. This is especially true if, for example, the tribes in the *Lyng* case had stressed how destroying their sacred sites would destroy their religion, thus destroying their culture and identity. "The trust doctrine incorporates a standard of affirmative protection—and indeed, promotion—of native cultural and religious vitality."[277]

As the trustee, the government owes an "uncompromising responsibility to the tribe and its members."[278] This fiduciary loyalty may be a stronger argument than what has been permitted under the court decisions or legislative acts. Two problems remain, though: (1) whether the fiduciary responsibility applies only to monetary damages, or can a tribe require specific performance (i.e., to stop tourism at a sacred site); and (2) can this same duty be applied to sites not on treaty, reservation or public lands. Therefore, even though "existing case law and modern statutes recognize a federal fiduciary duty to protect tribal culture"[279] it will be some time before these two issues will be addressed or solved.

Congressional Actions

Obviously, since broad sweeping acts that have the overriding goals of protecting religion and its practices are ineffective, it may be necessary for Congress to pass specific acts of protection. As of 1994, there have been four such acts that placed sacred sites in trust for various tribes.[280]

As an example, the El Malpais National Monument was created in 1987. Congress gave the Secretary of Interior the power to temporarily close sections of this park at the requests of any one of the four tribes (Acoma Pueblo, Laguma, Ramah Navajo and Zuni) who use the area for religious ceremonies.[281] At the same time, the park has been set up to permit non–Indians to observe and learn about the area's natural and cultural landscapes.[282]

The El Malpais National Monument Act of 1987 was the culmination of the Acoma Indian land claims. These claims were settled in 1972, and the Acoma ceded 1.5 million acres in return for $6.2 million, but never gave up their claim to the El Malpais area.[283] At hearings, Congress stated it would not return the area, but as a compromise would accommodate the religious needs of the tribes in the region.

Therefore, the 590 square miles of the El Malpais region had sections reserved as a national monument under the National Park Service (NPS) management; and another 263,000 acres set aside as wilderness/conservation areas under Bureau of Land Management control.[284] The NPS set up an advisory committee which submitted a plan in 1990 to Congress.[285]

This plan pays attention to the culture of the area as well as its attraction for tourism and development. El Malpais is a nature museum and the NPS has worked in alliance with the tribes so that respect and sensitivity for tribal ceremonies and traditions will be maintained.[286] Whatever the model used by the U.S. Congress, it is one step closer to protecting sacred sites than what seems to have been afforded by the court system.

As recently as December of 2003, the debate between recreationists and Indian sacredness continued. The U.S. Forest Service announced an immediate halt to climbing activities at Cave Rock, located near Lake Tahoe, Nevada. The site is held as extremely sacred to the Washoe Tribe.

The immediate reaction was a lawsuit filed by the Access Fund, a rock-climbing association, with the goal of keeping the site open.[287] However, it was not the tribe in this instance that forced the closure of the area. Instead, the USFS stated that their decision was based on the abuse and damage that the climbers have been doing to the site by installing permanent ladders, bolts, platforms and even cementing the cave floor, all without permission or authorization. This is in addition to the graffiti and other acts of vandalism defacing the site. Yet, the climbing association blamed the Washoe Indians and their religious beliefs for instituting the closure decision, without accepting any blame for themselves.

The USFS has continued to insist that its decision was not based on any religious criteria, but simply on the need to preserve the site for future generations.[288] Even the USFS sees the use of blaming the Washoe Tribe as a smokescreen obscuring the real issue, that of disrespect for a national treasure. Hopefully, a compromise can be achieved similar to that at Devil's Tower where the site is closed during certain times and access is limited and regulated to protect everyone's interests equally.

In 2007, the monument sitting on the remains of Chief Sitting Bull, which is within the borders of the Standing Rock Sioux Tribe but rests on private land since 2005, was being threatened by a multi-million-dollar complex to be built next door. The landowners promised that it would be done with dignity, but it was opposed by the tribe who did not want one of their most important leaders to become a tourist attraction. As of now, the plans have not been realized. Another large monument with mixed views is the

Crazy Horse Memorial being sculpted in the sacred Black Hills. Again, it is on private land, but the area is held sacred by the Lakota Indians.[289]

In the Southwest, another project has caused division among and in tribes over both the affront to sacredness of the land and profits. A skywalk (a glass-floored observation deck) has been constructed overlooking the Grand Canyon. The area is held sacred by the Hopi and Zuni Tribes as the point from which humans emerged into the current world. However, the area is now controlled by the Navajo and the project is theirs in partnership with a private company.[290] It is going to include a recreation center, a tramway, resorts, and shops. However, the appropriateness of the project, and maybe more importantly unfortunately how the profits are to be shared, has divided the tribe and has caused a rift with the developer.[291] Those who want to protect the sacredness of the area are pitted against those who see jobs and income as more important to the future. It is a shame that sacredness can be bought and sold, by even some the very same people who in the past fought so vehemently to keep their lands pure in the first place.[292] This may be the best demonstration yet of the loss of traditional spirituality and the victory of assimilation with its dedication to profits and instantaneous gratification.

Protecting the Past

American Indians are also suffering the same insults to their ancestors that have plagued the world for centuries. The looting, collecting and selling of grave objects, including human remains, is by no means limited to the Americas and their indigenous peoples. Just like other sites from around the world, sacred sites have been ransacked, dug up and have had their contents sold on the black market to both museums and private collectors. Typing the phrase "Indian Artifacts" into any search engine will result in hundreds, if not thousands, of sites including eBay and Amazon, that sell, trade, or buy these items. Granted, not all of these were obtained illegally by Indiana Jones wannabes, but few would disagree that there is an unknown portion that are robbed from gravesites around the nation. In addition, there are some items that are being sold legally by various tribal members for whatever reason or purpose.

However, the market in Indian relics is particularly disheartening, especially since the market is only a few hundred years old compared to other areas around the world. Museums, at one time, would actually pay for funerary objects, including skeletons. The Smithsonian Institution actually amassed a collection of over 18,000 American Indian remains, with some only finding their way to the museum as late as the 1960s.

Indian remains and artifacts became objects of curiosity, and at times questionable scientific inquiry. Nowhere was this more egregious than at Dickson Mounds in Illinois. The mounds were constructed and used until approximately 1250 CE. The site was excavated in 1927 by Donald Dickson and 237 Indian remains and other funerary objects were put on display in a private museum. In 1992, much to the dismay of many local residents and archeologists, the museum was closed and the bodies reburied thanks to popular support for protection of Native American graves. Yet, according to one white resident who visited the site on her honeymoon 25 years earlier, "those Indians are as much [her] ancestors as anybody's" and "this is just another case of minority rule."[293] Another white citizen expressed his disdain and disappointment by saying, "dead Indians do not vote, and out-of-state Indians (who pressured to have the site closed) do not vote either."[294] In essence, the local dissidents were more concerned with the economic impact of the closing of the mounds, than the fact that it was sacrilegious, racist and morally wrong to publicly display the bodies.

There are more than just a few examples of extreme hoarding by private citizens of Indian artifacts.[295] People do not understand that looting artifacts from private or national lands is illegal. Unlike a legitimate archeological study of a site, no care is taken to document and preserve the artifacts and the surrounding area. Collectors often deface and destroy burial and cremation gravesites without any regard to the effects upon the Indian peoples or to science as a whole. They do not understand that they are stealing from a people's history and culture. If Indians were to show up at a local cemetery and begin excavating the graves looking for souvenirs or bones to put on display or sell on the black market, the public outrage would be staggering and relentless.

As for the science angle, the mid– to late–1800s saw a pseudo-scientific movement extolling the idea that cranium size determined brain capacity and hence, intelligence. Obviously, the largest and hence the most intelligent brains belong to Caucasians, with African Americans and American Indians far behind. American Indians were mutilated and decapitated for this "Indian Crania Study" and their heads were sent to various museums for examination to prove the superiority of the white race. For a gruesome example, many of the Cheyenne and Arapaho from the now infamous 1864 Sand Creek, Colorado, massacre ended up as specimens in eastern museums, denying them, their families and their tribes the dignity of last rites and proper burials.[296]

Another area of concern are the ancient earthen works represented by sites like Cahokia, Illinois; Poverty Point, Louisiana; the Serpent Mound in Ohio; and literally hundreds of other sites spread throughout the United States. It is accepted that not all of these sites hold a sacredness attached to them by modern tribes, but they were constructed with a delineated purpose in the past. Many indicate advanced astronomical knowledge by being lined up with solar and lunar solstices and equinoxes. Some go way beyond being just a calendar, and actually track various stars and events with amazing precision demonstrating that ancient Indians were more than mere hunter-gatherers and capable of advanced calculations. Whether sacred or not, the historical importance of these sites cannot be dismissed. Yet, one site in particular is in an interesting predicament.

The Octagon Mounds in Newark, Ohio, consist of a large circle and octagon earthwork aligned to measure and show the solar and lunar cycles. What is interesting about of this site is it has a private golf country club built on and around the mounds. In fact, the country club acknowledges the historical importance of these mounds for the prehistory of the Indian peoples, and even boasts that their course was built incorporating the mounds in several of the holes. The club's website states in a somewhat bizarre manner that they have "a golf course on an unusual site, older than written history. Won't archeologists 2000 years from now be puzzled as they study the mounds and find all those lost golf balls?"[297] However, the club may not be very happy because in 2019, Licking County Municipal Court Judge David Branstool sided with the Ohio History Connection and stated they have the authority to reclaim the 134-acre mounds from the club.[298] He ruled that once compensation is agreed upon and paid, then the Connection may take over the historic site. The club had argued that opening the site to the public four days a year was adequate. However, the Judge ruled that years of manicured lawns does not immunize the country club from eminent domain to restore public access to the prehistoric earthworks.[299] Of course, the club is planning an appeal of this ruling basically due to the compensation amount that had been jury awarded in the fall of 2018.[300] The club wants more than what was originally decided upon.

The government finally responded to decades of pressure from Indian tribes and other groups against this grave robbing and curiosity displays of Indian remains with the National Museum of the American Indian Act in late 1989, and the Native American Graves Protection and Repatriation Act in late 1990. The National Museum Act openly acknowledges that 4,000 Indian human remains were sent to the Army Medical Museum by order of the army's Surgeon General which ended up at the Smithsonian. It also states in very clear language that the Smithsonian itself has a collection of approximately 14,000 additional Indian human remains and that Indian tribes, Native Alaskans and Native Hawaiians want to provide an appropriate resting place for their ancestors.[301] Therefore, the act detailed not only the specifics of the museum's location, structure, appropriations and governing board, but also helped set the stage for the process of reunification of these lost peoples with their tribes and homes.

The Native American Graves Protection and Repatriation Act made it illegal to remove Indian remains or artifacts from any federal or tribal lands. It also prohibits the purchase, sale, use for profit or transportation for sale or profit of Native American human remains or cultural objects without the right to possess these objects in the first place.[302] Furthermore, if a tribe or Native Hawaiian organization can establish that an item is of their culture, they can request it to be returned and this cannot be denied.

Because of these two acts, the Smithsonian Institution in 1989 began notifying tribes of human remains and funerary objects that they had in their collections for repatriation. The Institution agreed to disregard the guidelines of the American Anthropological Association which argued for the return of remains only to known relatives.[303] The obvious response is just how many remains are needed for research and how could almost 19,000 of them benefit the health and welfare of living Native Americans? As a result, the Smithsonian's National Museum of the American Indian now has an established protocol for inventorying, cataloging, identifying and considering remains and objects for return. The repatriation process actually boils down to six delineated steps that begin with a simple information request by a Native community representative and ends with the object and/or remains being repatriated if the request is approved after being found valid.[304] Finally, the long road home has begun.

Review and Conclusions

It is obvious that "the inherent difficulties of religion cases when combined with American society's ignorance of native religious practices severely handicap Indian people in the preservation of their religious identities. Indian people, by having to struggle against a pervasive lack of knowledge and against a sense of superiority that has generated years of preservation, are inextricably placed at a disadvantage."[305] As has been demonstrated, no area of government shows as much confusion and lack of rational direction as the court system. Justices have seemingly forgone common sense and even historical evidence to further the continuing tradition of conquest.

The suits brought forth by the various Indian plaintiffs have sought to halt progress which is seen as a valid government activity.[306] In contrast, non–Indian free exercise claims are rarely scrutinized for the centrality or indispensability of burdened religious conduct.[307] Yet, the "judicial application of the establishment clause to sacred site claims is perhaps the best illustration of unfair treatment of Indian free exercise claims."[308] What it does illustrate is how well the courts reflect the general public's lack of understanding of traditional Indian religions and the ethnocentric Anglo-Lockean conception of religion and property.

The substance of free exercise rights has been impermissibly circumscribed to only familiar and mainstream beliefs.[309] More importantly, the triggering mechanism for protection, the demonstratable centrality and indispensability of the beliefs, has been narrowed in focus so much that only familiar and well-documented religious tenets can hope for help.[310]

Even in this age of diversity and acceptance, the perception that traditional Indian religions are romantically primitive and thus contrary to national, religious and social ideals continues. The usurper tradition of relying upon Christianity as a justification also continues. "To the extent, therefore, that the judiciary is influenced by American civil religion and traditional monotheistic understandings of spiritual separation from the physical world, claims by Indians that development [for tourism, recreation, timbering, etc.] of public lands violates their religious beliefs would seem at once obstructionist and counterproductive."[311]

The First Amendment's establishment and free exercise clauses are universal and stand for the notion that *all* religions are equal and should be free from government interference. The government is the last entity that should have the right and the responsibility of judging and determining which religions are unorthodox. Furthermore, when sacred sites are threatened, "the freedom to believe and worship embodied in the First Amendment is rendered meaningless if government destroys the object of belief."[312] Sacred sites are as important to traditional Indian religions as churches are to the mainstream Judeo-Christian sects, and as such, should be afforded the same respect, acceptance and protection. Just because a site is naturally created, rather than constructed out of bricks and mortar, does not disqualify it from sacredness.

As such, protection of these sites must be diligent and constant. Failure to keep a watchful eye can be devastating. There are times when the tribes themselves are to blame for losing sites, due to their own complacency and disorganization. In the late 1980s, the University of Arizona and other scientific groups wished to build a telescope and astrophysical complex in Arizona's Mount Graham's Hawk and High Peaks. The U.S. Forest Service, in its 1985 study of the area, found only three shrines that may be of religious significance to local tribes.[313] Efforts were taken to avoid any adverse effects on these sites during construction. Nineteen local tribes were contacted by the University and USFS about the sites' significance and the feasibility of the mitigation plans. However, only two tribes responded, the AkChin and Hopi.[314] The San Carlos Apache did raise some issues concerning grazing, mineral and property rights, but made no mention of any religious concerns over the three sites.[315] The tribes in the area, including the San Carlos Apache, failed to respond to the USFS issuance of the Environmental Impact Statement, and in fact, asked to be removed from the USFS mailing list. Finally, in 1986, with all administrative avenues satisfied, the USFS and the State Historical Preservation Officer (SHPO) determined that the telescopes would have no impact on the cultural sites, but they would still be protected and would not be excavated.[316]

In 1993, the San Carlos Apache, under the Apache Survival Coalition, filed suit to stop the construction of the telescope complex. Their arguments stated that the 1988 Congressional act which authorized the construction was in fact, unconstitutional. They stated that the impact of the construction of the observatory would have on their religious practices and heritage was ignored.[317] The Court saw things otherwise. They believed that "the Tribe and its members exerted their rights in this action with inexcusable tardiness."[318] The Court determined that the tribe ignored the very processes which they were now contending to be inadequate. They had waited from 1985 to 1993 before filing any response or reaction to the construction of the telescopes. Therefore, in essence, the tribe's time for protest had expired and their claims were denied.

If tribes are to protect their spirituality and sacred sites for the future generations, they must pay attention to the happenings going on in the world around them. At times, compromises must be made for the encroaching world, and at other times, the battle must be immediate and fierce. In this instance, most of the surrounding tribes were seemingly satisfied with the government's actions, and the San Carlos Apache waited too long to enter the battle. The day was lost.

For some reason, the arguments and debates always boil down to a choice of sacredness verses jobs and money. Those that want to continue to follow, or at least pay homage to, the traditions of the past, wish to preserve the sacredness of sites. However, generations of assimilation have had an impact in convincing some that jobs, profits, and material goods are the best future for the Indian. In a way, the non–Natives are winning and are, in fact, killing the Indian. The American Indian is not perfect. They will never live up to the stereotypes of the idealized native, living one with nature and worshiping the environment. However, their spiritual and cultural sovereignty is important for them to be able to keep their identity and life.

As a concluding thought to this chapter, the Tennessee Supreme Court explanation in 1835 seems to summarize it best. The Court stated:

> We maintain, that the principle declared in the fifteenth century as the law of Christendom, that discovery gave title to assume sovereignty over, and to govern the unconverted natives of. .. North America, has been recognized as a part of the national law, for nearly four centuries, and that it is now so recognized by every Christian power, in its political department, and its judicial, unless the case of *Worcester* has formed an exception in these states. That, from Cape Horn to Hudson Bay, it is acted upon as the only known rule of sovereign power, by which the native Indian is coerced; for conquest

is unknown in reference to him in the international sense. *Our claim is based on the right to coerce obedience.* The claim may be denounced by the moralist. We answer, it is the law of the land. Without its assertion and vigorous execution, the continent never could have been inhabited by our ancestors. *To abandon the principle now, is to assert that they were unjust usurpers; and that we, succeeding to their usurped authority and void claims to possess and govern the country, should in honesty abandon it, return to Europe, and let the subdued parts again become a wilderness and hunting ground.* Similarly, in *Johnson*, the Court found Indian rights "Impaired" simply because the indigenous peoples of North America were not Christians at the time of European arrival.[319]

The future of sacredness remains uncertain in Indian Country. The battle will continue.

CHAPTER FOUR

Environmental Sovereignty in Indian Country

"No tribe has the right to sell, even to each other, much less to strangers ... sell a country! Why not sell the air, the great sea, as well as the earth? Didn't the Great Spirit make them all for the use of his children?"[1]
—TECUMSEH, SHAWNEE PROPHET

Introduction

Two dominant views have pervaded popular culture regarding the American Indian and the environment. First, the American Indian is seen as some sort of ecological superman, living in total and absolute harmony with nature and Mother Earth. He never built a fire too large, only killed what he could eat, and used every single part of every animal, all the while respecting the spiritual side of nature. The New Age movement has perpetuated this view to fulfill their own ecological yearnings. Yet, the other view in today's culture sees the Indian as a mindless child, either as a child that needs protection from the bullies of the corporate world that are trying to take advantage of him, or as a naive child who can be bought and sold to accept the newcomers' stealing and depleting the Indians' resources and leaving them their waste products.

Neither view is totally correct. While the American Indian does have a deep respect for Mother Earth and its forces, it could be argued that this was born out of need more than some sort of environmental consciousness. On the other hand, neither is the American Indian a mindless child. In the past, corporations and governments have taken advantage of them due to their trust, naiveté, and poverty, to destroy what little environment the Indians still controlled on their reservations, and the Indian is now aware of the consequences

116

and is fighting back. In this chapter, we will explore both these attitudes about the "eco–Indian" and how the Indians are fighting back.

The Eco-Indian: Myth and Reality

The 1960s really brought the image of the American Indian as a noble savage to a high point. Activists saw the Indian as someone who has always lived in harmony with nature and understood the intricacies of Mother Earth in a deep and spiritual manner that non–Indians are somehow incapable of grasping. During this time, "radical activists and philosophers began to articulate and implement their ideas for a truly ecological world, and they found themselves drawn, again and again, to the beliefs and traditions of the American Indian."[2] This eco–Indian is someone who took only what they needed from the world around them, used every single bit of any animal they hunted, wasted nothing whatsoever, could perceive the smallest nuance of nature and was a minimalist in the most environmentally sound way. It was believed, and still is, that the Indian holds certain environmental values that industrialized society has long ignored and forgotten in its pursuit of progress and comfort.[3]

The noble eco–Indian has saturated the public culture. "The image of the American Indian in nature who understands the systemic eco-consequences of his actions, feels deep sympathy with all living beings, and steps in to conserve so that earth's harmonies are never out of balance and resources never in doubt"[4] has continued to this day. This image has contributed to the Boy and Girl Scouts, the global green movement, the counterculture movement of the 1960s, the "rainbow tribe" and to the New Age spiritualists who want to be Indians. Yet, there is little understanding among these non–Indian groups of the actual relationship between the Indian peoples and their environments.

This view of the Indian as the first environmentalist has contributed to the reduction of the American peoples to a very simplistic myth. "The myth of the Indian as a peaceful, carefree, unshackled and wise people living innocent and naked in a golden world of nature"[5] started from the earliest contacts with the various tribes. This view has become ultimately dehumanizing, making Indians out to be child-like, naive and in need of being saved or led. Of course, this view justifies controlling every aspect of the Indian life and culture, and "it makes the Indian seem simply like an animal species, never leaving a trace upon nature, and thus deprives them of a culture."[6]

Archeologists and American Indians themselves differ in their opinions as to their origin and/or when they first walked upon North America. Needless to say, whether it was 15,000 years ago or a million, the estimated 10 to

12 million Indian people living in North America by the time of Columbus did have some impact upon the environment. Indians have made a mark upon the land and its plants, animals and landscape. Tribes depleted natural resources, such as trees, game animals, topsoil and water just like their white counterparts would and did do. Theories abound that several Indian civilizations, like the Anasazi, disappeared after their population outgrew its resources for survival. Villages up and down the East Coast would be regularly moved according to a set cycle to allow for the ground and game to restock itself. In the plains, the tribes were already nomadic, following game and resource needs. It would be hard to argue that a band of Lakota could carry off every single bit of dozens of buffalo killed during a hunt on their horses and travois. Something was wasted, albeit possibly with regret. There is evidence that the earliest Indians drove hundreds of buffalo and other game off of cliffs to their deaths, then skinned and took what they could, wanted and needed. Fires lit to drive the animals into the hunting traps at times burned out of control. It was surely wasteful in that the number of animals killed could not be controlled during these man-made stampedes, nor could the animals crushed from the weight of other animals falling upon them be retrieved or used.

Several recent theories have noted that the ancient peoples of the Americas were probably responsible for the extinction of numerous species. There seems to be a strong correlation between the appearance of humans and the disappearance of animals like the mammoth, mastodon, ground sloth, camels, horses and others.[7] These studies firmly place much of the responsibility on humans for these extinctions.

The impact of the ancient Americans even spread to the sea. Sea turtles, sea cows, and other species were decimated by man according to the theories.[8] This impact has been long lasting, even having an effect to this day. An example can be found among the coral reefs. The destruction of those species that had a symbiotic existence with the coral plant life is still having an effect in modern times. Therefore, man has always had an impact upon the environment, and it was not always one of balance and respect. This is due to a lack of knowledge as much as it is due to the need for survival.

Whereas the Indian may not have been as perfect an environmentalist as some would believe, there is a serious difference between living according to the cycles and at the will of nature, and attempting to control it at every opportunity. Iroquoian peoples routinely rotated crops and moved entire villages when resources became scarce. However, this did not prevent periods of starvation due to an unduly harsh winter or summer drought. What is important to note here is one major difference: The Indian peoples accepted the cycles of nature and tried to work within them, even if at times they were unsuccessful or imperfect. Indians both respected and valued nature and its forces, and realized that they were dependent upon it even if they did not understand it. The newcomers tried to force, change and control nature, with severe and drastic results at times. The difference is subjugating oneself to nature versus subjugating nature to yourself. The latter is far more likely to fail. The new arrivals to America did not see themselves as a part of the land, but something alien to it. Conquest of nature was imperative to survival. They viewed the Americas as vast and never-ending lands to explore and exploit, and it was their "manifest destiny" to inhabit these continents.

More importantly, with the arrival of the Europeans, many Indian peoples had the opportunity to create new roles for themselves, find new paths if you will, and were no longer totally dependent upon the unpredictability of nature for survival.[9] The Indian peoples quickly adopted new tools, techniques and materials, if they proved to be more useful and convenient than the old ways. Iron pots, axes, steel knives, guns and powder, alcohol,[10] the horse, and a myriad of other introduced items were quickly adopted by the Indians. More importantly, Indians began to participate in new roles as trappers, traders and scouts for the newcomer merchants and provided the new traders with beaver, deer and buffalo hides. This is not to say that there were no consequences for these adaptations, both good and bad, but its happening was inevitable. Over-hunting of deer and over-trapping of beaver occurred from New Jersey to the Dakotas, and the buffalo were nearly made extinct.[11]

"This image of connection between Indians and nature has been so tightly drawn over the past five-hundred years, that many non–Indians expect indigenous people to walk softly in their moccasins as conservationists and even preservationists. When they do not, then they are eagerly condemned, accused of not acting as Indians should, and held to standards that their accusers have seldom met."[12] If an Indian group favors the extraction of resources, the storage of wastes or other development projects—even if they have complete control over them—environmentalists rush in to deride the Indians for either betraying their eco-past or being the naive child-like dupes of some multinational corporation. These environmentalists often demean the Indians for wanting a landfill, a mine, or a timber contract as if the Indians have violated some age-old contract with Mother Earth. Then, when they have stopped the project and the economic benefits that it may have produced, they leave the reservation in its original poverty, content that they have saved the image of the eco–Indian for their future political usage,[13] all the while ignoring the economic realities and plights of the Indian peoples.

Western environmentalists have held the Indian up as a contemporary model of the way in which humans should learn to live in harmony with nature. However, this view is limited in its appreciation of the complexities in which the Indian peoples were integrated with the land and its forces. These groups must remember, that in their quest for the perfect role model, that as they turn to Indians for the answers, the Indians will not provide any instantaneous solutions to the problems being faced in today's world.[14] "Attempts to borrow culture, whether it be wholesale or piecemeal, are doomed to failure."[15] It has now become "Indian" to revere nature and want to protect it, but the concern has become, from whom?

Indian Control of Their Environment

When the "Great Chief in Washington" sent word to the Duwanish Indian Nation that the United States Government wished to purchase Indian lands, Chief Sealth [Seattle] is said to have replied,

> How can you buy or sell the sky, the warmth of the land? The idea is strange to us. If we do not own the freshness of the air and the sparkle of the water, how you buy them? ... We know that the white man does not understand our ways. One portion of land is the same to him as the next, for he is a stranger who comes in the night and takes from the land whatever he needs.... His appetite will devour the earth and leave behind only desert.[16]

For good or bad, the Indian tribes of the United States eventually found themselves as the "owners" of the land—or what was left of it after the Dawes Act. Tribal governments now find themselves faced with new problems of ownership: environmental problems and the necessity of regulating activities on the land which they now own, and the harsh economic realities of reservation life which some environmental projects could alleviate. Like states that have not assumed responsibility for the application of federal environmental laws, tribal lands fall under the authority of the U.S. Environmental Protection Agency. Representatives of the environmental justice movement in the past have misspoken when they claim that federal environmental laws do not apply to Indian Country.[17]

Tribal lands are not subject to regulation by the state in most respects because tribes are quasi-sovereign.[18] Like states, they are eligible to promulgate their own laws, including environmental laws, subject to federal preemption. During the early years of environmental regulation, however, tribes did not have the ability to assume control and responsibility for environmental regulation the way that states did. It has only been in the last decade or so that tribes have been able to receive authorization to administer federal environmental programs.

The environmental control debate is clouded by the issue of trust. The federal government has established a trust relationship with the tribes, for political, social, economic and environmental areas. This trust extends to every member of a tribe, whether it be on or off the reservation. Furthermore, all federal agencies must honor this trust or be liable for its breaches.[19] The

Cherokee cases have established the tribes as governments with inherent powers of self-government, even though these have been limited in future cases. Hence, the issue of federal and state jurisdiction over tribal environments has become unclear, and subject to numerous debates. Natural resources represent the conflict of interest between the interests of the country and tribal self-determination, but furthermore, the issue of the trust relationship between the federal government and the tribes. Because of this trust, it has been the federal government who has had control of what is to occur in Indian Country. By permitting financially questionable and environmentally irresponsible company activities on tribal lands, the federal government is being less than vigilant in fulfilling its trust responsibilities to the tribe.[20]

It has been argued several times that the Environmental Protection Agency (EPA) has not been enforcing environmental regulations on Indian lands. Part of this is due to the self-determination status of the tribes, but also due to the fact that the EPA has had serious resource issues itself. At times, the EPA has also been overridden by the concern of resource development as a source of tribal income to be less stringent in enforcing a regulation.[21] Yet, control over their environment is the key to exercising their sovereign authority over their lands. The EPA instituted a policy of ensuring environmental policies on Indian lands were sound, but coupled this with the gradual increase of regulation by the tribes themselves. Economic pressures have led some tribes to exploit their resources without consideration of the full impact—whether it be ecologically, socially and politically.

The move toward tribal recognition in environmental matters took on full steam with President Ronald Reagan in 1983 when he issued an Indian Policy Statement.[22] This policy explicitly recognized tribal governments and promised a government-to-government relationship between the federal government and Indian tribes. The statement also endorsed tribal self-government and tribal economic self-sufficiency. Self-government implies control over a group's resources and lands and self-sufficiency means that the group can determine their destiny through economic decision making and development. However, these definitions would remain unclear for the Indian peoples.

Budget cuts left many tribes scrambling for funds to sustain themselves. President Reagan's solution to meet tribal needs rested in the free market. Tribal self-government was an important component to this approach. As such, a state-to-state relationship had to be created and maintained when dealing with a tribal government. Of course, there may have been more than pure economic motive behind the President's policy, as Reagan said in 1988 that "maybe we made a mistake in trying to maintain Indian cultures. Maybe we should not have humored them in wanting to stay in that kind of primitive lifestyle. Maybe we should have said 'no,' come join us. Be citizens with the rest of us."[23] This demonstrates a paternalism that still existed between the federal government and the tribes, but also indicated that the marketplace was going to be used to finally assimilate the Indian into mainstream America.

Tribal governments must deal with underdeveloped economies and ones dependent upon federal monies as a primary resource. Of course, becoming independent due to casino revenues only opens a new plethora of problems and jealousies. Factionalism and arguments erupt over access and control of these funds. These problems have been further exacerbated by the BIA policy of treating tribal governments as mere appendages, including controlling their natural resources. However, thanks to President Reagan's stance on tribal self-sufficiency, tribes began to break away from this secondary role and became more in charge of their own environments.

In his federalism strategies, President Reagan initiated a transfer of federal trust responsibilities not only to the states, but also to the tribes and this was coupled by drastic cuts in domestic spending. However, his plan did permit state regulation of tribal natural resources unless it was in violation of federal laws or Congressional acts.[24] Non-Indians' use of Indian lands increased, as did Indian unemployment and poverty. Hence, natural resource development was encouraged by federal authorities as a means for economic development and self-sufficiency.[25] Tribes were urged to mine minerals, sell timber, and store solid and nuclear wastes, all under the promises that these activities would benefit them financially. Of course, the multi-national corporations that would "help" in these endeavors would also benefit, but that was secondary. Yet the irony of all this is that when a tribe did discover wealth in these efforts, or some other one such as a casino, a backlash was felt from jealous and greedy non–Indians who saw unfair competition or a new source of regulatory and income taxes for the government.

In furtherance of President Reagan's Indian policy, the EPA promulgated a policy with regard to the application and administration of environmental policy in Indian Country[26] in November of 1984.[27] Thereafter, in November of 1985, the EPA adopted the Interim Strategy for the Implementation of the EPA Indian Policy. The EPA placed primary authority for the regulation of the Indian environment within the control of tribal governments, rather than the state governments. In its policy, the EPA promised to "look directly to Tribal Governments to play this lead role for matters affecting reservation environments."[28] To carry out its new policy, the Indian Policy Implementation Guide[29] was issued as well. Pursuant to these new policies, the EPA instituted a legislative agenda of amending federal laws[30] to treat "tribes as states" (TAS).

These policy and economic tug-of-wars have had a disastrous effect on many tribes. Internal conflicts erupted as corporations and governments have sought to utilize and exploit reservation lands for their own benefits. These internal conflicts polarized tribes into three camps. First are the traditionalists. This group, usually influenced by outside groups, are the eco–Indians who seek to return to the old ways and reject all solutions to problems that face them. They also tend to dismiss the federally created tribal councils and do not recognize their authority over the tribe and its affairs. They are arguably somewhat naive in that they have forgotten or ignored what the past was really like, and they ignore the fact that most do not want to give up the modern conveniences that they have just for the sake of tradition. They also tend to ignore the fact that the skills of the past are lost, that the resources once relied upon are depleted or taken, and that the old days were not as majestic and serene as they believe. On the other end of the spectrum is the progressive camp. The progressives are only concerned with economic development, no matter what the cost or consequences. They openly negotiate with corporations and governments to take their waste, sell the timber and other natural resources so long as the price is right. Often times, it is the members of this group who fall to charges of corruption. Finally, somewhere in the middle of the traditionalists and the progressives are the pragmatists. These people are torn between the honoring of the old ways and traditions, and the need for economic development. They do realize that pollution will threaten what remains of their fragmented cultures. They are the ones who seek the balance between both sets of internal and external competing interests.

The result of many of these conflicts is that the tribes are being split apart. People, families, clans are being polarized due to competing interests and, of course, greed. The very legitimacy of tribal governments, for which battles have been fought, is now being challenged from both within the tribes and from outside sources. How can a tribe be trusted to regulate its environment, its lands, its people, if they are constantly fighting among themselves and being charged with bribery, favoritism or corruption? Some of these internal fights have led to bloodshed. The end of the trouble is far from sight.

As explained, the purpose of this chapter is to examine the status of environmental regulation in Indian Country, the progress tribes have made into establishing and enforcing environmental programs in Indian Country and the current developments in the TAS policy. In order to fully understand the unique atmosphere of regulation in Indian Country, it is first necessary to examine the sovereign power of tribal governments and the sources of that power. Once the question of who governs is answered, the next issue to be addressed is which environmental laws allow tribes to apply for TAS. Thereafter, is a discussion of what is happening under the Clean Water Act in Indian Country. The final section of this chapter is a look at what tribes are up against in the struggle to gain control of environmental regulation in Indian Country and some suggestions to implement programs.

Tribal Government

The power to regulate is a function derived from sovereignty.[31] Therefore, tribes must have some degree of sovereignty in order to enact and carry out environmental policies within their territories. The sovereignty of Indian tribes has been the issue in many Supreme Court cases. The jurisprudence indicates that tribes do have sovereignty, but the amount of sovereignty seems to vary depending on the issue over which a tribe wishes to assert its sovereignty. Sovereignty encompasses what land, what people and what actions tribes have control over.

Indian tribes were sovereign in the truest sense of the word long before the first European set foot on the shores of the American continent. However, tribes today are accorded a circumscribed version of sovereignty. At the heart of most sovereignty issues is land. Although it is certainly true that sovereignty also involves persons, in the context of Indian tribes the real issue of sovereignty is property. Who owns the property and who controls it are seminal issues for environmental enforcement.

The ensuing discussion will begin with a brief review of some cases already examined, but remain central to understanding how sovereignty affects environmental control in Indian Country. As mentioned previously, beginning in 1823 with *Johnson v. M'Intosh*,[32] Chief Justice John Marshall undertook to limit the inherent sovereignty of Indian nations. This decision represented a "conquest" theory[33] of ownership of land. According to Marshall, conquest gave the settlers ownership of the land, and Indians merely retained a "right of occupancy." Indians could inhabit the land, but they could not alienate the land by selling, donating or bequeathing it because they did not own it.[34]

Marshall had the opportunity to explore this issue further in what became known as the "Cherokee cases." In 1831, *Cherokee Nation v. Georgia*,[35] was decided by the Supreme Court. In these cases, Marshall described tribes as "domestic dependent nations." In effect, tribes were made wards of the federal government. This established a trust relationship between Indians and the federal government whereby the federal government would assume responsibility for the tribes. However, tribes retained the right of governing themselves and have been capable of doing so for centuries, so they do have some degree of inherent sovereignty within their own borders.

The final case in the Marshall trilogy is *Worcester v. Georgia*.[36] The *Worcester* case gave the Supreme Court the opportunity to apply the *Cherokee Nation v. Georgia* decision. In *Worcester*, the Court held that Georgia's laws were void in dealing with the Indians because all relations with Indians had to be carried out by the federal government. Thus, tribes have enough sovereignty to govern themselves *and* are not subject to state law or control.

Furthermore, the federal government has a duty to ensure that states do not attempt to subject Indians to state law or control.[37]

"Indian Country" is another issue of concern. While most sovereign nations have complete control over their lands, Indian tribes do not enjoy the same power. Indian tribes have long been considered both sovereigns and wards subject to the supervision and protection of the federal government, and they therefore derive power from their inherent sovereignty, treaties with the United States, and delegations from Congress.[38] Due to the unique sovereignty of tribes, the ownership of land on the reservation is important because who owns the land sometimes determines what government possesses enforcement power.[39]

Reservation lands are owned in a myriad of ways, which is a result of the Dawes Allotment Act of 1887.[40] The Dawes Allotment Act had a devastating effect on tribes. Under the Act, lands were divided up and allocated to individual Indians. The lands were then held in trust for 25 years, after which time a fee patent was issued.[41] Any lands which were left over after each tribal member received a share were deemed "surplus" and were sold to non–Indians. The result was the loss of some 90 million acres of reservation lands, fully two-thirds of the land originally held by tribes through reservations.[42] In addition to the loss of the land itself, the tribes lost a significant amount of control over the reservation as a whole because non–Indians living within the exterior boundaries of the reservation were not subject to all tribal control.[43] At best, it was a piecemeal ability to control what happens within the borders of Indian country.

The result of the Dawes Allotment Act[44] is a checkerboard of land ownership on some reservations: fee land, land held in trust for individuals ("allotments"), land held in trust for the tribe and land owned by non–Indians.[45] After the Dawes Allotment Act, there was an attempt to remedy the situation. Congress passed the Indian Reorganization Act of 1934, but none of the lands were given back to tribes. Indian policy flip-flopped again in the 1940s when there were attempts to assimilate Indians into mainstream culture. Finally, since the 1960s there has been a policy of allowing Indians the right to self-government without serious attempts to assimilate them.

A lot of issues deal with tribal control over non–Indians. It is well established that Indian tribes have considerable power over tribal members on the reservations.[46] The inherent power to regulate non–Indians on reservations is less clearly defined in federal jurisprudence. Two reasons in favor of supporting regulation of non–Indians on tribal lands are that the tribe has rights as a landowner and that the tribe, in its exercise of self-government, may regulate the relations between its members and other persons, consistent with federal law.

A series of three Supreme Court cases in the early 1980s bolstered tribal authority, but in the late 1980s and early 1990s, the Supreme Court has sought once again to narrow sovereignty. In *Washington v. United States*,[47] the Supreme Court opined that tribes had the power to collect state-imposed cigarette taxes on non-tribal members who made on-reservation purchases. This, of course, benefited the state more than the tribe. However, it began a trend in allowing tribes to assert authority over non–Indians on reservations.

In 1981, the Supreme Court handed down the decision in *Montana v. United States*.[48] In this case, the Court established that the Crow Tribe could prohibit non-members from hunting and fishing on the reservation land and charge a fee or establish bag limits.[49] The Court followed this same pattern in the 1985 decision in *Kerr-McGee v. Navajo*[50] when it allowed tribes to collect taxes on the value of leasehold interests on tribal lands and the sale of property produced or extracted from those lands.[51]

The 1851 treaty between the Crow Indians and the United States did not intend to convey this power to the tribe, the Court decided. This authority can only extend to land on which the tribe "exercises absolute and undisturbed use and occupation" and cannot apply to subsequently alienated lands held in fee by non–Indians.[52] In other words, the sovereignty of the tribe does not support its regulation of non–Indian hunting and fishing within non–Indian lands, even if these lands are within the borders of the reservation. The Crow, therefore, were denied regulatory powers over the Big Horn River, of which the title was passed to the state of Montana when it entered the union as a state and as the Court stated, the tribe had accommodated itself to the state.[53]

The *Montana* case in 1981 did more than just establish that tribes may set hunting and fishing limits and charge fees for non–Indians on tribal lands. It also established a test to determine whether the tribe retained regulatory power or lost it to the state or federal government. The Court determined that tribes retained the power to regulate the conduct of non–Indians on lands *within* the reservation owned in fee by non–Indians if the "conduct threatens or has some direct effect on the political integrity, the economic security, or the health and welfare of the tribe."[54] This was a huge step forward and reinforced sovereignty over their lands.

The *Montana* case espoused the general rule that "inherent sovereign powers of an Indian tribe do not extend to the activities of the tribe."[55] Yet, there are two exceptions to the general rule. These are:

1. An Indian tribe may regulate, through taxation, licensing, or other means, the conduct of nonmembers who enter consensual relationships with the tribe or its members, through commercial dealings, contracts, leases, or other arrangements.

2. A tribe may also retain inherent power to exercise civil authority over

the conduct of non–Indians on fee lands within its reservation when that conduct threatens or has some direct effect on the political integrity, the economic security, or the health or welfare of the tribe.[56]

However, the Supreme Court was not satisfied with that test and developed a new one in the next sovereignty case, *Brendale v. Confederated Tribes and Bands of the Yakima Nation.*[57] The Brendale case resulted in a troubling decision when the court held that a tribe lost the authority to zone fee lands in a reservation's open area which had significant ownership by non–Indians.[58] The case involved two independent proposed developments on the reservation by non-tribe members and the county Board of Commissioners' conclusions that neither required an environmental impact statement.[59] The Court said tribes cannot have extensive governing power over non–Indians because Indians are dependents of the federal government.[60] A new test was also formulated where "non–Indian activity on non–Indian land must be demonstrably serious and must imperil the political integrity, economic security or the health and welfare of the tribe."[61] The Court was evidently not happy with this test either, because it developed a new test in 1993.

The 1993 *South Dakota v. Bourland*[62] decision held that the Cheyenne River Sioux Tribe does not have the power to regulate non–Indian hunting and fishing in the reservoir behind the Oahe Dam which inundates a portion of the reservation.[63] For several years, both the tribe and the state regulated hunting and fishing.[64] However, when the tribe refused to recognize state game licenses and announced its intention to prosecute hunters without tribal licenses, the state sued and won.[65] The Cheyenne Sioux lands were taken under the Flood Control and Cheyenne River Acts of 1944. These acts abrogated the tribe's rights under the 1868 Fort Laramie Treaty to regulate hunting and fishing by non–Indians in the area (104,420 acres) taken for the dam and reservoir projects. In a rather circular argument, Justice Clarence Thomas attempted to justify the decision by declaring that tribal authority over non–Indians stems solely from the power to exclude. Therefore, tribal regulatory authority disappears when a tribe loses the power to exclude. However, a tribe may retain that authority over non–Indians if Congress expressly delegates it or if either of the two exceptions in the *Montana* case comes into play.[66] The Court dismissed tribal inherent sovereignty enabling it to regulate non–Indian hunting and fishing in the taken areas. These rights were eliminated by Congress, as is its right, pursuant to these acts. This action opened up the area to the general public and ended Indian control.

The *Bourland* case does indicate that an express delegation by Congress, such as in the TAS provisions and the designation of tribal control over all of Indian Country, endows the tribe with regulatory authority over non–Indians. While many commentators see the *Bourland* and *Montana* cases as decimating tribal control over tribal lands, the *Bourland* case in particular may mark the beginning of a jurisprudence which actually facilitates greater tribal control over the environment, and therefore the land.

The EPA and Congress have clearly announced their intention to give tribes jurisdiction over *all* of the land within the exterior boundaries of the reservation when it comes to environmental policy.[67] It remains to be seen whether the intention to give tribes environmental control over the entire reservation will be upheld by the courts after *Bourland*.

The *Montana, Brendale* and *Bourland* cases ignored the power that land has for a people and their futures. If the integrity of a tribe's culture is to be protected and respected, then their territorial sovereignty must be viewed and respected as a collective right.[68] Yet, the common theme in these three cases is that the tribe in question cannot regulate parcels of lands within the boundaries of the reservation because they are not owned by tribe members. This is difficult to support outside of Indian Country. Can not a city government regulate property within its limits, even if it is owned by someone who lives out of state? Of course they can regulate that land, for it falls within their territorial boundaries. In addition, the *Brendale* and *Bourland* cases were disputes that started when a state or local government refused to respect the authority of the neighboring tribal government. These cases rest on the assertion that inherent tribal authority over nonmembers is somehow inconsistent with the dependent status of the tribes and cannot exist without some act of Congress.[69] This dismisses sovereignty as nothing more than an abstract theory as applied to tribes and opens the door for a myriad of problems.

Federal Environmental Laws

As discussed, many federal environmental statutes have been amended to add language to allow primary enforcement of environmental provisions to Indian tribes on Indian lands. These amendments treat tribes as states and require that all tribal environmental standards meet minimum federal standards. Each federal statute covering a specific aspect of the environment now contains its own TAS provision. Therefore, the effect of each statute depends on the wording. This section briefly describes the language and impact of some of the major federal environmental legislation and how it deals with the TAS policy.

Many tribes have taken full advantage of the opportunity to run their own environmental programs, but are hampered by a lack of money and, sometimes, scientific information. However, by 1992, the EPA was providing technical assistance and limited funding for approximately 200 tribes that operated their own limited environmental protection programs.[70]

In 1986, the Safe Drinking Water Act (SDWA) was amended to provide that tribes recognized by the Department of Interior were eligible for TAS for certain SDWA programs.[71] The TAS amendment authorizes the EPA to delegate enforcement responsibility to the tribal governments for regulation of their public drinking water systems and protection of underground drinking water sources from dangerous or potentially dangerous underground injection.[72] In order to qualify for TAS, tribes must meet certain organizational and administrative requirements before they acquire control over the programs.[73]

In 1988, the EPA promulgated regulations to establish federal UIC program requirements for reservations that did not receive "primacy" to implement a SDWA program.[74] By 1993, only three tribes had submitted applications to the EPA for approval of drinking water programs. Two tribes, the Osage and the Navajo, received grants to operate federal UIC programs.[75]

Under the Clean Water Act (CWA), amended in 1987 by Section 518 to make Indian tribes eligible for the same treatment as states, the EPA is authorized to treat tribes as states only if:

1. the Indian tribe has a governing body carrying out substantial governmental duties and powers;

2. the functions to be exercised by the Indian tribe pertain to the management and protection of water resources which are held by an Indian tribe, held by the United States in trust for Indians, held by a member of an Indian tribe if such property interest is subject to a trust restriction on alienation, or otherwise within the borders of and Indian reservation; and

3. the Indian tribe is reasonably expected to be capable, in the Administrator's judgment, of carrying out the functions to be exercised in a manner consistent with the terms and purposes of this chapter and of all applicable regulations.[76]

The Act also specifically stated that Indian tribes may operate delegated federal programs over the entire reservation area, including fee lands owned by nonmembers.[77] Under the CWA, tribes qualify for TAS for purposes of grants for pollution control programs, grants for the construction of treatment facilities, establishment of water quality standards and tribal implementation plans, implementation of permit systems, and participation in the clean lakes program.[78]

The original Clean Air Act (CAA) did not allow tribes to participate, but Congress amended the CAA in 1990 to include a TAS provision.[79] The CAA allows tribal implementation plans to apply to all lands within the exterior boundaries of the reservation. Prior to the 1990 amendments, the EPA was allowed to delegate certain regulatory authority under the CAA to tribes, even though the tribe could then affect landowners off the reservation. These regulations allowed Indian tribes to redesignate their air quality classification from the automatic Class II category (moderate air quality deterioration allowed) to Class I (very little deterioration allowed) or Class III (air quality deterioration to the level of secondary ambient air quality standards allowed).[80] Litigation arose under the CAA's provisions for Indian tribes when the EPA approved a redesignation of air quality from Class II to Class I as requested by the Tribal Council of the Northern Cheyenne Tribe. The operator of a nearby strip mine brought suit alleging that the tribe's designation of air quality classification was not authorized under the CAA.[81] The Ninth Circuit upheld the delegation to the tribe as proper under the CAA, based on the inherent sovereignty of Indian tribes, deference to the EPA's interpretation of the statute and 1977 legislative history indicating Congress' approval of Indian authority to redesignate air quality classifications.[82]

Under CERCLA (Comprehensive Environmental Response, Compensation and Liability Act of 1980, commonly known as Superfund), the statute provides that Indian tribes shall be treated substantially the same as a state concerning specific provisions of the act,[83] including being eligible for Superfund monies. Even under the Federal Insecticide, Fungicide and Rodenticide Act (FIFRA), the EPA may grant the appropriate tribal governing body limited authority to regulate the use of restricted pesticides.[84]

Despite the fact that Indian tribes no longer possess all of the powers of a sovereign nation, they continue to possess some attributes of sovereignty over their members and territory.[85] Through TAS provisions, Congress explicitly granted tribes the authority to govern environmental concerns within the tribe's jurisdiction. This action creates a dichotomy by simultaneously recognizing the legitimacy of tribal government regulation and preempting state regulation. Due to the TAS provisions, environmental regulation by tribes goes beyond the inherent powers of the tribe to zone tribal lands. It clearly illustrates Congress' intent to grant the tribes the authority to govern their environments. The provisions also clearly recognize that the tribe's authority to control its environment is equal to the state's authority in that respect.

TAS Under the Clean Water Act

More than ten years after the move to treat Indian tribes as states (TAS), more and more tribes have begun to establish environmental programs on the reservation and request TAS status from the EPA. By 1993, approximately 91 tribes had received grants made available under section 1256 of the Clean

Water Act (CWA) to develop federally authorized water programs, along with federal assistance.[86] Several cases have come out of the CWA's TAS provision. For example, a significant water quality standards case was decided in New Mexico in 1993, *Albuquerque v. Browner*.[87] It involved the Isleta Pueblo, which is located on the Rio Grande River in New Mexico. The Pueblo is a community of about 4,500 people and straddles the Rio Grande some 10 miles south of Albuquerque.[88] The Pueblo uses the water from the river for various purposes, including irrigation, recreation and religious ceremonies.[89] It was the first tribe to be awarded TAS status by the EPA for purposes of the water quality standards program.[90]

At the time the EPA approved the tribe's application,[91] it indicated that upstream dischargers would have to comply with the Pueblo's water quality standards.[92] The EPA was also in the process of revising the City of Albuquerque's permit for its wastewater treatment facility to bring it into compliance with stricter state water quality standards. The wastewater treatment facility discharges five miles upstream of the Pueblo, and the EPA delayed issuing the permit to the city until the Pueblo's water quality standards could be approved.[93]

After some adjustments, the Pueblo's water quality standards were approved, despite the fact that the EPA believed some of the Pueblo's human health criteria when applied to all flows were stringent and scientifically unsupportable.[94] Of primary importance was an arsenic standard that was 1000 times more stringent than the state and almost 2500 times more stringent than the EPA dictates is safe for human consumption under the Safe Drinking Water Act.[95] There is high background arsenic around Albuquerque, and in order to comply with the Pueblo's water quality standards, the city would be required to build a reverse osmosis tertiary level treatment facility at a cost of $250 million, with a $26 million per year operating cost.[96]

The City of Albuquerque requested a preliminary injunction, arguing that the EPA's approval of the religious ceremonial use of the river by the Pueblo people violated the establishment clause of the Constitution.[97] While the Pueblo conceded that its goal was to ensure that water it used from the river would be fit for religious purposes, the EPA argued that the primary purpose of its approval of the tribe's standard was to achieve the secular goals of the CWA.[98] The Court agreed with the EPA. The District Court granted a Motion for Summary Judgment in favor of the EPA, finding that the EPA lacks the authority to reject stringent water quality standards on the grounds of harsh economic or social effect.[99] The City of Albuquerque appealed the case to the Tenth Circuit Court of Appeals where it lost in 1996.

In May of 2000, a federal district court in Montana rejected a challenge to the EPA's TAS policy. The state of Montana[100] sued the EPA after the Region VIII Administrator approved the application of the Confederated Salish and

Kootenai tribes for TAS to promulgate water quality standards on the Flathead Indian Reservation. The U.S. District Court for the District of Montana rejected arguments by Montana that the tribes lacked authority to apply clean water standards to the activities of nonmembers and that tribal standards should not apply to non–Indian activities on the reservation. The Tenth Circuit utilized the same reasoning as the District Court in Montana, as well as the decision in *Arkansas v. Oklahoma*,[101] and the City of Albuquerque is in the process of spending the $250 million to build a water treatment facility. However, whether tribes derive the same benefit as the Isleta Pueblo remains to be seen. One commentator has suggested that the tables would certainly turn if the tribes are "upstream" people instead of "downstream." If so, the current jurisprudence indicates that the tribe may be responsible for mitigation costs, cleanup costs, or the costs of forgone development.[102]

Waste in the Wastelands

It is ironic that in recent years, especially toward the end of the 1980s, the very wastelands that the tribes had been relegated to through forced removal, the allotment debacle, and treaty injustices became a hot commodity. As the country entered into an era of real or perceived landfill shortages, and a solid and nuclear waste disposal crisis in the 1990s, the wastelands of the reservation quickly became targets for corporations and governments to dump the waste produced by millions of non–Indians.

In no area has tribal environmental sovereignty been more challenged and lost than in the regulation of solid waste. This issue serves as another prime example of the loss of property rights. It has demonstrated the profound differences between the traditionalists, pragmatists and progressive camps among Indian tribes. The need for economic development to lift the Indian peoples out of unemployment and poverty weighs heavily against the needs and respect of the land and resources inculcated in the traditions and culture of the tribe.

The federal government has been failing in its trust duties to protect Indian lands from Alaska to Florida.[103] The third world status of many Indian nations have made them prime targets for manipulative corporations. Since Indian Country typically falls under less stringent environmental guidelines than state lands, corporations see this as a way of bypassing the barriers that hamper them locating waste disposal facilities elsewhere.[104] Greed and sovereign status have attracted the interest of waste merchants and the federal government for the disposal and storage of waste on Indian lands. Furthermore, federal policies remain out of touch with the Indian peoples and their needs, and only serve to compound the problems.

In 1965, Congress passed the Solid Waste Disposal Act to regulate for the first time, dumps and incinerators. However, solid waste remained a state issue rather than a federal concern. In 1976, reacting to environmental pressures, the Resource Conservation and Recovery Act (RCRA) was passed which now put the federal government in the middle of the hazardous waste and municipal solid waste (MSW) recycling and regulatory efforts. Subtitle C of RCRA dealt with comprehensive regulations of hazardous waste and its transportation, handling and disposal. This is administered by the EPA but responsibility can and has been given in some cases to the states to enforce the rules and regulations.

RCRA's Subtitle D, passed in 1988, centered on municipal solid waste, otherwise known as everyday household trash and garbage. Subtitle D established federal guidelines for municipal landfills and included stipulations for liners, leachate (particulate matter dissolved in water) and methane gas collection systems, vector controls (rodents, insects, etc.), coverings and insurance criteria (which was to last a minimum of thirty years) that the state and localities were charged to meet in order to protect human health and the environment. If a facility did not meet the Subtitle D rules, it was labeled an open dump and these were now illegal. It essentially made the controlling governmental authority liable for any environmental or health damages that the landfill caused, and subject to citizen lawsuits claiming damages. These rules, not really enforced for several years, created a stampede of local officials to create recycling programs, and close down their old landfills within the window of time before the subtitle went into full effect to avoid purchasing the mandatory insurance and equipment. With this rush of landfill closures came a search for other alternatives and new locales to dump their MSW. Obviously, the search was for a place with less stringent, or at least less clear, environmental regulations.

With the lack of straightforward regulatory authority and the vast acreage of what has been considered worthless land, Indian Country became a prime target for dumpers, both legal and illegal. Corporations quickly sought out tribal officials to get contracts permitting them to build landfills and dump MSW on tribal lands. Waste began to move into Indian Country, sometimes from thousands of miles away. Soon, scandals and charges of bribery followed, as did an outcry from tribal members themselves protesting this new conquest and usurpation of their lands.

In 1991, O&G Industries of Torrington, Connecticut, approached the Rosebud Reservation in South Dakota to establish a 5,760-acre (9 square miles) landfill. They courted the tribal leaders, who tended to be progressives, and swayed them with the usual promises of jobs and security to go along with the tons of trash to be disposed of in the poorest county in the United States. O&G had already been rejected by several tribes, so the Rosebud was their last hope.[105] Company officials had portrayed themselves as environmentalists and tried a marketing ploy exploiting the Indian heritage as caretakers of Mother Earth in order to convince them to allow the landfill project to go forward. The Rosebud leaders, seeing a means to get their own dumps cleaned up in the process and a solution for their own waste disposal needs, as well as avoiding federal fines if they did not get their dumps cleaned up, decided to allow the project to proceed. The O&G agreement with the Rosebud leadership stipulated that in no way would South Dakota state regulations be applied to the landfill, and if improvements were ever decided upon, the expense became the tribe's.[106] The result however, was a split within the tribe between the traditionalists, the pragmatists and the progressive tribal leadership that has had effects even to this day. Debates, angry protests and threats, and charges of bribery and corruption soon replaced the usual consensus on the reservation. Tribal government instability and mistrust has now become the common theme in the tribal political system. To further exacerbate things, the surrounding non–Indian ranchers have sided with the anti-landfill Indians which has only compounded the factionalism on Rosebud.[107] Yet, the grassroots opposition on the Rosebud Reservation was successful in stopping O&G and its landfill plans, but the political repercussions still resound today.

The Kaw Indians of Oklahoma were also placed in the middle of the waste wars. The tribal government initially accepted a contract with Waste-Tech (owned by Amoco) to operate an incinerator on their lands. However, after much outcry and opposition, the tribal council was forced to back out of the contract.[108] The effects of the factionalism were slow to wear off.

The Mississippi Choctaw have also felt the effects of polarization due to tribal council actions with a waste company. In 1991, National Disposal Systems bought 400 acres of land adjacent to the reservation and sold it to the tribe for the sole purpose of getting it out from under state regulatory control for use as a landfill.[109] The members of the tribe disliked this backdoor practice and demanded a popular referendum on the idea. The argument polarized the tribe, but it was eventually defeated.

Both the hazardous and solid waste regulations of RCRA have been held to apply in Indian Country. Since states in general lack authority over tribal lands, the federal government, through Congress and the EPA, maintains responsibility to monitor and regulate these lands. That is, of course, if the EPA has the staff and resources to do so. RCRA had not been originally amended to include treatment of Indian tribes as states, effectively leaving the tribes to deal with their environment and problems without federal assistance. Therefore, when a proposal comes from an outside source to build a landfill on reservation lands, the only government action required for such a project to proceed may be an approval from the Bureau of Indian Affairs for a land transaction deal. An environmental impact statement (EIS) would still have to be prepared under the auspices of the National Environmental Policy Act (NEPA), but this can be done separately from the original deal.

However, it is not the landfills on Indian land that are still a concern. Instead, it is the uncounted illegal open dumps that worry both tribal and environmental officials. Many of the 650 legal dumps[110] are operated by the Indian Health Service (IHS) and other quasi-sovereign Indian agencies and governments. Some tribes have undertaken comprehensive environmental planning to deal with this and other issues of pollution, but they have done so largely without federal financial or technical assistance. The illegal dumping is done due to the remoteness of most Indian lands and the indifference to prosecute the offenders.[111] Furthermore, federal agencies who have jurisdiction over this matter (the IHS, BIA, EPA, BLM, Congress and others) are uncoordinated and understaffed to handle the problem. As such, medical, household, hazardous and toxic wastes continue to wind up on Indian lands.

In 1994, Congress enacted the Indian Lands Open Dump Cleanup Act to address this problem in Indian Country. It directed the IHS to inventory open dumps on Indian lands and submit a funding proposal to Congress for cleanup. In addition, the EPA has gone ahead and begun to give tribes TAS standing so that they could regulate waste disposal on their lands and receive the help they need from the federal government.

However, as the *Blue Legs v. U.S. Bureau of Indian Affairs* (1989)[112] case demonstrated, even those directed to help protect the health of the Indian peoples have contributed to the pollution of their lands. In this case, citizens of the Oglala Sioux tribe of the Pine Ridge Reservation brought suit against the tribal government, the EPA, BIA and the IHS alleging their violation of RCRA statutes at the solid waste landfill in Wanblee, South Dakota, among others.

The landfill, really just an open dump, was operated by the tribe and was on tribal lands. Waste was collected from the tribe, the BIA and IHS, and hauled to the dump for disposal. The dumps were obviously being operated improperly, with a tacit sanction and participation of both the BIA and IHS. The issue was not who caused these conditions and threats, but who would be responsible for correcting them. The Court was asked to address and answer this issue.

The Court determined that it had the jurisdiction to enforce the provisions of RCRA regarding the prohibition of open dumps against the Oglala Tribe. They were ultimately held to be responsible for the regulation, operation and maintenance of the dumps found on their lands.[113] RCRA applied to Indian tribes and Indian Country.

In this case, the Court demonstrated that environmental sovereignty did come with inherent environmental responsibility, as it should. Even though

RCRA was considered a preemption upon tribal sovereignty, the Oglala were not being treated any differently than any other state or municipality in the nation. Tribal sovereignty still existed except where a treaty or Congressional act has eradicated it, and this was not the case here.

The Court did agree that the solution to the open dumping problem primarily resided with the tribal government. The EPA's role was to provide both technical and financial assistance to the tribe to overcome this problem. Whereas the plaintiffs had argued that the BIA and IHS bore some of the weight of responsibility for the dumps, especially since their waste was being hauled and disposed of in the dumps also, the Court limited their roles to providing assistance to the Oglala and enjoined them to cease sending their waste to the sites in question.[114] In conclusion, the Court ordered the tribe, the BIA and IHS to submit a plan to bring the dumps into compliance with the EPA.

Environmental sovereignty became a little less clear in the 1990s. In 1993, the Southern Missouri Recycling and Waste Management District of South Dakota filed for and obtained a landfill permit for a site on non–Indian lands within the boundaries of the Yankton Sioux Reservation. The boundaries of the reservation were set by treaty in 1858. The District was made up of four counties and contained some 25,000 residents. The tribe sued to halt the landfill on several environmental grounds.

The land selected for the site was not owned by the tribe as a result of the checkerboarding caused by the Dawes Act.[115] Though the land was not owned by an Indian, it was right in the middle of the reservation, Indian Country, and the waste would be hauled over tribal lands to get there. Furthermore, the effects of the landfill—air, noise, water, land and pest pollution—obviously could easily spill over into the surrounding Indian-owned lands.

The Yankton were rebuffed by the state and thus appealed to the federal District Court. The tribe argued that the landfill was in Indian Country and the state had no authority to grant a permit for this site. It fell to either the tribe or the federal government to grant such permission.[116] The District Court agreed that the landfill was in Indian Country, but ruled that the EPA, not the tribe, had the authority to grant permits for a landfill site.

The court utilized the "implicit divestiture" doctrine created in the *Montana* and *Brendale* cases. In the *Montana* case, the Court established the parameters of tribal regulatory authority when it came to non–Indian or non-tribal members. Of course, authority does exist if the person has entered into a consensual relationship with the tribe or if the conduct has some direct effect on core tribal interests.[117] In *Brendale*, the Court ruled that the Yakama Tribe was divested of its regulatory authority over fee lands, at least to those areas open to nonmembers, *unless* the tribe can show that the nonmember use of the land will impact the core governmental functions of the tribe.

Even though the Yankton Sioux had provided a list of concerns over the landfill, the District Court ruled that the tribe did not provide evidence of impact upon the tribal government's interests, such as health and welfare.[118] Therefore, since the tribe was divested of its authority due to where the landfill was to be located and the supposed failure to show impact, the court surmised that the tribe had no authority over the landfill, but the EPA did.

The EPA required evidence of serious and substantial impact and effects from fee-land activities to grant a tribe regulatory authority. In fact, a tribe only needed to demonstrate the potential that future pollution would have an impact instead of actually waiting for damages to occur before acting.[119] The Court examined the two-prong approach used by the EPA in situations like this.

The first prong: it was an accepted fact that non–Indians on fee lands may engage in activities regulated under federal laws and this may be enough to raise the presumption that the activity may have an impact upon a tribe and its interests.[120] Secondly, the tribe must provide supporting evidence that the activity in question has the potential to generate significant impacts on the health, welfare or governmental interests such as the economic security or political integrity of the tribe before regulatory authority can be granted.[121]

The Yankton provided information to this point which the District Court dismissed. It argued that the landfill's design, in particular its liner, would protect the tribe's environmental interests. As to the permit, if a state wished to assert primacy over Indian Country it must demonstrate their authority to regulate all sources within Indian territories, whether fee or Indian owned.[122] In order to get this authority, the state must show a clear delegation of authority from a treaty or a delegation of authority from Congress, and no state, the Court remarked, has been able to show this, including South Dakota.

Therefore, the Court's reading of the Indian and environmental laws found that the Yankton Sioux Reservation had remained intact and had not been diminished, and the state of South Dakota had no authority to grant a permit for a landfill in Indian Country.[123] The authority to do this resided with the EPA. This was especially true since RCRA treats tribes not as states (TAS) but rather as municipalities and only states have permitting powers.

South Dakota did not appeal the ruling, but instead began lobbying the EPA for a permit and a waiver for changing the liner of the landfill from composite to clay. They received approval of both in 1995. The Yankton once again disapproved in public hearings, and the issue ended up in court again.

The Supreme Court ruled that the EPA's actions were within the discretion of its powers. Furthermore, it ruled that the environment was not the tribe's to protect.[124] The site had been diminished from the reservation, and since the site was not on Indian land, it did fall within the state's jurisdiction. The site had been deeded to a non-Indian in 1904 under the Homestead Act.

The Court reviewed the treaties of 1892 and 1894 to determine that the Yankton had in fact diminished and ceded title to the land in question. The language of the act required the tribe to cede, sell, relinquish and convey to the United States all claim, right, title and interest in unallotted lands for a payment of $600,000.[125] The Court dismissed tribal arguments as absurd that the language contained in the treaties protected the 1858 boundaries; instead they claimed it only protected a continuation of annuities. The Court substantiated this conclusion by referring to a statement made by the treaty's negotiator, John J. Cole, who informed the Yankton that they could sign the treaty giving up the surplus lands or the government would see them starve. Cole told the Yankton that they had to remove all barriers and allow the white man and all elements of civilization onto the reservation.[126]

In addition to its reliance on Cole's candid remarks, the Court considered changes in the Indian population to reinforce the concept and intent of diminishment. The decline in the tribe's population and the decrease in the amount of land in incorporated municipalities was proof enough to validate the intent and fact of diminishment. The Court, however, conveniently ignored the post–1990 growth of Indian populations and the increasing economic importance of the area.

Therefore, in this case, the Court turned to selected demographic data to support its decision that diminishment of Indian lands was the intent of the treaties, instead of examining the treaties in the language and intent of the time. The treaties were nearly 150 and 100 years old. Obviously, the intent then may not be the same interpretation given now. The Court ignored the government-to-government approach that has emerged in modern Indian policy. Once again, by picking and choosing evidence to fit their conclusion, and with selective memories and perceptions, the Court has fulfilled the manifest destiny of the newcomers and allowed the Indian lands to be surrounded by wastes. The Yankton lost their lands, their authority to say not-in-my-backyard to a landfill like so many other communities have done, and the authority to regulate an activity that could have an everlasting impact upon the people of the tribe.

The Supreme Court seems to have ignored the *Montana* and *Brendale* issue of direct effect upon a tribe's health and welfare for making a decision about authority. Landfills are needed, but have serious environmental impacts. Just because they are on Indian lands does not make them safer, except to those not living on these lands.

Other Environmental Challenges
Facing Indian Tribes

While the City of Albuquerque and others may believe they are being held hostage by the extremely stringent regulation of Indian tribes, other commentators believe that "Indian land is the easiest place in the world to dump your wastes."[127] This, of course, implies that tribes have neither the will nor the financial resources to enforce environmental laws on the reservation.

> [M]any tribes no longer view the environment as a bank of natural resources that they must shield and shelter at any cost. Instead, the economic pressures of the twentieth century—particularly underdevelopment, unemployment and poverty—are forcing a growing number of Indian tribes to exchange the spiritual view of their once pristine environment for a commercial one. This shift from nurturing nature to exploiting the environment on a growing number of reservations results largely from a legal loophole that permits non-natives to pollute inside Indian country in ways they could not elsewhere.[128]

In many respects, it is true that many tribes lack the financial resources to implement and enforce environmental regulations. Tribes have been unable to remedy waste problems or comply with federal standards because they are not eligible for the type of support states receive for implementing and enforcing environmental laws.[129]

Despite the lack of funding, many tribes have attempted to make a profit while still enforcing strict environmental compliance on their reservations. A prime example of a recent case was the 600-acre Campo Landfill on the Campo Indian Reservation in southern California. When the Campo tribe proposed to build a landfill on the reservation, California politicians went berserk, attempting to pass specific legislative prohibitions making it illegal to dump waste in reservation landfills.[130] Environmentalists wanted any and all waste facilities on Indian lands to be regulated not only from a ecological standpoint, but to protect the Indians from waste merchants.[131] This opposition was in light of the fact that the Campo, as well as tribes all over the country, have well demonstrated the ability to make their own decisions concerning the best interests of their own people.

The Campo had done a very detailed and careful analysis of the feasibility for a landfill and filed the EIS with the BIA for their approval. This was a coproduced project from the start, meaning that all tribal factions and members were involved in all deliberations and discussions. All information was shared with every member of the tribe. The tribe proceeded to establish their own environmental codes and regulations, preempting the state in regulating their landfill both for environmental reasons, but also for the competitive advantage this would give the tribe over surrounding communities.[132]

They established an advisory board to negotiate contracts and monitor the facility. Liability was the company's responsibility, avoiding the costs for the tribe. The Campo also received an employment preference for any jobs the facility created.

A two-year battle began in which the state of California tried to assert jurisdiction over reservation waste projects. Environmental groups opposed any waste facility on Indian lands within the entire state, instead preferring to treat the Indians as naive, noble savages in need of the white man's protection from themselves and the outsiders.[133] Eventually, the state, environmental groups and the Campo Indian tribe entered into a voluntary agreement, but not without the state getting some egg on its face. It turned out that the regulations governing the design, construction and operation of the proposed landfill were at least as protective as state regulations, and in some cases even more so.[134]

Waste disposal can be a source of economic development, although maybe not an ideal one. Tribes have a resource that is needed, this being isolated land that is unused due to its condition or other reason. In addition, they lack the infrastructure to handle their own wastes, and the options touted to them can be used for their benefit. Like for the Campo Tribe, a waste facility can provide economic support for housing, schools, income supplements and investment capital for other needed projects. However, careful regulation and monitoring is needed for not only can pollution destroy a culture, it can destroy life itself.

One good reason for ensuring that there is strong regulation in Indian Country is that if tribes do not establish effective environmental regulatory programs, some states will assert that there is a void and state interests justify state regulatory jurisdiction. Some states can be expected to assert jurisdiction regardless of what tribes do. Consequently, Indian tribes must be aware of this problem and ascertain that the EPA is committed to federal enforcement so that there is no enforcement void into which a state may step. However, a reviewing court should find that tribal civil regulatory authority over non–Indian lands within the reservation boundaries has not been implicitly divested, and there is no need to engage in a balancing of governmental interests.[135]

Given the financial constraints of Indian tribes, the focus of tribal governments must be on how to build effective environmental regulation programs within those constraints.[136] In order to do this, two commentators have suggested a "mini–NEPA" process whereby a blanket review of all environmental development is utilized.[137]

It would be remiss not to mention the problem of hazardous and nuclear wastes on Indian lands. The Mescalero Apache of New Mexico have been fighting the disposal of spent nuclear waste on their lands for years under the Monitored Retrievable Storage (MRS) plan. The federal government has been peddling this idea to tribes just like a corporation seeking to dispose of its waste. It is ironic that tribes face millions of dollars in cuts in their federal assistance, but then are offered millions in return for storing nuclear waste on their lands. The federal government seems to be accepting tribal environmental sovereignty for waste disposal and storage, whereas it has fought to allow it for the regulations of hunting, fishing or other resources or practices.[138] As of 1993, 15 of the nation's 18 MRS sites were located on or near Indian lands.[139]

The Apache have been offered nearly $3 million to take the waste, not a small sum for the 3,000 members of the tribe. Communities surrounding the reservation, as well as the state government have opposed the plans. They claim the tribal leadership has been bribed, a charge vehemently denied.[140] However, the debate continues, the waste keeps piling up and other tribes have become interested due to the amount of money being offered to store this waste.

Finally, the Kaibob-Pauite Tribe of Arizona considered a hazardous waste incinerator on their lands. Neighboring communities opposed it, but the tribe saw this as an economic opportunity, albeit an imperfect one.[141] They pointed out that the opponents to the incinerator have been very slow to offer any alternatives to the tribe's economic problems. Waste-Tech offered $1 million a year for a 25-year contract for use of 640 acres. It also promised 120 jobs at $30,000 a year and extra payments if the amounts increased over 70,000 tons per year.[142] Tribal members were not exactly embracing the idea either, fearing health and cultural threats. Probably the most upsetting to the tribe was the condescending attitudes of both the opponents and proponents alike.[143]

It is ironic that the very lands that the Indians were forced onto are now valuable for dumping wastes, or for resources like coal or uranium. Companies have leased Indian lands and have built mines, processing plants and power plants often with total disregard to the environmental and health issues facing local residents. This movement can be traced to the NIMBY (Not In My Backyard) attitude that urban and suburban areas have toward these facilities.[144] No community wants these harsh and high polluting facilities near their homes, so what is the best option? Put them on barren land no one wants, lands where the Indians were removed to decades earlier. So with government assistance and blessings, private companies began to lobby tribal governments, both legally and illegally, dangling the modern equivalent of beads in exchange for the lands—the promise of money and jobs.

The effect has been to divide several tribes. It has pitted the people against their leaders, caused factionalism within the tribes where consensus had been the usual way of decision making. People see their leaders as too lenient with the companies, or even corrupted by them.[145] Outside environ-mental activists get involved, sometimes as tribal allies, sometimes as oppo-nents, but almost always as a third party to the actual issues at hand—who will win, the traditionalists or those who have been assimilated into the ways of mainstream America?

Recently, a four state, $3.8 billion project, the Dakota Access Pipeline was set to cross the Missouri River on the Standing Rock Sioux Reservation, but it ran into a roadblock. The Army Corps of Engineers had studies con-cerning the crossing site and had reported that at least five archeological and cultural sites would be violated by the crossing. However, in July 2016 the plan was still approved. The Corps approved the plan and claimed that no significant comments remained that were unresolved and the pipeline was not injurious to the public interest.[146] Obviously, the numerous Indians and environmentalists that decried the ruining of their lands, sacred sites and the threat to drinking water went unheeded.

The plans and construction met with immediate resistance, and when construction resumed, the Standing Rock people and hundreds of other sup-porters flocked to the site to protest. In August of 2017, Energy Transfer Part-ners, the company building the pipeline, filed a SLAPP (Strategic Lawsuit Against Public Participation) suit against the Standing Rock leaders claiming they were putting company employees, contractors, and law enforcement officials in danger by exercising their First Amendment rights. They tried to stop all opposition from the tribe and supporters while they continued to bulldoze gravesites and sacred sites.[147] The tribe did go to court, and in fact it would try to halt the construction through legal means several times, but each time its efforts were dismissed and the pipeline continued.

Eventually, the North Dakota governor would call out the National Guard, the company would hire a private security firm whose usual assignments were to deal with terrorism, and the number of protestors would increase. Many protestors would be attacked and arrested, and further legal attempts to stop the construction would be denied.

The pipeline would be finally built and the oil would flow despite protests and concerns when President Trump, in an unprecedented maneuver dealing with a private project, issued an executive order in January of 2017 to expedite the review and approval process for DAPL. This was immediately interpreted as permission to complete the project regardless of any issues or opposition. This is exactly what was done. The pipeline was completed, the civil lawsuits against the Standing Rock leaders were dropped, treaty rights were violated and once again, Indian sacred sites were violated.[148]

However, this battle may continue. The U.S. District Court of Washing-ton, D.C., has determined that the fast track approval process utilized by the U.S. Army Corps of Engineers to get the DAPL going violated several federal laws and procedures. In particular, it violated numerous key components of the National Environmental Policy Act (NEPA) because the Corps chose not to adequately consider the pipeline's impact on hunting, fishing, and cultural rights of the local tribes.[149] Instead, they ignored tribal rights and sovereignty and pushed the program forward. Obviously, the next step is uncertain except that once again, the American Indian has lost.

Conclusion

In order for Indian tribes to bring about successful environmental enforcement programs in Indian Country, they must work harder and plan harder than states. They must also carefully construct and diligently monitor their enforcement programs so that a court is not inclined to allow the state to come in. Hopefully, the state is precluded by the doctrine of preemption from asserting jurisdiction on tribal lands, and the federal jurisprudence to date supports this. However, with the Supreme Court slowly eroding away tribal sovereignty, Indian tribes must make the federal policy of putting environmental control in the hands of the tribe work in their favor.

Yet, "native peoples are under assault on every continent because their lands contain a wide variety of valuable resources needed for industrial development."[150] As a result, the Indian peoples in both North and South America have started to learn from their white counterparts. They are "blending their traditional forms of defending their cultures with the most sophisticated forms of political protest, coalition-building, and international networking with environmental and human rights organizations," and by doing so "the Indian groups have demonstrated that such ecologically-destructive megaprojects [such as timber harvesting, river damming, mining, etc.] can be slowed down, modified or even stopped."[151]

The environmental assaults and issues will continue. Recently, the Department of Interior has been examining the possibility of allowing oil drilling in Montana's Valley of the Chiefs which contains "numerous petroglyphs, historical and culturally important sites."[152] The BLM had approved a lease back in the 1980s, and when it was not used, permitted an extension to the company for exploration. Even though the BLM has publicly acknowledged that exploration would have significant adverse effects and impacts that could not be mitigated, they are still planning to permit the oil derricks to be placed in the Valley. In America's quest for energy independence, nothing is sacred, especially Indian Country. A solution may be at hand. Both the Blackfeet and Crow Tribes have offered a drilling swap to the oil company, permitting them to drill on the reservation if they agree not to drill and despoil the valley.[153] It remains to be seen if the company will take advantage of this offer.

One of the most pervasive and persistent images of the American Indian has been that of a natural being, people who lived in harmony with nature and whose identity is in congruence with the environment from thence they drew their sustenance. As has been discussed, this view is idealistic and utopian, but is no longer realistic. Life has changed for the Indian. Call it conquest, call it progress, but it cannot be denied. Living the traditional way is more and more difficult for the Indian peoples. For many, it is fast becoming a vague and blurry memory, only read about in books and seen in movies. Outside influences ranging from the encroachment of governments and multinational corporations to that of the eco-activists determining how a "real Indian" should live have ravaged the original inhabitants of this land.

New Age spiritualists have appropriated native religions because of their communion with nature. It is true that Indian religions had and still have a large part of their belief systems connected to nature. The forces of nature are honored and respected. Humans could please, influence and even offend these forces. Reciprocal relationships existed between man and his environment, so harmony and balance were the ideal. The Indian "utilized the environment extensively, realizing the differences between human and non-human persons, and felt guilt for their exploitation of nature's life-giving sustenance. Indian environmental religions were a means of idealizing and attempting to attain a goal of harmony with nature, for both participatory and manipulative reasons, but inherent in their religions was the understanding that they were not in fact at perfect harmony with nature."[154] However, things have changed over the centuries, due to a myriad of influences already discussed.

The Indian peoples must learn that dependence upon the government or environmental groups for ecological assistance may create more problems than expected. Each has their own views of the Indian and their own agendas. These are obviously not always in the best interest of the native people. As such, members of the National Indian Gaming Association decided to add environmental preservation and restoration to the list of items already funded from gaming profits.[155] By funding the protection and cleaning of their environments themselves, tribes will be able to better chart their own course and decide what is the best path for themselves.

Environmentalists will have to realize that Indians are not the mythical noble savages of literature and movies. Indian peoples require food, shelter, warmth and transportation and as a result of living in the modern world, they make waste and pollution. This is indeed an unfortunate consequence, but is must be accepted. Forcing the Indian peoples back to the old days, no matter how romantic, is unfair. It is also unfair to expect the Indian peoples to live up to some standards or expectations of ecological utopianism. Instead of touting the Indian as an ecological model, or condemning them if they fail to meet these unrealistic expectations, environmentalists need to understand that to help protect Indian environments and cultures, they should help the Indians get their treaties honored and enforced. Only through this power of control and sovereignty can the Indian peoples really hope to live in a clean and safe environment.

Turning back time to before the usurpers' arrival is impossible. Hence, a new respect for the environment must be born from and of the Indian, one in which they can live both in harmony with and respect for nature but balance the forces and needs of progress with this respect. The trespassers on Indian lands justified their conquest and dispossession of the Indian in part due to the belief that the Indian was just allowing the land and its resources to go to waste, remaining unused in their eyes. This justification is still being used today for the onslaught of attacks upon Indian environments—for the disposal of nuclear, toxic and solid wastes, or for flooding it to control the flow of rivers, or for a number of other reasons.

CHAPTER FIVE

The Battles Continue

"We are all poor because we are all honest."[1]
—RED DOG, OGLALA SIOUX

Introduction

The Indian wars are continuing. These wars focus more on property and its title. The denial of Indian property title is based on the fictional doctrines of discovery and conquest, or in other words, to the victor go the spoils. The indigenous peoples have never needed anyone else to bestow title to the lands they have occupied for thousands of years. European-Americans or American settlers use these legal fictions to justify the takings and occupations. These maneuverings to steal the land, ruin its sacredness, or cleanse the culture are not only illegal and immoral, but are a cause of wars all over the world against indigenous peoples. When a faraway country attempts to eliminate an ethnic group, the world, including the United States, rushes to the group's rescue with sanctions and military interventions. Yet, when the microscope is turned around onto the United States, the world fails to react. In the United States, it is not a bloody coup or chemical or biological warfare that is happening, at least not anymore. Maybe it is time for an international peacekeeping force to arrive on the shores of America and protect its indigenous peoples.

The Indian wars do continue, though the battles are smaller, more refined and focused. They take place in courtrooms, boardrooms, demonstrations and other gathering places. The warriors are now lawyers, advocates and activists. Yet, the goal is the same: let the indigenous people keep what they have and honor the promises that have been made over the past centuries. However, like arrows against guns, the odds are stacked against the Indian peoples since they almost always seem to be fighting a defensive action in the enemy's territory and have to follow the enemy's rules of engagement.

In this chapter, the remaining loose ends regarding sovereignty and property will be tied together. State governmental attacks in the new Indian wars will be discussed. Recent efforts to gain ground, and the recent losses will be examined. Finally, knowing that predication is a dangerous effort, a forecast for the outcome of the Indian wars will be discussed.

The New Battles

Each legislative session, states and the United States Congress invent new ways to eliminate American Indian sovereignty. From a redistribution of wealth among the tribes (obviously ignoring the diversity among Indian peoples) to calls for the tribes to forfeit their sovereignty or face the loss of federal funds (a position no state is ever placed in), the bills and acts continue to be debated and, unfortunately, sometimes passed.

In an attack on wealthy tribes with gaming, Senator Slade Gorton (R–Washington), chair of the United States Senate Appropriations Subcommittee on the Interior proposed a rider to the 1999 budget that would have redistributed half of the federal monies from the wealthier to the poorer tribes. It would have taken an estimated $12 million from the upper 10 percent of the tribes and given it to the bottom 20 percent. The idea was opposed by the BIA as being overly simplistic since it cannot adequately measure tribal wealth and it would pit one tribe against another.[2]

Whereas funding for Indian tribes has always been inadequate or poorly distributed, Gorton's plan merely put a Band-Aid on a gaping, bleeding battle wound. Furthermore, he was assuming that all Indians fall into a single homogeneous group with no differences, no tribal rivalries or self-determination plans. It is interesting that the same type of plan is never proposed so that the wealth from a "richer" state or community could be confiscated and given to a "poorer" one. This would violate state sovereignty, but more so would violate common sense. In sum, voters would not permit it.

Even in Hawaii the battle has raged on: Native Hawaiians are fighting to retrieve the land and sovereignty stolen from them over a hundred years ago. It is a fight against the actual physical conquest of Hawaii, rather than merely a jurisprudential exercise to justify its taking. In 1893, American businessmen backed by United States Marines invaded Hawaii, conquered it, overthrew its monarchy and set up their own provisional government. The islands were annexed in 1898 as a territory of the United States and over two million acres became governmental lands. This was not a war based on aggression, but one based solely on economic greed.

As a result, the Kanaka Maoli were removed from their lands, a mere 1.8 million acres, to make room for pineapple plantations, military bases and real estate developments.[3] They received no compensation for these losses. Another 2 million acres of their land was placed in trust under the control of the state Department of Hawaiian Home Lands (DHHL) for the supposed benefit of the 200,000 Kanaka Maoli. In 1921, Congress enacted the Hawaiian Homes Commission Act which set aside 200,000 acres of the confiscated lands into a Home Lands Trust for possible homesteading by Native Hawaiians.[4] Of course, the acreage chosen was the most barren and desolate, basically thought to be unusable. Although the state was to repatriate them onto their lands, as of 1998, only 7,000 have been repatriated while another 28,000 are still on the waiting list.[5] Most of the land is barren, remote and undeveloped without access to electricity, water or roads.

There has been a movement to restore the sovereignty of the Native Hawaiians and to gain compensation and justice for the illegal colonization of their islands. The United Nations had at one time "listed Hawaii as a colonized territory eligible for restoration of its independence," but the United States blocked this effort.[6] The United States government bypassed the United Nations declaration by sponsoring and holding a vote asking the Hawaiian population (and the United States military personnel stationed there) if they wanted statehood, and as a result, Hawaii joined the union in 1959, and the issue of decolonization seemed moot.

A state constitutional convention was held in 1978. At that time, an amendment was adopted that set a *pro rata* share (later established at 20 percent) of revenues collected from the Ceded Lands Trust and it also created the Office of Hawaiian Affairs (OHA) composed of "pure-blood" natives to manage these revenues.[7] The definition of a Native Hawaiian was set as anyone who was a direct descendent from those who suffered during the fall of Queen Liliʻuokalani's monarchy.

In 1993, Native advocates invited a panel of human rights and legal experts to investigate the predicament in Hawaii. Their judgment was that the Kanaka Maoli never relinquished their sovereignty nor had they voluntarily ceded their lands to the newcomers. Hence, the United States had violated their rights. As a reaction, the United States Congress issued a bill, which was signed by President Clinton into law in 1993, formally apologizing for depriving the Hawaiians of their self-determination and for other illegal acts.

The Hawaiian state legislature passed a law calling for a new plebiscite for the state's native population. The ballot asked only if there should be a proposal to select delegates to meet for the purpose of discussing whether to create a Native Hawaiian government and it had no provision for a return of land or compensation. Opponents claim that this is only going to continue to keep the Kanaka Maoli and others under state control.

The Kanaka Maoli wanted a process where they could work toward sovereignty and the proposed plebiscite did not satisfy these needs. They claimed that the process as stated kept them under state control.[8] As such, lawsuits were filed against the plebiscite and an injunction was issued preventing the results from being released. The Kanaka Maoli began a separate process to consider the issues of sovereignty and land compensation based upon the traditional methods of consensus building.[9] The eventual goal is independence, sovereignty and a return of their lands—in other words, self-determination and a future.

However, these goals were threatened by a series of recent court cases. Most notably, non–Native Hawaiians are also seeking their rights in these processes. In 1996, Harold E. Rice, the petitioner, applied to vote in the election of the OHA trustees. Rice was not a descendent or of Native blood. Thus, he was denied the right to participate in the election. His case went forward claiming a violation of the Constitution's 15th Amendment, denying him the right to vote in an election based on race. However, the lower court surmised that the OHA elections being limited to just Native Hawaiians was permissible under *Morton v. Mancari* (1974).[10]

The Supreme Court ruled that the OHA elections were a *state* function; thus the U.S. Constitution did apply and the denial of Rice's right to vote *was* in violation of the 15th Amendment. The *Mancari* case could not be applied in this instance, since the BIA preference was a special case. Race cannot be used to determine who could vote any more than determining who could not vote in an election. The OHA election was not a tribal election which could have a limited participation. The Native Hawaiians do not enjoy the same quasi-sovereign status that their American Indian counterparts enjoy. So, using ancestry as a qualifying factor was deemed by the Court as being the same as using race.[11] Ancestry was serving as a proxy for racial classification. This did, therefore, violate the U.S. Constitution's equal protection and right to vote clauses.

This case, along with some others,[12] have threatened not only the intent of finding justice and self-determination for the descendants of the native peoples of the Hawaiian Islands, but could also be expanded later to threaten any other function limited to those with Indian ancestry. Elections, tax decisions, and other efforts by Natives that may affect non–Indians may be challenged thanks to the federal decisions.

In 2007, a bill was introduced in Congress, the Native Hawaiian Government Reorganization Act, that would, as one critic pointed out, create a "permanent caste entitled to its own government with the United States."[13] George Will pointed out that the seeds of Native Hawaiians' problems were sown in 1993 when Congress passed a resolution apologizing for the U.S.'s involvement in what he called the "peaceful 1893 overthrow of Hawaii's monarchy."[14] He stated that the Native Hawaiians' lands were not taken by force like other American Indians, and that they chose to bring themselves under the U.S. Constitution by embracing statehood.[15]

This view, similar to that of the state's government, seemed to have been victorious when U.S. Supreme Court Justice Kennedy blocked the counts for the Native Hawaiian Self Governance referendum in 2015.[16] This was a vote to start the process of creating a self-government for Native Hawaiians. The entire process had been opposed by non-natives who saw it as being racially exclusive, and by the state government which decried that they were not a part of the process. Even some Natives opposed the idea because they did not want tribal status for themselves and their people.[17] However, this debate became essentially moot in 2016 when the U.S. Department of Interior under the Obama administration granted Native Hawaiians the right to choose to form a unified government and gave tribal status to them, along with self-determination which they had lost in 1893.[18]

As if attacks upon indigenous peoples from the national government were not enough, state governments also have often attempted to shrink American Indian landholdings as a way to divest or even void tribal sovereignty altogether.[19] States have sought court alliances to legitimize their claims for regulations and taxes on Indian lands so as to change the very size and status of these lands and replace tribal governmental authority with their own.[20] Rather than conquer, steal or cheat the Indians out of their lands, the new battle tactic is to make the tribes incapable of governing their own lands through legal and fiscal maneuvers so that the state can step in and take over. The attacks are on tribes, on the individual members and even on those who do business with the Indians.

In their attacks on their Indian populations and their rights, states have created the concept of a "coherent reservation community"[21] meaning that the state will only *respect* a tribal reservation that has a continuous, uninterrupted land base with no non–Indian holdings or owners. This is unrealistic, given the checkerboarding effects caused by the Dawes Act and other violations of treaties and the federal-tribal trust relationship. Furthermore, this concept has no legal standing or definition and it is not based on any clear federal policy. As such, even though it is wielded as a weapon over and over, the courts tend to ignore it—at least at the present time.

States attempting to take away Indian lands also rely on some construed instance of Congressional action which they claim has diminished or caused the disestablishment the reservation. Congress does have this power and has enacted legislation doing this to various parts of Indian Country. The courts, on deciding arguments about land takings, have relied on the salient language in the legislation and its intentions.[22] Especially important is whether payment was given for the lands taken. If there was compensation, then indications are present for the intentional diminishment of the tribal land base.[23] However, if the payment was transferred to a tribal account on the resale of the land, then the government was acting as a sales agent and the tribal land boundaries remain intact.[24]

The Indian territory of the 1800s became the state of Oklahoma, and this is where one example of these new battles has occurred. In *Oklahoma Tax Commission (OTC) v. the Sac and Fox Nation* (113 S.Ct. 1985 [1993]), the state (OTC) argued that distinctions of geography, membership status and residency should eviscerate tribal sovereignty in favor of the state. The OTC argued that the Allotment Act disestablished the reservation in 1891 and, as such, the Sac and Fox had no land base on which to exercise its governmental powers immune from the state.[25] Thus, the state could regulate and impose taxes on their land and, in this instance, on vehicles. The Sac and Fox fought to stop this collection and argued against the idea that their reservation had been disestablished.[26]

The OTC based its contentions on a previous case against the Citizens Band Pottawatomi[27] where the state of Oklahoma attacked the Pottawatomi Indians by claiming their trust lands did not qualify as a formally designated reservation.[28] In fact, the state went so far as to argue that the Allotment Act and corresponding statutes intentionally eliminated all reservations in the state. Therefore, the Pottawatomi, and by extrapolating this logic, all tribes in what was originally Indian territory would have their reservations eliminated and thus, be conquered by the state of Oklahoma. If the tribes did not have a land base for governing as sovereign entities, then obviously the war was over and won by the non–Indians. Since there is no reservation or tribal sovereignty, the state was not preempting or infringing on any aspect of tribal government.[29]

The Supreme Court dismissed this disestablishment argument. The OTC countered by arguing that the Sac and Fox did not have a sufficient land base to coincide with the level of power the tribe was claiming. In other words, geographic size was going to determine what powers a tribal government was to hold and exercise. To apply this argument to a state or municipal government would be ludicrous and absurd, yet this is the stance the OTC decided to pursue. Furthermore, to compound this stance, the OTC pointed out that the Sac and Fox lands were noncontiguous and were, in fact, just scattered trust plots.[30]

The Navajo filed an amicus brief and pointed out that their reservation was similar in areas in that it was also noncontiguous. Yet, just like the Sac and Fox, the Navajo explained that they, too, were the main service providers in these areas, and that these areas were still exempt from state jurisdiction. The OTC countered that, once again, size does matter. The Navajo holdings were much larger compared to the Sac and Fox, so their arguments should be dismissed. However, the Court also pointed out a small point that the OTC failed to mention from the *Pottawatomi* decision, that this decision stressed that tribal immunity from state jurisdiction was a power arising from trust lands, and not just from a formal reservation.[31] Therefore, the number of acres held by the tribe is of no consequence. Furthermore, the Court stressed its concern that a state thought it could impose a tax on a tribe without the tribe's consent, and as a result, remained unconvinced it could.

The OTC argued that the state provided all of the essential services for an ordered society. Therefore, using a balancing analysis, this outweighed the claims made by the Sac and Fox.[32] Yet, the OTC conveniently ignored the fact that there are numerous tribes throughout North America that have small populations, small land bases and not enough resources to be self-sufficient. Even with these facts, these tribes do not simply cease to function and continue to exist as long as they have a government and are federally recognized as a tribe. In this case, the Sac and Fox had taken advantage of and participated in federal legislation to strengthen their self-determination and sovereignty.[33] Furthermore, the Sac and Fox tribal government did provide police protection, street maintenance and education (using federal funds) for both tribal members and non–Indians living on the reservation.[34]

The Supreme Court struck down the OTC and its position. In a unanimous decision, the Court ruled that the state had no jurisdiction to tax tribal members who lived and worked in Indian Country.[35] Since the Sac and Fox Reservation was not disestablished as the state claimed, this effectively eliminated the OTC claims. However, the Court delineated that non–Indians were subject to state taxes. Contemporary tribal life means that some members must live and work off reservation, and this does not diminish their status as American Indians or tribal members, nor does it mean that the reservation is diminished because they leave the reservation to earn a living as the OTC contended.[36]

Even though the Sac and Fox won this battle, the war wages on to eliminate Indian sovereignty and their Indian lands. As mentioned, the new line of attack by various state governments was, and still is, the disestablishment argument.

It is a well-established fact, and practice, that Congress has the plenary power to take unilateral action to disestablish an Indian reservation or end a treaty arrangement. However, the courts have usually required clear and plain evidence that such an action had indeed taken place. As more and more states become upset that there is land within their borders, Indian Country,[37] that they have little or no jurisdiction over, the attacks will increase. Within this statutorily defined Indian Country, only the tribes and federal government share jurisdiction. Without Congressional authority, states have no power in Indian Country. They do have jurisdiction over non–Indians only as long as it does not affect or interfere with Indian property and/or rights, federal Indian programs, or treaty rights to self-government.[38] Hence, the states have sought to diminish, or even eliminate altogether all vestiges of Indian Country.

States, under the guise of protecting their citizens, are usually just frustrated over the lack of power in commerce or taxation in Indian Country. They claim that Congress has disestablished or diminished the reservation lands through the allotment statutes in order to justify their, at times, innocuous actions. According to these claims, the Allotment Act not only opened up the Indian lands for settlement, but it also ended the jurisdictional boundaries of the reservation and tribal government.[39] Indian lands are now fair game for the states to move into and seek control.

In 1994, the Supreme Court considered another case over the diminishment of a tribe's reservation. It ruled that the Ute Indians' Uintah Valley Indian Reservation in Utah had in fact been diminished by virtue of legislation passed in 1905. The Court, in *Hagan v. Utah*,[40] determined that the United States Congress had diminished the reservation in an ambiguously stated act back in 1905. There was no clear language or evidence of intent usually required in such cases as these.[41]

The 1905 legislation provided that the tribal lands be allotted to individual tribal members with all unallotted surplus lands being opened to non–Indian settlement.[42] The purpose of the surplus acts was a social experiment in ethnic cleansing designed to eliminate the American Indian culture by forcing them to assimilate into the cultural mainstream. The overall scheme was to give each individual Indian land and then expect them to act "white" by encouraging, and if necessary, coercing them to adopt the ways of their white neighbors. This would also subject them to the same laws and jurisdictions as the white citizens, ending tribal culture, authority, identity, and sovereignty. There was no mention of cession or payment for taking these surplus lands from the tribe.

The Court found intent to diminish the tribe's lands even though there was no explicit language in the act to do this. Instead, the Court relied on an act passed three years prior in 1902 which stated that all unallotted lands within the reservation should be returned to the public domain.[43] Thus, the Court went back into history to the Surplus Act to find a basis for justifying this decision. The Court weakly argued that the 1905 Act was merely an amendment to the one passed in 1902.

The Court also was blind to the fact that the Ute Indians never consented, nor agreed to any cession or relinquishment of their rights or interests in the reservation lands. In fact, the Utes had sent two delegations to Washington, D.C., to protest the allotment acts.[44] Tribal resistance was given no weight at all in the decision; nor was the fact that no compensation was ever received even considered.

As if to prove its own ineptitude at understanding American Indian history, the Court used the racial and political composition of the area to support its conclusions.[45] To the Court, the mere presence of whites in the area was indicative of Congress' intent to diminish the reservation in 1905![46] Using this logic, every reservation in the United States would be diminished by the end of the day unless each tribe expressly banished whites from living on or near tribal lands. Furthermore, the purpose of the 1905 Act was to *bring in* whites to the area, so this argument used by the Court appears to be the last vestiges of a tautological justification that was built on a shaky foundation from the start.

"The *Hagan* decision is all the more troubling because the Court seemed to rely on subsequent demographics to a significantly greater degree than ever before, probably in order to compensate for the dearth of direct evidence supporting its conclusion of diminishment."[47] The Court simply allowed the cannons of construction and the law to be made elastic, and stretched their supporting logic to the breaking point.

The Supreme Court had, up until this point, essentially required that Indian laws, treaties and executive orders be "liberally construed, [with] doubtful expressions being resolved in favor of the Indians."[48] This position is rooted in the unique trust relationship between the federal government and tribal members.

The result of the *Hagan* case is that the Court has "wreaked both jurisprudential and practical havoc on the all-important issues of jurisdiction."[49] It has caused further questions of criminal and civil jurisdiction between the state of Utah and the Ute Tribe, which will most likely reappear in the courts over and over again.

State governments are not the only entities that have attempted to further diminish Indian tribes and the agreements made with them in the past. Cities and individuals have reneged on their agreements with tribes which has forced legal showdowns. The Seneca Tribe of the Haudenosaunee (Iroquois) Confederacy has had a lease agreement with non–Indians to permit the City of Salamanca, New York, its very existence.

The 1784 Treaty of Fort Stanwix ended the war between the Americans and the Haudenosaunee (Iroquois) Confederacy with huge land cessions being made to the newly formed United States.[50] A separate treaty was signed with the Seneca in 1794 after their protests, and secured their lands in New York State. However, this did not stop private interests or the state of New York from attempting to alienate the tribe from their lands further.[51]

Railroad companies began to lease rights-of-way and other land from the Seneca Nation in the mid–1800s.[52] Soon, white settlers and railroad workers occupied these leased lands and when the leases were expired, refused to leave. Hence, the City of Salamanca developed on these expired leased lands.

The New York courts declared the leases void because the federal government had not approved of them, but the state refused to allow the return of the land to the Seneca at the end of the leases. By pressuring Congress, the leases were federally approved in 1875 and again in 1890 which granted a non-negotiable ninety-nine-year lease at very favorable rates.[53] Rent was set as low as one dollar per year for some parcels. Even at this bargain, as of 1939, nearly 25 percent of the lessees were ignoring or simply refusing payment to the Seneca.[54]

In *United States v. Forness* (1939), the Seneca were victorious in getting court approval for the termination of delinquent leases for nonpayment. Despite efforts by the state, politicians and landholders to extinguish Seneca title to the land altogether, a new lease for 3,300 parties with guaranteed payments was negotiated and finalized. This lease was set to expire in 1991.

The Seneca announced two decades in advance that new leases would be at market value and the failure to renegotiate, or make payments would result in the land being confiscated along with any and all improvements made on it.[55] The state of New York authorized the Salamanca Indian Lease Authority to negotiate a new lease in 1969, and settled it in 1989. Congress ratified this agreement in 1990.

The new forty-year leases, renewable for forty more, were at market rates and compensated the Seneca Nation for losses incurred up until this point of time. The federal government paid $35 million and the state paid another $25 million, with $14 million of this being earmarked for economic and community development programs within the Seneca Nation.[56] There was also a $10 million escrow account established of which one-third of the income went into a joint Anglo-tribal economic development program. The settlement money can be used to purchase land near the reservation, and it will receive special restricted status. This will permit the expansion of the tribe's holdings. The Seneca have planned to use the funds for elder care, youth programs, education, and environmental and economic development programs.[57]

There was a small group of dissenters who refused to sign the new leases and insisted on a new ninety-nine-year lease instead. Their lawsuit was dismissed in 1990, in which the court held that the Seneca Nation had sovereign immunity from suit and was an indispensable party to claims against non–Indian defendants.[58] However, the city council which negotiated the settlement was replaced in the 1991 elections. The new city council tried to get the United States Congress to reopen the settlement, but failed to do so. Instead, they tried to declare the settlement void on their own volition and authority in 1992.[59]

The Seneca, in response, threatened to evict the dissenters and confiscate buildings and land. Banks held up mortgages and titles until the problem was solved, essentially freezing the local real estate market. The state compounded the problem by trying to tax tobacco and gasoline sold on the reservation.[60] Eventually, the arguments died out, mainly due to public opinion being on the Seneca Nation's side. As of now, the city is paying its rent, the escrow account has been created, and new officials who wish to work with and honor the agreement with the Seneca Nation have been elected to office.

The federal government must approve and ratify any agreements that involve the alienation of Indian property rights. As the Seneca-Salamanca agreement shows, the federal government will not do so unless the state and local governments have first ironed out the details and have agreed to a burden of the costs.

Despite the Seneca "victory" for the natives, sovereignty issues still fuel many battles between tribes and the various levels of government. Due to both Congressional and judicial lack in clear lawmaking and reasoning, tribal sovereignty is very close to being subordinated to the sovereignty of the states.[61] This subjugation, even obliteration of tribes, their culture and ways is being achieved through trial and error methods.[62] Yet, the federal government has repeatedly affirmed respect for the principle of sovereignty while attempting to subjugate the Indian, leading to a "chaotic juxtaposition of sovereignty and subjugation."[63] As the battles ensue, the Indian continues to resist the imposition of more power over them and their affairs.[64]

The Oneida Tribe of the Iroquois Confederacy had won a judgment in the United States Supreme Court in 1985 against the state of New York. This was the second court action against the state of New York by the Oneida Indian Nation. In the first, the Oneidas sought fair rental value for approximately 100,000 acres of land in Madison and Oneida counties which they claimed was illegally taken by the state. Although they lost in the lower courts, the Supreme Court did affirm the Oneida claim to the land and that their right of possession was conferred by federal law, which was supreme to state law and claims. In addition, the Oneida could show that the 1794 Fort Stanwix Treaty recognized their right of possession to the lands. The case was remanded back to District Court.[65]

The District Court concluded that the Fort Stanwix Treaty was never ratified, and that the conveyance of land was void because it had violated the 1790 Indian Trade and Intercourse Act which was passed to prevent states from stealing Indian lands.[66] The Supreme Court granted certiorari to decide whether or not a tribe could lay claims to lands after nearly two centuries. The Court affirmed this right under the fact that the Doctrine of Discovery first recognized Indian title to the lands.

In the second court action brought by the Oneida Indian Nation, the state was ordered to return or pay for over 270,000 acres of land it illegally bought in the late 1700s and early 1800s in violation of the 1790 Indian Trade and Intercourse Act. The Supreme Court dismissed the counties' and state's arguments that there was a statute of limitations for such actions.[67] Furthermore, the Court did not agree with the counties or the state in that the Oneida Nation had had their title extinguished by subsequent treaties, nor had Congress intended this to be the case. Hence, the counties were liable, as was the state.[68]

Oneida and state officials attempted to negotiate an agreement, but talks stagnated forcing the tribe in 1998–1999, with federal blessings, to add over 20,000 individual landowners to the lawsuit in hopes of getting the state to settle. The backlash against the tribe has been vicious. Threats of death to the Oneidas have been made, landowners have erected mock missiles aimed at the reservation, and charges and counter-charges of racism abound.

Non-Indian homeowners have blamed the United States government for abandoning them and siding with the Indians. One homeowner stated that he and the others named in the lawsuit "view this as an invasion of our lives, of our homes, our traditions, our culture, our government, our American sovereignty. It is an invasion."[69] The Oneida simply saw this as a means to an end—getting the New York State government to finally settle a United States Supreme Court decision against them that was almost 15 years old. An attorney for some of the homeowners in Madison and Oneida counties, John Ben Carroll, stated:

> I think that this is a shock that the United States government has sued for judgments against us. This whole thing is absolutely explosive. And there was nothing in the world that made them file that action against all these people, except greed and retribution.
> When anybody talks to them [the Oneidas] they talk about "Well, this is what happened to our people." Well, because something happened to my great-grandfather doesn't give me the right to go do it to somebody else.[70]

Another attorney for the homeowners echoed this lack of historical knowledge when he derided the Oneidas and their leadership by saying it is the "Oneidas who want all the tax breaks and federal aid, yet they want to live as one race, apart from their white and black neighbors. You can't be separate and call yourselves equal. That's racism."[71] This shows a failure to understand Indian history, culture, land claims, and tribal sovereignty and a failure to grasp the very definition of cultural identity and racism. Rather than getting the state to settle, they have attacked the rightful heirs to the land, the Oneida Indians. Of course, the Oneidas are going to tell of how their ancestors were displaced illegally, for this is historical fact.

In April 2000, the settlement talks broke down. County officials blamed the Oneida Nation for the impasse. They have stated that the Oneida refused to lower their land acquisition claims, and the fact that the land would be property tax exempt (since it would become part of the reservation) was simply unacceptable.[72] Therefore, the argument was heading back to court even though the U.S. Supreme Court had already ruled that over 250,000 acres were illegally taken by the state back in the eighteenth century.

The county claims are unreasonable and unfounded. The Oneida had already agreed to set up a $25 million trust fund of state and federal monies to offset any property tax losses for the counties. Furthermore, they agreed to charge the same sales tax as the counties to offset unfair competition claims, and agreed to pay $1 million a year for 20 years to assist the communities impacted by the Oneida's business enterprises. They also agreed to limit and slow their land acquisition—to only 5,000 acres in the first 10 years, only up to 30,000 in the first 50 years and only up to another 10,000 acres after that.[73] The counties and the state of New York found this to be unreasonable. The state insisted on almost all gaming profits from the tribe in exchange for the settlement.[74] Never mind that they illegally took over 250,000 acres to start with, they want their money and land now too. The doctrine of conquest seems to be holding up in this case, supported by unreasonableness and greed.

This war of attrition has meant that the "inherent powers of the Native nations have been steadily and gradually reduced."[75] American Indian sovereignty and property rights have eroded over the last two centuries of American rule. While they are whittling away at the powers and rights of Indian tribes and individuals, the government keeps claiming respect for the basic principles of American Indian sovereignty.[76] Sovereignty is an issue of balance between independent nations. States especially see any tribal sovereignty as a threat to their power base, i.e., revenue sources.

To summarize, this onslaught over sovereignty, Steven Paul McSloy stated:

> For the greater part of American history, Indians have been explicitly excluded from any participation; as individuals or as groups, in any aspect of the national political process. This was not a denial of their rights, but rather a recognition of their status as separate sovereigns under international law.... Recognizing Indian sovereignty is not a matter of civil rights, equal protection or due process, nor is it a matter of privileges and immunities or the protection of discrete and insular minorities in a domestic sphere. It is instead a matter of international law and of limiting the authority of the United States to those powers that its founding charter recognizes and allows. The Framers declared that Native peoples were not citizens, and they did not intend them to become so except upon complete abandonment of their "Indian" character. Even such abandonment did not serve to make them citizens in the eyes of the Supreme Court. The Framers did not view Indian Nations as states of the Union, and despite stray promises over the years, they did not intend that Indian statehood would come to pass.[77]

The Future of Tribal Sovereignty

"The argument that Indian people are homogenized within a generalized citizenship, without distinctions warranting state recognition, is not unusual among states that have indigenous peoples within their boundaries."[78] Yet, this could not be further from the truth or from the dilemmas faced by the contemporary Indian. There are decisions that have to be made regarding the retention of tribal culture, community and identity that other ethnic groups are not forced to face. Among these decisions are: (1) determining the advantages and disadvantages of their distinctive political status; (2) dealing with their unique identity, benefits and drawbacks which tribal status confers on them; and (3) understanding and operating under a multi-governmental situation—tribal, local, state and federal.[79]

Sovereignty, the inherent right of self-government and self-determination, is the focal point of all Indian issues. These rights have been promised and guaranteed numerous times through legislation and judicial rulings. The 1975 Indian Self Determination Act[80] shifted authority to administer education, health, construction and other programs and services on the reservation to tribal governments which could only be achieved if the tribes were and are considered sovereign entities. This shift has continued in bits and pieces. Congress has enacted legislation giving tribes authority over education, health, child welfare and gambling.[81] The Indian Gaming Regulatory Act (1988) was passed in particular to promote tribal economic development, tribal self-sufficiency and strong tribal governments.[82] Yet, as we have seen, what Congress gives to the Indians, the courts find a way to take away.

The 1977 American Indian Policy Review Commission determined that Indian tribes are sovereign, with the power to determine their own membership and enact their own laws. In fact, the Commission determined that the concept of sovereignty is based in international law and is imperative for the federal-tribal trust relationship to continue.[83]

However, even the Commission had its dissenting opinions. The vice-chair, Representative Lloyd Meeks, condemned the report as "one sided Indian advocacy" rather than an examination of law.[84] He claimed that the fundamental error of the report is that it considered the American Indian tribe a body politic in the same nature and level as the United States and its individual states. Thus, the Commission failed to realize that the federal government *permits* the Indian tribes to govern themselves, but not the affairs of others.[85]

The Commission, according to Meeks, turned a political notion into a legal one. He stated that there is no theoretical basis for the assertion of inherent tribal sovereignty. "It would mean that whenever there is a group of American Indians living together on land which was allocated to them by the Federal Government, they would have the power to exercise general government powers. The source of those powers would then be some magical combination of their Indianness and their ownership of land. Governmental powers do not have as their source magic. Tribes govern themselves under federal power, and like federal power, their powers are specifically limited."[86]

Indian leaders speak of the sacredness of tribal sovereignty as if its meaning and interpretation were incontrovertible and self-evident. Obviously, this is not the case. They would argue, and correctly so, that just because the United States has unilaterally restricted their self-government powers, this does not mean that their nations lack the right and power to exercise full self-government.[87] For tribal sovereignty to be meaningful, Indian nations must be recognized as the sole governing authority inside their respective boundaries. If not, then the current jurisdictional chaos will continue with the ultimate victim being the tribe's government, culture, and identity.

"Although the principle of tribal sovereignty rests on the premise that modern tribes are the direct continuation of nations that predate the founding of the United States, the governments of all but a few are wholly a twentieth-century invention."[88] The federal government created these governments under the Indian Reorganization Act so it could deal with the tribes on some level of parity. Yet today, like the mad scientist that can no longer control the monster he has created, the federal government wants to deny this parity and revoke its promises and efforts at creating sovereign tribal governments. However, "political sovereignty and cultural sovereignty are linked inextricably, because the ultimate goal of political sovereignty is the protecting of a way of life."[89] And this way of life will never die in battle.

Despite the onslaught of attacks on Indian tribal sovereignty, the federal government has contradicted itself in this regard and has contributed to the legal, political, social and economic confusion over sovereignty and self-determination. The government has treated and affirmed Indian tribes as sovereign even while it battles to assimilate and subjugate them. While much of the discussion thus far has been concerning the attacks on sovereignty, it is fairly simple to point out how the federal government has affirmed tribal identity and sovereignty throughout its history. First, the United States has had a long history of treaty making with American Indian tribes. A nation does not make and enter into a treaty with its own citizens. Therefore, it can be safely assumed that a treaty is an agreement between two sovereign nations, and while the United States government may like to forget this part of its past, it did at one time consider Indian nations as independent and sovereign.

Second, the United States, both at the federal and state level, had initially refused to recognize American Indians as citizens, thus affirming that they were from a separate nation.[90] In fact, several states used this argument in order to deny resident Indians within their boundaries the right to vote. Even though there was a 3/5's Compromise regarding slaves, the only mention of Indians made in the Constitution is "Indians not taxed" in order to keep them from being counted in the census.[91] Yet, Indian nations have acted as independent and sovereign entities despite being ignored by the Constitution. In fact, the Haudensaunee proclaimed a separate declaration of war in World Wars I and II which demonstrates actions consistent with a sovereign nation.

The courts have given a third support to the fact that the government has respected the sovereignty of Indian nations. It has made decisions explaining that the Bill of Rights do not apply to Indian nations in the governing of their own peoples (hence implying a separateness); have upheld a tribe's right to choose and set their own membership and/or citizenship criteria (as a sovereign and independent nation would); and has permitted a combination of church and state. This clearly shows that the judiciary distinguishes between the American and Native nations.[92]

Finally, Indian nations have a long history of self-government.[93] Many Indian nations' governments have existed continuously centuries longer than the United States government. Just because the 1934 Indian Reorganization Act created governments similar in form to the ideal that the federal government wanted, this did not eliminate the fact that tribes have been governed for centuries before this. Indian governments have the powers of civil and criminal jurisdiction, taxation, environmental protection and a myriad of other regulatory duties.

Yet, while these practices and doctrines seem to support a federal acceptance of Indian sovereignty, as has been shown, there are corresponding attacks on this sovereignty at the same time. Congress voids American Indian laws and treaties with its plenary powers, while it also passes legislation to increase tribal self-sufficiency and determination. The Supreme Court chisels away at one side of sovereignty while patching up the other.[94] Overall, the result is a chaotic mixture of laws, acts and regulations that permit attacks on the very essence of Indian survival—sovereignty.

As has been demonstrated by the evidence, "opportunistic states thrive upon the uncertainty created when the federal government, acting in its self-prescribed role as national policy maker and trustee, fails to set clear limits on state power."[95] The states have become like vultures circling the reservations because of the federal government's failure to fulfill its promises to the first Americans. It is clear that there may be a conflict between the federal government's role as maker of policy regarding tribal sovereignty and economic self-sufficiency, and its role as trustee as derived from the Cherokee cases. It is not clear, though, that the federal government can handle both of these roles at once and in a fair manner.

The federal role of trustee makes it the protector of tribal sovereignty and lands. It is a role stemming from the guardian-ward relationship created nearly two centuries ago by Justice Marshall. Therefore, as protector, it is the federal government's duty to step in and side with the tribes in their battles against state encroachments. "Federal vacillation and equivocation about its dual roles aid the states who aggressively encroach upon tribal lands and undermine the authority of tribes to govern over the people, and events within their territory."[96] "The approaches used by Oklahoma, Alaska and other states only continue a historical pattern begun after the *Cherokee* and *Worcester* case, both the state and federal governments have failed to set clear boundaries on the reach of state power."[97]

Whereas the focus of this work has revolved around numerous facets of sovereignty, both tribal and individual, it would be remiss if Indian Boarding Schools escaped even a brief discussion. Volumes have been written on the history and ongoing effects of this abomination in the history of the American Indian peoples, so this work will not even attempt to duplicate these gallant efforts. Instead, just a brief overview will suffice as it will lead to the latest challenge to Indian sovereignty.

At one time, there were 357 American Indian Boarding Schools, mildly known as Indian Residential Schools, located throughout 30 states. Oklahoma, home to those tribes removed during the 1830s, led in numbers, closely followed by Arizona, Alaska, New Mexico and South Dakota. Most of these schools were headed and operated by several different religious groups, with the predominant number being operated by the Catholic Church. As of this writing, some 64 schools are still open and operating.[98]

Overall, the primary purposes of the boarding schools were twofold: to eliminate the Indian race and culture through forced assimilation of its children, and to Christianize the Indian children attending these schools. A secondary goal was the expectation that when the children left the school and went home, they would carry on the indoctrination and socialization that they had received at the school and would spread the effects onto the tribe as a whole and help "civilize" them. In other words, it was to make the American Indian more acceptable to the White European's Judeo-Christian beliefs and value systems.

Probably the most well-known school was at Carlisle, Pennsylvania. It was opened in 1879 by Captain Richard Henry Pratt, who practiced his techniques on captive Apache Indians in Florida, and coined the now infamous motto: "kill the Indian, and save the man."[99] When the child arrived at the school, all vestiges of their previous culture were quickly eradicated. Boys had to cut their hair, native languages were forbidden, they were given "white" names, and traditional songs, dress, foods, and religions were summarily banned. In other words, previous identities were erased and new ones that were more acceptable to American mainstream society created. Conversion to Christianity was a requirement. The children did receive traditional education, but the boys spent more time learning industrial arts and the girls, domestic skills.

The model included having the children produce goods that could be sold in the marketplace or to take in washing, all with the purpose of continuing to support the school. Additionally, the children would be loaned out to local residents purportedly to learn new job skills, but in reality they often became a source of cheap or even free labor.[100]

By the 1880s, the U.S. government itself was operating 60 similar schools utilizing this militaristic model and held over 6,200 Native children, in addition to the schools operated by the various religious orders. One estimate holds that by 1900, the schools were assimilating and indoctrinating nearly 20,000 children and the number would reach 61,000 by 1925,[101] and this number would remain somewhat consistent even into the early 1970s.

Reform to the system began in 1928 when the Merriam Report was presented to the U.S. Congress. The report noted the horrible conditions at the schools, the diseases, harsh living conditions, the lack of proper clothing and food, the lack of medical services and the unqualified teaching staffs.[102] Since many of these schools were now being operated by the government or its contractors, responsibility could not be avoided. To compound the problem, compulsory education rules required parents to send their children to school, but the entrenched racism of many local school systems often meant that parents had little option but to send their children to a boarding school or face sanctions from government agents. Parents were faced with sending their children away to school, sometimes even hundreds of miles away and not seeing them for years, and knowing at the same time they were giving their children a chance to survive in the "white world."[103]

The boarding school system became abused by social workers, government officials, missionaries and at times, tribal members themselves. Children were removed from their families for questionable reasons such as the family's poverty status, the fact that the parents did not speak English, or simply to meet some quota established by the area's school.

As a direct result to the horrors and traumas of removing children from their homes and tribes and sending them to boarding schools, the Indian Child Welfare Act was passed in 1978. It was a reaction to the obviously racist efforts to assimilate and indoctrinate Native children to make them non–Indian at the least, or white at the most. Although the act did not specifically focus on boarding schools, the act did address the issue of Native children being removed and placed in foster care or adoptions in extraordinary numbers compared to other minorities and for some dubious reasons. From 1969 to 1974, nearly one-third of Native children were in state care and 85 percent ended up in a non–Native home.[104] Therefore, in a nutshell, ICWA was enacted to keep Native children with their families, in their communities and their tribes.

The law gives preference to American Indian families when it comes to issues of foster care or adoption of an Indian child. The tribe must be notified when a need is present for the child to be placed elsewhere, and the tribe is given the opportunity to place the child in his/her extended family so as to maintain their community and cultural ties.[105] Exceptions for good cause are permitted. Congress had simply concluded the obvious: that Native children were being taken from their families, tribes and culture because state and local officials were incapable or unwilling to understand tribal cultures and societies.[106]

In October of 2018, ICWA was challenged over the adoption of a young Indian child, and if the lower court ruling is upheld by higher courts, it will dramatically change tribal sovereignty. In *Brackeen v. Zinke*, the District Court for the Northern District of Texas, the judge, in spite of the U.S. Constitution, Congressional intentions, and decades of well-established federal Indian law ruled ICWA unconstitutional.[107] The law is supported by 325 tribes, 21 states (except Texas, Louisiana and Indiana), 31 children's organizations as well as members of Congress, academicians and numerous others. The plaintiff's argument, which the judge supported, was that the law is unconstitutional because it is race based, and thus violated the equal protection clause.[108]

Tribes have countered that this ruling goes against the very essence of tribal sovereignty and is not race based since tribes are sovereign nations that work with the U.S. on a nation-to-nation basis. If the ruling stands, it will make tribes a racial entity and erode their status as sovereign governments, with repercussions well beyond the ICWA. The tribes point out the history of removal and state that ICWA's opponents "paternalistically contend they know what is better than Indian families and tribes what is best for their children."[109] They fail to understand the intricacies of the extended family in the Indian culture and the importance of culture to the self-identity and well-being of the child. Plaintiffs argue that ICWA subordinates what is best for the child in favor of the assumption that remaining in the tribe and community is best. In the appeal to the 5th Circuit, remarks made by the judges' panel were mixed, but tended to agree that ICWA protects the culture of the tribe through its children ad that the children do belong to the tribe.[110] For now, no clear path has been decided, but the battle will obviously continue. Tribes are a lot more than mere racial identities, and their sovereignty needs to be protected from challenges, while protecting the most valuable asset to any community and culture, their children.

Realizing Sacredness?

That the federal government's duty is to protect sacred sites cannot be really questioned. "It is both lawful and righteous for [it] to remove the barriers to free exercise of Native traditional religions and take the remedial actions to protect sacred places that can be protected."[111] Whereas in the past, many efforts were specifically targeting a certain site and done through executive orders or legislation, efforts are now taking shape to make the protection of these sacred areas more general and stringent.

The BIA hosted hearings throughout the year 2002 to discuss harsher sentencing guidelines for the desecration of a "cultural heritage resource."[112] The U.S. Congress has also tried to put some teeth into the AIRFA (1978) so actions can be taken to stop the destruction of a sacred site. At the same time, there have been calls for a pan-tribal effort to define and educate as to what exactly entails a sacred site and what makes it so.

Yet, some tribal leaders have been justly skeptical. They have supported the stronger guidelines but worry about prodding the government into protecting their sacred sites. Since many sites are secret, asking for assistance to stop a site's desecration or destruction may have the detrimental side effects of increasing publicity and this may cause unwanted visitors and vandalism.[113] From black marketeers in ancient Indian artifacts to Indian haters to New Agers who think they understand and deserve special access to Indian spirituality and sacredness, to the curious tourist, seeking public awareness for protection of these sites means revealing their presence and meaning and can open up the proverbial Catch-22. Seeking help to stop the desecration may only open the door for more of the same.

However, unlike many in the United States who can go and explore the "old country" to glimpse their heritage, American Indians cannot do the same. The petroglyphs, rock carvings, springs, caves, forests, and sacred sites are the Indian's heritage and are in this country. As such, they must be protected for the future of the peoples, as Europeans and others around the world, protect their own sacred places.

Whether Congress, the President or some federal or state agency can help stay the progress of desecration remains to be seen. Yet, it is the court system where the battle continues. It is unfortunate that "as a rule of thumb, when a decision is good for the Indians, it's usually interpreted as a single-issue ruling [and] when it's bad, it gets applied to every Indian."[114]

Sovereign Solutions

There is not an easy solution to this multi-faceted crisis facing Indian nations. It will depend more on a change in attitudes and thought than any single piece of legislation or policy doctrine. Federal Indian law will have to be decolonized, freed from the ideas like plenary power which only legitimizes and maintains majority force and coercion over the Indian nations.[115]

Federal Indian law must be put forth in a clear and definitive manner and enforced in a consistent way.

The Indian nations need to be treated as nations with all of the inherent rights and responsibilities due to them. Allowing self-determination to be just what it means, and not placing limits on it, will be a huge step in respecting the sovereignty and property of American Indians. Since geography is becoming an issue, a simple solution to many of the disputes would be for the United States to return all lands not freely given in fair and legal treaties.[116] At the same time, treaty commitments regarding land, compensation, sovereignty, jurisdiction and noninterference should also be respected. This is nothing more than any nation in the world would expect from its neighbors or fellow members of some alliance organization.

Finally, the United States will have to undo the imperialism resulting from the Manifest Destiny era and return to the Framers' respect for the Indian as independent nations, sovereign entities with international status.[117] This principle is nothing more than what Justice Marshall originally established and means that by logical consequence, every law passed and case decided about American Indians would probably be invalid due to the conflict with inherent and recognized sovereignty of American Indian nations.[118]

If this pattern of thought were adopted, then the American Indian nations would be able to fulfill their destinies of self-determination, economic self-sufficiency, and hopefully promote more tribal-state-local governmental cooperation.[119] Paternalistic policies thrust upon the various Indian nations needs to end. Indian nations suffer from poverty, pollution, illnesses and addictions, not because it is in their nature, but because their culture, their pride and their future have been replaced by one of dependency and despair. Given the proper opportunities, the first Americans can be a part of the nation that they helped create. True self-determination will require a federal-state-tribal cooperation that has yet to be truly in place. The control of one's resources is the key to self-determination, and the tribes must be willing to take on the duties and responsibilities of managing their environments in the soundest manner possible. Succumbing to the offers of money from corporations or governments is not the solution, nor is the solution to simply ignore the possibility of using their resources in a proper and ecological manner. A balance must be found.

The interdependence between the Indian peoples and their environments has been broken, and the mending may never occur. Control of this environment, tempered with the inherent respect that the native cultures had for Mother Earth and its forces, may be the only answer for bringing the balance and harmony back that we all seek.

Final Thoughts

"No person among us desires any other reward for performing a brave and worthy action, but the consciousness of having served his nation."[1]
—THAYENDANEGA (JOSEPH BRANT), MOHAWK IROQUOIS

In the preceding chapters, an exploration was undertaken of the numerous doctrines and maneuvers used to justify the taking of American Indian property, and as a result of the process, attempts to destroy their sovereignty and culture. After nearly 600 years of continual battles, it is a wonder that American Indians have persevered and survived as a people. However, their survival has not been without costs. Rather than simply summarizing the many points this work has reviewed and stressed, this chapter will espouse some final thoughts and ideas regarding the plight of the American Indian.

Of all the doctrines, theories, laws, legislation and decisions that have been covered, one reason for the attack on American Indians has been ignored in the various discussions until now. That reason is racism. The racism against the Indian has been well documented, and it is not the purpose of this chapter to set off on a broad sociological and psychological essay about the causes and instances of racism toward the Indian peoples. Instead, the aftermath, the effects of the centuries of racism can be summarized, especially as they pertain to the loss of property, culture and sovereignty. It is amazing that even to this day, most non–Indians do not know how to relate to living Indians.[2] Although it is simply pure racism, others have called the attitudes and actions taken toward the Indian genocide. Genocide is nothing but a "new word for an old tragedy, which can be defined simply as the deliberate, systematic destruction of a racial, political or cultural group."[3] Nowadays, it may be more appropriately called ethnic cleansing. However, whereas this term is used all over the world to describe horrific events and policies, no one wants to apply it to what was, and still is, being done to the American Indian peoples.

167

The genocide of the American Indian peoples began with the first explorers of the North American continent and continues to this day. From when Ponce de Leon first ventured onto the mainland in 1513, until the 1900s, approximately 99 percent of the indigenous population was eradicated.[4] Estimates vary, but scholars believe there were approximately 18.5 million Indians before the first Europeans arrived, and by the 1890s, this number had dropped to 237,000.[5] Arguments that the number of native peoples was not this high is usually due to an effort to minimize the effects of genocide on the peoples. It also gave justification to the idea that the land was wide open, just waiting for settlers and civilization. "After minimization, the most common mode of denying that genocide was perpetuated against the indigenous peoples of North America is what is referred to as the disease factor."[6]

No one can deny that disease did decimate large portions of the native population. While some was unintentional, there are numerous examples of deliberate germ warfare being perpetuated against various tribes.[7] Of course, the third part of genocide, and the part that most people equate with the term, is the direct murder of a people. The exact numbers killed through this process is almost impossible to determine, but the deaths began with Columbus and continued through the 1890s.

Whichever term is applied, the overall effect is appalling. American Indians continue to be the most poverty stricken and economically deprived segment of our population, a people whose plight dwarfs the situation of any other Americans, even those in the worst big city ghettos.[8] The efforts of the European settlers to remove and contain the Indians have had lingering consequences beyond nearly annihilating an entire race of people. So, by 1891, the American Indian population had been decimated to about 2.5 percent of its original size, and they had lost about 97.5 percent of their original land base.[9] The "fragments of geography left to the Indians by 1900 were considered worthless, unfavorable, arid patches of dust deemed remote enough to allow for the steady die-off of survivors, conveniently out of sight and mind of the dominant society. And there were, of course, federal policies designed to help the process along."[10]

The destruction of the American Indian continues, albeit in a more subtle manner than a massacre or battle. Due to the horrendous conditions of the reservations, the devastation of the loss of traditions and cultures, and the overall feeling of being conquered, the Indian could easily succumb, surrender and die. However, the Indian survives. The centuries of genocide have failed to completely erase their presence.

American Indians have undergone centuries of genocide—both formal and informal. Formal genocide consists of policies, programs and military efforts to end the sovereignty and existence of the people. Informal genocide can be subtler, consisting of media assaults like movies and books, infiltration of tribal religions and cultures by non-natives, and an educational system geared to dehumanize and trivialize the Indian peoples, their history and lives.

Therefore, only one conclusion can be reached. This is genocide. As Ward Churchill describes, genocide is any policy that is undertaken with the intention of bringing about the dissolution and ultimate disappearance of a targeted human group.[11] Genocide is much more than instances of mass murder, although history has more than enough examples of massacres of Indians from the time of Columbus onwards to the so-called Indian Wars of the late 1800s.[12] However, there are cultural dimensions to genocide also.

The objectives of cultural genocide would be the disintegration of the political, social, economic, cultural, linguistic, and religious aspects of the targeted group and, in essence, the very national feelings of the group destroyed.[13] American Indians have certainly experienced these assaults.

The cultural genocide of the American Indian has also included the forced removal, transfer and indoctrination of their children to a variety of boarding schools where their native languages, religions, dress, physical appearance, names and their very identities were destroyed all in the name of assimilation and civilization.[14] This was simply a program of education for the purpose of extinction.[15] In fact, up to the mid–1970s, up to 40 percent of native women were sterilized, often without their full understanding, knowledge or permission.[16] In addition, objects of historical, artistic and religious value have been destroyed, hidden away in museums, made into mere curiosities or even worse, commercialized by non-natives cheapening their original meanings and values.

Even though the total genocide of the American Indian peoples has not been successful, and although direct causality may be debated, the facts and figures remain clear: American Indians have suffered and are suffering more than any ethnic group in the United States. These are summarized in Charts A, B, and C. As can be observed, American Indians now suffer from among the highest rates of homicide, suicide, addictions, and disease among all American ethnic groups which is just one result of the long history of genocide against them. Among Indians, the tuberculosis rate is nearly 600 percent above the national average; the strep infection rate, 1,000 percent above the national average; meningitis cases, 2,000 percent above the national average; dysentery, 10,000 percent above; deaths from influenza and pneumonia over 300 percent above the national average; and, the venereal disease death rate is 500 percent above the national average.[17]

The maternal mortality rate is 11 per 100,000 live births and is 40 percent above the United States average.[18] The infant mortality rate is 11 per 1000, while the post-neonatal death rate is 40 percent higher among American Indians.

To compound these depressing figures, the homicide rate among Indians

Chart A

	United States	American Indian/ Alaska Native (AIAN)
Population (2004)	285,691,501	4,006,160 (1.4% of total)
Educational Attainment		
Less than High School	12% (2011)	0.9%
High School	88%	31.8%
Some College	59%	33.2%
Four Year Degree	32%	9.3%
Graduate/Professional	12%	4.8%
Median Income	$48,800 (2007)	$31,600
Poverty Rates		
Living Below Rate	9%	25%
Children Living in Poverty	11%	31%
Unemployment Rate	4.3% (2017)	12%
No Health Insurance	13.4%	29.2% (2014)
Need Drug/Alcohol Treatment	9.3% (2017)	17.5%
Family Status		
Single Parent Family	25% White	52%
66% African-American		
Unmarried Births	20%	29.2% (2014)
Unplanned Pregnancy	42.5% (2007)	59%

SOURCE: Data gathered from: U.S. Census Bureau. "American Fact Finder—Selected Population Profile in the U.S. 2015 American Community Survey"; Annie E. Casey Foundation, Kids Count Data Center, "Children In Single-Parent Families by Race," January 2017; SAMHSA, "Need for and Receipt of Substance Use Treatment Among American Indians or Alaskan Natives", *The NSDUH Report*, November 2012; The National Campaign to Prevent Teen and Unplanned Pregnancy; "American Indian/ Alaska Native Youth and Teen Pregnancy Prevention," *Science Says* 39, Brief, No. 39, August 2008.

Chart B

	United States	AIAN Community
No Electricity	1.0% (2017)	14%
No Running Water	1.0%	20%
No Sewer Service	1.0%	18%
No Telephone Service	5.0%	53.4%
Homeless Rate	0.5%	10.0%
Overall Poverty Rate	15.3%	
On Reservation		28.4%
On/Off Reservation Combined		22.0%

Chart C

Deaths/Diseases (per 100,000)	United States	AIAN Community
Diabetes Rates	21	63.6
Heart Disease Rates	11.8	14.7
Respiratory Diseases	42.7	47.2
Alcohol Deaths	7.4	51.9
Drug Deaths	12.6	23.9
Suicide Deaths	11.8	20.2
Homicide Deaths	5.5	11.6
Victim of Assault Rate	323.6	600.2
Victim of Domestic Violence	25%	56.1%

SOURCE: Data gathered from: Barnes, Patricia M. and Patricia F. Adams, Eve Powell-Griner. "Health Characteristics of American Indian or Alaska Native Adult Population: United States, 2004–2008," National Health Statistics Report No. 20, U.S. Department of Health and Human Services, Center for Disease Control and Prevention, No. 20, 9 March 2010. https://www.ncbi.nlm.nih.gov/pubmed/20583451; Center for Native American Youth, The Aspen Institute, "Fast Facts: Native American Youth and Indian Country", April 2014, https://aspeninstitute.org/.../Native%20 Youth%20Fast%20Update_04-2014; Indian Health Service. "Indian Health Disparities," April 2017, https://www.ihs.gov/newsroom/factsheets/disparities; Suicide Prevention Resource Center (SPRC), "Suicide Among Racial/Ethnic Populations in the U.S. American Indians/Alaska Natives," http://www.sprc.org/sites/default/files/ migrate/library/Ai_AN%20sheet%20Aug%2028%202013%20Final.pdf.

is nearly double that of non–Indians.[19] The suicide rate is anywhere from 1,000 to 10,000 percent above the national average depending on the age group and geographical location.[20] Deaths from alcoholism is six times (514 percent) higher than the national average.[21] Accidental deaths are 11.7 percent higher than the American average and vehicle crashes are 229 percent higher.[22] The amount of violence, domestic and other, is well above the average for any ethnic group in America.

In addition to this deplorable condition of Indian life, the dropout rate among Indian high school students ranks between 50 and 60 percent, while nationally it is closer to 20 percent.[23] Only 63 percent of Indians even have a high school education.[24] The average unemployment rate on the reservation is 25.6 percent, but on some reservations is as high as 80 percent.[25] Over one in four Indian families lives below the poverty level while the median income of Indian families is 16 percent lower than the national average.[26] The median household income for the American Indian population was $19,900, while the national median is $30,056, but both of these figures have increased over the past decade. Approximately 27 percent of Indian families or 31.2 percent of the population, or translated into numbers, 585,273 Indian people live in poverty compared to 10 percent of families in the non–Indian population.[27] Nearly 20 to 30 percent of reservation housing lacks electricity and/or plumbing, while one estimate states that 59 percent of Indian housing is substandard.[28]

The source for these problems is the loss of culture that genocide has caused. This is the primary effect of the internal colonialism that the newcomers have impressed upon the Indian peoples. As Robert Bachman stated, internal colonialism against the Indian can be typified by a history of brutalization, exploitation, segregation, expulsion and for some tribes, annihilation.[29] This has resulted in a policy of containment toward the Indian. The internal colonialism has contributed to the breakdown of social controls that used to exist in the Indian society. In connection to this, when one adds the economic deprivation and substance abuse suffered by the American Indian, the obvious result becomes poverty, disease, despair and death.

Those tribes with a higher level of community control have a lower rate of suicide and other social issues. This includes those communities with cultural continuity which includes an infrastructure, cultural facilities and sovereignty along with self-government.[30] In other words, those groups with better cultural identification, a more traditional way of life with family, religious and spiritual means to cope with stress were better prepared to face today's world.[31]

The "attempts to eliminate American Indian/Alaska Native (AIAN) culture—such as forced relocation, removal of children who were sent to boarding schools, prohibition of the practice of native language and cultural traditions, and outlawing traditional religious practices—have affected multiple generations of AIAN peoples and contribute to high rates of suicide among them."[32] And assimilation is not the answer since studies of Natives trying to adapt to the white culture reported more stress, less happiness, lower self-esteem, higher rates of depression and more substance abuse due to having to cope with being stuck between two worlds, belonging totally to neither one.[33]

The alienation of culture is paramount and seemingly insurmountable. The Indian peoples have lost their customs, traditions and sacredness to the continual usurpations leveled against them. The problems described are not because the Indian is an inferior race, but because their culture with its norms, morals, traditions and social controls has been banned, condemned, stolen or simply ignored and forgotten. The American public romanticizes over their image of the Indian, but the Indian peoples are a contemporary people with contemporary problems, and are seeking solutions in both their past and present. Traditions, customs and spirituality are the very linkages from the past that must be examined to help solve our present ills and prevent the problems from occurring in the future. The problems are the result of the incessant paternalism exercised by the government toward a people it has considered inferior and conquered for decades.[34]

To demonstrate this, in 1876 the U.S. Supreme Court ruled that the 1834 Trade and Intercourse Act did not apply to the Pueblo Indians since they were "peaceable, industrious, intelligent and honest.... Indians in feature, complexion and a few of their habits," but since they were not like other Indians, they were not subject to the same restrictive laws. Yet, in 1913, the Court overruled a lower court in its allowing the sale of liquor to the Pueblo Indians because the Pueblo Indians "are Indians in race, customs, and domestic government ... adhering to primitive modes of life, largely influenced by superstition, and chiefly governed according to the crude customs inherited from their ancestors, they are essentially a simple, uninformed and inferior people." Are not all Americans following the government of their ancestors when they refer to the United States Constitution? To further the argument, in 1922, the head of Indian Services Charles Henry Burke became dedicated to changing all Indian beliefs through education and force. He banned native dances because they "still had enough evil tendencies to furnish a retarding influence and at times a troublesome situation which calls for careful consideration and right-minded efforts."[35]

This ethnic cleansing of a conquered and forgotten people continues from non-governmental sources as well. The latest fashion and cultural fad is "Indian"—in decorating, jewelry, spirituality and ceremonies. "New Agers" easily appropriate Indian spirituality, modifying it to fit their needs and then portray themselves as Indian ceremonial experts writing books, creating web sites on the Internet where they espouse "Indian" teachings infused with New Age mysticism and reveal so-called "Indian" secrets, and even forming "tribes" for their followers while declaring themselves "chief."[36] This theft of cultural property is just another example of racism and another phase of the ethnic cleansing in that the distinct cultural boundaries are being blurred. No one is sure who is legitimate anymore. If non–Indians stole from other ethnic groups, it would be labeled as blatant racism, but if they steal from a conquered people, it is called the freedom of religion.

To this very day, as DeLoria has stated, dealing with the living Indian is a conundrum for many Americans. It is easier to learn from so-called experts on Indians than from the Indian people themselves. It may be that this helps avoid seeing the history and results of racism in the eyes of the Indian. The stereotypes of a horse-riding, tepee-living, feather-wearing Indian still abound in many imaginations and wishful thoughts. As Vine Deloria stated, "the general attitude of the whites [is] that they are the true spiritual descendants of the original Indians and the contemporary Indians are foreigners who have no right to complain about their activities,[37] no matter how disgusting or ignorant they may be. Today, Indians have to war against these conceptions of them by others as much as anything else. This means they have to continually protect their cultural sovereignty.

There has been a new eagerness to incorporate the American Indian in a positive way into the national narrative and image. The Indian is a defeated enemy, but fought well as warriors, were loyal and had some virtues that deserve some place in this new revised version of the national character.[38] They have been used to show that the United States has an ancient heritage and is not just a land of immigrants.[39] However, the Indian has not really actively sought to be included in the new dominant society, but instead this role has been imposed upon them through centuries of forced assimilation and genocide.[40] So the dichotomy that now exists has created serious repercussions and tensions. Whites see the Indian as noble savages and warriors, or sexy and obliging maidens,[41] where the Indian sees the Whites as conquerors, eradicating their culture, sovereignty, their very lives.

Businesses and sports teams can use American Indian symbols as logos, promotions and product names. If a sports team were to name itself after the African American, Jewish, Caucasian or other race, or use some derogatory racial slang term for them as their team name, riots would surely ensue. Yet, people easily dismiss any furor over the use of Indian names, or even the use of "Indian" itself, racial slurs, sacred images, or racial caricatures as a mere nuisance with the protestor being too sensitive. To be honest, as one person stated to the author, if Indians get upset over these matters, they are being selfish for taking away the material for some good jokes and fun from everyone.

There are those who continue these myths and misinterpretations about the American Indian out of innocence, such as a child. The child who sees the cowboy movies, hears the "ugg" and "how" language used, and unless they are taught otherwise, believe this view of the Indian peoples to be true. Even as they grow older, the belief that all Indians live in teepees and ride horses is prevalent. However, there are those who are ignorant in their thinking about the Indian peoples, not wanting to know the truth even though they could learn it. They are more comfortable in maintaining their misperceptions about Indians than disrupting them with truths and understanding. Finally, there are those who are just plain arrogant, refusing to accept the truth about the sovereignty and integrity of American Indian culture, spirituality and values. Instead, the arrogant uses the old "white is right" argument to justify their prejudices and racism toward the Indian peoples.

Just recently, a Catholic all-girls high school in New Orleans decided to drop the use of "Sioux Indians" as a mascot for their ninth-grade class after using this since 1948. The other grades use Leprechauns, Skippers and the Merry Macs which implies that the Sioux, or as they wish to be called Lakota, peoples are nothing more than a pep rally mascot. The students at the school gave themselves tribal names, posed "Indian" style for yearbook photos, and wore the stereotypical single feather in their hair. When the school administration decided to end this practice, many alumni were upset, calling the move bowing to political correctness or revisionist history.[42] However, the question remains: Why are American Indians always the culture that are romanticized and trivialized into mascots? Why are no other ethnic groups used? Are there no other cultures or ethnicities worthy of this "honor"? To be honest, if any other racial group suffered this humiliation, there would likely be a national outcry.

In a very interesting and poignant article, Michael Mark Cohen aptly points out that one does not hear white racial slurs because they are the ones who possess the privileges. According to Cohen, "white privilege is the right of whites, and only whites, to be judged as individuals, to be treated as an unique self, possessed of all the rights and protections of citizenship."[43] It is amazing that American society has become sensitive to all the different and, at times, antiquated, racial slurs that have existed for Asian Americans, Italian Americans, Irish Americans, and especially African Americans and they have been deemed socially unacceptable in a modern colorblind society. However, the terms redskin, squaw, and other derogatory labels can continue to be used for American Indians and their use is even defended as right and somehow part of the American heritage. It is seen as cute when schoolchildren dress up as Indians for Thanksgiving or Halloween, but it would cause riots if the same parents allowed their children to dress up using blackface or some other cultural accouterments. Ethnicity is not a costume that can be removed when it becomes uncomfortable. Claiming an ethnic heritage means to take on its representation and its burdens, both good and bad.[44]

Whereas volumes more could be written on the theft of American Indian cultural property by both individuals and corporations, this has not fallen within the scope of this work. However, it would be remiss not to at least briefly point to its continuation.

Cultural symbols are essential to the survival of the Indian. This appropriation and misuse of Indian names, symbols and sacred images falls within the context of group intellectual property.[45] If American Indians are able to claim group rights in the context that their cultural survival is at stake, they would be able to exert more control over their cultural symbols and hopefully prevent the devaluation and depletion of their culture. Indians would be able to prevent the use of the prayer pipe, eagle feathers, medicine wheel and other sacred objects to garnish food items, clothing and sports teams. Preventing the loss of cultural identities, a very important part of the collective consciousness of a people, means that their individual rights will remain protected and respected.

That there are harmful psychological impacts on the Indian peoples and their culture by seeing their symbols and myths used inappropriately must be accepted. For African Americans, the history of slavery and civil rights and the struggles over these issues is well known. Racist caricatures on television and radio, and in other media have been fought against and almost erased. Yet, the struggle for Indians to gain the same goal goes on. Between Hollywood and other industries including the NFL, MLB, NHL and the NCAA, the racist imagery that Indians are a savage inferior, child-like people whose names and sacred objects can be used to sell anything will continue.[46]

This is demeaning the American Indian peoples through the use of words rather than actual physical attacks, but the effects can be the same. The Indian peoples are left off-balance, fighting to find their self and identity again.[47] This has left generations seeking meaning for themselves. This is especially true when shows, movies and cartoons that depict other ethnic groups in a demeaning, stereotypical manner are removed from the public domain, but those treating American Indians in a similar fashion are still seen. Disney's "Song of the South" has been locked away as being racist for its treatment of Southern African Americans; the cartoon character Speedy Gonzales has been removed from the air for showing Mexican-Americans in a demeaning fashion; and cartoons created during World War II showing Japanese in a racist manner are no longer shown, or are shown with a disclaimer. However, shows and cartoons that depict Indians as savages, inferior intellectually and culturally still appear regularly. Just think, when children revert to acting like savages and without morals, they become "Indian" such as in the 1953 Disney movie, *Peter Pan*, and its racist songs about why Indians are red, say "ugg" and "how." Schools have homecoming themes of cowboys and Indians, but would never ever consider a day dedicated to masters and slaves.[48] It is seen as a cute tradition to have little children dress up as Pilgrims and Indians for Thanksgiving, but nothing is taught about the decimating wars waged by those same Pilgrims against the very tribes that showed them compassion on that day. At Halloween, people can go and buy Indian costumes, including the "Sexy Maiden" version. However, if the same costumes were offered of slaves, African natives, Hispanics, Jews, or even Nazi soldiers, that store's judgment would be questioned and public action and protests would surely follow. So, why is the American Indian still considered a proper costume? If anything, this demonstrates the institutional racism that exists in America today. At best, it has reduced the American Indian to a commodity that can be bought and sold for entertainment.

The misuse and demeaning display of American Indian symbols is dehumanizing to so many Indians. This blatant racism renders the Indian as subhuman, depriving them of their history and present reality, relegating them to "relics of the past."[49] The overall effect of all this is the disenfranchisement and alienation of the Indian peoples from their own culture and history, and thus, genocide. In fact, the U.S. Supreme Court has recently ruled that denying trademark protection to disparaging racial slurs is unconstitutional and violates the freedom of speech. Hence, teams such as the Redskins now have governmental protection and the right to continue to use racist terms for their names and mascots.[50] Teams that use these terms always claim they are honoring the Indian peoples. Using this logic implies other races are not as honorable. More likely, the teams know they would face harsher and more stringent opposition if they chose to use another ethnic slur as their mascot.

There are those people who will not agree that the entire fault for the genocide of the American Indian rests with the U.S. Supreme Court and its rulings. While they may not be totally at fault for the plight and genocide of the American Indian in North America, they are, at the very least, compliant and have been very much complacent in the treatment of the country's native peoples. The Court's rulings have confused and muddied the relationships between the tribes and the various levels of government, and have often given contradictory directions as to the paths that need to be followed. According to David E. Wilkin, the U.S. Supreme Court has used the most "egregious examples of precedent, have applied linguistic semantics, rhetorical strategies and other devices to disempower tribal governments and to disenfranchise individual Indians."[51] The Supreme Court, and other government officials, have acted out of self-interest, political expediency and cultural arrogance in countless decisions and policies. As Wilkins points out, of the 90 cases he examined involving tribal sovereignty, only five had a dissenting opinion, which demonstrated an ideological consensus based on cultural biases among other things.[52] The Court's legal consciousness has stressed the Indian's allegedly inferior cultural, political, technological, social and spiritual status in relation to the prevailing invaders.[53] So, simply put, yes, the U.S. Supreme Court, the last vestige of recourse and justice, is to blame for much of the genocide that has taken place over the centuries.

As if to further demonstrate the consequences of these acts of alienation and disenfranchisement, little concern is shown for America's forgotten minority even by its intellectual elite. The author was an invited speaker at a conference dedicated to civil rights and social justice at a prestigious university.[54] As the conference progressed, the author found that there were sessions dedicated to Hispanic rights, African American rights, even heated and emotional debates over the rights of illegal aliens, but besides himself, not a single presenter or discussion was held regarding the American Indians and their rights. The irony was that the conference was held in a state with 11 Indian reservations (roughly 764,240 acres) within its borders, which hold a population of over 20,000 out of the state's population of 50,000 Indians.[55]

American Indians have not, in acutality, been conquered, just swindled and cheated because they tended to be honorable and trustful of the newcomers. The many nations, even confederations, still exist and thrive. However, it may be just that the goals of assimilation have been achieved all too well. Many Indians and their leaders now act just like their oppressors—displaying greed, power struggles, jealousy, backstabbing, corruption, nepotism, drug and alcohol abuse, domestic abuse, murder, suicide, and all in all, cowardice. Tribes are being ripped apart over gaming profits and the struggle for control of these assets. Tribes fight with each other and oppose the others' chances for recognition because they do not wish to share their slice of the proverbial pie. Instead, they should be banding together and making a new pie that will feed everyone. Tribal leaders are bickering and fighting for control of the tribal assets. They are becoming individuals and forgetting the community that once meant the tribe. Honor is gone in some instances altogether, never to return. Assimilation has arrived full force.

In 2015, in one of the final acts of the Obama Administration, the Bureau of Indian Affairs made a positive change in the process in which a group could gain official federal recognition as an Indian tribe. Recognition is important, not just for the social and cultural status, but so the tribe can apply for health, economic and justice assistance from the federal government. This is the very foundation of sovereignty in all of its forms. The new process is more transparent with full public access to the materials submitted by the tribe for recognition and on all decisions made in the process.[56] Before, groups had to prove existence as a tribe from their first contact with non-natives; now they only have to prove and verify that they have been a cohesive, recognized and separate native group since 1900. This means the documentation needed as evidence of tribal status will be easier to gather and present, especially since many tribes have been scattered due to removal and other state and federal policies. Finally, specific types of evidence have been finalized and an appeal process has been instituted if the status if not approved.[57]

As the 2020 U.S. presidential election approaches, there is a lot of discussion among various candidates concerning repatriations for the descendants of slavery. The plans differ—from outright monetary payments to housing and education assistance. Whatever the plan, one group of people that seem to be left out of the discussion are the nation's original inhabitants. There does not seem to be much concern about how the American Indians were the original slaves[58]; lost millions of acres of homeland; had their cultures, religions and very existence attacked; had their children removed and sent to boarding school; had their graves robbed; and so much more. Can there even be a fair and just repatriation system for the indignities and problems caused for the native peoples?

The arguments and issues reviewed throughout this work can be attributed to those pillars of a modern civilized society: power, money and control.[59] Much of the dysfunction in the Indian communities is due to the influence of alien forms of government, justice and culture. The IRA insti-tuted forms of governance and laws that were unnatural to most tribes. The system of solving disputes through an adversarial structure was new to the Indians. In this system, there's more concern on winning than on reaching a compromise or agreeable solution among the involved parties. This adver-sarial structure has wormed its way into the Indian community and weakened the linkages among its members. This is not to claim there were no problems or injustices before the arrival of the new peoples. Instead, the purpose of justice was to regain balance and harmony, not to prove someone a wrongdoer and punish them for their error. By losing one's interconnectiveness with other tribal members, the process of assimilation or Americanization has been accomplished.[60] For many, the loss of tribal identity and sovereignty has been completed, never to be regained.

By losing one's interconnectiveness with the other members of the tribe, the process of assimilation, in other words Americanization, has been accom-plished. The loss of tribal identity and sovereignty has been completed.[61] The decades of assimilation have resulted in a new breed of Indian, the self-hating kind.[62] Due to personal alienation and disaffection, the self-hating Indian hides behind the destruction of himself and things around him. He becomes a racist, self-righteous, despising those whom he sees as being a lesser–Indian than himself. He begins to hide behind traditions and ceremonies, often times interpreted by New Agers or just plain made up. These ceremonies are often performed for others at a cost so as to fill the void within himself, as an ego satisfier.[63] Other self-hating Indians resort to traditions in what they see as the "pure" form, not realizing that this cannot be achieved. For just as the drum's skin tightens, the gourd rattle yellows and cracks, and the sweat lodge ages, so do the ceremonies change over time. As Leslie Marmon Silko states in her book, "in many ways the ceremonies have always been changing. When the white people came, the elements in this world shifted, and it became nec-essary to create new ceremonies. Only growth will keep the ceremonies strong. Things that do not shift and grow are dead things. [If] we cling to the ceremonies the way they were, the people will be no more."[64] Claiming a ceremony is not traditional simply because a song was performed incorrectly or a word missed does not make the ceremony any less important. Instead, seeking refuge in the purity of traditions is only another way of avoiding reality. Things change, and so must the ceremonies to meet the new needs and challenges of the Indian peoples.

The self-hating Indian becomes so anxious to get approval that he often ignores those closest to him, his family and friends. This causes even more alienation and thus, the cycle of self-hatred and destruction continues. One of the greatest hindrances to the reestablishment of the Indian people and their spirituality is their failure to understand their own history.[65] It is only after the origins and causal factors of self-hate are grasped that true healing can begin.

A tribe's ancestral homeland and sacred sites are the very heart of their existence. When you remove and condemn the traditions, values and religion of the tribe, in addition to depriving them of their heart, they become nothing more than a loose conglomeration of individuals, many who are now self-hating Indians. Ceremonies become hollow and meaningless since they are no longer connected to and performed on the same ground that the elders used. Outsiders invade the ceremonies, attending sweat lodges and powwows. Whether they be New Agers seeking verification in others, charlatans seeking new ways to extort money from the unsuspecting and lost, or Boy Scouts dressing up as Indians and dancing at a powwow, the usurpation and rein-forcement of self-hatred continues.

The gap between the tribal elders and the newest generation of Indians is ever widening. The elders are trying to pass the traditions and knowledge along, but they are battling the forces of assimilation. The problem is even greater for the generation of Indians who do not live on or near their home reservation. These urban Indians have become even more lost than their reservation counterparts. The rates of drug and alcohol abuse, suicide, domes-tic violence and other ills are highest among this group. The vicious cycle of self-hatred has taken its toll upon them also.

There are efforts to regain the tribal collective consciousness needed to stop the cycle of self-hatred. Deep down, the connectiveness of the Indian to each other and to the lands still exists, it just needs to be rekindled. Tribal colleges are rebuilding their languages and traditions, and tribes are running cultural programs to guarantee that their people do not forget the lessons of the past, both good and bad. It is time to stop allowing anthropologists, his-torians, economists, educators, and politicians from dictating the identity of the American Indian. If not, it will remain fragmented forever.[66] The Indian peoples need to embrace the tools needed to move forward, to create a new path in this world, to end the victim mentality and find a new inner strength based on unity of the individual, the clan and the tribe. The Indian needs to be free. We have heard the proverbial "it is a good day to die" statement, but today's Indian peoples must believe it is a good day to live. The cycle must be broken. To break out of the traps of fear, failure, mistrust, sorrow and anger means life can begin. This may seem clichéd, but seeking the path in the light of life means a better future. We, the Indian peoples, must under-stand that there is still a life for us in this country and we must have the cour-age to live it. It is in this manner that a return to the best of the old ways—community, support, caring, empowerment, ceremony and spirituality—will eventually replace the racism, loneliness, complacency and self-loathing that we suffer from today. One writer has summed it up simply by saying, "it is imperative that the Indian create their own path using the best tools of both their and the white world."[67] The Indian people can no longer portray the victim and must once again decide to live in this world. There needs to be a return to traditions, in ceremonies, spiritualism, family and leadership. It must be adapted if necessary, not diluted, for the modern era, but it can cleanse and redirect the people so as the universe will return to balance.

It is now, this life, that we as a people must stand up and be responsible for ourselves. Corruption, greed, laziness, and self-hatred have to be replaced with the quiet pride of a people who have survived over 500 years of genocide, and we are still here. We must take the moral high ground in this continuing battle, and this does not mean self- or tribal immolation when we lose. It is time to, as Andrew Iron Shell has written, to take the best of both worlds and use them in the struggles of the people. The struggle for sovereignty, cultural identity, ceremony and spirituality requires all the weapons that can be mustered. The people must, once again, dictate who they are and what they will be to the land from which they were born.

The Indian people must remember that "history is a merciless judge. It lays bare our tragic blunders and foolish missteps and exposes our most intimate secrets, wielding the power of hindsight like an arrogant detective who seems to know the end of the mystery from the onset."[68] This is true of *all* cultures. However, for the Indian, "today our hearts are divided between two worlds. We are strong and courageous, learning to walk in two worlds, hanging onto the threads of our culture and traditions as we live in a predominantly non–Indian society. Our history, our culture, our heart, and our homes will always be stretching our legs across the plains, singing songs in the morning light, and placing our feet down with the ever-beating heart of the world. We walk in two worlds."[69]

Breaking the cycle of self-hatred and pain will be a difficult process. The Indian's ties to their land will have to ultimately find respect for themselves and their histories. Sovereignty in all its dimensions must be fought for and restored. Only weakness awaits in being silent and passive. The cycle begins and ends with the people, and to borrow a phrase from a song by Robbie Robertson, "the people need to start making a noise in this world."[70]

American Indian Religious Freedom, Public Law 95-341

Joint Resolution American Indian Religious Freedom

Whereas the freedom of religion for all people is an inherent right, fundamental to the democratic structure of the United States and is guaranteed by the First Amendment of the United States Constitution;

Whereas the United States has traditionally rejected the concept of a government denying individuals the right to practice their religion and, as a result, has benefitted from a rich variety of religious heritages in this country;

Whereas the religious practices of the American Indian (as well as Native Alaskan and Hawaiian) are an integral part of their culture, tradition and heritage, such practices forming the basis of Indian identity and value systems;

Whereas the traditional American Indian religions, as an integral part of Indian life, are indispensable and irreplaceable;

Whereas the lack of a clear, comprehensive, and consistent Federal policy has often resulted in the abridgement of religious freedom for traditional American Indians;

Whereas such religious infringements result from the lack of knowledge or insensitive and inflexible enforcement of Federal policies and regulations premised on a variety of laws;

Whereas such laws were designed for such worthwhile purposes as conservation and preservation of natural species and resources but were never intended to relate to Indian religious practices and, therefore, were passed without consideration of their effect on traditional American Indian religions;

Whereas such laws and policies often deny American Indians access to sacred sites required in their religions, including cemeteries;

Whereas such laws at times prohibit the use and possession of sacred objects necessary to the exercise of religious rites and ceremonies;

Whereas traditional American Indian ceremonies have been intruded upon, interfered with, and in a few instances banned: Now, therefore, be it

Resolved by the Senate and House of Representatives of the United States of America in Congress assembled, That henceforth it shall be the policy of the United States to protect and preserve for American Indians their inherent right of freedom to believe, express and exercise the traditional religions of the American Indian, Eskimo, Aleut, and Native Hawaiians, including but not limited to access to sites, use and possession of sacred objects, and the freedom to worship through ceremonials and traditional rites.

Sec. 2. The President shall direct the various Federal departments, agencies and other instrumentalities responsible for administering relevant laws to evaluate their policies and procedures in consultation with native traditional religious leaders in order to determine appropriate changes necessary to protect and preserve Native American religious cultural rights and practices. Twelve months after approval of this resolution, the President shall report back to the Congress the results of his evaluation, including any changes which were made in administrative policies and procedures, and any recommendations he may have for legislative action.

APPENDIX II

Chief Seattle's Speech

Yonder sky has wept tears of compassion on our fathers for centuries untold, and which, to us, looks eternal, may change. Today it is fair. Tomorrow it may be overcast with clouds. My words are like the stars that never set. What Seattle says, the great chief, Washington can rely upon, with as much certainty as our pale-face brothers can rely upon the return of the seasons.

The son of the white chief says his father sends us greetings of friendship and good will. This is kind, for we know he has little need of our friendship in return, because his people are many. They are like the grass that covers the vast prairies, while my people are few, and resemble the scattering of trees on a storm-swept plain.

The great, and I presume also good, white chief sends us word that he wants to buy our lands but is willing to allow us to reserve enough to live on comfortably. This indeed appears generous, for the red man no longer has rights that he need respect, and the offer may be wise, also, for we are no longer in need of a great country.

There was a time when our people covered the whole land, as the waves of a wind-ruffled sea cover its shell-paved floor. But that time has long since passed away with the greatness of tribes now almost forgotten. I will not mourn over our untimely decay, nor reproach my pale-face brothers for hastening it, for we, too, may have been somewhat to blame.

When our young men grow angry at some real or imaginary wrong, and disfigure their faces with black paint, their hearts, also, are disfigured and turn black, and then their cruelty is relentless and knows no bounds, and our old men are not able to restrain them.

But let us hope that hostilities between the red man and his pale-face brothers may never return. We would have everything to lose and nothing to gain.

True it is, that revenge, with our young braves, is considered gain, even

185

at the cost of their own lives, but old men who stay at home in times of war, and old women, who have sons to lose, know better.

Our great father Washington, for I presume he is now our father as well as yours, since George has moved his boundaries to the north; our great and good father, I say, sends us word by his son, who, no doubt, is a great chief among his people, that if we do as he desires, he will protect us. His brave armies will be to us a bristling wall of strength, and his great ships of war will fill our harbors so that our ancient enemies far to the northward, the Simsiams and Hydas, will no longer frighten our women and old men. Then he will be our father and we will be his children.

But can this ever be? Your God loves your people and hates mine. He folds his strong protecting arms lovingly about the white man and leads him as a father leads his infant son, but he has forsaken his red children; he makes your people wax strong every day, and soon they will fill the land; while my people are ebbing away like a fast-receding tide, that will never flow again. The white man's God cannot love his red children or he would protect them. They seem to be orphans and can look nowhere for help. How then can we become brothers? How can your father become our father and bring us prosperity and awaken in us dreams of returning greatness?

Your God seems to us to be partial. He came to the white man. We never saw Him; never even heard His voice; He gave the white man laws but He had no word for His red children whose teeming millions filled this vast continent as the stars fill the firmament. No, we are two distinct races and must ever remain so. There is little in common between us. The ashes of our ancestors are sacred and their final resting place is hallowed ground, while you wander away from the tombs of your fathers seemingly without regret.

Your religion was written on tablets of stone by the iron finger of an angry God, lest you might forget it. The red man could never remember nor comprehend it.

Our religion is the traditions of our ancestors, the dreams of our old men, given them by the great Spirit, and the visions of our sachems, and is written in the hearts of our people.

Your dead cease to love you and the homes of their nativity as soon as they pass the portals of the tomb. They wander far off beyond the stars, are soon forgotten, and never return. Our dead never forget the beautiful world that gave them being. They still love its winding rivers, its great mountains and its sequestered vales, and they ever yearn in tenderest affection over the lonely hearted living and often return to visit and comfort them.

Day and night cannot dwell together. The red man has ever fled the approach of the white man, as the changing mists on the mountain side flee before the blazing morning sun.

However, your proposition seems a just one, and I think my folks will accept it and will retire to the reservation you offer them, and we will dwell apart and in peace, for the words of the great white chief seem to be the voice of nature speaking to my people out of the thick darkness that is fast gathering around them like a dense fog floating inward from a midnight sea.

It matters but little where we pass the remainder of our days. They are not many.

The Indian's night promises to be dark. No bright star hovers about the horizon. Sad-voiced winds moan in the distance. Some grim Nemesis of our race is on the red man's trail, and wherever he goes he will still hear the sure approaching footsteps of the fell destroyer and prepare to meet his doom, as does the wounded doe that hears the approaching footsteps of the hunter. A few more moons, a few more winters, and not one of all the mighty hosts that once filled this broad land or that now roam in fragmentary bands through these vast solitudes will remain to weep over the tombs of a people once as powerful and hopeful as your own.

But why should we repine? Why should I murmur at the fate of my people? Tribes are made up of individuals and are no better than they. Men come and go like waves of the sea. A tear, a tamanawus, a dirge, and they are gone from our longing eyes forever. Even the white man, whose God walked and talked with him, as friend to friend, is not exempt from the common destiny. We may be brothers after all. We shall see.

We will ponder your proposition, and when we have decided we will tell you. But should we accept it, I here and now make this the first condition: That we not be denied the privilege, without molestation, of visiting at will the graves of our ancestors and friends. Every part of this country is sacred to my people. Every hill-side, every valley, every plain and grove has been hallowed by some fond memory or some sad experience of my tribe.

Even the rocks that seem to lie dumb as they swelter in the sun along the silent seashore in solemn grandeur thrill with memories of past events connected with the fate of my people, and the very dust under your feet responds more lovingly to our footsteps than to yours, because it is the ashes of our ancestors, and our bare feet are conscious of the sympathetic touch, for the soil is rich with the life of our kindred.

The sable braves, and fond mothers, and glad-hearted maidens, and the little children who lived and rejoiced here, and whose very names are now forgotten, still love these solitudes, and their deep fastnesses at eventide grow shadowy with the presence of dusky spirits. And when the last red man shall have perished from the earth and his memory among white men shall have become a myth, these shores shall swarm with the invisible dead of my tribe, and when your children's children shall think themselves alone in the field, the store, the shop, upon the highway or in the silence of the woods they will not be alone. In all the earth there is no place dedicated to solitude. At night, when the streets of your cities and villages shall be silent, and you think them deserted, they will throng with the returning hosts that once filled and still love this beautiful land. The white man will never be alone. Let him be just and deal kindly with my people, for the dead are not altogether powerless.

SOURCE: Paul S. Wilson, "What Chief Seattle Said," *Environmental Law*, Vol. 22, 1992, pp. 1464–1468.

Chapter Notes

Chapter One

1. The term American Indian, preferred by most tribal members, will be interchangeable with the terms Native American, Indian, Native, and Native People for this work. The diversity among the North American Indian tribes makes treating them as a monolithic group very difficult and erroneous. Therefore, references made in this work are general, and may not apply to each tribe.

2. Seneca. Translates as "The Great Teacher." His common name was Handsome Lake. He was Seneca Iroquois (Nundawáono Haudenosaunee, People of the Gray Rocks of the People of the Longhouse). Iroquois is a French version of the Algonquian term for the League who were their enemies and roughly translates as "rattlesnakes." Handsome Lake's visions and teachings established a new code of religious belief for the Iroquois Confederacy during the early 1800s. The Code of Handsome Lake, the Gaiwiio, is still followed to this day by a good number of the Haudenosaunee.

3. Commonly and inappropriately called the Chippewa, which means "puckered foot" and refers to the type of moccasin worn by members of the nation.

4. Indians conceptualize guardian spirits in the forms of various animals and even design their clan structures around them. The application of human qualities to plants and animals is a common thread throughout most tribal beliefs; see Christopher

Vecsey and Robert W. Venables, eds., *American Indian Environments: Ecological Issues in Native American History* (Syracuse: Syracuse University Press, 1980), pp. 20–21. Vecsey continues by stating that American Indians "utilized the environment extensively, realized the differences between human and nonhuman persons, and felt guilt for their exploitation of nature's life-giving life. Indian environmental religions were means of idealizing and attempting to attain a goal of harmony with nature, for both participatory and manipulative reasons, but inherent in their religions was the understanding that they were not in fact at perfect harmony with nature" (p. 23). A criticism of this statement is that this belief and understanding is still strong and central in Indian cultures as is the desire for harmony with nature.

5. Bernard Bailyn, *The Barbarous Years* (New York: Vintage Books, 2012), p. 11.

6. Peter J. Longo and Christina E. Miewald, "Native Americans, the Courts and Water Policy: Is Nothing Sacred?" *Great Plains Research*, Vol. 2/No. 1, 1992, p. 54.

7. *Ibid.*, p. 55. John Locke in the *Second Treatise of Civil Government* (1690) stated that God had given the world in common, but He did not intend for it to remain that way. In other words, humans were to go out and utilize what nature had to offer for the benefit of themselves. However, most proponents of this belief fail to read on where Locke states that when a person becomes wasteful of what nature has to

offer, they can be limited in what they own or control. Yet, as we will see, this argument cuts both ways against the American Indians.

8. Indian nations had systems of land ownership which stressed a communal use of the land, yet personal property was held privately. The tribes had systems of citizenship, decision making, leadership and alliances which rivaled the newly arrived European powers.

9. Recent research and theories have indicated that the Mayan Culture may have collapsed and been absorbed into surrounding cultures due to overpopulation and overuse of the land compounded with long periods of drought.

10. Eugene F. Pickette et al., "Cultural Identification of American Indians and Its Impact on Rehabilitation Services," *Journal of Rehabilitation*, Vol. 65/No. 3, July–September 1999, p. 3.

11. *Ibid.*, p. 6.

12. John R. Wunder, *Retained By the People: A History of American Indians and the Bill of Rights* (New York: Oxford University Press, 1994), p. 8. American Indian nations also had a system of laws, although they were not written out on paper.

13. Vecsey, *op. cit.*, p. 34. As Vecsey states, "white policy has been and continues to be a three-pronged attack on nature, nature folk and nature religions" (p. 37).

14. Vecsey, *op. cit.*, p. 22. Whereas the Indians viewed the environment as nourishing, they realized it was, and is, not indestructible. One can please, influence, or even offend Mother Earth. Hence, harmony is the ideal. (See p. 22.)

15. Later, there would even be an utopian communitarian venture established at Rugby, Tennessee in 1880 for the "second sons" to provide them a place to live and prosper in skills and trades, such as farming, that their class would frown upon back in England. The community was organized by Thomas Hughes. However, the residents' lack of the necessary skills to make a living, coupled with financial woes and disastrous fires caused the community collapse by the turn of the century. For a full account, see: John Egerton, *Visions of Utopia* (Knoxville: University of Tennessee Press, 1977).

16. Francis Jennings, *The Invasion of America: Indians, Colonialism, and the Cant of Conquest* (Chapel Hill: University of North Carolina Press, 1975), pp. 15, 30. Jennings states that certain tribes were almost completely wiped out by epidemics, thus leaving a "virgin" land for the newcomers. For example, the Hurons dropped from 32,000 to 10,000 in only 10 years; the Susquehannocks in Pennsylvania numbered 6,500 in 1647, but only 250 in 1698; and the Pequots only numbered 300 in 1674, down from 4,000 (see p. 30).

17. Pickette et al., *op. cit.*, p. 5.

18. John S. Harbison, "The Broken Promise Land," 14 *Stanford Environmental Law Journal*, May 1995, n.p.

19. *Ibid.*

20. *Ibid.*

21. *Ibid.*

22. Robert A. Porter, "Strengthening Sovereignty Through Peacemaking," paper presented at the Federal Bar Association Indian Law Conference, Albuquerque, NM (April 1995).

23. *Ibid.*

24. Dan Philpatt, "Sovereignty," *The Stanford Encyclopedia of Philosophy*, Summer 2003 Edition, http://plato.stanford.edu/archives/sum2003/entries/soverignty/.

25. *Ibid.*

26. Peter d'Ericco, "American Indian Sovereignty: Now You See It, Now You Don't," 1997, http:www.nativeweb.org/pages/legal/sovereignty.html.

27. David E. Wilkins, *American Indian Sovereignty and the U.S. Supreme Court* (Austin: University of Texas Press, 1997), p. 20.

28. *Ibid.*, p. 21.

29. *Ibid.*

30. BIA, *FAQs*, updated 11 April 2017, https://www.bia.gov/FAQs/.

31. Mark A. Chavaree, "Tribal Sovereignty," *Wabanaki Legal News*, Winter 1998, http://www.ptla.org/ptlasite/wabanaki/sovereign.htm.

32. *Ibid.*

33. Charles F. Wilkinson, *Fire on the Plateau* (Washington, D.C.: Island Press, 1999), p. 112.

34. *Ibid.*, p. 110, and *Merriam v. Jicarilla Apache Tribe*, 455 U.S. 130 (1982).

35. D'Ericco, *op. cit.*

36. *Ibid.*

Chapter Two

1. Kent Newburn, ed., *The Wisdom of the Native Americans* (Navato, CA: New World Library, 1999).

2. Lewis Lord, "How Many People Were Here Before Columbus?" *U.S. News and World Report*, 18–25 August 1997, pp. 68–70, http://www.bxscience.edu/ourpages/auto/2009/4/5/34767803/Pre-Columbian%20population.pdf.

3. Bailyn, *op. cit.*, p. 12.

4. *Ibid.*, pp. 22, 26.

5. Jennings, *op. cit.*, p. 39.

6. *Ibid.*, pp. 39–41.

7. Yet, as this book will point out, "by the twentieth century, the order of arrival to America will become a curious piece of information, obvious, but commonly dismissed." See Jill Norgren, "Protection of What Rights They Have: Original Principles of Federal Indian Law," *North Dakota Law Review*, Vol. 64, 1988, p. 75.

8. Jennings, *op. cit.*, p. 4.

9. Robert A. Williams, Jr., *The American Indian in Western Legal Thought: The Discourse of Conquest* (New York: Oxford University Press, 1990), pp. 44–45; and Steven T. Newcomb, "The Evidence of Christian Nationalism in Federal Indian Law," *New York University Review of Law and Social Change*, Vol. 20, 1993, pp. 309–310. The Catholic Church devised political theories to rationalize expansionism. Thus, discovery and conquest became intertwined.

10. *Ibid.*, p. 45.

11. *Ibid.*, p. 67.

12. Portugal would dispute the claims for Spain that Columbus made and appealed to the Pope for resolution. In 1494, the Pope divided the lands between the two nations. In addition, the Pope placed those peoples disposed to embrace Christianity under his guardianship. See Williams, *ibid.*, p. 80–81. Pope Nicholas V, in 1455 empowered Portugal via a Papal Bull, to enslave persons and seize lands and property of all pagans whatsoever, and all enemies of Christ wheresoever placed which was used to justify the conquest of the Holy Land, and eventually, the world (Jennings, *op. cit.*, p. 4). Pope Alexander VI in 1493 granted Spain all the world not already possessed by a Christian nation, so that the abandoned heathen could

be made to embrace the Catholic faith and be trained in good morals (Jennings, *op. cit.*, p. 5). Henry VII of England commissioned John Cabot in 1496 to conquer and possess the heathen's lands.

13. Norgren, *op. cit.*, p. 76. The Arawak's greeting of Columbus and his men with gifts apparently reinforced his perception that the Natives were submitting to a recognized superior. See Judith Nies, *Native American History* (New York: Ballentine Books, 1996), p. 69.

14. Williams, *op. cit.*, p. 83.

15. *Ibid.*, p. 84. Within twenty years, slavery and flight from the Spanish had reduced the estimated 250,000 Indians on Hispaniola to 15,000.

16. There were some Christian sects that disagreed with the need for slavery to convert the natives. The Dominicans appealed to the royal court, but lost the argument to the Aristotelean dictum that the Indians were natural slaves with no ability to reason. The result of this was a set of codes which justified the Eurocentric views of the Indians and their need for subjugation by peaceful, and if needed, forceful means. These codes legitimized the appropriation of all Indian resources, including labor for all purposes of assimilation.

17. Jennings, *op. cit.*, p. 6. The Arawaks, over three million in number in 1492, were all but extinct within five decades of their fateful rescue of Columbus and the crew of the *Santa Maria*. See Nies, *op. cit.*, p. 71. Their extinction gave rise to the African slave trade by 1509 to replace the loss of Indian slaves. Columbus would be tried, but acquitted of the charges of excessive cruelty to the Indians in 1500. See Nies, *op. cit.*, p. 75.

18. Jennings, *op. cit.*, pp. 48–49.

19. *Ibid.*, p. 78. Catholic priest Bartoleme de Las Casa recorded in 1502 how Columbus decapitated innocent Arawaks for their refusal to be subjugated. See Nies, *op. cit.*, p. 76.

20. Nies, *op. cit.*, p. 76.

21. Williams, *op. cit.*, p. 91. This was to be read to the Indians before hostilities could legally begin. It remained in effect until 1556. The document asked that the Indians acknowledge the Church as the ruler of the world with the Pope as its high priest, and the Kings and Queens of Spain as the superiors of the discovered lands. If they accepted,

the document continued, they would be accepted in love; but failure to do so meant that the Spaniards would forcibly enter the Indians' country, make war against them in all manners possible, make them into slaves, and seize their goods. See Marvin Lunenfield, *1492: Discovery, Invasion Encounter* (Lexington, MA: D.C. Heath and Co., 1991), pp. 188–190; and also Albert L. Hurtado and Peter Iverson, *Major Problems in American Indian History* (Lexington, MA: D.C. Heath and Co., 1992), pp. 83–85.

22. Williams, *op. cit.*, p. 97.

23. Lunenfield, *op. cit.*, p. 192.

24. Vitoria did state that the Indians' low level of civilization (lack of proper laws, magistrates, governments) may lead to a change in this argument. Governance may have to be entrusted to those with more intelligence; it was their duty to do so, like adults over children. However, he was not sure if this was the case and so stated. *Ibid.*, pp. 197–198.

25. *Ibid.*, p. 194.

26. *Ibid.*

27. Williams, *op. cit.*, p. 99; Jennings, *op. cit.*, p. 45.

28. Lunenfield, *op. cit.*, p. 196.

29. *Ibid.*, p. 103.

30. Norgren, *op. cit.*, p. 77.

31. Lunenfield, *op. cit.*, p. 196.

32. *Ibid.*, p. 106. Only the European Christians could offer the Indians the chance at a rational existence which they were obliged to accept and live.

33. Nies, *op. cit.*, p. 103. These "illegal" works included those by de Las Casas who, as stated, had documented the crimes of Columbus and other Spanish settlers.

34. Lunenfield, *op. cit.*, p. 236. In 1588, France began its mercantilist policies of granting fur trade monopolies in Canada (Nies, *op. cit.*, p. 106).

35. Jennings, *op. cit.*, p. 5.

36. *Ibid.*, p. 10. Spain's terror continued. In 1600, it began kidnapping Apache, Diné (Navajo), and Ute Indians to be sold as slaves in its colonies (Nies, *op. cit.*, p. 112). The Dutch routinely sent severed Indian heads back as trophies. See Fergus Bordewich, *Killing the White Man's Indian* (New York: Anchor Books, 1996), p. 35.

37. *Ibid.*, pp. 46, 48.

38. Bailyn, *op. cit.*, p. 218.

39. *Ibid.*, pp. 222, 249–297.

40. This had to do with the split from the Catholic Church as well as a development in colonization justification theories. See Bailyn, *loc. cit.*, pp. 38–40. The English views of the Indian changed from one that held the Indian as satanic, barbaric, cannibalistic and weak of mind and spirit to one of the "noble savage," a simple but unsophisticated people that were uncorrupted, but needed to be civilized.

41. Williams, *op. cit.*, p. 194. The English may have used the Dutch West Indies Company as an example in their land acquisition practices. The company had declared that all parties to a treaty were indeed sovereign, and as such, the Indians had transferable title to their lands. However, the Dutch realized that individual acquisitions would lead to confusion and held that a government should control the process (Norgren, *op. cit.*, p. 78). The 1493 Cabot Charter from King Edward VII gave Cabot the authorization to seek out, discover, subdue and occupy the lands of heathens and infidels (Newcomb, *op. cit.*, p. 311). England authorized Sir Gilbert in 1578 and Sir Walter Raleigh in 1584 to seize remote and heathen lands, and neither grant mentioned conversion to Christianity as a purpose, but the grants did go into great detail regarding the taking of property and the imposition of government (Jennings, *op. cit.*, p. 45).

42. Lunenfield, *op. cit.*, p. 237. This is why the Shawnee ended up in Ohio and the Tuscarora joined the Haudenosaunee Confederacy in the early 1600s.

43. *Ibid.*, p. 237.

44. Ward Churchill, "The Earth Is Our Mother: Struggles for American Indian Land and Liberation in the Contemporary United States," in M. Annette Jaimes, ed., *The State of Native America: Genocide, Colonization and Resistance* (Boston: South End Press, 1992), pp. 140–141. This would explain why the French, British and American armies constantly sought out the various tribes for either military alliances against their enemies, or at least promises of neutrality in the various wars fought around them.

45. *Ibid.*, p. 206. The confederacy consisted of an estimated 30 tribes with over 9,000 members.

46. Powhatan had died in 1618. His son,

Opechancanough, inherited his rule, and his dislike for the new settlers. The idea of getting Indian permission to expand the company's holdings was soundly rejected by London. Thus, a legal doctrine was sought to deny the need for permission rather than looking at the reality of things (Wunder, *op. cit.*, pp. 13–14).

47. Williams, *op. cit.*, p. 215.

48. Jennings, *op. cit.*, pp. 78–79. Of the 8,000 settlers who died, only 347 were killed by the Indians. Smith and Purchas would use these reasons to justify retaliatory massacres in 1625 (p. 80). Once again, by helping the colony survive in 1607, the natives sealed their fate. See also Bordewich, *op. cit.*, p. 36.

49. *Ibid.* Roger Williams was an exception to the common thought that Indians were soulless and their lands were free for the taking. He believed in the rationality and sovereignty of the Indians and their rightful title to their lands. He purchased land from the local tribes to establish the colony of Rhode Island. See also Jennings, *op. cit.*, p. 140; and Bailyn, *op. cit.*, pp. 106–110.

50. These same ideas would appear in Justice John Marshall's rulings in a number of Supreme Court cases in the early 1820s and 1830s.

51. Williams, *op. cit.*, p. 238.

52. These included the Hurons who were conquered by the Seneca and Mohawk in the 1640s; the Erie in 1656; the Anishinabé (Chippewa) were pushed westward in 1654; the Delawares (Lenapes), and Shawnee in the early 1700s. See Nies, *op. cit.*, pp. 143–165.

53. John Locke, *Of Civil Government Second Treatise* (South Bend: Gateway, 1955), p. 26. This work was first published in 1690.

54. *Ibid.*, p. 22; Jaimes, *op. cit.*, p. 28. John Cotton used this argument to justify the Puritans' taking of Indian lands. Man must improve the land, not just hunt on it, in order to have a just claim of ownership. See William T. Hagan, "Justifying Dispossession of the Indian: The Land Utilization Argument," in Vecsey and Venables, *op. cit.*, p. 66. The Puritans used biblical justifications such as Psalms 2:8 and Romans 13:2 to claim that the surrounding Indian lands were vacant, and thus theirs; or to declare the Indian as an outlaw to humanity, and thus, not deserving of the lands according to the Christian God (Jennings, *op. cit.*, pp. 83, 135).

55. This, however, was not true of all tribes. The Haudenosaunee were agriculturally based. They moved every few seasons, leaving the land to go wild, in order to allow it to rejuvenate. Still, there were large cities of Indians in some areas, some with amenities that even the whites did not have, such as glass windows. This may have appeared to be a nomadic existence to the white settlers who farmed the same piece of land for generations, and only moved when the land was dead.

56. Locke, *op. cit.*, p. 27.

57. Williams, *op. cit.*, pp. 250–251. Virginia went further when the House of Burgesses appropriated funds for the extermination of the Indians as far back as 1711. See Bordewich, *op. cit.*, p. 35.

58. Benjamin Franklin was proficient at aiding land syndicates in securing Indian lands. He was involved in numerous ventures to get the lands that the French had abandoned in the late 1760s. One venture involved Sir Johnson who helped press the Haudenosaunee for 2.4 million acres of land on the north side of the Ohio River near Fort Pitt as compensation for traders who suffered during the French and Indian War. The Haudenosaunee were to agree or risk losing all trading rights. Franklin was to get Parliament's blessing for this deal and attempted to do so by circulating rumors of a new Indian war unless it was approved. The deal was finalized in the Fort Stanwix Treaty in 1768. The colony of Vandalia was established on this land in spite of opposition from Virginia, Maryland and Pennsylvania. However, due to Franklin's radical connections and events in the colonies, the colonial endeavor was abandoned. Virginia, under Governor Lord Dunmore's direction, filled the vacuum around Fort Pitt and thus, controlled the upper Ohio Valley. (See Williams, *op. cit.*, pp. 255–265.)

59. Williams, *op. cit.*, p. 272. Another issue was that often the Indian seller did not have the right to do so, or did not understand what the transaction actually involved.

60. Williams, *op. cit.*, p. 272.

61. *Ibid.*, p. 279.

62. *Ibid.*, p. 280.

63. As an example, when Samuel Wharton, a speculator who worked with Franklin, attempted to bribe members of Congress to

reconfirm the old Vandalia grant and Haudenosaunee land transfers, he found that most members already agreed with his position and believed that the Indians had the necessary sovereignty to sell and grant land title to whomever they pleased. (*Ibid.*, pp. 273–274.) Also see: Steven Paul McSloy, "Back to the Future," 20 *New York Review of Law and Social Change*, 1993, pp. 235–238.

64. *Ibid.*, p. 291.

65. *Ibid.*, pp. 297–298.

66. "Plain Facts: Being an Examination into the Rights of the Indian Nations of America, to Their Respective Countries." *Ibid.*, p. 298.

67. *Ibid.*, p. 303.

68. Ironically, the new United States Constitution was based in part on Benjamin Franklin's efforts on the Albany Plan. Franklin in turn had used his observations and analyses of the Haudenosaunee system of democratic government and its Great Law of Peace to develop this plan. For a full accounting of the Indian influences upon the Constitution, see: Bruce Johansen, *Forgotten Founders* (Boston: Harvard Common Press, 1982) and Oren Lyons et al., *Exiled in the Land of the Free: Democracy, Indian Nations and the United States Constitution* (Sante Fe: Clear Light Publishers, 1992).

69. *Ibid.*, p. 306.

70. Norgren, *op. cit.*, p. 80.

71. *Ibid.*, p. 81. Article III. This was important since many states were giving Indian lands to their troops as bounty without deference to the fact that various tribes already owned and occupied these lands. Obviously, this practice could, and most likely would, have resulted in another war between the infant United States and the usually militarily stronger Indian nations.

72. Richard A. Monette, "Governing Private Property in Indian Country," *New Mexico Law Review*, Vol. 25, Winter 1995, n.p.

73. Hurtado and Iverson, *op. cit.*, pp. 170–171.

74. Williams, *op. cit.*, p. 320, n. 88. In fact, Georgia had earlier passed a law in 1789 declaring that it was legal to kill any Indian within its borders! This effort was aimed at the Creek Nation, whereas legal efforts would turn toward the Cherokee Nation. See Rennard Strickland, "Genocide-at-Law," *University of Kansas Law Review*, Vol. 34, 1986, pp.

720–721. The federal government had to promise that all Indians would be removed from the Georgia territory in 1802 in order to get it to end its claim to lands in Alabama and Mississippi. President Monroe agreed to this stipulation in 1817. See Bordewich, *op. cit.*, pp. 43, 44.

75. Norgren, *op. cit.*, p. 83.

76. U.S. 6 Cranch 87 (1810).

77. *Ibid.*, pp. 83, 84. However, this status would soon become, and remains, fluid.

78. *Ibid.*, p. 84.

79. "Indian title is not such as to be absolutely repugnant to seizing in fee on the part of the state." *Ibid.* Peck's argument was that the Indians only occupied the land, "it is overrun by them rather than inhabited," and as such, they do not have true legal possession of the lands. See James E. Falkowski, *Indian Law/Race Law: A Five Hundred Year History* (New York: Praeger, 1992), p. 96. Also see: John P. Lowndes, "When History Outweighs Law: Extinguishment of Abenaki Aboriginal Title," *Buffalo Law Review*, Vol. 42, Winter 1994, pp. 77–118, at p. 84.

80. *Ibid.*, p. 85. As will be discussed, the denial of the right to evict the Indians would lead to the infamous "Cherokee Cases." Justice Marshall's opinion meant that if Georgia did indeed have discovery rights, it could merely be preemptive rights to acquire the land or it amounted to de facto dominion over the territory regardless of the acquisition process (see Monette, *op. cit.*).

81. Williams, *op. cit.*, pp. 309, 320.

82. Norgren, *op. cit.*, p. 86.

83. *Ibid.*, p. 83. It is ironic that the early settlers treated the Indians as "autonomous, although alien cultures" (p. 75), but now were seeking ways to evict them as inferior heathens.

84. U.S. 7 Cranch 164 (1812).

85. Norgren, *op. cit.*, p. 87.

86. *Ibid.*, p. 88.

87. U.S. 8 Wheat. 543 (1823).

88. Falkowski, *op. cit.*, p. 97. Johnson could not take possession of the land due to the Revolutionary War. The original sale did take place with the complete knowledge of British civilian and military officials.

89. *Ibid.*, p. 98.

90. *Ibid.*, and Williams, *op. cit.*, p. 311.

91. Falkowski, *op. cit.*, p. 97; Norgren, *op. cit.*, p. 89.

92. Norgren, *op. cit.*, p. 90. Marshall reasoned that conquest had given the settlers ownership over vacant Indian lands, but was subject to the continued right of Indian occupancy. Vine Deloria and Clifford M. Lytle, *American Indians, American Justice* (Austin: University of Texas Press, 1983), p. 26. Hereafter cited as Deloria.

93. McSloy, *op. cit.*, pp. 230–233.

94. David E. Wilkins, "*Johnson v. M'Intosh* Revisited: Through the Eyes of *Mitchel v. United States*," *American Indian Law Review*, Vol. 19, 1994, pp. 159–183, at p. 162.

95. Norgren, *op. cit.*, p. 90; Deloria, *loc. cit.*, p. 4. Marshall further states that the doctrine of discovery was an exclusive right to end Indian title of occupancy either by purchase or conquest, Williams, *op. cit.*, p. 313. Marshall said that the Indian title of occupancy did end via justified military conquest and/or voluntary cessations or transfers. Only the federal government could undertake these negotiations. Conveyance of fee simple title to the federal government did not end title of occupancy. Joseph W. Singer, "Well Settled? The Increasing Weight of History in American Indian Land Claims," *Georgia Law Review*, Vol. 28, 1994, pp. 493, 499. In essence, the doctrine of discovery limited European powers in their competition for America. However, the U.S. was their successor sovereign and now had the same right to exclusive purchase power of Indian lands. Fee simple title can only be gained through a grant of the sovereign, hence, the U.S. Lowndes, *op. cit.*, pp. 86, 87.

96. Norgren, *op. cit.*, p. 90. Obviously, the discoverers were, and would have to be Christian and white.

97. Falkowski, *op. cit.*, p. 98. In addition, Marshall pointed out that "Indian title was flawed by their character and habits." Hagan in Vecsey and Venables, *op. cit.*, p. 69. Since the needs of the white usurpers were assumed to be superior over the Indians, the land utilization argument that either make good use of the land or lose it was still strong in legal thought (p. 68). Also: Wilkins, *op. cit.*, pp. 166–167. See also Kathryn C. Wyatt, "The Supreme Court, Lyng and the Lone Wolf Principle," *Chicago-Kent Law Review*, Vol. 65, 1989, p. 633.

98. Wyatt, *op. cit.*, p. 633.

99. Churchill, in Jaimes, *op. cit.*, p. 142.

Deloria, *op. cit.*, p. 4. This decision traded a vested property right for a recognized property right, for the political right of quasi-sovereignty for the Indian tribes. Marshall did note that there are legal limits on the future conduct of the conquerors, and though conquest gave them title, it did not settle the legality of doing this. Singer, *op. cit.*, p. 489.

100. Deloria, *op. cit.*, p. 26. Therefore, Indian property rights are not really rights, but revocable licenses to occupy the land. Singer, *op. cit.*, p. 490.

101. Williams, *op. cit.*, p. 313.

102. *Ibid.* Also see Robert A. Williams, Jr., *Savage Anxieties* (New York: Palgrave Macmillan, 2012), p. 224.

103. Singer, *op. cit.*, p. 492.

104. Wilkins, *op. cit.*, pp. 163–164. As stated, the landlord-tenant relationship of the federal government toward the American Indian tribes had now been created by "this unilateral transmutation of Indian property and political rights based solely on the self-generated notions of the Supreme Court" (p. 164).

105. *Ibid.*, p. 165.

106. *Ibid.*

107. Newcomb, *op. cit.*, p. 308. The Christian and heathen distinction found in Marshall's opinions makes it possible to understand why federal–Indian relationships are difficult to define (p. 305).

108. *Ibid.*, p. 309.

109. *Ibid.*, p. 320.

110. *Ibid.*, p. 327.

111. Monette, *op. cit.*

112. *Ibid.*, p. 333.

113. Norgren, *op. cit.*, p. 95.

114. Melvin Urofsky, *A March of Liberty* (New York: McGraw Hill, 1988), pp. 268–269.

115. *Ibid.*, p. 269.

116. Bordewich, *op. cit.*, p. 44.

117. *Ibid.* The Cherokee had always faced pressures even after they readily adapted to the ways of the invader's culture, such as forming a Constitution in 1827, a written language, and an agrarian economy. Jefferson had earlier argued for their removal due to the fact that the white and Indian races could not coexist. Deloria, *op. cit.*, p. 6.

118. Andrew Jackson's humane Indian policy was simply to move them as far west as possible. The 1830 Indian Removal Act

encompassed 94 treaties and over $500,000 in order to achieve this goal. This attitude was reinforced by wars with other Indian nations such as the Black Hawk War in 1832 and the Seminole War from 1835 to 1842. See Urofsky, *loc. cit.*, pp. 269–270. Of course, it is often forgotten that both the Creek and Cherokee fought alongside Jackson during the War of 1812 and in subsequent battles to subjugate rebellious tribes in the South.

119. U.S. 5 Pet. 1 (1831).

120. Falkowski, *op. cit.*, p. 100; Norgren, *op. cit.*, pp. 101, 102.

121. Norgren, *op. cit.*, p. 102; Falkowski, *op. cit.*, p. 101. According to Marshall, the Indians are "domestic dependent nations and are in a state of pupilage; their relations to the United States resembling that of a ward to his guardian" (p. 101). The Cherokee did have rights to the lands they occupied until they voluntarily extinguished these by cession to the federal government, who had the sole right as the discoverer, to purchase these lands. Singer, *op. cit.*, pp. 493, 494. See also Wunder, *op. cit.*, p. 26.

122. Norgren, *op. cit.*, p. 104. The justices defined the Cherokee as a state, "men united together to provide safety and advantages by means of union." Deloria, *op. cit.*, p. 31.

123. *Ibid.*, p. 105. Justices Baldwin and Johnson argued that the Indians had no sovereignty whatsoever. Deloria, *op. cit.*, p. 30.

124. In addition, laws were passed forbidding the Cherokee to mine the gold on their lands, testify against any white person in court, or even hold political assemblies. See Nies, *op. cit.*, p. 244.

125. U.S. 6 Pet. 515 (1832).

126. Norgren, *op. cit.*, p. 106. Worcester, in his defense, claimed to be a federal employee. This could have worked since the federal government originally supported missionaries into Cherokee lands. However, the governor of Georgia arranged for him to be fired so that he could be tried. Wunder, *op. cit.*, p. 26. The Cherokee argued that Georgia's actions violated not only their sovereignty, but treaties and the U.S. Constitution.

127. *Ibid.*, p. 107.

128. *Ibid.*

129. *Ibid.*, p. 108; Churchill, in Jaimes, *op. cit.*, p. 142; Falkowski, *op. cit.*, p. 102; Deloria, *op. cit.*, p. 4. In other words, the Indians kept their land titles only if the U.S. agreed; and if they resisted encroachments on their lands, this became aggression against the U.S. and the conquest doctrine may be justified.

130. Norgren, *op. cit.*, p. 108. The Court found the Cherokee to be "a people distinct from others" and a "distinct political community, retaining original natural rights" like "other nations on Earth." Wunder, *op. cit.*, p. 27.

131. Worcester was not released from prison. More importantly, Jackson told the Cherokee to accept Georgia's rule over them or leave the state.

132. In 1830, the first Indian Removal Law was passed by the Congress, and the Treaty of Dancing Rabbit Creek effectively removed the Choctaw from their Alabama and Mississippi lands. Of the 13,000 removed, 4,000 died making the journey. The Creeks would be forced out to Oklahoma in 1832; the Cherokee in 1836; the Chickasaw in 1837; and the Seneca would be forced onto reservations in Pennsylvania and New York in 1842. See Nies, *op. cit.*, pp. 244–254.

133. Deloria, *op. cit.*, p. 33.

134. U.S. 9 Pet. 711 (1835). Justice Henry Baldwin wrote the unanimous opinion, even though Marshall was still on the Court. Baldwin's position in earlier cases was that the Indians had recognized their dependent status through treaties and they were not sovereign entities. As a side note, his fellow justices questioned his sanity, Justice Story called him deranged, and he did miss the 1833 term due to mental illness.

135. Wilkins, *op. cit.*, p. 173.

136. *Ibid.*, p. 175.

137. Norgren, *op. cit.*, p. 112.

138. *Ibid.*

139. Wilkins, *op. cit.*, p. 175. The sale and title held by Mitchel was valid by acts of Congress, the law of nations, and by U.S.-Spanish treaties according to the Court.

140. *Ibid.*, p. 176.

141. *Ibid.*, pp. 176–178.

142. *Ibid.*, p. 160.

143. U.S. 4 Haw. 567 (1846).

144. Norgren, *op. cit.*, pp. 112–113.

145. *Ibid.*, p. 113.

146. *Ibid.* The Court would continue in these efforts. In *United States v. Holliday* 70 U.S. 3 Wall. 407 (1865) the Court allowed

Congress to extend its authority forbidding liquor to the Indians to include even those not living on a reservation. *United States v. 43 Gallons of Whiskey* 93 U.S. 188 (1876) was similar in that the Supreme Court concluded that the power to regulate commerce with the Indians was as broad and free from restriction as it would be with foreign nations. However, state jurisdiction is limited, as was the Indians.' Indian rights were limited when off the reservation in that legislative regulations apply to them even if they have become state citizens (essentially giving up their Indian affiliation) and had fee simple title to their land. In *Smith v. Stevens*, 77 U.S. 10 Wall. 321 (1870), Congress was allowed to safeguard the Kansas Indians on the reservations from their own improvidence. This included the right to restrict their powers of property title alienation. Finally, *Cherokee Tobacco*, 78 U.S. 11 Wall. 616 (1870) stated that an act of Congress could supersede a treaty. The debate was on taxes levied against tobacco, an exemption guaranteed to the Cherokee by treaty.

147. Hagan, in Vecsey and Venables, *op. cit.*, p. 71. This was said in relation to the removal of the Sac and Fox Indians from the Kansas and Iowa territories—a compassionate statement from an anti-slavery activist.

148. *Ibid.* This same mode of thought exists to this day.

149. Scott W. Berg, *38 Nooses: Lincoln, Little Crow, and the Beginning of the Frontier's End* (New York: Pantheon Books, 2012), p. 66.

150. *Ibid.*

151. *Ibid.*, p. 67.

152. *Ibid.*, p. 68.

153. *Ibid.*

154. Elizabeth Prine Pauls, "Trail of Tears," 5 April 2017, https://britannica.com/event/Trail-of-Tears. The Seminoles would fight their removal and this would culminate in the 1835–1842 Seminole Wars and most of the tribe eluding removal by retreating into Florida's swamps. According to Ward Churchill, the Choctaws and Chickasaws would lose about 15 percent of their population due to the march, the Creeks and Seminoles about 50 percent and the Cherokees, over 55 percent; see *A Little Matter of Genocide* (San Francisco: City Lights Books, 1997), p. 144. Thirty years later, the Navajo

would suffer their 1864 Long Walk where about half of the tribe would die either on the march or as a direct result of the 300-mile forced march to Bosque Redondo (see p. 145). Other tribes like the Cheyenne, Ponca and others would suffer similarly during their periods of internment while awaiting their fates (p. 145).

155. Berg, *loc. cit.*, p. 68.

156. *Ibid.*, p. 69.

157. David A. Nichols, *Lincoln and the Indians* (St. Paul: Minnesota Historical Society Press, 2012), p. 6.

158. *Ibid.*, p. 7.

159. *Ibid.*, p. 8.

160. *Ibid.*, pp. 10–16.

161. For example, Samuel Pomerary (Kansas) received 9,000 acres of Pottawatomie lands and another 50,000 from the Kickapoo Tribe as part of the treaties *he* negotiated on "their behalf" and he would later use this wealth to become an U.S. Senator. Henry Sibley (Minnesota) negotiated the treaty with the Sioux where they received a lump sum payment of $475,000 and he received $145,000 for his efforts. This was approved by the Indian agent, Alexander Ramsey. Sibley would go on to be the state's first governor, and Ramsey the second. There are even cases of the federal Indian commissioner being involved in numerous scandals, but there were no consequences, even in face of evidence to the contrary. *Ibid.*, pp. 18, 19.

162. Hampton Sides, *Blood and Thunder* (New York: Anchor Books, 2006), p. 400.

163. *Ibid.*, p. 401.

164. *Ibid.*, pp. 405, 408.

165. U.S. 19 Wall. 591 (1873).

166. Norgren, *op. cit.*, p. 117.

167. Many treaties were procured by the threat of military force so great that the Indian tribes had little choice—either cede the lands or perish. Overall, an estimated two billion acres were given up by treaties to the United States. See Nell Jessup Newton, "Compensation, Reparations and Restitution: Indian Property Claims in the United States," *Georgia Law Review*, Vol. 28, 1994, p. 459. Treaty protocol was developed primarily with the Indian nations of the northeast. Indian speakers at these negotiations would not always be leaders, but those known for their oratory skills. Thus, they had no

authority to sign as representatives of their tribe (Jennings, *op. cit.*, pp. 120–124). Furthermore, treaties usually had to be read to the attendees, and the signatories signed papers supposedly detailing what they heard. This was not always the case, in that the papers were purposely changed by the United States representatives, by Congress at a later date, or by the interpreter who may not have known the lingual nuances of the local language.

168. These tribes are commonly, and as a group, known as the Sioux. However, the term Sioux has its meaning from French trappers, and means cutthroats or killers. It is rarely used by the members of the three nations when referring to themselves.

169. Wunder, *op. cit.*, p. 30.

170. Sharon O'Brien, *American Indian Tribal Governments* (Norman: University of Oklahoma Press, 1989), p. 71. This was also due in part to the efforts of Congress to establish a policy of assimilation. This meant the dissolving of tribal identity and sovereignty and integrating the Indians into white society and culture forcefully and completely. This process of genocide continues.

171. *Ibid.*, p. 29.

172. Newton, *op. cit.*, p. 460. Since treaties recognized the sovereignty of the signing parties, the way to end sovereignty would be to attack the very basis of treaties, including the people who signed them. Wunder, *op. cit.*, p. 18.

173. The entire state of California was taken in this manner. Later, in 1944, the U.S. Court of Claims would decide what damages were due the Indians of California. The Indians were entitled to receive 8,518,900 acres of land with a value of $1.25 per acre and goods guaranteed by treaty for a total due of $17,053,941.98. However, after deducting the costs for goods and services (including health, education and civilization supports) that they had received, the court settled on a total of $5,024,842.34 for the entire state of California. *Indians of California v. U.S.*, 102 Ct. Cl. 837, December 4, 1944. In total, nearly one billion acres of land was taken with no, or little compensation.

174. U.S. 375 (1886).

175. Jaimes, *op. cit.*, p. 18; O'Brien, *op. cit.*, p. 73. *Lonewolf v. Hitchcock*, 187 U.S. 553 (1903) would complete the process. Here,

the plenary powers of Congress allowed it to pick and choose which sections of any treaty they would follow, getting rid of those sections it found inconvenient. Of course, the Indians need not consent to this. In effect, Congress chose to find those treaty aspects which gave the U.S. lands inviolate, but sections dealing with compensation or obligations to be inconvenient and thus, dispensed with at their will. It also made federal control over the Indians absolute, thus increasing dependency and depriving them of the needed sovereignty to manage their own affairs. The U.S. attempted to get 2.5 million acres of land owned by the Kiowa, Comanche and Apache tribes in violation of the 1867 Treaty of Medicine Lodge. Congress had authorized the sale of excess lands in 1889, but with the stipulation that three-quarters of all adult males must agree. The vote failed, but the Senate went ahead with the land sale anyway. Lone Wolf sued claiming this was a treaty abrogation, as was the allotment process as a whole. He lost when the Court ruled Congress had unlimited power over Indian lands regardless of treaty statements. In other words, Justice White justified unilateral termination of treaties and secured an era of new colonialism. See Wunder, *op. cit.*, pp. 39–40; Deloria, *op. cit.*, pp. 40–44; Jaimes, *op. cit.*, p. 19; O'Brien, *op. cit.*, p. 74–75.

176. Wunder, *op. cit.*, p. 17; Hurtado and Iverson, *op. cit.*, pp. 370–372.

177. Deloria, *op. cit.*, p. 9; Wunder, *op. cit.*, p. 32; Rebecca L. Robbins, "Self-Determination and Subordination: The Past, Present and Future of American Indian Governance," in Jaimes, *op. cit.*, p. 93. The Cherokee, Choctow, Seneca and some other tribes were exempted from the Act. Issues such as non–Indians marrying into the tribe and heirship of lands already allotted would have to be settled through the courts in the coming years.

178. Wunder, *op. cit.*, p. 32. Benefits did not apply to off-reservation Indians. Mixed-blood Indians had to become U.S. citizens to receive their parcel. See also O'Brien, *op. cit.*, p. 77. The Indians had to choose allotment, for if they did not, the BIA did it for them after four years. Terry L. Anderson and Dean Lueck, "Land Tenure and Agricultural Productivity on Indian Reservations,"

Journal of Law and Economics, vol. 35, October 1992, p. 429. Note: Anderson's and Lueck's article stresses a non–Indian view of the land and argues that the overall purpose of the land should be economic profit and productivity, a goal which land trusteeship hampers. He lays some of the blame on tribal governments (p. 434), but fails to point out that most of these were set up by the federal government in the first place by the 1934 IRA.

179. Deloria, *op. cit.*, p. 9.

180. Newton, *op. cit.*, p. 465.

181. *Ibid.*, p. 466.

182. *Ibid.*, p. 461. The courts would now rule that land disputes between the Indians and the government were political issues, immune from judicial review and subject to the overriding presumption that the government always acted in good faith toward the Indians (p. 467).

183. *Ibid.*

184. Rennard Strickland, "Genocide-at-Law," *University of Kansas Law Review*, Vol. 34, 1986, pp. 723–725.

185. *Ibid.*, p. 728.

186. *Ibid.*

187. *Ibid.*, p. 729. Many families would declare themselves to be white and hide their tribal affiliations so as to keep their families intact. Thus, destruction of the Indian was accomplished one way or another.

188. *Ibid.*

189. For a good summary of the IRA sections, see: Arlene Hirschfelder and Martha Kreipe de Montano, *The Native American Almanac* (New York: Prentice-Hall, 1993), pp. 72–75.

190. Wunder, *op. cit.*, p. 62–63. Among some of the findings: The Indian death rate was more than double the average death rate, 25.6 to 54 as compared with 11.8 per 1000; the infant mortality rate was 26.2 compared to 13.6/1000 for non–Indians; the children's death rate 36.9 to 16.2/1000; and the annual per capita income was under $500 per year. Additionally, the allotment process had created a new social ill of homelessness. For example, the Oklahoma tribes lost 13.5 million of their 15 million acres thanks to the Dawes Act. Collier sought to return not only economic benefits, but also social and cultural benefits back to the Indians. He ended religious discrimination, compulsory

religious education, the forcing of Indian children to attend boarding schools away from their homes, and expanded the rights of the accused in state and tribal courts. Wunder, *op. cit.*, pp. 63–65.

191. *Ibid.*, p. 68; Hurtado and Iverson, *op. cit.*, pp. 451–454.

192. Wunder, *op. cit.*, p. 68.

193. The Cheyenne River Sioux in South Dakota drew up its own constitution which carefully deleted the BIA's powers over the tribe. Its nine articles are dedicated to territory, membership criteria, the council and its election, council powers, duties and removal, land, and amendment and referendum processes. Frank Ducheneaux pointed out at the time that the IRA did not give them anything they already did not have as a sovereign nation, and by accepting the IRA they would be losing authority and self-determinative powers. Collier sent an Indian Organization Unit made up of anthropologists and lawyers to convince them to approve the IRA. Opponents were branded as agitators. All Collier and the BIA did succeed in doing was set up a division between the older, traditional leaders and the younger, educated mixed bloods who saw the IRA as a means of gaining power. Wunder, *op. cit.*, pp. 74–77; Robbins, in Jaimes, *op. cit.*, p. 96.

194. Wunder, *op. cit.*, p. 71–72. Those males not voting or abstaining in the election were counted as "yes" votes, thereby guaranteeing the acceptance of the IRA. Robbins, in Jaimes, *op. cit.*, p. 96.

195. Wunder, *op. cit.*, p. 73.

196. Properly known as the Diné.

197. Robbins, in Jaimes, *op. cit.*, p. 94.

198. Wunder, *loc. cit.*, pp. 73–74.

199. Wunder, *op. cit.*, p. 99.

200. *Ibid.*, p. 100.

201. *Ibid.*, p. 101.

202. Some examples of losses due to termination: The Menominee had 3,270 members and 33,881 acres lost by 1961, status and partial lands restored in 1973; the Klamath had 2,133 members and 862,662 acres lost, with partial restoration in 1986; Utah Paiute had 232 members with 42,839 acres lost by 1957, restored in 1980; Utah Mixed Blood Utes, 490 members with 211,430 acres lost in 1961, never restored; and the last tribe to be terminated, the Northern Ponca in 1966, had 442 members and 834 acres restored in

1990. See Wunder, *op. cit.*, pp. 102, 175. The Menominee were forced into termination. They had sued and won $7.6 million from the U.S. government for its mismanagement of tribal timber resources. In order to get the money (which could not be released without Congressional approval), they had to accept termination. They did, mainly because the Menominee had gone corporate earlier and it was controlled by non–Indians (*ibid.*, pp. 103–105).

203. *United States v. Joseph,* 94 U.S. 616 (1876).

204. Wunder, *op. cit.*, p. 43.

205. U.S. 28 (1913).

206. *Ibid.*, p. 43. The case involved the sale of liquor to the Pueblos.

207. John Collier responded to the Bursum Bill and its effects on the Pueblo Indians with disdain in that it would "deprive the Pueblos of their land and water and leave several thousand Mexicans and Americans" to legally fight it out for the possession of these. Hurtado and Iverson, *op. cit.*, pp. 443–447.

208. U.S. 371 (1905).

209. *Ibid.*, p. 52.

210. *Winters v. United States,* 207 U.S. 564 (1908). Wunder, *op. cit.*, p. 52. See also Hurtado and Iverson, *op. cit.*, p. 408.

211. Wunder, *op. cit.*, p. 54.

212. U.S. 219 (1923). In *U.S. ex rel. Hualpai v. Santa Fe Railroad,* 314 U.S. 339 (1941) this issue of Indian title would take a slight detour. Justice Douglas relegated the justness of a title extinguishment, regardless of its manner, to something not open to judicial review. However, even though the Hualpai were forced to relocate in 1874, there was no plain intent to give up their lands and thus, title was not ended. In other words: no consent, no extinguishment. In *U.S. v. Alcea Band of Tillamooks,* 329 U.S. 40 (1946), the Court ruled that the Tillamooks could recover for lands taken by executive order for the same reason. They were initially awarded $3 million with $14 million in back interest. The government appealed the award on the grounds it was not a Fifth Amendment compensatory taking, and was able to get the interest waived. Lowndes, *op. cit.*, pp. 92–95.

213. Felix S. Cohen, "Original Indian Title," *Minnesota Law Review,* Vol. 32, 1947, p. 32.

214. U.S. 272; 75 S. Ct. 313; 99 L. Ed. 314; 15 Alaska 418 (1955).

215. U.S. at 277. Economics may have been the real premise for Reed's logic in that the claim was for $9 billion. Falkowski, *op. cit.*, p. 105.

216. U.S. at 278.

217. *Ibid.*

218. *Ibid.* Also see Lowndes, *op. cit.*, p. 96.

219. U.S. at 281–282.

220. He noted that there were only 65 members of the tribe left, no women of child-bearing age in a matriarchal system; and the system of property ownership was communal not individual. Furthermore, he stated that the Tee-Hit-Ton's use of the land was not sufficiently intensive. Singer, *op. cit.*, pp. 520–521. Of course, these observations really had no bearing on the legality of the issue at hand. Since when does proper use necessarily determine property rights.

221. U.S. at 290.

222. Newton, *op. cit.*, p. 472.

223. See *United States v. Alcea Band of Tillamooks,* 341 U.S. 48 (1951).

224. Singer, *op. cit.*, pp. 519–520.

225. Falkowski, *op. cit.*, p. 105. Case cite: 358 U.S. 217 (1959).

226. Allen, *op. cit.*, pp. 864, 868–869. The case involved a challenge to Public Law 280 passed in 1953 which permitted states to take civil and criminal jurisdiction away from the tribes without their consent. Six states were required to do this, some had to use their state constitution to take jurisdiction while the others merely had to pass legislation to do so. States were prohibited from assuming control over taxes, real property or water rights and, any tribal custom or law in conflict with the state's civil law was voided. In *Williams,* Arizona sued a federally licensed trader on the Diné reservation for taxes due on goods sold on credit. The state supreme court affirmed this action, but the U.S. Supreme Court stated Arizona had overstepped its bounds and violated the procedures for PL 280. It had no jurisdiction *in this matter.* Wunder, *op. cit.*, pp. 107–110.

227. The Tuscarora joined the League in 1722 after fleeing North Carolina. They left after a war with English slave traders. Nies, *op. cit.*, p. 169. Their voice in the council is through the Onondaga.

228. *Federal Power Commission v. Tuscarora Indian Nation,* 362 U.S. 99, 80 S. Ct. 543-567 (1960).

229. *Ibid.,* p. 545.

230. *Ibid.,* pp. 548, 550. Obviously, the Indian community did not count.

231. *Ibid.,* pp. 552, 553.

232. *Ibid.,* p. 557.

233. *Ibid.,* p. 559.

234. *Ibid.,* p. 563. This means, it falls under the power of eminent domain.

235. Nies, *op. cit.,* p. 359.

236. *Seneca Nation v. Brucker,* 162 F. Supp. 580 (1958), p. 581.

237. *Ibid.,* p. 580.

238. *Ibid.*

239. *Seneca Nation v. Brucker,* 262 F.2d 27, 104 U.S. App. D.C. 315 (1958).

240. *Ibid.,* p. 316.

241. Other members, rather than accept the poor land or face the humiliation of losing their homes, simply left the reservation and some, even the Iroquois League. They chose to live among their white neighbors. This meant that they had to deny (at least publicly) their own heritage to avoid discrimination and/or having their children removed to boarding schools. Some members of the author's family followed this path, and it was not until decades later that they admitted and embraced their cultural heritage and beliefs. As a side note, the Seneca cemetery was dug up by archeologists through an arrangement with the Army Corps of Engineers and over any opposition by the Seneca (who, it was stated, were in the minority), who analyzed and categorized their findings on 361 bodies. This included Cornplanter himself. See George H. Abrams, "The Cornplanter Cemetery," *Pennsylvania Archeologist,* Vol. 35/No. 2, 1965, pp. 59–73.

242. F.2d 1194 Ct. Cl.; cert. denied 400 U.S. 819 (1970).

243. Nell Jessup Newton, "Indian Claims in the Courts of the Conqueror," *American University Law Review,* Vol. 41, Summer 1992, p. 778. Hereafter cited as Newton-A.

244. *Ibid.*

245. *Ibid.* Judge Davis would make other profound statements. In *Fort Sill Apache Tribe v. United States,* 477 F.2d 1360 (Ct. Cl.) 1973, he stated that allowing the tort claim in this case would open the door for a multitude of claims from other tribes. In *Fort Sill,* the Apache Tribe sued for damages caused by their imprisonment after Geronimo's rebellion. During the 27 years in prison, the tribe was nearly wiped out. Davis stated that the claim allowed for the destruction of the tribe's existence would mean the government had no power to terminate existence by unilateral, but peaceful, means and insist that tribal members assimilate into the general population. *Ibid.,* pp. 779–781.

246. Churchill, in Jaimes, *op. cit.,* p. 148. The *Passamaquoddy Tribe v. Morton,* 528 F.2d 370 (1st Cir. 1975) reversed the 1974 ruling in *Morton v. Mancari* where the Court ruled that tribes were a political, not racial classification. The Passamaquoddy had a history in Maine for over 3,000 years. They first sued to retrieve their land in 1892 but the Maine Supreme Court ruled they were not a tribe even though they had two reservations and over 800 members at the time. The First Circuit Court overruled the state and said the tribe was entitled to trust benefits and protections as a recognized tribe. The Passamaquoddy did agree not to press for full return of the land if they got monetary compensation and unoccupied lands. In 1980, Congress agreed and granted them $27 million in cash and a land acquisition fund of $54 million to be shared with the neighboring Penobscot and Maliseet tribes. Wunder, *op. cit.,* pp. 166–168. By the mid-1970s, other tribes were seeking restoration of their status and compensation for lands stolen through policy or court decision. The Department of Interior created rules for federal recognition as an Indian tribe in 1978–1980. This is in itself ironic, that the same culture that destroyed the Indians would now determine who is an Indian. The Menominee (1973) and Ponca (1990), and some others, had specific Congressional acts passed restoring their status and property. Note: Native Hawaiians were excluded from these processes (see Chapter Five).

247. Paul Van Develder, "A Coyote For All Seasons," *Native Peoples,* Vol. 11/No. 4, Summer 1998, p. 44.

248. *Ibid.,* p. 47.

249. *United States v. Sioux Nation of Indians,* 448 U.S. 371; 100 S. Ct. 2716 (1980). For a full accounting of this case and its underlying history, see Edward Lazarus, *Black Hills White Justice* (New York: Harper Collins, 1991).

250. Hurtado and Iverson, *op. cit.*, pp. 331–337.

251. U.S. at 378. General Sheridan let it be known he would give cordial support to the settlement of the Black Hills should Congress decide to open up the territory for settlement by ending the treaty with the Indian tribes.

252. Food rations were cut until the signatures were acquired. The Court of Claims remarked on this pattern of duress to get an agreement of sale by stating that "a more ripe and rank case of dishonorable dealings will never, in all probability, be found in our history, which is not, taken as a whole, the disgrace it now pleases some persons to believe." 448 U.S. at 388.

253. The Act took approximately 7 million acres. 448 U.S. at 382 n. 14.

254. Nell Jessup Newton, "The Judicial Role in Fifth Amendment Takings of Indian Land: An Analysis of the Sioux Nation Rule," *Oregon Law Review,* Vol. 61, 1982, p. 252, 255. Hereafter cited as Newton-B.

255. U.S. at 371. The Indian Claims Commission was formed in 1946 and initially ruled that the tribes failed to prove their case in 1950. The claim was reheard in 1974 by the Indian Claims Commission on the grounds that past counsel for the Sioux was inadequate. It was at this time that they ruled that the government had made no effort to compensate the tribes for the lands taken in 1877. Congress had acted pursuant to its power of eminent domain, and not as a trustee. Thus, compensation due with value of land at the time. The Government appealed to the Court of Claims. 448 U.S. at 385, 387.

256. References were made to *Shoshone Tribe v. U.S.,* 299 U.S. 476 (1937) which stated that Congress has paramount power over Indian lands, but that power does not extend so far as to giving tribal lands to others, or taking it for itself without just compensation.

257. Newton-B, *op. cit.*, p. 256.

258. *Ibid.*, p. 259.

259. *Ibid.*, p. 248.

260. *Ibid.*, pp. 261, 265. According to the BIA, the "federal trust responsibility is a legal obligation under which the U.S. has charged itself with the moral obligations of the highest responsibility and trust towards Ameri-

can Indian tribes." See BIA, "FAQs," *op. cit.* Many would argue with this assessment.

261. U.S. at 427.

262. U.S. at 433.

263. U.S. at 435.

264. U.S. at 436–437.

265. U.S. at 437.

266. This was another chapter in a series of events that the Abenaki staged in order to win a homeland in western Vermont.

267. Vt. 102; 616 A.2d 210 (VT 1992); cert. denied 507 U.S. 911, 113 S. Ct. 1258 (1993).

268. Singer, *op. cit.*, p. 482.

269. A.2d at 212. The trial court found that the evidence presented by the Abenaki of their existence in the area since 9300 BCE, based on culture, governance, familial traditions and other points, disproved the state's assertion that the Abenaki had abandoned the lands (p. 214).

270. A.2d at 213. The sovereign's intent to end the Indian's rights need not be express, but there must be evidence that demonstrates a plain and unambiguous intent to extinguish the Indian's exclusive rights (p. 213). Also, Lowndes, *op. cit.*, pp. 78–81. The Abenaki were not a federally recognized tribe but did qualify and receive federal grants and programs designed solely for American Indians.

271. Singer, *op. cit.*, p. 482.

272. *Ibid.*, p. 483.

273. *Ibid.*

274. *Ibid.*, p. 486.

275. The court quoted *U.S. ex rel. Hualapai Indians v. Santa Fe Railroad,* 314 U.S. 339 (1941) where the Court stated: "Aboriginal title may be extinguished by treaty, by the sword, by purchase, by the exercise of complete dominion adverse to the right of occupancy, or otherwise, its justness is not open to inquiry in the courts."

276. The court misquoted, or took out of context, statements made in the Cherokee cases where Marshall claimed that discovery gave exclusive title to those who made the discovery, and this constituted the conquest of America. "History carried out this preordained outcome." Singer, *op. cit.*, p. 490. Marshall only meant the discovery principle to apply to and between the European powers and applied to the Indians only so far as these powers were attempting to influence them. *Ibid.*

277. A.2d at 215. The Royal Proclamation of 1763 revoked these grants and established a firm border along the Appalachian and Green Mountain ranges, while further stipulating the Crown's policy of banning further expansion onto Indian lands. Lowndes, *op. cit.*, pp. 102, 103.

278. A.2d at 215, 218.

279. A.2d at 218, 220; Lowndes, *op. cit.*, pp. 112–114.

280. A.2d at 218.

281. *Ibid.*, pp. 504–506.

282. *Ibid.* The Court called these Royal Proclamations "paper tigers," and since Britain did not enforce them, this was de facto evidence of their intent to extinguish aboriginal title to the land. The sovereign's recognition of the inevitability of white settlement constituted implied consent to the Indian title being ended. Lowndes, *op. cit.*, p. 103.

283. *Ibid.*, p. 510.

284. *Ibid.*, p. 515. The Court agreed that the Abenaki never withdrew from the area. In fact, it agreed that the mere withdrawing from a land due to white encroachment may not end property titles. However, it stated the Abenaki had lost control of the lands by the 1790s. 616 A.2d at 219.

285. Lowndes, *op. cit.*, pp. 115–117.

286. *Ibid.*, p. 529.

287. *Ibid.*, p. 530.

288. *Ibid.*, p. 532. One final point: the Vermont Supreme Court's opinion seems to have ignored that Marshall, in *Cherokee Nation v. Georgia* (1831) stated that the Indians could only cede lands to the discoverer, the federal government, and not to any other party. The Court was quick to accept the discovery doctrine, but apparently failed to apply it according to earlier Supreme Court rulings.

289. Newton-B, *op. cit.*, p. 246.

290. *Ibid.*, p. 247.

291. Newton-A, *op. cit.*, p. 754.

292. *Ibid.* This is especially true that since the early Marshall rulings, there has been doubt as to whether the Indians could sue the federal government on their own behalf. It would not be until 1965 that Congress would allow tribes to bring suit against the federal government without U.S. permission. Until this time, tribes needed a private bill from Congress granting them the right

to litigate. The 1946 Indian Claims Commission was created to grant the tribes equal access to the Court of Claims and to settle historic wrongs and grievances for all time. This was dissolved in 1978 and cases now go to the Court of Claims (*ibid.*, pp. 769–774).

293. Newton, *op. cit.*, p. 456.

294. *Ibid.*, p. 457.

295. *Ibid.*, pp. 457–458.

296. *Ibid.*, p. 457.

297. Cohen, *op. cit.*, p. 35.

298. *Ibid.*, pp. 38–39.

299. *Ibid.*, pp. 39–40. He points out that the New Netherlands, New Jersey, Connecticut, Rhode Island and others had these laws as early as the 1620s.

300. Newton, *op. cit.*, p. 480. According to the BIA, as of 2017, there is 56.2 million acres held in trust by the U.S. government, and 326 Indian land areas currently administered by the federal government. In addition, there is allotted land (areas broken up and taken by the Dawes Allotment Act of 1887), and this consists of over 10 million acres of land held in trust for individuals or their heirs. This does not include restricted lands that can only have their title conveyed with government approval or lands held in trust by a state. See BIA, "FAQs," *op. cit.*

301. Churchill, in Jaimes, *op. cit.*, p. 174.

302. *Ibid.*, pp. 175–177. Since 1970, approximately 540,000 acres of land have been returned to the tribes. For example, in 1988: The Puyallup, 321 acres; Hannahville Indian Community, 3,359 acres; Potawatomi, 11,300 (WI); Confederated Tribes of Oregon, 9,811; the Paiute in Utah, 4,765; and the Quinault, 11,905 acres. In addition, tribes are receiving monetary damages for stolen lands: Rhode Island, $3.5 million (1988); Connecticut, $900,000 (1983); Massachusetts, $5 million (1988); Florida $6.5 million (1987); and the Micmacs, $900,000 in 1991. See Newton, *op. cit.*, p. 475, nn. 98, 100. However, even with these successes, the losses are still much greater.

303. Aviam Soifer, "Objects In Mirror Are Closer Than They Appear," *Georgia Law Review*, Vol. 28, 1994, pp. 533–553, at p. 533. Soifer goes on to criticize the courts in the manner in which they employ history in an inconsistent way. The "routine ways in which judges emulate soldiers and settlers in a rush to establish a new reality" is disparaging (p.

535). He points out the way in which Justices Scalia and Thomas simply wave away relevant texts and language, claiming that they must do so in the service of history.

304. *Ibid.*, p. 537. Soifer uses the Noatok Indian case to demonstrate this point. Whereas Justice Marshall made clear that the Indian tribes *were not foreign nations*, the Supreme Court, in order to protect the state of Alaska, determined that the Indians *were foreign nations* and protected from these suits by the Eleventh Amendment. Yet, this is a grant of sovereignty without authority. They claimed to be relying on history, but betray their ability to remember (*ibid.*, pp. 537–552).

305. Steven P. McSloy, "Revisiting the 'Courts of the Conqueror': American Indian Claims Against the United States," *American University Law Review*, Vol. 44, Winter 1994, pp. 537–644, at p. 642. McSloy is referring to the Court of Claims which developed out of the Indian Claims Commission. It was created to adjudicate breach of trust claims arising out of the guardianship doctrine between the government and the Indian tribes, as well as any other claim against the government from disgruntled civil servants, etc. This court was renamed the Court of Federal Claims in 1992 (*ibid.*, pp. 541–547).

306. *Ibid.* McSloy states: "The courts are left to enforce the letter of laws whose spirits have long since departed" (p. 643).

307. *Ibid.*, pp. 642–643.

308. Dissenting Opinion, *Federal Power Commission v. Tuscarora Indian Nation* (1960), *op. cit.*, p. 567. Italics added.

Chapter Three

1. Newburn, *op. cit.*, p. 35.

2. Don L. Boroughs, "Mickey Mouse Walks Away From a Fight," *U.S. News and World Report*, Vol. 117/No. 14, 10 October 1994, p. 103.

3. Hugh Sidey, "When Mickey Comes Marching Home," *Time*, Vol. 143/No. 23, 21 March 1994, p. 61. Disney spent nearly $50,000 per day on its lobbying and public relations efforts. It employed former Carter press secretary, Jody Powell, to lead this campaign. Powell, in an obviously hypocritical move, was the same person who worked to "stop millionaire developer Til Hazel from

dropping a shopping mall onto the Second Manassas Battlefield in 1988" (*ibid.*).

4. *Ibid.*

5. C. Vann Woodward, "A Mickey Mouse Idea," *The New Republic*, Vol. 120/No. 4144, 20 June 1994, p. 16.

6. *Ibid.*

7. Charles Krauthammer, "Who's Afraid of Virginia's Mouse?" *Time*, Vol. 143/No. 12, 6 June 1994, p. 76.

8. Connie Farrow, "Site of Mo. Civil War Battle Now Fighting Encroachment," *The Advocate*, 7 November, 2004, p. 13B.

9. *Ibid.*

10. *Ibid.*

11. David Dishneau. "Battlefield Billboards Causing New Fighting," *The Advocate*, 5 December 2004, p. 25A.

12. *Ibid.*

13. *Ibid.*

14. Deb Riechmann, "Millennium Fireworks Plans for Monument Spark Debate," *The Advocate*, 28 December 1999, p. 2A.

15. *Ibid.* In recent years, many southern states have had to face the symbols of the Confederacy and the Civil War and what they mean to both the African American and white communities. The city of New Orleans has finally finished a long political, social and legal battle by removing four monuments that commemorated leaders of the Confederacy and the segregationist era of its aftermath (Robert E. Lee, Jefferson Davis, P.G.T. Beauregard and the White League Uprising). However, its statue of Andrew Jackson and Jackson Square remain undisturbed.

16. Bear Butte, SD, is held sacred by the Northern Cheyenne, Lakotas, Crow, Kiowa and 20-plus other tribes. It has been a state park since 1962 and a National Historical site since 1965, yet the state "built observation platforms so tourists would have a good place to ogle the Indian ceremonies that take place there" and built a concert/beer hall within shouting distance to cater to the 500,000 bikers that flock there every year for the Sturgis Bike Festival. See Jake Page, "Sacred Ground: Landscapes as Living Spirit," *Native Peoples*, Vol. 20/No. 3, May/June 2007, p. 30. Other sites that Page refers to include: Woodruff bluff—sacred to the Hopis but is being dug up to use as paving material for Interstate 40; Rice Lake, Wisconsin used by the Sakaogen, Ojibwe, Menominee, and Pot-

tawatomies for harvesting wild rice has been threatened by a huge zinc and copper mining operation; as are several others around the United States.

17. Amendment 1 of the U.S. Constitution states: "Congress shall make no law respecting an establishment of religion, or prohibiting the free exercise thereof...." These are the establishment and the free exercise clauses referred to throughout this chapter.

18. John Rhodes, "An American Tradition: The Religious Persecution of Native Americans," *Montana Law Review*, Vol. 52, Winter 1991, p. 18.

19. Sharon O'Brien, "Freedom of Religion in Indian Country," *Montana Law Review*, Vol. 56, Summer 1995, p. 453. Hereafter cited as O'Brien, "Freedom."

20. Rhodes, *loc. cit.*, p. 19.

21. C. S. Locust, "American Indian Beliefs Concerning Health and Unwellness," University of Arizona, Native American Research and Training Center, 1985, as quoted in Eugene F. Pickette et al., "Cultural identification of American Indians and Its Impact on Rehabilitation Services," *Journal of Rehabilitation*, Vol. 65/No. 3, July–September 1999, p. 4.

22. Deward E. Walker, "Protection of American Indian Sacred Geography," in Christopher Vecsey, ed., *Handbook of American Indian Religious Freedom* (New York: Crossroad, 1993), p. 102. See also: Rupert Ross, *Dancing With a Ghost* (New York: Penguin Books, 2006), pp. XII–XV, 59–77.

23. Rhodes, *loc. cit.* This belief obviously affects many tribes' views on resource development on their lands.

24. *Ibid.* Also see Kirsten Boyles, "Saving Sacred Sites," *Cornell Law Review*, Vol. 76, July 1991, p. 1124. Unless the ceremonies are performed to maintain the balance, the world will descend into chaos according to the Hopi. Under American Indian teleology, the peoples on Earth (the Red, White, Yellow and Black which also represent the four sacred colors and directions), are precisely and properly placed and must live in balance with all of the creatures, plants and elements. See Robert Charles Ward, "The Spirits Will Leave," *Ecology Law Quarterly*, Vol. 19, 1992, p. 800.

25. Rhodes, *loc. cit.*, p. 20.

26. *Ibid.*, p. 21.

27. Annie L. Booth and Harvey M. Jacobs, "Ties That Bind," *Environmental Ethics*, Vol. 12, Spring 1990, p. 31.

28. Rhodes, *op. cit.*, p. 21; Ward, *op. cit.*, p. 801.

29. Booth and Jacobs, *op. cit.*, p. 31.

30. *Ibid.*, p. 33.

31. O'Brien, "Freedom," *op. cit.*, p. 453.

32. Rupert, *Dancing*, *op. cit.*, p. 63.

33. *Ibid.*, p. 64.

34. *Ibid.*, pp. 75–76.

35. Booth and Jacobs, *op. cit.*, p. 34.

36. Christopher Vecsey, ed., *Handbook of American Indian Religious Freedom* (New York: Crossroad, 1993), p. 103.

37. A vision quest is a personal ceremony performed in order to seek a vision from the Great Spirit. It is usually done under the guidance of a "medicine man" (a generic term). The quest can generally last up to four days and nights in which the participant deprives himself of food and water, and prays continuously seeking guidance, direction or other messages. The location for the quest needs to be isolated and untarnished to provide the proper setting for the dream visions. Purification ceremonies include sweat lodges, among others. Medicine plants include sage, cedar, sweet grass, and other herbs and roots used in healing practices and cultural medicines.

38. Vecsey, *op. cit.*, p. 111.

39. *Ibid.*, p. 112.

40. Celia Byler, "Free Access or Free Exercise," *Connecticut Law Review*, Vol. 22, Winter 1990, p. 410.

41. Arlene Hirschfelder and Martha Kreipe de Montano, *The Native American Almanac* (New York: Prentice-Hall, 1993), p. 111.

42. Boyles, *op. cit.*, p. 1124.

43. Byler, *loc. cit.*, p. 411.

44. Ward, *op. cit.*, p. 800.

45. *Ibid.*, p. 799.

46. O'Brien, "Freedom," *op. cit.*, p. 453.

47. *Ibid.*, p. 454. It is this fact that has played the most havoc among the Indian nations on both the North and South American continents.

48. Sarah B. Gordon, "Indian Religious Freedom and Governmental Development of Public Lands," *Yale Law Journal*, Vol. 94, May 1985, pp. 1448–1449.

49. *Ibid.*

50. *Ibid.*, p. 1450.

51. *Ibid.* Even though there are religious sites important to Western religions, they are usually in the Middle East and are seen as mystical and separate from the everyday worship system.

52. Rhodes, *op. cit.*, p. 15.

53. O'Brien, "Freedom," *op. cit.*, p. 454. "The U.S. Commission on Civil Rights noted in 1983 that the federal government's failure to protect Native American religion stems from its long history of antagonism and refusal to treat them as significant as western religions." Hirshfelder and Montano, *op. cit.*, p. 112.

54. U.S. 145 (1878).

55. O'Brien, "Freedom," *op. cit.*, p. 456.

56. Mark S. Cohen, "American Indian Sacred Religious Sites and Government Development," *Michigan Law Review*, Vol. 85, February 1987, p. 772. Hereafter cited as M. Cohen.

57. Kathryn C. Wyatt, "The Supreme Court, Lyng and the Lone Wolf Principle," *Chicago-Kent Law Review,* Vol. 65, 1989, p. 626. The separation of church and state would only apply to beliefs, not religious practices.

58. U.S. 624 (1943).

59. *Minersville v. Gobitis* 310 U.S. 586 (1940).

60. Ironically, the Pledge of Allegiance was written in 1892 by Francis Bellamy, a utopian socialist and Baptist minister, to commemorate the 400th anniversary of Columbus. It did not become officially adopted until 1942, and the words "under God" where added in 1954. He proposed it be accompanied by a salute that was eerily similar to that used by the Nazi regime in the 1930s. The salute was quickly replaced.

61. U.S. 624 (1943).

62. U.S. 398 (1963); and O'Brien "Freedom," *op. cit.*, p. 456.

63. M. Cohen, *op. cit.*, pp. 773, 774.

64. John Gillingham, "Native American First Amendment Sacred Land Defense," *Missouri Law Review*, Vol. 54, Summer 1989, p. 780.

65. U.S. 205 (1972).

66. Byler, *op. cit.*, pp. 412–413.

67. M. Cohen, *op. cit.*, p. 775. Again, the majority held the yardstick to determine whether a religion was recognizable, and thus accepted as mainstream.

68. *Ibid.*

69. *Ibid.*

70. *Ibid.*, p. 777.

71. *Ibid.*

72. *Ibid.*, p. 778.

73. M. Cohen, *op. cit.*, p. 782, and Wyatt, *op. cit.*, p. 631.

74. Gillingham, *op. cit.*, p. 779.

75. *Ibid.*

76. Wyatt, *op. cit.*, p. 632.

77. *Ibid.*, p. 781.

78. *Ibid.* David E. Wilkins puts it bluntly: the Court has "seriously jeopardized the practice, nay, the very existence of Indian spiritual ways." See David E. Wilkins, *American Indian Sovereignty and the U.S. Supreme Court* (Austin: University of Texas Press, 1997), p. 3.

79. *Ibid.*, p. 786.

80. *Ibid.*, pp. 786–787.

81. Ward, *op. cit.*, p. 803.

82. Gordon, *op. cit.*, p. 1451.

83. Vine DeLoria, Jr., *God Is Red: A Native View of Religion* (Golden, CO: Fulcrum Publishing, 1994), p. 278.

84. *Ibid.*, p. 1453. American Indians unsuccessfully argued that the courts should enforce the government's fiduciary responsibilities owed to them (p. 1454).

85. Gordon, *op. cit.*, p. 1454.

86. *Ibid.*, p. 1456.

87. Rhodes, *op. cit.*, p. 22.

88. *Ibid.*, p. 35.

89. *Ibid.*

90. *Ibid.*, p. 46.

91. F.2d 1159 (6th Cir.), cert. denied 480 F. Supp. (608) [E. TN] (1979); 449 U.S. 953 (1980).

92. Wyatt, *op. cit.*, p. 639. As stated, this relationship between belief, practice and a certain site is not generally recognized in the Judeo-Christian systems (*ibid.*).

93. M. Cohen, *op. cit.*, p. 784; O'Brien, "Freedom," *op. cit.*, p. 468; Rhodes, *op. cit.*, p. 48. When the TVA impounded the land, the remains in the cemeteries were reinterred. However, the Indian remains were sent to a museum as "matters of scientific interest" (Wyatt, *op. cit.*, FN 98, p. 636). The Tellico Dam is probably best remembered for the cause of the infamously endangered snaildarter fish more than for the Cherokee land claims.

94. M. Cohen, *op. cit.*, p. 784. Also see: Vecsey, *op. cit.*, pp. 35–36.

95. *Ibid.*, p. 785.

96. *Ibid.*; Rhodes, *op. cit.*, p. 50; Wyatt, *op. cit.*, p. 640; O'Brien, "Freedom," *op. cit.*, p. 468; Ward, *op. cit.*, p. 809; Gillingham, *op. cit.*, p. 787. Once again, the Court failed to understand the intertwining between religion, history and culture in Indian life. Of course, protection for historical and cultural reasons should have been enough reason to halt the dam.

97. O'Brien, "Freedom," *op. cit.*, p. 468. Again, religion can be personal and an individual matter for most Indian nations.

98. Wyatt, *op. cit.*, p. 640; Gillingham, *op. cit.*, p. 787.

99. Rhodes, *op. cit.*, p. 50.

100. *Ibid.*, p. 51.

101. Peter J. Longo and Christiana E. Miewald, "Native Americans, the Courts and Water Policy," *Great Plains Research*, Vol. 2, 1992, pp. 62–63.

102. M. Cohen, *op. cit.*, p. 783.

103. F.2d 172 (10th Cir. 1980), cert. denied 452 U.S. 954 (1981).

104. Rhodes, *op. cit.*, p. 53; M. Cohen, *op. cit.*, p. 792. The area was taken by the federal government via executive order in 1910 without tribal permission (Vecsey, *op. cit.*, p. 35).

105. Brenda Norrell. "Rainbow Bridge is the 'True Bridge of Life,'" *Indian Country Today*, 6 June 2001, p. B1.

106. Rhodes, *loc. cit.*, p. 53.

107. *Ibid.*; M. Cohen, *op. cit.*, pp. 792–793; Wyatt, *op. cit.*, p. 641; O'Brien, "Freedom," *op. cit.*, p. 468. Economic growth outweighed religious claims (Longo and Miewald, *op. cit.*, p. 62).

108. O'Brien, "Freedom," *op. cit.*, p. 468.

109. O'Brien, "Freedom," *op. cit.*, p. 468; Rhodes, *op. cit.*, p. 53. It is unique that the Diné sought relief under one religious clause, yet the Court used the other to deny it! It was forgotten who owned this land before it was taken from them in the first place. Selective memory is a useful tool when deciding in favor of the usurpers and their goals.

110. Rhodes, *op. cit.*, p. 54.

111. Gillingham, *op. cit.*, p. 788.

112. *Ibid.*

113. F. Supp. 785 (D.S.D. 1982), aff'd 706 F.2d 856 (8th Cir. 1983); cert. denied 464 U.S. 977 (1983).

114. Rhodes, *op. cit.*, p. 54.

115. *Ibid.*, p. 55.

116. *Ibid.*

117. Vecsey, *op. cit.*, p. 37.

118. Rhodes, *op. cit.*, p. 55. No one ever considered that to avoid this conflict, the Butte could be returned to the tribes from whom it was originally taken.

119. O'Brien, "Freedom," *op. cit.*, p. 469.

120. Rhodes, *loc. cit.*, p. 56.

121. Wyatt, *op. cit.*, p. 642.

122. M. Cohen, *op. cit.*, p. 790.

123. F.2d 735 (D.C. Cir. 1983), cert. denied 464 U.S. 956 (1984).

124. *Wilson v. Block*, *op. cit.*, p. 737.

125. *Ibid.*, p. 738.

126. *Ibid.*, p. 740.

127. *Ibid.*

128. M. Cohen, *op. cit.*, p. 787.

129. *Wilson v. Block*, *op. cit.*, p. 744. Try to imagine a court entertaining testimony about Christianity from a non–Christian expert.

130. *Ibid.*, *op. cit.*, p. 740.

131. *Ibid.*

132. *Ibid.*

133. *Ibid.*, p. 741; and Gordon, *op. cit.*, p. 1460.

134. *Wilson v. Block*, *loc. cit.*, p. 741.

135. *Ibid.*

136. *Wilson v. Block*, *op. cit.*, p. 744.

137. See Appendix I for the complete act.

138. AIRFA (1978).

139. Gordon, *op. cit.*, p. 1457; Wyatt, *op. cit.*, pp. 637, 638; and Boyles, *op. cit.*, p. 1127.

140. Gordon, *op. cit.*, p. 1458.

141. *Ibid.* In *Wilson*, the agency merely had to *solicit and consider* Indian opinions for they were not binding on their actions. In the *Fools Crow* case, it was decided that the AIRFA did not create a cause of action for Indian religious right violations (Boyles, *op. cit.*, p. 1128).

142. *Wilson v. Block*, *op. cit.*, p. 745.

143. *Ibid.*, p. 747.

144. Gillingham, *op. cit.*, pp. 789–790.

145. U.S. 439, 108 S. Ct. 1319 (1988).

146. Robert J. Miller, "Correcting Supreme Court Errors," *Environmental Law*, Vol. 20, 1990, p. 1049.

147. *Lyng*, *op. cit.*, p. 442. In its recommendation against building the road, the report stated that approximately 147 archeological sites would be destroyed and requested

that the area be nominated for the National Register of Historic Places (Miller, *op. cit.*, p. 1049).

148. *Ibid.*, p. 443.

149. Several environmental groups as well as the state of California sided with the American Indian plaintiffs in this case.

150. *Lyng, op. cit.*, p. 445; Wyatt, *op. cit.*, p. 624; and Miller, *op. cit.*, p. 1052.

151. Miller, *op. cit.*, p. 1050.

152. Vecsey, *op. cit.*, p. 39.

153. *Ibid.*

154. *Lyng, op. cit.*, p. 447.

155. *Ibid.*, p. 448.

156. U.S. 693 (1986).

157. *Lyng, op. cit.*, pp. 448–449.

158. Byler, *op. cit.*, p. 421; and Boyles, *op. cit.*, pp. 1128–1129.

159. *Lyng, op. cit.*, pp. 449–450. It would most likely also be extremely difficult for any Christian to prove beyond the shadow of doubt that there is a god, or that events in the Bible occurred literally. Instead, these are accepted on faith. So why cannot the Indian be accepted on the same criterion?

160. *Ibid.*, p. 451.

161. *Ibid.*, p. 452; and Wyatt, *op. cit.*, p. 624. The Supreme Court held that, "even if the governmental interference were virtually to destroy the Native American's religion…, the Constitution simply does not provide a principle that would justly upholding the Native American's legal claims" (Wyatt, *op. cit.*, p. 624).

162. *Ibid.*, p. 453. Italics added.

163. Ann M. Hooker, "American Indian Sacred Sites on Federal Public Lands," *Yale Law Journal*, Vol. 19, 1994, p. 139.

164. *Lyng, op. cit.*, p. 460.

165. *Ibid.*, p. 461.

166. *Ibid.*, p. 465.

167. *Ibid.*, p. 475.

168. Rhodes, *op. cit.*, p. 66.

169. *Ibid.*, p. 68.

170. *Lyng, op. cit.*, p. 476.

171. Ward, *op. cit.*, p. 811.

172. *Ibid.*

173. *Ibid.* Drawing the line between practice and belief in American Indian religion is antagonistic to their very belief structure.

174. DeLoria, *op. cit.*, p. 269.

175. Ward, loc cit. Members of the world's major religions have been able to separate from specific places and move elsewhere

and furthermore, one can be a follower without ever visiting or seeing their holy places. As an example, American history points to the Puritans and Pilgrims who came here for religious reasons, albeit they only sought freedom for themselves while condemning any other religion and its followers.

176. Wyatt, *op. cit.*, p. 624.

177. *Ibid.*, p. 625.

178. F.3d 856 (1995).

179. *Pueblo, loc. cit.*, p. 856.

180. *Ibid.*, p. 857.

181. *Ibid.*, p. 860.

182. *Ibid.*, pp. 856, 858.

183. *Ibid.*, p. 859.

184. *Ibid.*

185. *Ibid.*, p. 860.

186. *Ibid.*, p. 961.

187. *Ibid.*

188. *Ibid.*, p. 862.

189. Brenda Norrell, "Sandia Mountain Support Grows," *Indian Country Today*, 21 February 2001, p. A2.

190. *Ibid.*

191. Rhodes, *op. cit.*, p. 22.

192. *Ibid.*, p. 23.

193. Gillingham, *op. cit.*, p. 778.

194. Hirshfelder and Montano, *op. cit.*, p. 111.

195. Michael J. Simpson, "Accommodating Indian Religions," *Montana Law Review*, Vol. 54, Winter 1993, p. 19.

196. *Ibid.*, pp. 28–29. As the motto of the Carlisle Indian School in Pennsylvania aptly stated, "Kill the Indian and Save the Man," the courts have taken up this creed as their own.

197. *Ibid.*, p. 34. Other sites are, or have been, placed in danger or outright destroyed. For example, Badger Two Medicine in Montana, held sacred by the Blackfeet is threatened by oil drilling; Medicine Wheel, Wyoming, sacred to the Lakota, Arapaho, Crow, Cheyenne, and Shoshone tribes was threatened by the Forest Service's tourism development plans in 1991; and Celilo Falls, Oregon was lost to the Umatella, Nez Perce and Yakima tribes when it was flooded by the Dalles Dam in 1957. See Hirshfelder and Montano, *op. cit.*, p. 113. The loss of the Seneca sacred sites has been discussed elsewhere in this work. Bears Ears, an area held sacred by five tribes, is threatened by President Trump's directive to have all large

monuments reviewed to make sure it does not infringe upon economic growth and development. See Terry Williams, "Will Bears Ears Be the Next Standing Rock?," *New York Times*, 6 May 2017.

198. DeLoria, *God Is Red*, p. 43.

199. "Many Native Americans Do Not Like New Age Religions," broadcast transcript of National Public Radio / All Things Considered, 24 November 1993, Executive Producer Ellen Weiss. Hereafter cited as NPR/ATC. Simply observing a ceremony or reading a book on American Indian religion and then believing one can go out and practice it as an "expert" only serves to trivialize and reduce centuries-old spiritual traditions into a child-like understanding of the truths and values. Would anyone attempt this after only attending a Christian church once?

200. Alan Trachtenberg, *Shades of Hiawatha: Staging Indians, Making Americans 1880–1930* (New York: Wang and Hill, 2004), p. 10.

201. A very good example was Iron Eyes Cody who played an Indian in movies during the 1960s and became an icon for national anti-pollution campaigns of the 1970s. In reality, he was an Italian-American born in Louisiana. See Philip J. Deloria, *Indians in Unexpected Places* (Lawrence: University Press of Kansas, 2004) for an excellent examination of the effects and impacts of Indian stereotypes and expectations.

202. *Ibid.*, p. 11.

203. *Ibid.*, p. 10.

204. "Germany's Obsession with American Indians is Touching—and Occasionally Surreal," *Indian Country Today*, 24 May 2013, https://newsmaven.io/indiancountrytoday/archive/germany-obsession-with-american-indians-is-touching-and-occasionally-surreal-1lsvYURPGEKcX1JAFPUP4g.

205. *Ibid.*

206. *Ibid.*

207. *Ibid.* German museums also have collections of American Indian scalps and other sacred artifacts and are reluctant to return them to their tribes. See Melissa Eddy, "Lost in Translation: Germany's Fascination with the American Old West," *New York Times*, 17 August 2014, https://www.nytimes.com/2014/08/18/world/europe/germmanys-fascintation-with-american-old-west-native-american-scalps-human-remains.html.

208. *Ibid.*

209. As mentioned, there have been instances when a New Ager has performed the Indian Sacred Healing Sweat Ceremonies which have ended up in the rape and even the death of one or more of the participants. The Men's Movement of the 1990s was notorious for using corrupted versions of Indian spirituality and ceremonies for its own purposes. A detrimental side effect of these copycat ceremonies is that the participants come away with the belief that what they just experienced was truly Indian, and this may cause a stereotypical view and misinterpretation of "what Indians are like and do," or at its worst, cause a disdain and mistrust for Indians and their ceremonial practices. American Indians have had to fight this problem thanks to Hollywood, and now they face it again thanks to the New Agers and the Men's Movement.

To show the other side of the coin, Annette Jaimes states in *The State of Native America* (Boston: South End Press, 1992): "Evidence of the colonialist content of much Euroamerican feminist practices has been advanced not just at the material level, but in terms of cultural imperialism. [F]eminism of the 'New Age' persuasion for ripping off native ceremonies for their own purposes. .. that as long as they take part in Indian spiritual abuse, either by being consumers of it, or by refusing to take a stand on it, Indian women will consider white 'feminists' to be nothing more than agents in the genocide of [the Indian] peoples" (p. 333).

210. Wendy Rose, "The Great Pretenders," in Jaimes, ed., *State of Native America*, *op. cit.*, p. 404.

211. DeLoria, *op. cit.*, p. 42.

212. Rose, *loc. cit.*, p. 404.

213. *Ibid.*

214. Relma Hargus, "Patton Boyle at Ease With Miracles, 'Mystic Double Talk,'" *The Advocate*, 8 January 2000, p. F1. Not knowing an American Indian religious leader or one of the hundreds of American Indian religions before writing a book about it assumes that all Indians are the same, have the same practices and beliefs, and whatever the belief system, it is simple and childish enough to be explained without doing a bit of research

or background examination. This only serves to perpetuate the stereotype that all Indians are alike, and that our beliefs are so simple anyone can write about them without even speaking to us Indians. This is racism and cultural rape for Indian beliefs were bastardized for the author's own power and profit.

215. NPR/ATC.

216. *Ibid.* It is always amazing and somewhat humorous how "tribal elders" always seem to pick a non–Indian to spread the "truth" and educate the people about Indian ways rather than a member of their own tribe or family. Of course, when asked what elders in particular gave them this charge, the plastic shaman becomes secretive and elusive, or names someone who is not known to the tribe they supposedly represent.

217. Book clubs sell "genuine" Indian smudge sticks, manuals, and Indian tarot cards. There is a company that sells a portable sacred Indian sweat lodge. There are even manuals on how to perform certain ceremonies and on how to become a real Indian medicine man! In addition, there are numerous examples of New Agers charging admission to their bastardized versions of sacred Indian ceremonies. Usually, it is couched in terms of a *required minimum donation* so that they can continue to do their work and "spread the word." Another common theme is that these spiritual thieves, these cultural rapists, learned their trade from some unnamed tribal elder who chose them over someone in their own tribe or culture to go out and preach the Indian sacred way. It is amazing to the author that there never seems to be an Indian willing to learn from these elders, and only white New Agers can receive their lessons. Add this group to those fake Indian tribes which can be joined for a fee, get an Indian name, and claim some sort of pseudo–Indianness, and you have the formula for cultural rape.

Some non-recognized tribes sell memberships claiming having more members will help their efforts to achieve federal status. The Kaweah and Pembina Nation Little Shell Tribes were selling memberships online for hundreds of dollars. They are wrong to believe or tell anyone that paid membership will increase any chance of federal recognition as a legitimate Indian tribe. See

Oskar Garcia, "Unofficial Indian Tribes Selling Memberships to Illegal Immigrants," *The Advocate*, 18 April 2007, p. 10A.

A prime example of these internet-based pseudo–Indians is the Nemenhah Band. The band is just one of the numerous internet Indians that promise spirituality and more while having absolutely no legitimate, legal or historical connection to any true and recognized Indian tribe. In essence, the band blurs the lines of traditional religions and tribes by making tenuous references to federal laws and policies that have no real standing in law. The band does not claim to be a tribe because this would make them subject to the federal government, and because that is a term that Indians never really used for themselves. Instead, they claim legitimacy by stating if a member is a member of a recognized tribe, then the band gets legitimacy through them. To become a member, one applies for spiritual adoption and will become a medicine man or woman as long as they make the suggested monetary donation and supposedly, but erroneously, will be protected by AIFRA. Of course, annual fees and further purchases are expected to advance one's spiritual and healing knowledge. See the Nemenhah Band website.

It must be made clear, this band *is not* a true American Indian tribe or group. It has no connection whatsoever to a legitimate tribe. Its leader at one time claimed he was related to the Nez Perce Chief Seattle, but that tribe had disavowed itself of him stating there is no connection whatsoever. Instead, these are white people who steal and adopt what they believe are American Indian ways and names and give true Indians a bad reputation for their actions and behaviors. In other words, it is just another way in which the culture and spirituality of the American Indians has been usurped and used for personal power and profits.

218. One can readily see the pop-culture Anglicizing of the American Indian. Dream catchers are sold everywhere. Plates, statues, and paintings abound showing a shapely Indian girl, sexily posed with her perfectly tanned skin and cleavage in a revealing white buckskin dress. Even Heidi Klum posed as a bikini-clad Indian with headdress and warpaint in 2014. To be fair, she apologized and agreed it was insensitive when backlash

erupted calling this racist. The Indian men are all muscular, stoic warriors. Nowhere does one see the elderly, the sick, the true facial features of the Indian peoples, but only what the non–Natives want to believe all Indians look like—the perfect and noble savage, or at least a tanned version of themselves.

219. DeLoria, *op. cit.*, p. 43.

220. This may be partly due to the environmental movement's iconization of the Indian as the perfect environmentalist, the "noble savage" living in harmony with the world and its creatures. However, it ignores the discrimination and oppression suffered for just being an Indian. See: Booth and Jacobs, *op. cit.*, pp. 27–43.

221. NPR/ATC. An art center in Minnesota has advertised a "Ghost Dance," even showing pictures of non–Indians dressed in tribal garb at previous dances. When local Indians responded negatively on social media, the director of the center, who lists herself as an intuitive counselor, medium, and psychic, claimed to not understand why Indian peoples would be insulted by non–Indians doing this sacred dance and ceremony of the Plains Indians. In fact, the "medicine man" in charge, claimed to have roots in the Wamponoag tribe, but admitted he did not know if the tribe still existed. He, however, is qualified, because he "knows" the culture. See Sara Sunshine Manning, "New Age 'Ghost Dance' Held in Southwest Minnesota," *Indian Country Today*, 2 September 2017, http://indiancountrymedianetwork.com/.

222. DeLoria, *op. cit.*, p. 271.

223. *Ibid.*, p. 270.

224. NPR/ATC.

225. DeLoria, *op. cit.*, p. 43. People buy "peace pipes" and drums and hang them on the wall for decorations. Christians would be outraged if non–Christians purchased crucifixes and holy objects just to put them on display as simple home decorations. If these pipes and drums are just collectable symbols, objects to be collected, then so are holy statues, parts of saints and crosses. Some claim that this is their way of honoring the Indian, but there is no honor to have one's religion made into a hobby and flea market finds. The demand for Indian items has led to a black market for stolen artifacts or family items too numerous to estimate.

226. "New Age Groups Accused of Disrupting Archaeology," *Star Tribune*, 3 July 1994, p. 20A.

227. *Ibid.*

228. Larry Oakes, "Sacred Roots," *Star Tribune*, 9 October 1994, pp. 1, 18A.

229. Martha Sawyer Allen, "Religious Freedom," *Star Tribune*, 5 March 1993, p. 1B.

230. Michael Haederie, "Homage or Ripoff?" *Star Tribune*, 11 May 1994, pp. 1, 8E. Of course, unlike a church or a man-made monument, a mountain or tree cannot be locked up at night to keep out unwanted and disrespectful intruders who would defile them and haul off chunks and pieces as souvenirs. Defiling a sacred place is an odd way of showing respect for its sacredness and the native religion one claims to follow.

231. Peter Hecht, "Deaths Raise Questions About Spiritual Quests," *Sacramento Bee*, 26 June 2002, p. A1. The group did respond to state that they did have liability insurance—obviously something no good Indian spiritual leader would be without. See also the editorial, "Ceremonies Require Respect," *Indian Country Today*, 10 July 2002, p. A2. In 2009, a self-help guru performed a sweat ceremony as part of his spiritual warrior program which ended up with 21 people needing medical attention and three dying. The leader, James Arthur Ray would eventually be convicted for these deaths. See Felicia Fonseca, 22 June 2011, www.nbcnews.com/id/43501833/ns/us_news_crime_and_courts/t/self-help-guru-convicted/.

232. Ann Rovin, "Devils Tower," *Star Tribune*, 16 October 1994, p. 22A. Also see "Sacred Ground," *Native Peoples*, May/June 2007, p. 26.

233. Rovin, op cit. One must wonder if this owner would also find the prayer scrolls and papers left in Jerusalem's Wailing Wall nothing more than a bunch of trash.

234. DeLoria, *op. cit.*, p. 276.

235. *Federal Register*, Vol. 61/No. 154, 8 August 1996, p. 41424.

236. *Ibid.*

237. "Saving the Sacred Lands and Monuments," *Indian Country Today*, 26 July 2000, p. C7.

238. *Federal Register*, Vol. 61/No. 104, 29 May 1996, p. 26771.

239. *Ibid.*

240. The four directions to many tribes

represent the Grandfathers. Colors are associated with each direction, and although they vary somewhat, they include red for healing (East), black for peace (West), yellow for power and strength (South) and white for wisdom (North). Again, these vary from tribe to tribe and this is a generalization.

241. "Saving the Sacred Lands," *op. cit.*

242. O'Brien, "Freedom," *op. cit.*, p. 470.

243. Ward, *op. cit.*, pp. 817–818.

244. *Ibid.*, pp. 818–819.

245. DeLoria, *op. cit.*, p. 268.

246. Public Law, 42 U.S.C. §200066 (Supp. V. 1993).

247. Luraline D. Topahe, "After the Religious Restoration Act," *New Mexico Law Review*, Vol. 24, Spring 1994, p. 331.

248. *Ibid.*, p. 336.

249. O'Brien, "Freedom," *op. cit.*, p. 471.

250. Bruce Epstein, "Religious Freedom Act Struck Down," *Philadelphia Inquirer*, 26 June 1997, p. A13. See also: Richard Carelli, "Justices Overturn Religious Freedom Law," *Baton Rouge Advocate*, 26 June 1997, p. A2; and O'Brien, "Freedom," *op. cit.*, p. 451.

251. Kenneth L. Karst, "Religious Freedom and Equal Citizenship," *Tulane Law Review*, Vol. 69/No. 2, December 1994, p. 342; and Bob Cohen and David A. Kaplan, "A Chicken On Every Altar?" *Newsweek*, Vol. 120/No. 19, 9 November 1992, p. 79.

252. Karst, *loc. cit.*, p. 352.

253. *Ibid.*

254. Bruce Nolan, "Church Wins a Round Vs. State," *Times-Picayune*, 25 January 1996, p. A10.

255. *Ibid.*

256. Epstein, *op. cit.*, p. A13; and Corelli, *op. cit.*, p. 2A.

257. *City of Boerne v. Flores* WL 345322 (U.S. Tex.), 1997, p. 2.

258. David O. Stewart, "Power Surge: Asserting Authority Over Congress," *ABA Journal*, Vol. 83, September 1997, p. 47.

259. *Ibid.*

260. *Ibid.*

261. Epstein, *op. cit.*, p. A13. Obviously, O'Connor had either a change of heart between the *Lyng* decision and this case, or her own ethnocentrist bias allowed her to side with an established Christian church while not allowing her to understand or protect an Indian religion.

262. *City of Boerne, op. cit.*, p. 25.

263. *Ibid.*, p. 26.

264. *Ibid.*, p. 29.

265. *Ibid.*, p. 32.

266. Topahe, *op. cit.*, p. 345.

267. Jeri Beth K. Ezra, "The Trust Doctrine," *Catholic University Law Review*, vol. 38, Spring 1989, pp. 706–707. The trust doctrine has been accepted in federal legislation, e.g., 1978 Indian Child Welfare Act, AIRFA and others, and in speeches made by political leaders, e.g., Clinton in 1994. See O'Brien, "Freedom," *op. cit.*, pp. 482–483; and Mary Christina Wood, "Protecting the Attributes of Native Sovereignty," *Utah Law Review*, Vol. 1995, 1995, p. 217.

268. Ezra, *op. cit.*, p. 710.

269. See: *Lone Wolf v. Hitchcock*, 187 U.S. 553 (1903); *United States v. Creek Nation*, 295 U.S. 103 (1935); *Seminole Nation v. United States*, 316 U.S. 286 (1942); *Menominee v. United States*, 391 U.S. 404 (1968); *Pyramid Lake Paiute Tribe v. Morton*, 354 F. Supp. 252 (D.D.C. 1972); and *United States v. Sioux Nation*, 448 U.S. 371 (1980). In *United States v. Kagima* [118 U.S. 375 (1886)], invalidating the Major Crimes Act, the Court rejected dual sovereignty and established the government as the trustee of a helpless and weak people, thus starting the policy of paternalism. *Lone Wolf* affirmed the right of Congress to abrogate treaties with the tribes if it was in the best interest of the Indians, and the United States Congress' trusteeship allowed it to change the form of Indian investment from land to cash without violating its fiduciary duty. In *United States v. Creek Nation*, the Court ruled that Congress' power was subject to the limits of the trust relationship in this land valuation dispute. The *Seminole* case allowed the Court to delineate the principles of a private trust and the fiduciary responsibility of the government, as well as accountability to individual tribal members. The *Menominee* case limited *Lone Wolf*, while the *Pyramid Lake* case imposed a strict fiduciary duty on the federal government to *protect and accommodate* Indian interests. The *Tribal Council of Passamaquoddy Tribe v. Morton* [528 F.2d 370 (1st Cir. 1975)] held that the nonintercourse act established a trust relationship between the U.S. and Indian nations. Finally, in the *Sioux* case, the Court rejected

government paternalism in favor of a true trust relationship. See: Ezra, *op. cit.*, pp. 715–731; and O'Brien, "Freedom," *op. cit.*, pp. 479–482.

270. Ezra, *op. cit.*, p. 731.

271. O'Brien, "Freedom," *op. cit.*, pp. 474–475.

272. Ezra, *op. cit.*, p. 734.

273. O'Brien, "Freedom," *op. cit.*, p. 474.

274. *Ibid.*; and Wood, *op. cit.*, pp. 210–213.

275. O'Brien, "Freedom," *op. cit.*, p. 478. This obligation stems from the cession of lands from the tribes to the Unites States. "The unique guardian-ward relationship between the federal government and Native American tribes precludes the degree of separation of church and state ordinarily required by the First Amendment." Also see: Wood, *op. cit.*, p. 214.

276. Wood, *op. cit.*, p. 210.

277. *Ibid.*, p. 211.

278. *Ibid.*

279. *Ibid.*, p. 221.

280. Hooker, *op. cit.*, p. 139. These are: 48,000 acres around Blue Lake in the Carson National Forest as part of the Pueblo de Taos Reservation; 185,000 acres of the Grand Canyon National Park in trust for the Havasupai Indians with access to the area only with tribal permission; part of the Six Rivers National Forest as a wilderness area; and the El Malpais Lava Flow in New Mexico as a national monument and a public trust site which can be closed to the public for Indian ceremonial use (pp. 139–140).

281. *Ibid.*, p. 134. Several myths are connected to this lava flow.

282. *Ibid.*, p. 140.

283. *Ibid.*, p. 146.

284. *Ibid.*, p. 147.

285. *Ibid.*, p. 150. Ninety-five percent of the park was zoned for primitive use; 3 percent with trails and 2 percent for development.

286. *Ibid.*, p. 152.

287. Ryan Slattery, "Climbing Banned at Sacred Washoe Site," *Indian Country Today*, 31 December 2003, pp. B1.

288. *Ibid.*

289. Charles Michael Ray, "The Slow Carving of the Crazy Horse Monument," NPR-ATC, 1 January 2013, www.npr.org/2013/01/01/167988928/the-slow-carving-of-the-crazy-horse-monument/.

290. David Roberts, "Grand Canyon on the Edge." *Smithsonian*, Vol. 45/No. 11, March 2015, p. 64.

291. *Ibid.*, p. 68.

292. *Ibid.* As of January 2017, according to the *Navajo-Hopi Observer*, the Navajo Government had tabled the developer's plans. See www.nhomews.com/news/2017/jan/17/resource-and-development-committee-table.

293. Hugh Dellios, "Controversy Laid to Rest as Dickson Mounds Closes," *Chicago Tribune*, 4 April 1992, https://www.chicagotribune.com/news/ct-xpm-1992-04-04-9201310139-story.html.

294. *Ibid.*

295. Theresa Braine, "California MD Indicted on 21 Felony Counts was Hoarding 30,000 Indian Artifacts," *Indian Country Today*, 14 October 2015, https://mewsmaven.io/indiancontrytoday/archive/california-md-indicted-on-21-felony-counts-was-hoarding-30-000-indian-artifacts-HIpdIjL0aUuEi9j-pLNwdg/, and see Theresa Braine, "Native American Remains Among 2,000 Bones Found at Indiana home Containing 42,000 Artifacts," *New York Daily News*, 27 February 2019, https://www.nydailynews.com/news/national/ny-news-artifacts-remains-native-americans-indiana-hoarding-bones-20190226-story.html.

296. Suzan Shown Harjo, "Last Rites for Indian Dead: Treating Remains Like Artifacts Is Intolerable," *Los Angeles Times*, 16 September 1989, https://www.latimes.com/archive/la-xpm-1989-09-16-me-21-story.html. Chiefs Black Kettle, White Antelope and Left Hand arrived at Fort Lyon seeking peace and were directed to wait at Sand Creek until arrangements could be made. Meanwhile, the Reverend John M. Chivington, a Colonel in the Union Army and his 750 men attacked the Indian camp. Estimates differ on the exact number of Indians killed, but there is no dispute about the treachery and brutality of the attack, especially since it was reported that Black Kettle was flying a white flag along with the American flag in his camp. Men, women and children were slaughtered in the attack.

297. See the Moundbuilder Country Club website, "The Beginning," 23 May 2019, http://moundbuilderscc.com/Default.aspx?p=Dynamicmodule&pageid=367884&ssid=280003&vnf=1.

298. Kent Mallet, "Judge Rules OHC Can Reclaim Octagon Mounds from Moundbuilders," *Newark Advocate*, 10 May 2019, https://www.newarkadvocate.com/story/news/2019/05/10/judge-rules-ohc-can reclaim-octagon-mounds-country-club/1170949001/.

299. *Ibid.*

300. Kent Mallet, "Moundbuilders Plans Appeal of Judge's Eminent Domain Ruling," *Newark Advocate*, 13 May 2019, https://www.newarkadvocate.com/story/news/2019/05/13/moundbuilders-country-club-plans-appeal-ruling-octagon-mounds/1188321001/.

301. National Museum of the American Indian Act, Public Law 101-185, 28 November 1989, Section 2, Parts 7 and 8.

302. Native American Graves Protection and Repatriation Act, Public Law 101-601, 16 November 1990.

303. Irvin Molotsky, "Smithsonian to Give Up Indian Remains," *New York Times*, 13 September 1989, https://www.nytimes.com/1989/0913/us/smithsonian-to-give-up-indian-remains.html.

304. Smithsonian National Museum of the American Indian, Repatriation Process, https://americanindian.si.edu/explore/collections/repatriation.

305. O'Brien, "Freedom," *op. cit.*, p. 474.

306. Gordon, *op. cit.*, p. 1459.

307. Topahe, *op. cit.*, p. 338.

308. *Ibid.*, p. 339.

309. Gordon, *op. cit.*, p. 1459.

310. *Ibid.*, p. 1461.

311. *Ibid.*, p. 1464.

312. *Ibid.*, p. 1468.

313. *Apache Survival Coalition v. United States*, 21 F.3d 895 (1994) at 898.

314. *Ibid.*

315. *Ibid.* at 899.

316. *Ibid.*

317. *Ibid.* at 901.

318. *Ibid.* at 907.

319. *State of Tennessee v. Foreman*, 16 Tenn. (8 Yer.) 256 (1835). In Newcomb, *op. cit.*, pp. 304–305. Italics added.

Chapter Four

1. Newburn, *op. cit.*, p. 41.

2. Annie L. Booth and Harvey M. Jacobs, "Ties That Bind," *Environmental Ethics*, vol. 12, Spring 1990, p. 30.

3. *Ibid.*

4. Shepard Krech, *The Ecological Indian: Myth and History* (New York: W.W. Norton, 1999), p. 21.

5. *Ibid.*, p. 17.

6. *Ibid.*, p. 26. Rousseau referred to the Indians of America as noble savages.

7. Paul Recer, "Study: Early Hunters Caused Extinctions," *The Advocate*, 8 June 2001, p. 10A.

8. Paul Recer, "Ecological Sea Damage," *The Advocate*, 27 July 2001, p. 9A.

9. *Ibid.*, p. 152.

10. It is another myth that Indians never drank alcoholic beverages before the white man introduced them to the "devil-whiskey." Several tribes made beers and fruit brandies that were used as normal refreshments or in special ceremonies.

11. Krech, *loc. cit.*, pp. 152–163, 177.

12. *Ibid.*, p. 216.

13. This is not to say that such projects do not polarize tribes. Often times, as will be examined later in this chapter, tribal leaders wish to construct such a project, but the members oppose it, questioning its real economic benefits and environmental impacts. The results can sometimes be devastating for the stability of the tribe. See Krech, *op. cit.*, pp. 220–225.

14. Booth and Jacobs, *op. cit.*, p. 42.

15. *Ibid.*

16. Attributed to Chief Seattle, Duwanish Indian Nation, to President Franklin Pierce, 1854. To illustrate this entire episode of the eco–Indian, the now famous speech of Chief Seattle has been known for years to be a work of fiction. Chief Seattle did make a speech in the 1850s, but it has been reworked, rewritten and refocused several times until its rebirth in the 1970s as part of the environmental movement. The present speech has made Chief Seattle out to be an eco–Indian. See Paul S. Wilson, "What Chief Seattle Said," *Environmental Law*, Vol. 22, 1992, pp. 1451–1460. The full, true text of Chief Seattle's speech can be found in Appendix Two.

17. Dean B. Suagee, "The Turtle's War Party," *Journal of Environmental Law and Litigation*, Vol. 9, 1994, pp. 465–466. Statements such as these only serve to add fuel to the fires of opposition for legitimate and safe projects, as well as help in attacks on Indian sovereignty.

18. See the discussion of tribal sovereignty within this chapter and elsewhere.

19. Mark Allen, "Native American Control of Tribal Natural Resource Development," *Boston College Environmental Affairs Law Review*, Vol. 16, Summer 1989, p. 859.

20. *Ibid.*, p. 879.

21. *Ibid.*, p. 824.

22. Reagan Administration Indian Policy Initiatives, 19 *Weekly Comp. Pres. Doc.* 98, 99 (January 24, 1983).

23. "In the Red," *The Economist*, Vol. 310/ No. 7591, 25 February 1989, p. 26.

24. *Ibid.*, pp. 70–71.

25. *Ibid.*, p. 72. This may be one reason why, if a tribe decides to build a casino instead, it meets such opposition from citizens and governments.

26. U.S.C.A. §1151—Indian Country "...means (a) all land within the limits of any Indian reservation under the jurisdiction of the United States Government, notwithstanding issuance of any patent, and, including rights-of-way running through the reservation (b) all dependent Indian communities within the borders of the United States whether within the original or subsequently acquired territory thereof, and whether within or without the limits of a state, and (c) all Indian allotments, the Indian titles to which have not been extinguished, including the rights-of-way running through the same."

27. William D. Ruckleshaus, "EPA Policy for the Administration of Environmental Programs on Indian Lands" (8 November 1984).

28. *Ibid.*, p. 2.

29. Environmental Protection Agency, Indian Policy Implementation Guidance (8 November 1984).

30. Currently, nearly every federal environmental law provides that tribes may apply for and be treated as states in the assumption of environmental programs.

31. Sovereignty is defined by Black's Law Dictionary as "a person, body or state in which independent supreme authority is vested."

32. U.S. (8 Wheat.) 543 (1823).

33. Generally, three theories have been used to relieve Indians of their land. The first of these is the conquest theory wherein it was reasoned by Europeans and, later,

American courts, that Indians lost their claim to the land through the conquest of the Europeans. See the discussion of this doctrine in Chapter Two.

34. U.S. (8 Wheat.) 543 (1823).

35. U.S. (5 Pet.) 1 (1831).

36. U.S. (6 Pet.) 515 (1832).

37. U.S. (6 Pet.) 515 (1832).

38. Walter E. Stern, "Environmental Compliance Considerations for Developers of Indian Lands," *Land & Water Law Review*, Vol. 28, 1993, pp. 77, 79.

39. As discussed in this chapter and elsewhere, while Indian tribes do not always maintain control over all of the lands or peoples within the exterior boundaries of the reservation, the EPA has made it clear that, as far as environmental policy is concerned, tribes shall have control over all lands within the reservation, regardless of the ownership.

40. U.S.C. §§331-34 et seq.

41. Judith V. Royster, "Environmental Protection and Native American Rights: Controlling the Land Through Environmental Regulation," *Kansas Journal of Law & Policy*, Vol. 1, Summer 1991, pp. 89, 90.

42. *Ibid.*, p. 90.

43. *Ibid.*

44. Not all reservations were carved up by the Dawes Act. Those tribes who own reservations which were not subject to the Act have a good deal more control over their land because there are no non–Indian landowners within the exterior boundaries of the reservation.

45. Royster, *op. cit.*, p. 90.

46. *New Mexico v. Mescalero Apache Tribe*, 462 U.S. 324 (1983). *Cf. Worchester v. Georgia*, 31 U.S. (6 Pet.) 515 (1832).

47. U.S. 134 (1980).

48. 450 U.S. 544 (1981), 101 S. Ct. 1245 (1981).

49. *Ibid.*, p. 566. The Court also upheld the right of tribes to regulate non–Indians on non–Indian lands when the non–Indian enters into a consensual relationship with the tribe or its members. Non-Indians who enter into such consensual relationships, generally through business dealings, are subject to regulation through "taxation, licensing or other means." *Ibid.*, p. 565.

50. 471 U.S. 195 (1985).

51. U.S. 195, 198 (1985).

52. 450 U.S. at 545.

53. C. E. Willoughby, "Native American Sovereignty Takes a Back Seat to the 'Pig in the Parlor': The Redefining of Tribal Sovereignty in Traditional Property Law Terms," *Southern Illinois Law Review*, Vol. 19, Spring 1995, pp. 593ff.

54. U.S. at 566.

55. Ben Harrison, "Montana and Its Progeny," Proceedings, ABA Key Environmental Issues in U.S., EPA Region VI Conference, May 1999.

56. 450 U.S. at 566.

57. 492 U.S. 408 (1989).

58. In *Brendale*, the Court split 4–3–2: four justices found that the county had exclusive zoning authority over all non–Indian land within the reservation; three justices found that the Indian tribe had exclusive zoning authority over all land within the reservation, regardless of ownership; and two justices, the swing votes, found that the county's right to zone non–Indian lands depended on the extent of non–Indian land ownership.

59. When it is determined that tribes do not have the authority to govern on the reservation, state law may govern in some instances when a non–Indian owns land within the exterior boundaries of the reservation.

60. The logic of this statement escapes the authors.

61. U.S. 408, 428 (1989). See also Harrison, *op. cit.*

62. S. Ct. 2309 (1992).

63. Ironically, the tribe relinquished and was compensated for some 104,000 acres of land to develop the reservoir with the understanding that it would remain part of the reservation. The 1944 Flood Control Act took over 104,000 acres of Indian land, but only 18,000 of non–Indian lands along the Missouri River.

64. S. Ct. at 2313.

65. *Ibid.*

66. S. Ct. at 2319–2320. Justice Thomas asserts that after *Montana*, tribal authority over non–Indians cannot survive without Congressional delegation and is therefore not inherent. This is flatly contradicted by the language of *Montana*. It is also contradicted by the result in *Bourland. Cf.* James M. Grijalva, "Tribal Government Regula-

tion of Non-Indian Polluters of Reservation Waters," *North Dakota Law Review*, Vol. 71, 1995, p. 433, n. 97. See also John S. Harbison, "The Broken Promise Land," *Stanford Environmental Law Journal*, Vol. 14, May 1995, pp. 347–367+.

67. Some federal laws, such as the CWA, explicitly state that tribes shall have such jurisdiction over their entire reservation.

68. Harbison, *op. cit.*, n.p.

69. *Ibid.*

70. Charlotte Uram and Mary J. Decker, "Jurisdiction Over Water Quality on Native American Lands," *Journal of Natural Resources & Environmental Law*, Vol. 8, 1992/1993, pp. 1, 9.

71. *Ibid.*, p. 7.

72. *Ibid.*

73. U.S.C. §300j-11(b). The Administrator (1) is authorized to treat Indian tribes as States under this subchapter (2) may delegate to such Tribes primary enforcement responsibility for public water systems and for underground injection control, and (3) may provide such Tribes grants and contract assistance to carry out functions provided by this subchapter.

74. Fed. Reg. 43084 (1988).

75. Uram and Decker, *op. cit.*, p. 8.

76. U.S.C. §1377(e)(1)-(3).

77. *Ibid.* at §1377(h)(1). *Cf. Brendale v. Confederated Tribes and Bands of Yakima*, 492 U.S. 408 (1989).

78. U.S.C. §1377(e).

79. U.S.C. §7602(r).

80. Uram and Decker, *op. cit.*, p. 15.

81. *Nance v. EPA*, 645 F.2d 701 (9th Cir. 1981), cert. denied *Crow Tribe of Indians Montana v. EPA*, 454 U.S. 1081 (1981).

82. *Ibid.*, pp. 713–714.

83. U.S.C. §9626 (a).

84. C.F.R. §171.10.

85. John L. Williams, "The Effect of EPA's Designation of Tribes as States on the Five Civilized Tribes in Oklahoma," *Tulsa Law Journal*, Vol. 29, Winter 1993, pp. 345, 351.

86. Uram and Decker, *op. cit.*, p. 6. In 1987 when Congress amended the Clean Water Act, it did not provide additional funds to support tribal water programs. See 56 Fed. Reg. 64, 876 at 64,889-90 (1991).

87. *Albuquerque v. Browner*, 865 F. Supp. 733 (D.N.M. 1993).

88. John S. Harbison, "The Downstream

People: Treating Indian Tribes as States Under the Clean Water Act," *North Dakota Law Review*, Vol. 71, 1995, pp. 473, 475.

89. Mark A. Bilut, "Albuquerque v. Browner, Native American Tribal Authority Under the Clean Water Act: Raging Like A River Out of Control," *Syracuse Law Review*, Vol. 45, 1994, pp. 887, 889.

90. *Ibid.*

91. The water quality standards were approved in December 1993. See New Mexico: Indian Pueblo Granted Authority by EPA to Set Water Quality Standards for River, 23 *Environmental Reporter* (BNA), 1685, 1993.

92. Harbison, *loc. cit.*, p. 474. This is an outgrowth of cases involving states with separate water quality standards, *International Paper Co. v. Ouellette*, 479 U.S. 481 (1987) and *Arkansas v. Oklahoma*, 112 S. Ct. 1046 (1992).

93. *Ibid.*

94. *Ibid.*

95. *Ibid.*, p. 889.

96. *Ibid.* Also see Harbison, *op. cit.*, p. 475. The EPA was unable to consider Albuquerque's cost of coming into compliance with the Pueblo's water quality standards. Cf. *Homestake Mining Co. v. EPA*, 477 F. Supp. 1279, 1283 (S.D. Fla. 1988).

97. *Albuquerque v. Browner*, 865 F. Supp. 733, 740 (D.N.M. 1993).

98. *Ibid.*

99. *Ibid.*

100. *Montana v. EPA* (D.C. Mont. No. CV-95-56-M-CCL, 27 March 1996), reported in the *Environmental Reporter*, 12 April 1996, p. 2347.

101. S. Ct. 1046 (1992). Therein, the court asserted that upstream permittees may be forced to meet downstream water quality standards. Cf. *International Paper Co. v. Ouellette*, 479 U.S. 481 (1987).

102. Hardison, *op. cit.*, p. 477.

103. In 1991, the BIA had only 5 people to cover environmental issues for the 53 million acres of Indian Country in the lower 48 states. See Bill Lambrecht, "Poisoned Mandate," *St. Louis Post-Dispatch*, 17 November 1991, p. A10.

104. Robert Allen Warrior, "Dancing with Wastes," *Christianity and Crisis*, Vol. 51, 15 July 1991, pp. 216–217.

105. They had been rejected by the Na-

vajo, the Kaw of Oklahoma, the Pauite-Kaibob of Arizona, the Choctaw in Mississippi, the Mohawk of New York (nine times to be exact), the Chikaloon of Alaska, the Moapa Paiute, Campo, the Lakota of Standing Rock, La Posta Indians and the Cabazon in Palm Springs, California. See Paul Schneider and Dan Lamont, "Other People's Trash," *Audubon*, Vol. 93/No. 4, July 1991, p. 111.

106. *Ibid.*, pp. 113, 114.

107. Conger Beasley, Jr., "Of Landfill Reservations," *Buzzworm*, Vol. 3/No. 5, September/October 1991, p. 41.

108. Bill Lambrecht, "Land Vs. Money: Trash Debate Rips Tribe," *St. Louis Post-Dispatch*, 20 December 1990, pp. A1, 13. It was discovered that Waste-Tech had a less than exemplary record in maintaining safe and non-polluting facilities and this added fuel to the opposition to the company and to the council that signed with it. The Kaibob-Paiute had also rejected offers from company opposition from the members and some council members. The opponents argue that tradition and spirituality won out over economics. See Bill Lambrecht, "Indian Tribe Rejects Waste-Disposal Plan," *St. Louis Post-Dispatch*, 3 February 1991, pp. A1, 4.

109. Warrior, *op. cit.*, p. 218.

110. *Ibid.* See also Saugee, *op. cit.*, p. 477.

111. Bill Lambrecht, "Illegal Dumpers Scar Indian Lands," *St. Louis Post-Dispatch*, 17 November 1991, p. A11.

112. *Blue Legs v. U.S. EPA*, 668 F. Supp. (DSD 1987), pp. 1329–1342.

113. *Ibid.*, p. 1337.

114. *Ibid.*, pp. 1340, 1341.

115. The tribe had lost nearly 60 million acres thanks to the Dawes Act. See Judith V. Royster, "Of Surplus Lands and Landfills," *South Dakota Law Review*, Vol. 43, 1998, p. 284.

116. *Ibid.*, p. 287.

117. *Ibid.*, p. 288.

118. *Ibid.*, p. 290.

119. *Ibid.*, p. 292.

120. *Ibid.*

121. *Ibid.*

122. *Ibid.*, p. 295.

123. *Ibid.*, p. 296.

124. This type of statement indicates the inequality of the bargaining positions, maybe even duress.

125. *Ibid.*, p. 304.

126. *Ibid.*, p. 309. Obviously, civilization includes hosting dumps for white man's trash also.

127. Ward Stone, Wildlife Pathologist for New York State, quoted in Roger Romulus Martella, Jr., "'Not in My State's Indian Reservation'—A Legislative Fix to Close an Environmental Law Loophole," *Vanderbilt Law Review*, Vol. 47, 1994, pp. 1863, 1867.

128. Martella, *loc. cit.*, pp. 1864–65.

129. A. Cassidy Sehgal, "Indian Tribal Sovereignty and Waste Disposal Regulation," *Fordham Environmental Law Journal*, Vol. 5, Spring 1994, pp. 431, 432.

130. Dan McGovern, "The Battle Over the Environmental Impact Statement in the Campo Indian Landfill War," *Hastings W.-N.W.J. Environmental Law & Policy*, Vol. 3, Fall 1995, p. 145.

131. This only demonstrates again the paternalism that Indians face. They need protecting from not only themselves, but from outside forces. See Ralph Frammalino, "Pact Reached to Regulate Dumps on Indian Lands," *Los Angeles Times*, 11 September 1991, p. A18.

132. Kevin Grover and Jana L. Walker, "Escaping Environmental Paternalism," *University of Colorado Law Review*, Vol. 63, 1992, p. 938.

133. *Ibid.*, p. 942. This self-appointed guardianship of the Indians is nothing more than another form of racism and arrogance. Their assumption that if an Indian tribe accepts waste then they were bamboozled and too stupid to understand the contracts and consequences of their decisions. Unfortunately for these self-righteous eco-racists, the Indian peoples are uniquely qualified to protect their own interests; after all, they have centuries of experience and learning about being cheated and lied to.

134. *Ibid.*

135. Dean A. Suagee and Christopher T. Stearns, "Indigenous Self-Government, Environmental Protection and the Consent of the Governed: A Tribal Environmental Review Process," *Colorado Journal of Environmental Law & Policy*, Vol. 5, Winter 1994, pp. 59, 84.

136. *Ibid.*

137. *Ibid.*, p. 90.

138. Valerie Taliman, "The Toxic Waste of Indian Lives," *Covert Action*, No. 40, Spring 1992, p. 21.

139. Al Gedicks, *The New Resource Wars* (Boston: South End Press, 1993), p. XIII.

140. Thomas Lippman, "On Apache Homeland, Nuclear Waste," *Washington Post*, 28 June 1992, p. A3. Also see Taliman, "The Toxic Waste of Indian Lives," *op. cit.*, pp. 21–22.

141. Thomas Grof, "Tribal Showdown Over Incinerator," *Denver Post*, 22 July 1990, p. A15.

142. In 2000, the reported median income was $20,000 a year and there were only 196 residents on the reservation.

143. *Ibid.*

144. John M. Gliona, "In Navajo Country, Coal Gives Life—And Takes It, Some Say," *The Advocate*, 21 December 2014, p. 24A.

145. Felicia Fonseca, "40-Year Ban Keeps Navajo Land Barren," *Advocate*, 25 December 2007, p. 14A.

146. Rebecca Hersher, "Key Moments in the Dakota Access Pipeline Fight," 22 February 2017, www.npr.org/sections/thetwo-way/2017/02/22/514988040/key-moments-in-the-dakota-access-pipeline-fight/. There were reports of President Trump's ownership of stock in the companies that held a vested interest in the pipeline and that he divested himself of these in May of 2016. In addition, reports show that company CEOs donated over $100,000 to his campaign. See: Steven Mufson, "Trump Dumped His Stock in the Dakota Pipeline Owner Over the Summer," *Washington Post*, 23 November 2016, https://www.washingtonpost.com/news/energy-environment/wp/2016/11/23/trump-dumped-his-stock-in-dakota-access-pipeline-owner-over-the-summer/?utm_term=.a74bc5416b17, and Liz Hampton and Valerie Volcovici, "Top Executive Behind Dakota Access has Donated More than $100,000 to Trump," Reuters.com, 26 October 2016, https://www.reuters.com/article/us-usa-election-trump-dakota-access/top-executive-behind-dakota-access-has-donated-more-than-100000-to-trump-idUSKCN12Q2P2.

147. *Ibid.* Also see "DAPL Civil Suit Dropped Against Archambault, Council Members," *Indian County Media Network*, 19 May 2017, https://indiancountrymedia

network.com/news/native-news/dapl-civil-suit-dropped/; James MacPherson, "Government Intervention in Oil Pipeline Project Unprecedented," *The Advocate*, 11 September 2016, p. 2A.

148. In May of 2017, there was a small leak in the pipeline which was dismissed by the company as inconsequential, but is seen by opponents as a warning for what will happen in the future. See Matt Egan, "Dakota Access Pipeline Suffered Minor Oil Spill In April," 10 May 2017, www.money.cnn.com/2017/05/10/investing/dakota-access-pipe line-oil-spill/index.html.

149. *Indian Country Media Network*, "DAPL Approval Illegal, Judge Finds," 14 June 2017, https://indiancountrymedia network.com/news/native-news/dapl-approved-illegal-judge-finds/.

150. Gedicks, *op. cit.*, p. 13.

151. *Ibid.*, p. 15.

152. Brian Stockes, "Montana Sacred Site Enters Energy Debate," *Indian Country Today*, 20 June 2001, p. A1. Only about one-third of the Valley's 4,268 acres has been inventoried, but have shown researchers over 79 significant sites.

153. "Montana Tribes Offer Oil Drilling for Weatherman Draw," *The Circle*, July 2001, p. 4. This offer claims it would create tribal jobs and help reduce the 62 percent unemployment rate among the Blackfeet.

154. Christopher Vecsey and Robert W. Venables, eds., *American Indian Environments* (Syracuse: Syracuse University Press, 1980), p. 23.

155. David Melmer. "Gaming Now Supports the Environment," *Indian Country Today*, 16 May 2001, p. B1.

Chapter Five

1. Newburn, *op. cit.*, p. 22.

2. Native American Report, "Gorton's 'Robin Hood' Plan Would Shift Funds From Richest to Poorest Tribes," n.p., 1998, pp. 2–3.

3. Mary Gray Davidson, "Hawaiian Independence," *Common Ground Radio Series*, Program #9638, 9 September 1996. See also: Meki Cox, "Hawaiians Resettling Ancestors' Land," *The Advocate*, 17 March 1997, p. 4A.

4. Alan and Christina Parker, "Native Hawaiians Are at a Political Crossroads," *In-dian Country Today*, 23 May 2001, p. B2. Hereafter cited as "Crossroads."

5. *Ibid.*

6. *Ibid.*

7. Alan and Christina Parker, "Native Hawaiian Grass-Roots Movement Born," *Indian Country Today*, 30 May 2001, p. B5. Hereafter cited as "Grass-Roots."

8. *Ibid.*

9. *Ibid.* At this time, the results are still unknown and the future still uncertain.

10. "Grass-Roots," *op. cit.* This case upheld the Indian hiring preference in the BIA since this was an obligation the United States had to the Indian peoples.

11. *Ibid.*

12. See Alan and Christina Parker, "Tribes, Native Hawaiians Endangered," *Indian Country Today*, 20 June 2001, p. B4. The Rice case has opened the pathway for others to challenge the DHHL and OHA roles and services. Federal delegation of its role to the state set the stage for problems for the island natives. See also: Bruce Dunford, "Lawsuit Challenges Rules That Benefit Native Hawaiians," *The Advocate*, 3 July 2001, p. 9A.

13. George F. Will, "Let 'Native Hawaiian' Stand," *The Advocate*, 29 November 2007, p. 7B.

14. *Ibid.*

15. *Ibid.*

16. Jennifer Sinco Kelleher, "Court Justice Blocks Native Hawaiians Vote Count," *The Advocate*, 28 November 2015, p. 4A.

17. *Ibid.*

18. Merritt Kennedy, "Native Hawaiians Now Have Pathway to Form a Government," 23 September 2016, http://www.npr.org/sections,thetwo-way/2016/09/23/495212183/.

19. Gloria Valencia-Weber, "Shrinking Indian Country: A State Offensive to Divest Tribal Sovereignty," *Connecticut Law Review*, Vol. 27, Summer 1995, p. 1281.

20. *Ibid.*

21. *Ibid.*, p. 1302.

22. Lauren Natasha Soll, "The Only Good Indian Reservation Is a Diminished Reservation?" *Federal Bar News and Journal*, Vol. 41, September 1994, pp. 546, 547.

23. *Ibid.*

24. *Ibid.*, p. 547.

25. Valencia-Weber, *op. cit.*, p. 1285. The Sac and Fox Reservation is 800 acres separated into two parcels.

26. The Sac and Fox has an earnings tax on Indians and non–Indians who worked within the reservation borders, and had a vehicle tax. The state, via OTC, wanted to impose its own vehicle tax on those vehicles owned by tribal members living on tribal lands. Anyone not paying the tax was to be considered delinquent and fined. *Ibid.*, p. 1288.

27. *OTC v. Citizens Band Potawatomi Tribe of Oklahoma* [498 U.S. 505 (1991)].

28. Valencia-Weber, *op. cit.*, p. 1286.

29. *Ibid.*, p. 1289.

30. *Ibid.*, p. 1295.

31. *Ibid.*, p. 1294.

32. *Ibid.*, p. 1297.

33. *Ibid.*

34. *Ibid.*, p. 1298.

35. *Ibid.*, p. 1290.

36. *Ibid.*, p. 1302.

37. See 18 U.S.C. §1151 (1988) for a legal definition of Indian Country. It states: "... Indian Country means (a) all land within the limits of any Indian reservation under the jurisdiction of the United States Government, notwithstanding the issuance of any patent, and including rights-of-way running through the reservation (b) all dependent Indian communities within the borders of the United States whether within the original or subsequently acquired territory thereof, and whether within or without the limits of a state, and (c) all Indian allotments, the Indian titles to which have not been extinguished, including rights-of-way running through the same."

38. Soll, *op. cit.*, p. 545.

39. *Ibid.*

40. S. Ct. 958 (1994).

41. Soll, *op. cit.*, p. 544.

42. *Ibid.*, pp. 547, 548.

43. *Ibid.*; 114 U.S. 958, 966 (1994).

44. Soll, *op. cit.*, p. 548.

45. *Ibid.*

46. *Ibid.*

47. *Ibid.*

48. *Ibid.*, p. 545.

49. *Ibid.*, p. 544.

50. Some tribes and bands of the Iroquois Confederacy had sided with the British during the war. They lost their lands or resettled in Canada. Those that were allied with the Americans lost their lands anyway.

51. This constitutes a different attack on Seneca lands than the one with the Kinzua Dam project already discussed.

52. Katherine F. Nelson, "Resolving Native American Land Claims and the Eleventh Amendment: Changing the Balance of Power," *Villanova University Law Review*, Vol. 39, 1994, p. 578.

53. *Ibid.*

54. *Ibid.*

55. *Ibid.*

56. *Ibid.*

57. This account has caused major disputes and violent conflicts over its control within the Seneca Nation. It has helped fuel a "civil war" over the tribe's leadership. See: Robert McFadden, "Tribal Politics Flare in Violence," *Times-Picayune*, 26 March 1995, p. A2.

58. Nelson, *op. cit.*

59. *Ibid.*

60. *Ibid.* See also: Ben Dobbin, "Senecas Set Aside Feuding to Join Against New York State," *The Advocate*, 28 April 1997, p. 7A. New York took this action because the Indian tribes in the state have an unfair advantage over non–Indian businesses. Six of the state's nine resident tribes had agreed to the new taxes and regulations. The Senecas had not. The Seneca believed this was a matter of sovereignty and self-reliance. Furthermore, due to religious and traditional reasons, gaming is not a feasible solution to economic progress.

61. Willoughby, *op. cit.*, n.p.

62. *Ibid.*

63. Steven Paul McSloy, "Back to the Future: Native American Sovereignty in the 21st Century," *New York University Review of Law and Social Change*, Vol. 20, 1993, p. 220.

64. *Ibid.*

65. Nelson, *op. cit.*, p. 542. See *Oneida Indian Nation v. State of New York,* 414 U.S. 661 (1974).

66. Nelson, *op. cit.*, p. 543.

67. *Ibid.* See *Oneida Indian Nation v. State of New York,* 470 U.S. 226 (1985).

68. Nelson, *op. cit.*, p. 545.

69. NPR/ATC, "Oneida Land Claims in New York," 21 December 1999.

70. *Ibid.*

71. *Ibid.*

72. David Melmer, "Oneida Land Talks Fall Through," *Indian Country Today*, Vol. 19/No. 43, 12 April 2000, p. A1.

73. *Ibid.*, p. A3.

74. *Ibid.*

75. McSloy, *op. cit.*, p. 224.

76. *Ibid.*

77. *Ibid.*, pp. 260, 279–280.

78. Velencia-Weber, *op. cit.*, p. 1300.

79. *Ibid.*, pp. 1302, 1303.

80. Francis Paul Prucha, *Documents of United States Indian Policy* (Lincoln: University of Nebraska Press, 1990), pp. 274–276.

81. As examples: The Education Assistance Act of 1975; Indian Health Care Improvement Act of 1976; Tribally Controlled Community College Assistance Act of 1978; the Indian Child Welfare Act of 1978; Tribally Controlled Schools Act of 1988; and the Indian Gaming Regulatory Act of 1988. See Prucha, *loc. cit.*, pp. 278–288, 314–316.

82. *Ibid.*, p. 316.

83. *Ibid.*, p. 282. The Final Report can be found on pages 281–283. See also: Fergus M. Bordewich, *Killing the White Man's Indian* (New York: Anchor Books, 1996), pp. 84–85.

84. Prucha, *loc. cit.*, p. 282.

85. *Ibid.*, p. 283.

86. *Ibid.*

87. Bordewich, *op. cit.*, p. 106.

88. *Ibid.*, p. 71.

89. *Ibid.*, p. 171.

90. McSloy, *op. cit.*, p. 221.

91. *Ibid.*

92. *Ibid.*, pp. 222–223.

93. *Ibid.*, p. 223.

94. This confusion can be attributed in part to: *Oliphant v. Suqumesh Indian Tribe* (1978) where the Court ruled that tribal courts have no criminal jurisdiction over non–Indians; *U.S. v. Wheeler* (1978)—the Court ruled that the Navajo never relinquished its right to punish its members for violations of tribal criminal laws; *Duro v. Reina* (1990) in which the Court stated that through an extension of *Oliphant*, the tribe would have no jurisdiction over a nonmember Indian either; *Montana v. U.S.* (1981) where it was decided that the Crow Tribe had no power to regulate the hunting and fishing activities of nonmembers on reservation lands; and yet, in *Merriam v. Jicarilla Apache Tribe* (1982) the Court stated that tribes enjoy the power to tax and regulate businesses on the reservation by virtue of their inherent tribal sovereignty. Finally, in *Brendale v. Confederated Tribes of Yakima Indians* (1989) the Court limited the tribe's right to regulate land owned by nonmembers in open areas of the reservation. Hence, the Court's wavering in support of sovereignty has only added to the confusion. See Willoughby, *op. cit.*, pp. 593ff.

95. Valencia-Weber, *op. cit.*, p. 1308.

96. *Ibid.*

97. *Ibid.*, p. 1318–1319.

98. National Native American Boarding School Healing Coalition, https://boarding schoolshealing.org/wp-content/uploads/2018/09/NABS-map-2018-web-2-jpg. Hereafter cited as NABSHC.

99. The school operated from 1879 to 1918. It is believed that over 10,500 students passed through the school from over 140 tribes. David Murray, "Six Facts About the Carlisle Indian Industrial School," *Great Falls Tribune*, 2 July 2018, https://www.great fallstribune.com/story/news/2018/07/02/native-american-students-carlisle-indian-industrial-school-pennsylvania/745715002/.

100. "The Challenges and Limitations of Assimilation," *Brown Quarterly*, Vol. 4/No. 3, Fall 2001, p. 1, https://brownvboard.org/content/brown-quarterly-archives-vol-1-5.

101. NABSHC, *op. cit.*

102. "Challenges," *loc. cit.*, p. 4. Also, "A Brief History of American Indian Boarding Schools," *The Circle News*, 10 August 2017, https://thecirclenews.org/news/education/a-brief-history=-of American-indian-board ing-schools/.

103. *Ibid.* "Separate but Equal" was often also applied to American Indian children in many school systems throughout the nation (p. 5). Canada used the U.S. schools as their model, but in 2015 openly took responsibility for this travesty and apologized to its indigenous peoples for doing so. Canada had 130 schools and 150,000 students passed through them, with an estimated 6,000 passing away in them. Canadian studies, reflected by those done in Indian Country in the U.S., link higher rates of suicide, substance and alcohol abuse, domestic violence and a myriad of other mental and physical health issues to the residential school experiences. See Mary Amber Pember, "When Will U.S. Apologize for Boarding School Genocide?" *Indian Country Today*, 20 June 2015, https://newsmaven.io/indiancountrytoday/archive/

when-will-u-s-apologize-for-boarding-
school-genocide-Xs4lcrge5Eypq8mBzl
HZBQ/.

104. Pauly Denetclaw, "Appeals Court
Hears Texas Case Challenging Indian Child
Welfare Act," *Indian Country Today*, 13 March
2019, https://newsmaven.io/indiancountry-
today/news/appeals-court-hears-texas-case-
challenging-indian-child-welfare-act-judge-
says-they-are-not-your-children-they-are-
the-children-of-the-tribes-hWmbRAMrMk
6Lp-uBpmVvrw/. Also see: Native American
Rights Fund Annual Report 2018, 25 March
2019, www.narf.org/nill/documents/narf-
ar/2018.pdf; and Felicia Fonseca, "The Indian Child Welfare Act Is Facing Its Biggest
Legal Challenge Yet," *Salt Lake Tribune*, 12
March 2019, https://www.sltrib.com/news/
nation-world/2019/03/12/indian-child-
welfare-act/.

105. *Ibid.*

106. NARF Annual Report, *loc. cit.*, p. 20.

107. *Ibid.*

108. Denetclaw, *op. cit.*

109. Kevin McGill, "U.S. Court Hears
Native American Adoption Case," *Advocate*,
14 March 2019, p. 3A. One must ask themselves—what could be more important that
preserving the child's ethnic awareness and
heritage? This does not happen to any other
racial, religious or cultural group.

110. Denetclaw, *op. cit.*

111. Suzan Shawn Harjo, "Protecting Native People's Sacred Sites," *Indian Country
Today*, 3 April 2002, p. A5.

112. Robert Taylor and Valerie Taliman,
"Feds Tighten Penalties on Abuse of Sacred
Land," *Indian Country Today*, 27 March
2002, pp. A1, 3.

113. Ron Seldon, "Elders Defend Secrets
of Sacred Sites," *Indian Country Today*, 10
April 2002, p. A6. Also see "Auction of Items
from Reservations Raises Questions," *The
Advocate*, 5 June 2016, p. 11A. Items in private collections are not regulated by the Native American Graves Protection and Repatriation Act (1990) and this causes concern
for many since a lot of these items may have
been stolen or swindled from tribes in the
first place.

114. Harjo, *op. cit.*, p. A5.

115. Valencia-Weber, *op. cit.*, p. 1317.

116. McSloy, *op. cit.*, p. 280.

117. *Ibid.*, p. 281.

118. *Ibid.*, p. 219.

119. Willoughby, *op. cit.*, n.p.

Conclusion

1. Newburn, *op. cit.*, p. 27.

2. DeLoria, *God Is Red*, p. 3.

3. Rennard Strickland, "Genocide-at-
Law," *University of Kansas Law Review*, Vol.
34, 1986, p. 713.

4. Ward Churchill, *A Little Matter of
Genocide* (San Francisco: City Lights Books,
1997), p. 129.

5. *Ibid.*, p. 97. Although this work focused on North America, the treatment of
the South American Indians is even more
horrible and the genocide continues up to
this very day. See *ibid.*, pp. 98–116, for a
much more detailed description of their
plight and eradication.

6. *Ibid.*, p. 137.

7. *Ibid.*, pp. 139, 151–157.

8. Strickland, *op. cit.*, p. 716.

9. Churchill, *loc. cit.*, p. 245.

10. *Ibid.* These policies have been discussed, and include the General Allotment
Act of 1887, the banning of Indian religions
in 1894, the 1924 Indian Citizenship Act, and
the 1934 Indian Reorganization Act among
numerous others.

11. Ward Churchill, *Kill the Indian, Save
the Man* (San Francisco: City Lights Books,
2004), p. 3.

12. Some sources list as many as 375 instances of a massacre occurring. Ward Churchill in *A Little Matter of Genocide* gives a
good description of the wars between the
Spanish, Dutch, French, English and Americans and the Native populations. See pp.
157–245.

13. Ward, *Kill the Indian, Save the Man*,
loc. cit.

14. *Ibid.*, pp. 6, 16–17. The boarding
school removal program led many American Indian families to deny their culture and
heritage to avoid having their children taken
away from them.

15. *Ibid.*, p. 13. In 2015, Canada released
its report on the effects of its boarding school
program from 1883 to 1998. It stated that the
schools and the treatment received by the
students there are directly correlated to the
problems of addiction, poverty, suicide,
health and incarceration rates suffered by

the Native peoples. The schools left the children culturally, emotionally, physically and spiritually adrift, with no sense of self. Hence, the effect of Canada's efforts to extinguish the Indian culture within their borders. The report led to the Prime Minister formally apologizing to the Native peoples of Canada. See Mary Annette Pember, "Cultural Genocide," 3 June 2015, https://indiancountry-medianetwork.com/2015/06/03/coming-full-circle-tyruth-and reconciliation-calls-residential-schools-cultural-genocide/. Even Pope Francis has apologized to the Native peoples for their treatment "in the name of God" by members of the church. See: "Pope Francis Apologizes to Indigenous Peoples," *Indian Country Today Media Network*, 10 July 2015, http://indiancountrytoday medianetwork.com/2015/07/10/pope-francis-apologizes-indigenous-peoples-grave-sins-colonialism-161030/.

16. *Ibid.*, p. 11.

17. Strickland, *op. cit.*, p. 717. Also see National Congress of American Indians (NCAI), "Demographics/NCAI," 12 April 2017, http://www.ncai.org/about-tribes/demographics.

18. Ronet Bachman, *Death and Violence on the Reservation* (New York: Auburn House, 1992), p. 6.

19. *Ibid.*, p. 7.

20. Strickland, *op. cit.*, p. 717.

21. *Ibid.*

22. Patricia M. Barnes, Patricia F. Adams, and Eve Powell-Griner, "Health Characteristics of American Indian or Alaska Native Adult Population: United States, 2004–2008," National Health Statistics Report No. 20, U.S. Department of Health and Human Services, Centers for Disease Control and Prevention, no. 20, 9 March 2010, https://www.ncbi.nlm.nih.gov/pubmed/205834.

23. Bachman, *op. cit.*, p. 7.

24. Kevin Galvin, "Clinton Sees Dire Poverty on Indian Reservation," *The Advocate*, 8 July 1999, p. A2. Roughly 1.43 million Indians live on or near a reservation. The 1990 U.S. Census reports that there are 1,937,391 Indians in the United States.

25. Strickland, *op. cit.*, and Bachman, *op. cit.*

26. Strickland, *op. cit.*, and Bachman, *op. cit.*

27. U.S. Census Data for 1990, released August 1995.

28. Galvin, *op. cit.*, and Bachman, *op. cit.*

29. Bachman, *op. cit.*, p. 37. Refer to the model in the article for the connections between internal colonialism and homicide, suicide and addiction rates.

30. Suicide Prevention Resource Center (SPRC), "Suicide Among Racial/Ethnic populations in the U.S. American Indians/Alaska Natives," http://www.sprc.org/sites/default/files/migrate/library/Ai_AN%20sheet%20Aug%2028%202013%20Final.pdf.

31. *Ibid.*

32. *Ibid.*

33. *Ibid.*

34. John R. Wunder, *Retained by the People* (New York: Oxford University Press, 1994), p. 43.

35. *Ibid.*, p. 54.

36. There is a so-called tribe in Louisiana where one can join for a fee, can participate in a collage of generic and pseudo–Indian ceremonies and practices, and even receive an Indian name. It is led by a self-proclaimed medicine man and chief. The group is disdainful of full-blooded Indians, claiming their non–Indian group will be the only group around in five hundred years. In essence, they are to be Indians through self-declaration, not heritage. This is nothing more than self-aggrandizement on the leader's part, and wishful thinking for the members. The "tribe" is more like a cult than anything else. Blood and family lineage, not a membership fee, make you an Indian and a member of a tribe. Also see the previous discussion of the Henondah Band.

37. Deloria, *op. cit.*, pp. 14, 35.

38. Trachtenberg, *op. cit.*, p. 22.

39. *Ibid.*

40. *Ibid.*

41. *Ibid.*, p. 26. The author's own university had an Indian mascot until 2007. Recently, several prominent political leaders have become embroiled in controversy for wearing blackface. Questions and accusations of racism have erupted over these instances. Yet, red and painted Indian faces and mascots still remain acceptable to many team supporters and fans.

42. Aubry Killion, "Ursuline Academy Decides to Retire Sioux Mascot, Alumni Reacts," WDSU-TV News, 16 August 2019; and

"Ursuline Academy to Remove Sioux as Class Mascot After This Year," WWL-TV News, 16 August 2019.

43. Michael Mark Cohen, "Douchebag: The White Racial Slur We've Been Waiting For," 13 November 2014, https://medium.com/human-parts/douchebag-the-white-racial-slur/.

44. *Ibid.*

45. Terrence Dougherty, "Group Rights to Cultural Survival," *Columbia Human Rights Law Review*, Vol. 29, Spring 1998, p. 376.

46. At the time of researching and writing this section, there were 94 registered trademarks using Cherokee, 35 with Navajo, and 206 with Sioux and these numbers do not include team names or product images. In contrast, "moonies" was denied for toy dolls which exposed their behinds because it was determined to be an affront to an organized religious sect, and the use of the term "Madonna" for the name of a wine because it was deemed blasphemous. See *ibid.*, pp. 376, 379–380. The author was interviewed on a radio talk show about the use of Indian names for teams and callers claimed that their local high school team called the "Indians" was to honor a brave culture. However, when it was pointed out that this "brave culture" was still alive, and the consequence of their logic was that the other cultures were not brave, the callers' opinions seemed less sure. A key counterpoint is why aren't there any teams named after African Americans, those of European descent or other ethnic groups? Plus, the NFL endorses and permits a racist term to be used in naming one team—the Redskins; and Major League Baseball has a team named for the race of Indians, with a cartoon chief (Chief Wahoo) as its mascot, which to their credit, the team has recently decided not to use anymore. At least the National Collegiate Athletic Association has asked its members to end the use of these racist terms for teams and mascots, excepting those teams that are named after a particular tribe with their permission. See: "Native American Mascots," *NCAA Press Release*, 29 October 2010, http://www.ncaa.org/wps/portal/ncaa home?WCM_GLOBAL_CONTEXT=/ncaa/NCAA/In most states, public schools have already begun the process of renaming those teams originally using a derogatory name or mascot for American Indians.

47. Andrew Iron Shell. "Americanized Thought Eroding Traditional Ways," *Indian Country Today*, 1 August 2001, p. A4.

48. It is amazing how many white actors have played Indians in the movies: Rock Hudson, Burt Lancaster, Audrey Hepburn, Johnny Depp, Jeff Chandler, Tony Curtis, William Shatner, Anthony Quinn, Dennis Weaver, and Chuck Connors; even Boris Karloff played a Seneca chief in the movie "Unconquered" in 1947. However, if a white actor were to play an African American or Hispanic character today, society would be appalled.

49. Dougherty, *op. cit.*, pp. 376, 377. The author was accused of not being an Indian because he no longer lived in a teepee and had electricity and running water. This is the type of ignorance that seems to pervade the public regarding the Indian peoples and their lives. Even the Hamilton Collection, known for making decorative plates and ceramic figurines, has a porcelain kitten dressed up as a Native American wearing buckskin, a feathered headdress and jewelry, called "Chief Runs with Paws" who is a "chosen guardian of the spirit world," for sale. If it were any other race or ethnicity, there would be a public outcry.

50. See: Lynn Cordova, "Supreme Court: Yes, You Can Trademark Disparaging Racial Words Like the R-Word," *Indian Country Media Network*, 19 June 2017, https://indiancountrymedianetwork.com/news/native-news/supreme-court-yeas-trademark-racial-slurs/.

51. Wilkins, *op. cit.*, p. 3.

52. *Ibid.*, p. 7. He continues to point out that the Court has almost always adhered to historically and constitutionally inaccurate ideas that place tribes in a subservient political and legal position in regards to the federal government, and even to the states at times (p. 10).

53. *Ibid.*, p. 10. The Indian peoples have often been viewed as pagans and savages to some degree, obviously depending upon which tribe they came from and how hostile they were to the invaders.

54. The National Conference on Race Relations and Civil Rights at the Roy Wilkins Center for Human Relations and Social Justice sponsored by the University of Minnesota and the Humphrey Institute of Public Affairs, Minneapolis, October 1994.

55. There are nearly 300 federal, state and self-proclaimed (unrecognized) Indian reservations within the United States. In Minnesota, of the eleven, four are Lakota or Dakota (Sioux) and the rest are Anishinabe (known as Ojibwe or Chippewa). These figures are from the 1990 U.S. Census Report. Minnesota reported 94,944 African Americans, 77,886 Asian Americans, 49,909 American Indians, and 21,965 other races.

56. 25 CFR 83, Department of Interior, Bureau of Indian Affairs, "Procedures For Establishing that an American Indian Group Exists as an Indian Tribe," June 2015. Of course, not everyone is happy with this new streamlined procedure. States and opposing groups who fear the loss of tax revenue or property control have spoken out. Often, the effort to recognize a tribe is equated with the increase in gambling via casinos and all the vices that may be connected to this. For example, see Rob Hotakainer, "New Rules Might Recognize More Tribes, Create Casinos," *The Advocate*, 17 August 2014, p. 13A. The federal recognition process was first established in 1978 and revised in 1994. Prior to Part 83, recognition was through treaty.

57. The new rules state that suitable evidence (newspapers, books, state or local government documents, self-identification documents) can be presented that the group has been treated, acted, or recognized as a distinct Indian tribe or community rather than very specific and detailed criteria that were required before the changes. Plus, this separateness only has to be proved to have been in existence from 1900 rather than from 1789. Social and cultural patterns must be proven, such as residing in the same land(s). Historical and political impacts can be taken into account, such as the effects of removal policies and/or boarding schools. There must be a history of leadership, however informal, with a certain degree of political autonomy. Members of the applicant groups still cannot be a member of any other recognized tribe, and cannot be a previously terminated tribe by Congressional Act. Whereas this still sounds like a daunting process, it is much easier than previous requirements. Some level of evidentiary criteria must be maintained to prevent fake tribes from seeking recognition and the accompanying benefits.

58. See Andres Resendez, *The Other Slavery* (New York: Houghton Mifflin Books, 2016) for an excellent history of Native American slavery.

59. Robert A. Porter, "Strengthening Sovereignty Through Peacemaking," paper presented at the Federal Bar Association Indian Law Conference, Albuquerque, NM, April 1995, p. 2. At this time, Mr. Porter was the Attorney General for the Seneca Nation.

60. *Ibid.*, p. 11.

61. *Ibid.*

62. The author would like to thank Glenn Longie, Turtle Mountain Anishinabe, for his help developing this concept.

63. The Sauk leader Black Hawk said it best: "We have men among us, like the whites, who pretend to know the right path, but will not consent to show it without pay. I have no faith in their paths, but believe that every man must make his own path."

64. Leslie Marmon Silko, *Ceremony* (New York: Viking Press, 1977), p. 126.

65. DeLoria, *op. cit.*, p. 248.

66. Shell, *op. cit.*

67. Andrew Iron Shell, "Americanized Thought Eroding Traditional Ways," *Indian Country Today*, 1 August 2001, p. A4. See also Timberly Ross, "Indian Tribes Buying Back Land," *Times-Picayune*, 28 December 2009, p. A2. Tribes are using casino and other revenues to buy back lands because they are tired of waiting for treaties to be honored, and this is one way to protect and preserve cultural and environmental sovereignty.

68. David Grann, *Killers of the Flower Moon* (New York: Vintage Books, 2017), p. 277.

69. *Ibid.*, p. 289.

70. Robbie Robertson, "Making a Noise," song from *Contact from the Underworld of Redboy*, Capital Records, Inc., Hollywood, CA, 1998; *and* at: robbie-robertson.com/lyrics/Robbie-robertson/contact-from-the-underworld-of-redboy/making-a-noise/.

Bibliography

Court Cases and Government Documents are in separate sequences at the end.

Abrams, George H. "The Cornplanter Cemetery." *Pennsylvania Archeologist.* Vol. 35/No. 2, 1965, pp. 59–73.

"ACLU: Teen Suspended Over Hair." *Times-Picayune*, 20 March 2011, p. A7.

Adams, Jim. "Sacred Lands Campaign Comes to U.S. Capital." *Indian Country Today*, 24 July 2002, pp. A1, 3.

Alexie, Sherman. *The Lone Ranger and Tonto Fistfight in Heaven.* New York: Harper Perennial, 1994.

Alfred, Gerald R. *Heeding the Voices of Our Ancestors.* New York: Oxford University Press, 1995.

Allen, Mark. "Native American Control of Tribal Natural Resource Development in the Context of the Federal Trust and Tribal Self-Determination." *Boston College Environmental Affairs Law Review* 16: 857–895, Summer 1989.

Allen, Martha Sawyer. "Religious Freedom." *Star Tribune*, 5 March 1993, pp. 1, 2B.

Almendrala, Anna. "Native American Youth Suicide Rates Are at Crisis Levels." 19 December 2016. http://www.huffingtonpost.com/entry/native-american-youth-suicide-rates-are-at-crisis-levels_us_560c3084e4 6768127005591.

Ambler, Marjone. "On the Reservations: No Haste, No Waste." *Planning*, Vol. 57/No. 11, November 1991, pp. 26–29.

Anderson, Jack, and Dale Van Atta. "Waste Merchants Target Reservations." *Washington Post*, 22 February 1991, p. E3.

Anderson, Terry L., and Dean Lueck. "Land Tenure and Agricultural Productivity on Indian Reservations." *Journal of Law and Economics*, 35: 427–454, October 1992.

Annie E. Casey Foundation, Kids Count Data Center. "Children in Single-Parent Families by Race." January 2017. http://datacenter.kidscount.org/data/tables/107-children-in-single-parent-families-y# detailed/1/any/false/573,869,36,868,867/ 10,11,9,12,1,185,13/432,431.

Aquinas, Robert. "Four More Heads for the Indian Trophy Room." *Indian Country Today*, 15 June 2016. https://newsmaven.io/ indiancountrytoday/archive/four-more-heads-for-the-indian-trophy-room-vrst HkemDOegXmmOu66U3w/.

Arrandale, Tom. "Environmentalism and Racism." *Governing*, Vol. 5/No. 5, February 1992, p. 63.

Bachman, Ronet. *Death and Violence on the Reservation: Homicide, Family Violence, and Suicide in American Indian Populations.* New York: Auburn House, 1992.

Bailyn, Bernard. *The Barbarous Years.* New York: Vintage Books, 2012.

Barnes, Ian. *The Historical Atlas of Native Americans.* New York: Chartwell Books, 2017.

Barnes, Patricia M., Patricia F. Adams, and Eve Powell-Griner. "Health Characteristics of American Indian or Alaska Native Adult Population: United States, 2004–2008." National Health Statistics Report No. 20, U.S. Department of Health and Human Services, Center for Disease Control and Prevention, No. 20, 9 March 2010. https://www.ncbi.nlm.nih.gov/pubmed/20583451.

Beasley, Conger, Jr. "Of Landfill Reservations." *Buzzworm*, Vol. 3/No. 5, September/October 1991, pp. 36–42.

Berg, Scott W. *38 Nooses: Lincoln, Little Crow, and the Beginning of the Frontier's End.* New York: Pantheon Books, 2012.

Beschizza, Rob. "U.S. Patent Office Cancels Redskins Trademark." 18 June 2014. http://boingboing.net/2014/06/18/us-patent-office-cancels-redsk.html.

Bilet, Mark A. "*Albuquerque V. Browner*, Native American Tribal Authority Under the Clean Water Act: Raging Like a River Out of Control." *Syracuse Law Review*, 45: 887, 1994.

Bilharz, Joy A. *The Allegany Senecas and the Kinzua Dam: Forced Relocation Through Two Generations.* Lincoln: University of Nebraska Press, 1998.

Blaisdell, Bob, ed. *Great Speeches by Native Americans.* Mineola, NY: Dover Publications, 2000.

Booth, Annie L., and Harvey M. Jacobs. "Ties That Bind: Native American Beliefs as a Foundation for Environmental Consciousness." *Environmental Ethics*, 12: 27–43, Spring 1990.

Bordewich, Fergus M. *Killing the White Man's Indian: Reinventing Native Americans at the End of the Twentieth Century.* New York: Anchor Books, 1996.

Boroughs, Don L. "Mickey Mouse Walks Away from a Fight." *U.S. News and World Report*, Vol. 117/No. 14, 10 October 1994, p. 103.

Boyles, Kristen L. "Saving Sacred Sites: The 1989 Proposed Amendment to the American Indian Religious Freedom Act." *Cornell Law Review*, 76: 1117–1149, July 1991.

Braine, Theresa. "California MD Indicted on 21 Felony Counts Was Hoarding 30,000 Artifacts." *Indian Country Today*, 14 October 2015. https://newsmavem.io/indiancountrytoday/archive/california-md-indicted-on-21-felony-counts-was-hoarding-30-000-indian-artifacts-HlpdIjL0aUuEi9j-pLNwdg/.

_____. "Native American Remains Among 2,000 Bones Found at Indiana Home Containing 42,000 Artifacts." *New York Daily News*, 27 February 2019. https://www.nydailynews.com/news/national/ny-news-artifacts-remains-native-american-indiana-hoarding-bones-20190226-story.html.

"Brief History of American Indian Boarding Schools." *The Circle News*, 10 August 2017. https://the circlenews.org/news/education/a-bried-history-of-american-indian-boarding-schools/.

Bruce, Elyse. "Idle nor More: Who's Scalping Who?" 13 December 2013. https://elysebruce.wordpress.com/tag/indian-cranis-study/.

Bureau of Indian Affairs. "Frequently Asked Questions." 11 April 2017. https://www.bia.gov/FAQs/.

Byler, Celia. "Free Access or Free Exercise: A Choice Between Mineral Development and American Indian Sacred Site Preservation on Public Lands." *Connecticut Law Review*, 22: 397–435, Winter 1990.

Canby, William C. *American Indian Law.* St. Paul: West Publishing, 1988.

Carelli, Richard. "Justices Overturn Religious-Freedom Law." *Baton Rouge Advocate*, 26 June 1997, p. A2.

Center for Native American Youth, The Aspen Institute. "Fast Facts: Native American Youth and Indian Country," April 2014, https://aspeninstitute.org/.../Native%20Youth%20Fast%20Update_04-2014.

"The Challenges and Limitations of Assimilation: Indian Boarding Schools." *Brown Quarterly*, Vol. 4/No. 3, Fall 2001. https://brownvboard.org/content/brown-quarterly-archives-vol-1-5.

Churchill, Ward. *Kill the Indian, Save the Man.* San Francisco: City Lights Books, 2004.

_____. *A Little Matter of Genocide: Holocaust and Denial in the Americas 1492 to the Present.* San Francisco: City Lights Books, 1997.

Cohen, Bob, and David A. Kaplan. "A Chicken on Every Altar?" *Newsweek*, Vol. 120/No. 19, 9 November 1992, p. 79.

Cohen, Felix S. "Original Indian Title." *Minnesota Law Review*, 32: 28–59, 1947.

Cohen, Mark S. "American Indian Sacred Religious Sites and Government Development: A Conventional Analysis in an Unconventional Setting." *Michigan Law Review*, 85: 771–808, February 1987.

Cohen, Michael Mark. "Douchebag: The White Racial Slur We've All Been Waiting For." 13 November 2014. https://medium.com/human-parts/douchebag-the-white-racial-slur/.

Cordova, Lynn. "Supreme Court: Yes, You Can Trademark Disparaging Racial Words Like R-Word." *Indian Country Media Network*, 19 June 2017. https://indiancountry medianetwork.com/news/native-news/supreme-court-yes-trademark-racial-slurs/.

Cornell, Stephen. *The Return of the Native: American Indian Political Resurgence.* New York: Oxford University Press, 1988.

Cox, Meki. "Hawaiians Resettling Ancestors' Land." *The Advocate* (Baton Rouge, LA), 17 March 1997, p. 4A.

Craig, Robin Kundis. "Borders and Discharges: Regulation of Tribal Activities Under the Clean Water Act in States with NPDES Program Authority." *UCLA Journal of Environmental Law and Policy*, 16: 1–68, 1997–1998.

Davidson, Mary Gray. Producer. "Hawaiian Independence." *Common Ground Radio Series*, Program #9638, 27 September 1996.

Dellios, Hugh. "Controversy Laid to Rest as Dickson Mound Closes." *Chicago Tribune*, 4 April 1992. https://www.chicago tribune.com/news/ctxpm-1992-04-04-9201310139-story.html.

Deloria, Philip J. *Indians in Unexpected Places.* Lawrence: University of Kansas Press, 2004.

Deloria, Vine, Jr. *God Is Red: A Native View of Religion.* Golden, CO: Fulcrum Publishing, 1994.

Deloria, Vine, Jr., ed. *American Indian Policy in the Twentieth Century.* Norman: University of Oklahoma Press, 1985.

_____. *Custer Died for Your Sins: An Indian Manifesto.* Norman: University of Oklahoma Press, 1988.

Deloria, Vine, Jr., and Clifford M. Lytle. *American Indians, American Justice.* Austin: University of Texas Press, 1983.

Denetclaw, Pauly. "Appeals Court Hears Texas Case Challenging Indian Child Welfare Act." 13 March 2019. https://newsmaven. io/indiancountrytoday/news/appeals-court-hears-texas-case-challenging-indian-child-welfare-act-judge-says-they-are-not-your-children-they-are-the-children-of-the-tribes-hWmbRAMr Mk6Lp-uBpmVvrw/.

Dishneau, David. "Battlefield Billboards Causing New Fighting." *The Advocate*, 5 December 2004, p. 25A.

Dobbin, Ben. "Senecas Set Aside Feuding to Join Against New York State." *The Advocate* (Baton Rouge, LA), 28 April 1997, p. 7A.

Dougherty, Terrence. "Group Rights to Cultural Survival: Intellectual Property Rights in Native American Cultural Symbols." *Columbia Human Rights Law Review*, 29: 355–400, Spring 1998.

Eddy, Melissa. "Lost in Translation: Germany's Fascination with the American Old West." *New York Times*, 17 August 2014. https://www.nytimes.com/2014/08/18/world/europe/germmanys-fascintation-with-american-old-west-native-american-scalps-human-remains.html.

"Effort to Recognize Virginia Tribe Draws Ire Over Racism." *The Advocate* (Baton Rouge, LA), 4 January 2015, p. 10A.

Egan, Matt. "Dakota Access Pipeline Suffered Minor Oil Spill in April." 10 May 2017. www.money.cnn.com/2017/05/10/investing/dakota-access-pipeline-oil-spill/index.html.

Egerton, John. *Visions of Utopia.* Knoxville: University of Tennessee Press, 1977.

Ehle, John. *Trail of Tears: The Rise and Fall of the Cherokee Nation.* New York: Anchor Books, 1988.

Ellwood, Lisa J. "NJ Superior Court Rules Naticoke Lenni-Lenape Are Sovereign Tribe." *Indian Country Today*, 31 August 2017. https://indiancountrymedia network.com/history/events/nj-superior-court-rules/.

Epstein, Bruce. "Religious Freedom Act Struck Down." *Philadelphia Inquirer*, 26 June 1997, pp. A1, 13.

Evans, Murray. "Cherokees Vote to Restrict Tribal Membership." *The Advocate*, 4 March 2007, p. 15A.

Ezra, Jeri Beth K. "The Trust Doctrine: A Source of Protection for Native American Sacred Sites." *Catholic University Law Review*, 38: 705–736, Spring 1989.

Falkowski, James E. *Indian Law/Race Law: A Five Hundred Year History*. New York: Praeger, 1992.

Farrow, Connie. "Site of Mo. Civil War Battle Now Fighting Encroachment." *Advocate*, 7 November 2004, p. 13B.

Fedarko, Kevin. "Why We Must Return to Wounded Knee." *Parade Magazine, Times-Picayune*, 16 May 2004, pp. 4–7.

"Federal Protection for Utah National Monument Threatened." National Public Radio, Host Robert Siegel, 24 August 2017. www.npr.org/templetes/transcript.php?storyid=545901850.

"FFF: American Indian and Alaska Native Heritage Month." Release Number CB16-FF.22, 2 November 2016. https://www.cemsus.gov/newsroom/facts-for-features/2016/cb16ff22.html.

Fonseca, Felicia. "40-Year Ban Keeps Navajo Land Barren." *Advocate*, 25 December 2007, p. 14A.

_____. "The Indian Child Welfare Act Is Facing Its Biggest Legal Challenge Yet." *Salt Lake Tribune*, 12 March 2019. https://www.sltrib.com/news/nation-world/2019/03/12/indian-child-welfare-act/.

_____. "Lawsuit Planned in Death at Retreat." *Times-Picayune*, 19 October 2009, p. A-3.

_____. "Native Americans Say Movement to End 'Redface' Is Slow." *Advocate*, 18 March 2019, p. 6A.

_____. "Self Help Guru Convicted." 22 June 2011. www.nbcnews.com/id/43501833/ns/us_news-crime_and_courts/t/self-help-guru-convicted/.

_____. "3rd Person Dies in Arizona Sweat Lodge Ceremony Case." Associated Press, 18 October 2009. http://news.yahoo.com/s/ap/20091018/ap_on_re_us/us_sweat_lodge_deaths/print.

Frosch, Dan. "Custer's Last Stand Was Only the Beginning." *Times-Picayune*, 19 December 2010, p. A21.

Gadoua, Renee K. "Pope Urged to Rescind Doctrine." *The Advocate*, 13 September 2014, p. 8A.

Gaffney, Dennis. "Indian Artifacts: Understanding the Law." PBS, 7 April, 2014. https://www.pbs.org.wgbh/roadshow/stories/articles/2014/4/7/indian-artifacts-understanding-law/.

Gallay, Alan. *The Indian Slave Trade*. New Haven: Yale University Press, 2002.

Garcia, Oskar. "Unofficial Indian Tribes Selling Memberships to Illegal Immigrants." *The Advocate*, 18 April 2007, p. 10A.

Gedicks, Al. "Multinational Corporations and Internal Colonialism in the Advanced Capitalist Countries: The New Resource Wars." *Political Power and Social Theory*, 5: 169–205, 1985.

_____. *The New Resource Wars: Native and Environmental Struggles Against Multinational Corporations*. Boston: South End Press, 1993.

"General Dynamics Corp." *Wall Street Journal*, 9 September 1991, p. C14.

"Germany's Obsession with American Indians Is Touching—and Occasionally Surreal." *Indian Country Today*, 24 May 2013. https://newsmaven.io/indiancountrytoday/archive/germany-obsession-with-american-indians-is-touching-and-occasionally-surreal-11svYURPGEKcX1JAFPUP4g.

Gillingham, John. "Native American First Amendment Sacred Lands Defense." *Missouri Law Review*, 54: 777, Summer 1989.

Glavin, Kevin. "Clinton Sees Dire Poverty on Indian Reservation." *The Advocate*, 8 July 1999, p. A2.

Glionna, John M. "In Navajo Country, Coal Gives Life—and Takes It, Some Say." 21 December 2014, *The Advocate*, p. 24A.

Gordon, Sarah B. "Indian Religious Freedom and Governmental Development of Public Lands." *Yale Law Journal*, 94: 1447–1471, May 1985.

Gover, Kevin, and Jana L. Walker. "Escaping Environmental Paternalism: One Tribe's Approach to Developing a Commercial Waste Disposal Project in Indian Country." *University of Colorado Law Review*, 63: 932–943, 1992.

Gramm, David. *Killers of the Flower Moon*. New York: Vintage Books, 2017.

Grijalva, James M. "Tribal Government Regulation of Non-Indian Polluters of Reservation Waters." *North Dakota Law Review*, 71: 433, 1995.

Grof, Thomas. "Tribal Showdown Over Incinerator: Proposed Project a Blessing or Curse?" *Denver Post*, 22 July 1990, pp. A1, 15.

Gubernick, Lisa. "The Third Battle of Bull Run." *Forbes*, Vol. 154/No. 9, 17 October 1994, pp. 67–71.

Gugliotta, Guy. "A Linguist's Alternative History of 'Redskin.'" *Washington Post*, 3 October 2005, http://www.washington post. com/wp-dyn/content/article.

Haederie, Michael. "Homage or Ripoff? Indians Resent Spiritual 'Wannabes,' but Who Owns Spirit?" *Star Tribune*, 11 May 1994, pp. 1, 8E.

Hampton, Liz, and Valerie Volcovici. "Top Executive Behind Dakota Access has Donated More Than $100,000 to Trump," Reuters.com, 26 October 2016. https://www.reuters.com/article/us-usa-election-trump-dakota-access/top-executive-behind-dakota-access-has-donated-more-than-100000-to-trump-idUSKCN12Q2P2.

Harbison, John S. "The Broken Promise: An Essay on Native American Tribal Sovereignty over Reservation Resources." *Stanford Environmental Law Journal*, 14: 347ff, May 1995.

_____. "The Downstream People: Treating Indian Tribes as States Under the Clean Water Act." *North Dakota Law Review*, 71: 473ff, 1995.

Hargus, Relma. "Patton Boyle at Ease with Miracles, 'Mystic Double Talk.'" *Advocate*, 8 January 2000, pp. 1, 2F.

Harjo, Suzan Shown. "Last Rites for Indian Dead: Treating Remains Like Artifacts Is Intolerable." *Los Angeles Times*, 16 September 1989. https://www.latimes.com/archives/la-xpm-1989-09-16-me-story.html.

Harrison, Ben J. "Montana and Its Progeny: The Status of Tribal Jurisdiction in Indian Country." American Bar Association Key Environmental Issues in U.S. EPA Region VI Conference (Published in Proceedings), Dallas, TX, 7 May 1999.

Harvey, Christine. "School Chief Backs Off Hair Ruling." *Times-Picayune*, 20 November 2008, pp. B1, 3.

Hass, Nancy. "Learning Its Lessons Well." *Newsweek*, Vol. 123/No. 7, 14 February 1994, p. 37.

Hecht, Peter. "Deaths Raise Questions About Spiritual Quests." *The Sacramento Bee*, 26 June 2002, p. A1.

Hendricks, Maggie. "Aboriginal Leaders: Russian Ice Dancers' Routine Still Offensive." 22 February 2011. http://sports.yahoo.com/olympics/vancouver/blog/fourth_place_medal/Aboriginal-Ice.

Hersher, Rebecca. "Key Moments in the Dakota Pipeline Fight." 22 February 2017. www.npr.org/sections/thetwo-way/2017/02/22/514988040/key-moments-in-the-dakota-access-pipeline-fight/.

Highwater, Jamake. *The Primal Mind: Vision and Reality in Indian America*. New York: Penguin Books, 1982.

Hill, Gord. *The 500 Years of Resistance Comic Book*. Vancouver: Arsenal Pulp Press, 2010.

Hirschfelder, Arlene, and Martha Kreipe Montano. *The Native American Almanac: A Portrait of Native America Today*. New York: Prentice-Hall, 1993.

Hooker, Ann M. "American Indian Sacred Sites on Federal Public Lands: Resolving Conflicts Between Religious Use and Multiple Use at El Malpais National Monument." *American Indian Law Review*, 19: 133–158, 1994.

Hoover, William. *Kinzua: From Cornplanter to the Corps*. Lincoln, NE: iUniverse, 2006.

Hotakainer, Rob. "New Rules Might Recognize More Tribes, Create Casinos." *Advocate*, 17 August 2014, p. 13A.

Hurtado, Albert L., and Peter Iverson. *Major Problems in American Indian History*. Lexington, MA: D.C. Heath and Company, 1994.

"In the Red." *The Economist*, Vol. 310/No. 7591, 25 February 1989, pp. 25–26.

Indian Country Media Network. "Archambault Acquitted on DAPL Charges." 2 June 2017. https://indiancountrymedia network.com/news/native-news-archambault-acquitted/.

_____. "DAPL Approval Illegal, Judge Finds," 14 June 2017. https://indiancountrymedia network.com/news/native-news/dapl-approved-illegal-judge-finds/.

_____. "DAPL Civil Suit Dropped Against Archambault, Council Members." 19 May 2017. https://indiancountrymedianetwork.com/news/native-news/dapl-civil-suit-dropped.

_____. "National Council Does Not Condone Faux Native American Churches or Marijuana Use." 19 May 2017. https://indiancountrymedianetwork.com/history/events/national-council-does-not-condone.

Indian Country Today. Editorial. "Ceremonies Require Respect." 10 July 2002, p. A2.

Indian Health Service. "Indian Health Disparities." April 2017. https://www.ihs.gov/newsroom/factsheets/disparities.

Ishou, Hunan. "A Sad, Curious Tale of Rampant Duplicity and Stupidity." 12 May 2009. Downloaded 19 May 2011. https://whistlingelk.blogspot.com/2009/05/sad-curious-tale-of-rampant-duplicity.html.

Jaimes, Annette, ed. *The State of Native America: Genocide, Colonization, and Resistance*. Boston: South End Press, 1992.

Jennings, Francis. *The Invasion of America: Indians, Colonialism and the Cant of Conquest*. Chapel Hill: University of North Carolina Press, 1975.

Johansen, Bruce. *Forgotten Founders: How the American Indian Helped Shape Democracy*. Boston: Harvard Common Press, 1982.

Johnson, Kirk. "Indian Claims Whittled Down." *Times-Picayune*, 8 August 2008, p. A3.

"Justices Order Child Returned to Adoptive Parents." *Times-Picayune*, 26 June 2013, p. A7.

Kaplan, Sarah. "Moving Mountains." *Times-Picayune*, 24 July 2015, pp. C6–7.

Karst, Kenneth L. "Religious Freedom and Equal Citizenship: Reflections on Lukumi." *Tulane Law Review*, 69/2: 335–372, December 1994.

Kelleher, Jennifer Sinco. "Court Justice Blocks Native Hawaiian Vote Count." *The Advocate*, 28 November 2015, p. 4A.

Kennedy, Merritt. "Native Hawaiians Now Have Pathway to Form a Government." 23 September 2016. http://www.npr.org/sections/thetwo-way/2016/09/23/495212183/.

Killion, Aubry. "Ursuline Academy Decides to Retire Sioux Mascot, Alumni Reacts." WDSU-TV News, 16 August 2019.

King, Ledyard, and Shelby Fleig. "2020 Democrats Are Stepping Up Their Courtship of Native American Voters. Here's Why." *Des Moines Register*, 17 August 2019. https://www.desmoinesregister.com/story/news/elections/presidential/caucus/2019/08/17/native-american-vote-2020-increase-influence-turnout-oj-semans-swing-states-voting-rights-trump-iowa/1857159001/.

Kollmorgan, Sarah. "Freeze Frame." *Discover Magazine*, Vol. 37/No. 4, May 2016, pp. 70–72.

Kral, Debra Utaica. "Keeping Hawaiian Lands in Native Hawaiian Hands." *Indian Country Today*, 31 August 2017. https://indiancountrymedianetwork.com/nes/politics/keeping-hawaiian-lands-native.

Krauthammer, Charles. "What Happens When Words Become Tainted." *Times-Picayune*, 18 October 2013, p. B7.

_____. "Who's Afraid of Virginia's Mouse?" *Time*, Vol. 143/No. 12, 6 June 1994, p. 76.

Krech, Shepard. *The Ecological Indian: Myth and History*. New York: W.W. Norton, 1999.

Kunzelman, Michael. "Court Hears Suit Over Kindergartner's Hair." *Times-Picayune*, 5 December 2009, p. A10.

Lambrecht, Bill. "Illegal Dumpers Scar Indian Lands." *St. Louis Post-Dispatch*, 17 November 1991, p. A11.

_____. "Indian Tribe Rejects Waste Disposal Plan." *St. Louis Post-Dispatch*, 3 February 1991, pp. A1, 4.

_____. "Indian Tribes Lurred by Money from Toxic Waste Incinerators." *St. Louis Post-Dispatch*, 24 June 1990, pp. A1, 11.

_____. "Land Vs. Money: Trash Debate Rips Tribes." *St. Louis Post-Dispatch*, 20 December 1990, pp. A1, 13.

_____. "Poisoned Mandate." *St. Louis Post-Dispatch*, 17 November 1991, pp. A1, 10.

Lame Deer, John, and Richrad Erdoes. *Lame Deer: Seeker of Visions*. New York: Simon & Schuster, 1972.

Laskaw, Sarah. "The Racist History of Peter Pan's Indian Tribe." *Smithsonian*, 2 December 2014. www.smithsonian.com/arts-culture/racist-history-peter-pan-indian-tribe/.

Lazarus, Edward. *Black Hills White Justice: The Sioux Nation Versus the United States, 1775 to the Present*. New York: HarperCollins, 1991.

Lewis, Jack. "An Indian Policy at EPA." *EPA Journal*, Vol. 12, January/February 1986, pp. 23–26.

Lippert-Martin, Kristen. "When Mickey Comes Marching Home." *Time*, Vol. 143/No. 23, 21 March 1994, p. 61.

Locke, John. *Of Civil Government Second Treatise*. South Bend: Gateway, (1690) 1955.

Longo, Peter J., and Christiana E. Miewald. "Native Americans, the Courts and Water Policy: Is Nothing Sacred." *Great Plains Research*, 2: 51–66, 1992.

Lowndes, John P. "When History Outweighs Law: Extinguishment of Abernaki Aboriginal Title." *Buffalo Law Review,* 42: 77–118, Winter 1994.

Lunenfield, Marvin. *1492: Discovery, Invasion, Encounter.* Lexington, MA: D.C. Heath and Company, 1991.

Lyden, Fremont J., and Lyman H. Letgers, eds. *Native Americans and Public Policy.* Pittsburgh: University of Pittsburgh Press, 1992.

Lyons, Oren, and John Mohawk, et al. *Exiled in the Land of the Free: Democracy, Indian Nations and the United States Constitution.* Sante Fe: Clear Light Publishers, 1992.

MacPherson, James. "Government Intervention in Oil Project Unprecedented." *The Advocate,* 11 September 2016, p. 2A.

_____. "In North Dakota, People vs. Oil Pipeline Protest Strengthens." *The Advocate,* 14 August 2016, p. 10A.

_____. "Our Cause is Just Says Tribal leader in Pipeline Protest." *The Advocate,* 4 September 2016, p. 4A.

Mallett, Kent. "Judge Rules OHC Can Reclaim Octagon Mounds from Moundbuilders." *Newark Advocate,* 10 May 2019. https:www.newarkadvocate.com/story/news/2019/05/10/judge-rules-ohc-can-reclaim-octagon-mounds-country-club/1170949001/.

_____. "Moundbuilders Plans Appeal of Judge's Eminent Domain Ruling." *Newark Advocate,* 13 May 2019. https://www.newarkadvocate.com/story/news/2019/05/13/moundbuilders-country-club-plans-appeal-ruling-octagon-mounds/1188321001/.

Manning, Sarah Sunshine. "New Age 'Ghost Dance' Held in Southwest Minnesota, Indigenous People Respond." *Indian Country Today,* 2 September 2017. https://indiancountrymedianetwork.com/native-news/new-age-ghost-dance-minnesota.

"Many Native Americans Do Not Like New Age Religions." National Public Radio / All Things Considered (broadcast story transcript). Executive Producer, Ellen Weiss. Washington, D.C., 24 November 1993.

Marcelo, Philip. "Interior Department Rules Against Tribe in Trust Land Bid." 8 September 2018. www.wbur.org/news/2018/09/08/interior-department-wamponoag-tribe-trust-land.

Marcelo, Philip, and Felicia Fonseca. "Land-Trust Case for Mashpee Tribe Raises Concerns Across Indian Country." 4 July 2018. www.wbur.org/news/2018/07/04/mashpee-wamponoag-trust-case.

Martella, Roger, Jr. "Not in My State's Indian Reservation—A Legislative Fix to Close an Environmental Law Loophole." *Vanderbilt Law Review,* 47: 1863, 1994.

Marx, Jane, Jana L. Walker, and Susan M. Williams. "Tribal Jurisdiction Over Reservation Water Quality and Quantity." *South Dakota Law Review,* 43: 315–380, 1998.

"The Massacre at Sand Creek." Retrieved 21 May 2019. https//ushistory.org/us/40a.asp.

McClam, Erin. "Sitting Bull Battle." *The Advocate,* 17 June 2007, p. 23A.

McFadden, Robert D. "Tribal Politics Flare in Violence." *Time-Picayune* (New Orleans, LA), 26 March 1995, p. A2.

McGill, Kevin. "U.S. Court Hears Native American Adoption Case." *Advocate,* 14 March 2019, p. 3A.

McGovern, Dan. "The Battle Over the Environmental Impact Statement in the Campo Indian Landfill War." *Hastings W.—N.W. Journal of Environmental Law and Policy,* 3: 145, Fall 1995.

_____. *The Campo Indian Landfill War.* Norman: University of Oklahoma Press, 1995.

McSloy, Steven P. "Back to the Future." *New York University Review of Law and Social Change,* 20: 217–302, 1993.

_____. "Revisiting the 'Courts of the Conquerors': American Indian Claims Against the United States." *American University Law Review,* 44: 537–644, Winter 1994.

Meredith, Howard. *Modern American Indian Tribal Government and Politics.* Tsaile, AZ: Navajo Community College Press, 1993.

Miheswuah, Devon A. *American Indians: Stereotypes and Realities.* Atlanta: Clarity Press, 1996.

Miller, Robert J. "Correcting Supreme Court 'Errors': American Indian Response to *Lyng V. Northwest Indian Cemetery Protective Association.*" *Environmental Law,* 20: 1037–1062, 1990.

Miniclier, Kit. "Will Waste Be Dumped on Indians?" *Denver Post,* 29 July 1991, pp. B1, 6.

Molotsky, Irvin. "Smithsonian to Give Up Indian Remains." *New York Times*, 13 September 1989. https://nytimes.com/1989/09/13/us/smithsonian-to-give-up-indian-remains.html.

Monette, Richard A. "Governing Private Property in Indian Country; the Double-Edged Sword of the Trust Relationship and Trust Responsibility Arising Out of Early Supreme Court Opinions and the General Allotment Act." *New Mexico Law Review*, 25: 35ff, Winter 1995.

Montana, Cate. "Yakama Nation Fighting to Preserve Sacred Land." *Indian Country Today*, Vol. 19/No. 43, 12 April 2000, pp. A1, 2.

"Montana Tribes Offer Oil Drilling for Weatherman Draw." *The Circle*, Vol. 22/No. 7, July 2001, p. 4.

Moquin, Wayne, and Charles Van Doren, eds. *Great Documents of American Indian History*. New York: DaCapo Press, 1995.

Moundbuilder Country Club. "The Beginning." n.d. http://www.moundbuilderscc.com/Default.aspx?p=DynamicModule&pageid=367884&ssid=280003&vnf=1.

Moya-Smith, Simon. "I Am a Native American. I Have Some Questions for Elizabeth Warren." *CNN*, 15 October 2018. https://www.cnn.com/2018/10/15/opinions/Elizabeth-warren-native-heritage-where-has-she-been-moya-dsmith/index.html.

Mufson, Steven. "Trump Dumped His Stock in the Dakota Access Owner Over the Summer." *Washington Post*, 23 November 2016. https://www.washingtonpost.com/news/energy-environment/wp/2016/11/23/trump-dumped-his-stock-in-dakota-access-pipeline-owner-over-the-summer/?utm_term=.b3240c700f42.

Murphy, Sean. "Elizabeth Warren's DNA Claims Inflames Some Tribes." *The Advocate*, 17 October 2017, p. 5A.

_____. "Vote Angers Descendants." *The Advocate*, 5 March 2007, p. 3A.

Murray, David. "Six Facts About the Carlisle Indian Industrial School." *Great Falls Tribune*, 2 July 2018. https://www.greatfallstribune/story/news/2018/07/02/native-american-students-carlisle-indian-industrial-school-pennsylvania/7457 15002.

Myers, Amanda Lee. "Lawsuit Settled Over Az Tribe Blood Samples." *Times-Picayune*, 22 April 2010, p. A14.

Myers, J. Jay. "Sand Creek Massacre." Retrieved 21 May 2019. https://www.hisorynet.com/sand-creek-massacre.

The National Campaign to Prevent Teen and Unplanned Pregnancy. "American Indian/Alaska Native Youth and Teen Pregnancy Prevention." Science Says 39 Brief, No. 39, August 2008. https://thenationalcampaign.org/sites/default/files/resource-primary-download/ss39_nativeamericans.pdf.

National Congress of American Indians (NCAI). "Demographics/NCAI." 12 April 2017. http://www.ncai.org/about-tribes/demographics.

National Museum of the American Indian, Smithsonian Institute. "Repatriation Policy." https://americanindian.si.edu/explore/collections/repatriation.

National Native American Boarding School Healing Coalition. https://boardingschoolhealing.org/wp-content/uploads/2018/09/NABS-map-2018-web-2.jpg.

National Public Radio. *All Things Considered*. "Oneida Land Claims in New York." 21 December 1999.

"Native American Mascots." *NCAA Press Release*, 29 October 2010. http://ncaa.org/wps/portal/ncaahome?WCMGLOBALCONTEXT=/ncaa/NCAA.

Native American Report. "Congress' Proposed Funding." 1998, pp. 1–3.

Native American Rights Fund. Annual Report 2018. 25 March 2019. www.narf.org/nill/documents/narf-ar/2018.pdf.

_____. "NARF Brings Historical Tribal Trust Claims to Historic Settlements." *Native American Rights Fund Legal Review*, Vol. 37/No. 1, Winter/Spring 2012, pp. 1–10.

_____. "Shinnecock Indian Nation of New York." 5 May 2017. http://www.narf.org/cases/shinnecock-indian-nation-new-york/.

Nelson, Katherine F. "Resolving Native American Land Claims and the Eleventh Amendment." *Villanova Law Review*, 39: 525ff, 1994.

"The Nemenhah Band and the Daniel Hauser Controversy." *Mountain Sage*, 20 May 2009. Downloaded 19 May 2011. http://mountainsageblog.com/2009/05/20/the-nemenhah-band-and-the-daniel-hauser-controversy.

"Nemenhah Band in Spotlight." *Columbia*

Daily Tribune, 24 May 2009. Downloaded 19 May 2011. http://www.columbitribune.com/news/2009/may/24/nemenhah-band-in-spotlight.

"Nemenhah Band: Spiritual Adoption." 13 June 2009 and 10 May 2011. http://www.nemenhah.org/internal/spiritual_adoption.html.

"New Age Groups Accused of Disrupting Archaeology." *Star Tribune*, 3 July 1994, p. 20A.

Newcomb, Steven T. "The Evidence of Christian Nationalism in Federal Indian Law: The Doctrine of Discovery, *Johnson V. McIntosh*, and Plenary Power." *New York University Review of Law and Social Change*, 20: 303–337, 1993.

Newton, Nell Jessup. "Compensation, Reparations and Restitution: Indian Property Claims in the U.S." *Georgia Law Review*, 28: 453–480, 1994.

_____. "Indian Claims in the Courts of the Conquerors." *American University Law Review*, 41: 753–854, Spring 1992.

_____. "The Judicial Role in Fifth Amendment Takings of Indian Land: An Analysis of the Sioux Nation Rule." *Oregon Law Review*, 61: 245–265, 1982.

Nichols, David A. *Lincoln and the Indians: Civil War Policy and Politics*. St. Paul: Minnesota Historical Society Press, 2012.

Nies, Judith. *Native American History: A Chronology of a Culture's Vast Achievements and Their Links to World Events*. New York: Ballantine Books, 1996.

Nolan, Bruce. "Church Wins a Round Vs. State." *The Times-Picayune* (New Orleans, LA), 25 January 1996, p. A10.

Nordhaus, Hannah. "Battle for the American West." *National Geographic*, Vol. 234/No. 5, November 2018, pp. 42–67.

Norgren, Jill. "Protection of What Rights They Have: Original Principles of Federal Indian Law." *North Dakota Law Review*, 64: 72–120, 1988.

Oakes, Larry. "Sacred Roots." *The Star Tribune*, 9 October 1994, pp. 1, 18A.

O'Brien, Sharon. *American Indian Tribal Governments*. Norman: University of Oklahoma Press, 1989.

_____. "Freedom of Religion in Indian Country." *Montana Law Review*, 56: 451–484, Summer 1995.

Office of Minority Health, U.S. Department of Health and Human Services. "Infant Mortality and American Indian/Alaska Natives," 2015. https://minorityhealth.hhs.gov/omh/browse.aspx?lvl=4&lvlid=38.

Orbey, Eren. "In Iowa, Democrats Court the Long-Overlooked Native American Vote." *The New Yorker*, 21 August 2019. https://www.newyorker.com/news/campaign-chronicles/in-iowa-democrats-court-the-long-overlooked-native-american-vote.

Page, Jake. "Sacred Ground: Landscapes as Living Spirit." *Native Peoples*, Vol. 20/No. 3, May/June 2007, pp. 26–32.

Pauls, Elizabeth Prine. "Trail of Tears." 5 April 2017. https://britannica.com/even/Trail-of-Tears.

Pember, Mary Annette. "'Cultural Genocide,' Truth and Reconciliation Commission Calls Residential Schools." 3 June 2015. https://indiancountrymedianetwork.com/2015/06/03/coming-full-circle-truth-and-reconciliation-calls-residential-schools-cultural-genocide.

_____. "When Will U.S. Apologize for Boarding School Genocide?" *Indian Country Today*, 20 June 2015. https://newmaven.io/indiancountrytoday/archive/when-will-u-s-apologize-for-boarding-school-genocide-Xs4lcrge5Eypq8mBz1HZBQ/.

Pevar, Stephen L. *The Rights of Indians and Tribes*. Carbondale: Southern Illinois University Press, 1992.

Philpott, Dan. "Sovereignty." The Stanford Encyclopedia of Philosophy (Summer 2003 Edition), Edward N. Zolta, ed. http://plato.stanford.edu/archives/sum2003/entries/sovereignty/.

Pickette, Eugene F., Michael T. Garrett, John F. Kosciulek, and David A. Rosenthal. "Cultural Identification of American Indians and Its Impact on Rehabilitation Services." *Journal of Rehabilitation*, 65: 3–10, July–September 1999.

"Planned Auction of Items from Reservations Raises Questions." *The Advocate*, 5 June 2016, p. 11A.

Pommersheim, Frank. *Braid of Feathers: American Indian Law and Contemporary Tribal Life*. Los Angeles: University of California Press, 1995.

_____. "The Crucible of Sovereignty: Analyzing Issues of Tribal Jurisdiction." *Arizona Law Review*, 31: 329–363, 1989.

"Pope Francis Apologizes to Indigenous

Peoples for 'Grave Sins' of Colonialism." *Indian Country Media Network*, 10 July 2015. http://indiancountrymedianetwork. com/2015/07/10/pope-francis-apologizes-indigenous-peoples-grave-sins-colonialism-161030.

Porter, Robert A. "Strengthening Sovereignty Through Peacemaking." Paper presented at the Federal Bar Association Indian Law Conference, Albuquerque, NM, April 1995.

"The Problem with Heidi Klum's Native American Photo Shoot." 11 April 2014. https://shine.yahoo.com/fashion/heidi-klum-redface-native-americans-germanys-next-top-model.

Prucha, Francis Paul. *American Indian Treaties: The History of a Political Anomaly*. Los Angeles: University of California Press, 1994.

_____. *Documents of United States Indian Policy*. Lincoln: University of Nebraska Press, 1990.

Ray, Charles Michael. "The Slow Carving of the Crazy Horse Monument." NPR—ATC, 1 January 2013. www.npr.org/2013/01/01/16788928/the-slow-carving-of-the-crazy-horse-monument/.

Recer, Paul. "Ecological Sea Damage Said Very Old." *The Advocate*, 27 July 2001, p. 9A.

_____. "Study: Early Hunters Caused Extinctions." *The Advocate*, 8 June 2001, p. 10A.

Redman, Samuel. "When Museums Rushed to Fill Their Rooms with Bones." Smithsonian.com., 15 March 2016. https://www.smithsonianmag.com/history/when-museums-rushed-fill-their-rooms-bones-180958424/.

Regan, Mary Beth. "Mickey Does Manassas." *Business Week*, No. 3348, 29 November 1993, p. 46.

Reilly, William K. "Environmental Equity: EPA's Position." *EPA Journal*, Vol. 18, March 1992, pp. 18–22.

"Reservation Poverty." *Wikipedia*, 11 April 2017. https://en.wikipedia.org/w/indes. php?title=Reservation_poeverty&oldid=774964888.

Rhodes, John. "An American Tradition: The Religious Persecution of Native Americans." *Montana Law Review*, 52: 13–72, Winter 1991.

Riechmann, Deb. "Millennium Fireworks Plans for Monument Spark Debate." *The Advocate*, 28 December 1999, p. 2A.

Roberts, David. "Grand Canyon on the Edge." *Smithsonian*, Vol. 45/No. 11, March 2015, pp. 58–69, 94.

Robertson, Robbie. "Making a Noise." Song from *Contact from the Underworld of Redboy*, Capital Records, Inc., Hollywood, CA, 1998; *and* at: robbie-robertson.com/lyrics/Robbie-robertson/contact-from-the-underworld-of-redboy/making-a-noise/.

Rosay, Andre B. "Violence Against American Indian and Alaskan Women and Men: 2010 Findings from the National Intimate Partner and Sexual Violence Survey." National Institute of Justice, Office of Justice Programs, U.S. Department of Justice, NCJ 249736, May 2016. https://www.ncjrs.gov.

Rosenbaum, Ron. "The Shocking Savagery of America's Early History." *Smithsonian*, Vol. 20, February 2017. http://www.smithsonianmag.com/history/the-shocking-savagery-of-americas-early-history.

Ross, Rupert. *Dancing with a Ghost: Exploring Aboriginal Reality*. New York: Penguin Books, 2006.

_____. *Returning to the Teachings: Exploring Aboriginal Justice*. Toronto: Penguin Canada, 2006.

Ross, Timberly. "Indian Tribes Buying Back Land." *Times-Picayune*, 28 December 2009, p. A2.

Rovin, Ann. "Devils Tower: A Climb or Shrine?" *Star Tribune*, 16 October 1994, p. 22A.

Royster, Judith V. "Environmental Protection and Native American Rights: Controlling the Land Through Environmental Regulation." *Kansas Journal of Law and Policy*, 1: 89, Summer 1991.

_____. "Of Surplus Lands and Landfills: The Case of the Yankton Sioux." *South Dakota Law Review*, 43: 283–314, 1998.

SAMHSA. "Need for and Receipt of Substance Use Treatment Among American Indians or Alaskan Natives." *The NSDUH Report*, November 2012. https://www.samhsa.gov/data/sites/default/files/NSDUH120/NSDUH120SR120-treatment.

"Sand Creek Massacre." History Channel. 13 November 2009. https://www.history.com/this-day-in-history/sand-creek-massacre.

Schake, Kori. "Lessons from the Indian Wars." *Hoover Institution Policy Review*, February–March 2013. https:hoover.org/research/lessons-indian-wars/.

Schneider, Paul, and Dan Lamont. "Other People's Trash." *Audubon*, Vol. 93/No. 4, July 1991, pp. 108–119.

Sehgal, A. Cassidy. "Indian Tribal Sovereignty and Waste Disposal Regulation." *Fordham Environmental Law Journal*, 5: 431, Spring 1994.

Shell, Andrew Iron. "Americanized Thought Eroding Traditional Ways." *Indian Country Today*, 1 August 2001, p. A4.

Sheyahshe, Michael A. *Native Americans in Comic Books*. Jefferson, NC: McFarland, 2008.

Sides, Hampton. *Blood and Thunder: The Epic Story of Kit Carson and the Conquest of the American West*. New York: Anchor Books, 2006.

Silko, Leslie Marmon. *Ceremony*. New York: Penguin Books, 1986.

Simpson, Michael J. "Accommodating Indian Religions: The Proposed 1993 Amendment to the American Indian Religious Freedom Act." *Montana Law Review*, 54: 19–55, Winter 1993.

Singer, Joseph William. "Well Settled? the Increasing Weight of History in American Indian Land Claims." *Georgia Law Review*, 28: 481–532, 1994.

"Skywalk Dragged Down by Dispute." *Times-Picayune*, 24 April 2011, p. A16.

Slattery, Ryan. "Climbing Banned at Sacred Washoe Site." *Indian Country Today*, 31 December 2003, pp. B1, 4.

Soifer, Aviam. "Objects in Mirror Are Closer Than They Appear." *Georgia Law Review*, 28: 533–553, 1994.

Soll, Lauren Natasha. "The Only Good Indian Reservation Is a Diminished Reservation?" *Federal Bar News and Journal*, 41: 544–549, September 1994.

Solomon, Jolie. "Disney: A Sudden Surrender in Virginia." *Newsweek*, Vol. 124/No. 15, 10 October 1994, p. 46.

"Sovereign Immunity Cannot be Evaded by Sleight of Hand." Native American Rights Fund (NARF), 14 February 2018. https://www.narf.org/sovereign-immunity-cannot-be-evaded.

Stannard, David E. *American Holocaust*. New York: Oxford University Press, 1992.

Stern, Walter E. "Environmental Compliance Considerations for Developers of Indian Lands." *Land and Water Law Review*, 28: 77, 1993.

Stewart, David O. "Power Surge: Asserting Authority Over Congress in Religious Freedom Case." *ABA Journal*, Vol. 83, pp. 46–47, September 1887.

Strickland, Rennard. "Genocide-at-Law: An Historic and Contemporary View of the Native American Experience." *University of Kansas Law Review*, 34: 713–755, 1986.

Suagee, Dean B. "Turtle's War Party: An Indian Allegory on Environmental Justice." *Journal of Environmental Law and Litigation*, 9: 461–497, 1994.

Suagee, Dean B., and Christopher T. Stearns. "Indigenous Self-Government, Environmental Protection and the Consent of the Governed: A Tribal Review Process." *Colorado Journal of Environmental Law and Policy*, 5: 59, Winter 1994.

Suicide Prevention Resource Center (SPRC). "Suicide Among Racial/Ethnic Populations in the U.S. American Indians/Alaska Natives." http://www.sprc.org/sites/default/files/migrate/library/Ai_AN%20sheet%20Aug%2028%202013%20Final.pdf.

"Sweat Lodge Lacked Building Permit." *Times-Picayune*, 13 October 2009, p. A4.

"Sweat Lodge Victim's Kin Say She Was in Top Shape." *Times-Picayune*, 11 October 2009, p. A4.

Taliman, Valerie. "The Toxic Waste of Indian Lives." *Covert Action*, No. 40, Spring 1992, pp. 16–22.

Time-Life Books, eds. *The American Indian: The European Challenge*. Alexandria, VA: Time Inc., 1992.

Tocqueville, Alexis de. *Democracy in America*. New York: Random House, 1981.

Topahe, Luralene D. "After the Religious Restoration Act: Still No Equal Protection for First American Worshipers." *New Mexico Law Review*, 24: 331–363, Spring 1994.

Trachtenberg, Alan. *Shades of Hiawatha: Staging Indians, Making Americans 1880–1930*. New York: Wang and Hill, 2004.

"Trump Administration Moves to Shrink National Monuments." National Public Radio, Host Ari Shapiro, 24 August 2017. http://www.npr.org/templetes/transcript/ytranscript.php?storyid=545901843.

"2 Die, Others Sickened at Arizona Sweat

Lodge." *Times-Picayune*, 10 October 2009. p. A4.

Uram, Charlotte, and Mary J. Decker. "Jurisdiction Over Water Quality on Native American Lands." *Journal of Natural Resources and Environmental Law*, 8: 1ff, 1992/1993.

Urofsky, Melvin I. *A March of Liberty: A Constitutional History of the United States, Volume I: Tto 1877*. New York: McGraw-Hill, Inc., 1988.

U.S. Census Bureau. "The American Community—American Indians and Alaska Natives: 2004." https://www.census.gov/prod/2007pubs/acs-07.pdf.

_____. "American Fact Finder—Selected Population Profile in the U.S. 2015 American Community Survey." 50201. https://factfinder.census.gov/.

Valencia-Weber, Gloria. "Shrinking Indian Country: A State Offensive to Divest Tribal Sovereignty." *Connecticut Law Review*, 27: 1281–1322, Summer 1995.

Van Develder, Paul. "A Coyote for All Seasons." *Native Peoples*, Vol. 11/No. 4, Summer 1998, pp. 42–48.

Vecsey, Christopher, ed. *Handbook of American Indian Religious Freedom*. New York: Crossroad, 1993.

Vecsey, Christopher, and Robert W. Venables, eds. *American Indian Environments: Ecological Issues in Native American*. Syracuse: Syracuse University Press, 1980.

Vecsey, Christopher, and William A. Staina, eds. *Iroquois Land Claims*. Syracuse: Syracuse University Press, 1988.

Wallace, Anthony F. C. *The Long, Bitter Trail: Andrew Jackson and the Indians*. New York: Hill and Wang, 1993.

Ward, Robert Charles. "The Spirits Will Leave: Preventing the Desecration and Destruction of Native American Sacred Sites on Federal Lands." *Ecology Law Quarterly*, 19: 795–843, 1992.

Warrior, Robert Allen. "Dancing with Wastes." *Christianity and Crisis*, 51: 216–218, 15 July 1991.

Wilkins, David E. *American Indian Sovereignty and the U.S. Supreme Court: The Masking of Justice*. Austin: University of Texas Press, 1997.

_____. "*Johnson V. M'Intosh* Revisited: Through the Eyes of *Mitchel V. United States*." *American Indian Law Review*, 19: 159–183, 1994.

Wilkinson, Charles F. *Fire on the Plateau*. Washington, D.C.: Island Press, 1999.

Will, George F. "Agency Withdrew Redskins' Trademark Despite Absence of Revulsion." *Times-Picayune*, 29 June 2014, p. E2.

_____. "Let 'Native Hawaiians' Stand." *The Advocate*, 29 November 2007, p. 7B.

Williams, John L. "The Effect of EPA's Designation of Tribes as States on the Five Civilized Tribes in Oklahoma." *Tulsa Law Journal*, 29: 345ff, Winter 1993.

Williams, Robert A., Jr. *The American Indian in Western Legal Thought: The Discourse of Conquest*. New York: Oxford University Press, 1990.

_____. *Savage Anxieties: The Invention of Western Civilization*. New York: Palgrave MacMillan, 2012.

Williams, Terry Tempest. "Will Bears Ears be the Next Standing Rock?" *New York Times*, 6 May 2017. https://www.nytimes. will-bears-ears-be-the-next-standing-rock.html.

Willoughby, C. E. "Native American Sovereignty Takes a Back Seat to the 'Pig in the Parlor': The Redefining of Tribal Sovereignty in Traditional Property Law Terms." *Southern Illinois University Law Review*, 19: 593, Spring 1995.

Wilson, Paul S. "What Chief Seattle Said." *Environmental Law*, 22: 1451–1468, 1992.

Wood, Mary Christina. "Protecting the Attributes of Native Sovereignty: A New Trust Paradigm for Federal Actions Affecting Tribal Lands and Resources." *Utah Law Review*, 1995: 109–237, 1995.

Woodward, C. Vann. "A Mickey Mouse Idea." *The New Republic*, Vol. 120/ No. 4144, 20 June 1994, pp. 15–16.

Wright, J. Bart. "Tribes v. States: Zoning Indian Reservations." *Natural Resources Journal*, 32: 195–206, Winter 1992.

Wright, Ronald. *Stolen Continents: The "New World"/"New World" Through Indian Eyes*. New York: Houghton Mifflin Company, 1992.

Wunder, John R. *Retained by the People: A History of American Indians and the Bill Of Rights*. New York: Oxford University Press, 1994.

WWL-TV News. "Ursuline Academy to Remove Sioux as Class Mascot After This Year." 16 August 2019.

Wyatt, Kathryn C. "The Supreme Court, Lyng and the Lone Wolf Principle." *Chicago-Kent Law Review,* 65: 623–655, 1989.

Court Cases

Apache Survival Coalition V. United States. 21 F.3d 895 (1994).

Arkansas V. Oklahoma. 112 S. Ct. 1046 (1992).

Atlantic States Legal Foundation V. Salt River Pima-Maricopa Indian Community. 827 F. Supp. 608 (1993).

Badoni V. Higginson. 638 F.2d 856 (8th Cir. 1982), cert. denied 452 U.S. 954 (1981).

Blue Legs V. U.S. Bureau of Indian Affairs. 867 F.2d 1094 (1989).

Bowen V. Roy. 476 U.S. 693 (1986).

Brendale V. Confederated Tribes of Yakima Indians. 492 U.S. 408 (1989).

Cherokee Nation V. Georgia. 30 U.S. 5 Pet. 1 (1831).

Cherokee Tobacco. 78 U.S. 11 Wall. 616 (1870).

Choctaw Nation V. Oklahoma. 397 U.S. 620, 90 S. Ct. 1328, 25 L. Ed. 2d 615 (1970).

Citizens Interested in Bull Run, Inc. V. EPA. 992 F.2d 1219 (1993).

City of Albuquerque V. Browner. 865 F. Supp. 733 (D.N.M. 1993).

City of Albuquerque V. Browner. 97 F.3d 415 [C.A. 10 Cir. (N.M.)] (1996).

City of Boerne V. P.F. Flores. WL 345322 (U.S. Tex.) 1997.

City of Sherrill V. Oneida Nation of New York. 544 U.S. 197 (2005).

Coeur D'Alene Tribe of Idaho V. State of Idaho. 42 F.3d 1244 (1994).

Cramer V. United States. 261 U.S. 219 (1923).

Crow Tribe of Indians Montana V. EPA. 454 U.S. 1081 (1981).

Duro V. Reina. 495 U.S. 676 (1990).

Employment Division, Oregon Department of Human Resources V. Smith. 494 U.S. 872 (1990).

Federal Power Commission V. Tuscarora Indian Nation. 362 U.S. 99, 80 S. Ct. 543 (1960).

Fletcher V. Peck. 10 U.S. 6 Cranch 87 (1810).

Fools Crow V. Gullet. 706 F.2d 856 (8th Cir. 1982), cert. denied 464 U.S. 977 (1983).

Fort Sill Apache Tribe V. United States. 477 F.2d 1360 Ct. Cl. (1973).

Gila River Pima-Maricopa Indian Community V. United States. 427 F.2d 1194 (Ct. Cl.), cert. denied 400 U.S. 819 (1970).

Henry Chouteau V. Patrick Molony. 57 U.S. 203 (1853).

Homestake Mining Company V. EPA. 477 F. Supp. 1279 (S.D. Fla. 1988).

Indians of California V. United States. 102 Ct. Cl. 837 (December 4, 1944).

International Paper Company V. Ouellette. 479 U.S. 481 (1987).

Johnson V. M'Intosh. 21 U.S. 8 Wheat. 543 (1823).

Kerr-McGee Corporation V. Farley. 915 F. Supp. 273 (1995).

Kerr-McGee Corporation V. Navajo. 471 U.S. 195 (1985).

Kescoli V. Babbitt. 101 F.3d 1304 (1996).

Lonewolf V. Hitchcock. 187 U.S. 553 (1903).

Lyng V. Northwest Indian Cemetery Protective Association. 485 U.S. 439, 108 S. Ct. 1319 (1988).

Menominee V. United States. 391 U.S. 404 (1968).

Merriam V. Jicarilla Apache Tribe. 455 U.S. 130 (1982).

Minersville V. Gobitis. 310 U.S. 586 (1940).

Mississippi Band of Choctaw Indians V. Holyfield. 490 U.S. 30, 109 S. Ct. 1597 (1989).

Mitchel V. United States. 34 U.S. 9 Pet. 711 (1835).

Nance V. EPA. 645 F.2d 701 (9th Cir. 1981), cert. denied.

Oliphant V. Suqumesh Indian Tribe. 435 U.S. 191 (1978).

Oneida Indian Nation V. State of New York. 414 U.S. 661 (1974).

Oneida Indian Nation V. State of New York. 470 U.S. 226 (1985).

Passamaguoddy Tribe V. Morton. 528 F.2d 370 (1st Cir. 1975).

Plains Commerce Bank V. Long Family Land and Cattle Co., Inc. 556 U.S. 287 (2008).

Public Service Company of Colorado V. Shoshone-Bannock Tribes. 30 F.3d 1203 (1994).

Pueblo of Sandia, Et Al. V. United States. 50 F.3d 856 (1995).

Pyramid Lake Paiute Tribe V. Morton. 354 F. Supp. 252 (D.D.C. 1972).

Ray Jones V. Patrick Meehan. 175 U.S. 1, 20 S. Ct. 1 (1899).

Razore V. Tulalip Tribes of Washington. 66 F.3d 236 (1995).

Seminole Nation V. United States. (1942). https://www.law.cornell.edu/supreme court/text/316/286.

Seminole Nation V. United States. 316 U.S. 286 (1942).

Seneca Nation of Indians V. United States. 338 F.2d 55 (1964).

Seneca Nation of Indians V. Wilber Brucker. 162 F. Supp. 580 (1958).

Seneca Nation of Indians V. Wilber Brucker. 262 F.2d 27, 104 U.S. App. D.C. 315 (1958).

Sequoyah V. Tennessee Valley Authority. 620 F.2d 1159 (6th Cir.), cert. denied 449 U.S. 953 (1980).

Sherbert V. Verner. 374 U.S. 398 (1963).

Shoshone Tribe V. U.S. 299 U.S. 476 (1937).

Smith V. Stevens. 77 U.S. 10 Wall. 321 (1870).

State of Alaska Ex Rel. Ukon Flats School District V. Native Village of Venetie. 101 F.3d 1286 (1996).

State of Alaska V. Native Village of Venetie. 856 F.2d 1384 (1988).

State of Montana V. EPA. (D.C. Mont. No. CV-95-56-M-CCL, 27 March 1996).

State of Montana V. United States. 440 U.S. 544, 101 S. Ct. 1245 (1981).

State of Montana V. United States. 137 F.3d 1135 (1998).

State of New Jersey V. Wilson. 11 U.S. 7 Cranch. 164 (1812).

State of New Mexico V. Mescalero Apache Tribe. 462 U.S. 324 (1983).

State of South Dakota V. Bourland. 508 U.S. 679, 113 S. Ct. 2309 (1993).

State of South Dakota V. U.S. Department of Interior. 69 F.3d 878 (1995).

State of South Dakota V. Yankton Sioux Tribe. 118 S. Ct. 789 (1998).

State of Tennessee V. Foreman. 16 Tenn (8 Yer.) 256 (1835).

State of Vermont V. Elliot. 159 Vt. 102; 616 A.2d 210 (1992).

State of Washington V. United States. 447 U.S. 134 (1980).

State of West Virginia Board of Education V. Barnette. 319 U.S. 624 (1943).

State of Wisconsin V. Yoder. 406 U.S. 205 (1972).

Strate V. A-1 Contractors. 520 U.S. 438, 117 S. Ct. 1404 (1997).

Tee-Hit-Ton Indians V. United States. 348 U.S. 272; 75 S. Ct. 313; 99 L. Ed. 314; 15 Alaska 418 (1955).

Turtle Mountain Band of Chippewa Indians, Et Al. V. United States. 490 F.2d 935 (1974).

United States V. Alcea Band of Tillamook. 341 U.S. 48 (1951).

United States V. Cook. 86 U.S. 19 Wall. 591 (1873).

United States V. Creek Nation. 295 U.S. 103 (1935).

United States V. Forness. 2nd Cir., 125 F.2d 928 (1943).

United States V. 43 Gallons of Whiskey. 93 U.S. 188 (1876).

United States V. Gemmill. 535 F.2d 1145 (1976).

United States V. Holliday. 70 U.S. 3 Wall. 407 (1865).

United States V. Joseph. 94 U.S. 616 (1876).

United States V. Kagima. 118 U.S. 375 (1886).

United States V. Klamath Indians. 304 U.S. 119 (1938).

United States V. Klamath Indians. 44 F.3d 758 (1994).

United States V. Lara. 54 U.S. 193 (2004).

United States V. Navajo Nation. 537 U.S. 488 (2003).

United States V. Navajo Nation. 556 U.S. 287 (2009).

United States V. Rogers. 45 U.S. 4 Haw. 567 (1846).

United States V. Sandavol. 231 U.S. 28 (1913).

United States V. Sioux Nation of Indians. 448 U.S. 371; 100 S. Ct. 2716 (1980).

United States V. Wheeler. 435 U.S. 313 (1978).

United States V. Winans. 198 U.S. 371 (1905).

Wagnon V. Prairie Band of Potawatomi Indians. 546 U.S. 95 (2005).

Williams V. Lee. 358 U.S. 217 (1959).

Wilson V. Block. 708 F.2d 735 (D.C. Cir. 1983), cert. denied 464 U.S. 956 (1984).

Winters V. United States. 207 U.S. 564 (1908).

Worcester V. Georgia. 31 U.S. 6 Pet. 515 (1832).

Yankton Sioux Tribe of Indians V. Kenneth Nelson, Et Al. 604 F. Supp. 1146 (1985).

Yankton Sioux Tribe V. Southern Missouri Waste Management District. 890 F. Supp. 878 (1995).

Government Documents

Federal Register. Vol. 61/No. 18, 26 January 1996, p. 2584. Proposed Rule, Environmental Protection Agency, Subtitle D Landfill Regulations.

Federal Register. Vol. 61/No. 104, 29 May

1996, p. 26771. Executive Order 13007 of 24 May 1996. "Indian Sacred Sites."

Federal Register. Vol. 61/No. 154, 8 August 1996, p. 41424. Notice, Department of Interior, National Park Service. "Climbing Management Plan for Devils Tower National Monument, Wyoming."

Public Law 95-341 [S.J. Res. 102]. 11 August 1978. "American Indian Religious Freedom."

Public Law 101-185. 28 November 1989. "National Museum of the American Indian Act."

Public Law 101-601. 16 November 1990. "Native American Graves Protection and Repatriation Act."

25 Code of Federal Regulations (CFR) Part 83. *Procedures for Establishing That an American Indian Group Exists as an Indian Tribe.* Bureau of Indian Affairs, Department of Interior (updated 2017).

Index

243

O'Connor, Justice Sandra Day 89, 105
Oklahoma Tax Commission v. Sac and Fox Nation (1993) 151, 152
Oneida Indians 156, 157, 158

Paine, Thomas 31
Pauite Indians 49
Pennsylvania 29, 30
Peublo Indians 50, 131; and Intercourse Act 173
Pilgrims 28
Polk, James K. 43
Porter, Robert 16
Portugal 24, 28; dispute with Spain 191*n*12
Powhatan, and Confederacy 28, 29, 192*n*46
Pratt, Richard Henry 162
Primogeniture, Doctrine of 14
Pueblo of Sandia v. U.S. (1995) 91
Puritans 28

Quest, Vision 205*n*37

Raritan Tribe 27
Reagan, President Ronald 121, 122
Red Cloud, Chief 45
Religious Freedom Restoration Act (RFRA) 103
Reservation: Pine Ridge 135; Rosebud 133, 134; Standing Rock Sioux 142
Resource Conservation and Recovery Act (RCRA)(1976) 133, 134, 135, 136, 137; subtitle D 133
Reynolds v. U.S. (1878) 76
Rhenquist, Justice William 57
Rights 15, 16

Sacred Circle 10
Sacred Sites: in danger 208*n*197; protection of 20
Safe Drinking Water Act (SDWA) (1986) 131
San Carlos Apache Indians 113, 114
Schools, Boarding 162, 163; in Canada 233*n*15
Seattle (Sealth), Chief 120; speech 185
Seganagatha 10
Seminole Indians 40, 43
Seneca Indians: and Cornplanter Band 54; and Kinzua 201*n*241; and Kinzua Dam 54; reservation 54; and Salamanca 154, 155, 156
Sequoyah v. TVA (1980) 80, 81
Sherbert v. Verner (1963) 77, 80

Sioux, Oglala 135
Sioux, Yankton 136, 137, 138
Slavery: and Indians 24, 25; and wars 197*n*154
Solid Waste Disposal Act (1965) 133
South Dakota v. Bourland (1993) 127, 128
Sovereignty: concept of 16, 17; cultural 19; dimensions of 18; environmental 132, 135; future of 158, 159, 160; government and 17; inherent 18; tribal 17–18, 20, 21
Spain 23, 24, 26, 27, 40, 41; crimes 192*n*36
Spirituality, American Indian 71, 72
Squanto 23
Standard Oil Company 48
State of Vermont v. Elliot (1992) 58, 59
Symbols, Sports 174, 176; list of 224*n*46

Tecumseh 32, 33
Tee-Hit-Ton Indians 51, 52
Tee-Hit-Ton Indians v. U.S. (1955) 51, 59
Tennessee Supreme Court 114–115
Termination 10; losses 199*n*202; policy of 47
Thomas, Justice Clarence 127
Tlingit Indians 51
Trail of Tears 43
Treaty, Fort Stanwix 154, 156
Tribes-as-States (TAS) 122, 123, 128, 129, 130
Trust Doctrine 105, 106
Tsitsistas (Cheyenne) Indians 83
Tuscarora Indians 53, 54, 200*n*227

U.S. v. Cook (1873) 44
U.S. v. Forness (1939) 155
U.S. v. Kagima (1876) 46
U.S. v. Rogers (1846) 42
U.S. v. Sandoval (1913) 50
U.S. v. Winans (1905) 50
Ute Indians 153

Valley of Chiefs, Montana 143
Vermont 58, 59, 60
Views, World 14, 15, 20
Virgina Company 28, 29
Virginia 30, 31, 67

Washington, George 43, 55
Washington Monument 69
Washington v. U.S. (1980) 126
Waste: municipal (MSW) 133; nuclear 132; solid 132
West Virginia Board of Education v. Barnette (1943) 77